June 15 1975

THE MOVIE STARS

Other books by Richard Griffith

THE WORLD OF ROBERT FLAHERTY
ANATOMY OF A MOTION PICTURE
THE MOVIES, with Arthur Mayer
THE FILM TILL NOW, with Paul Rotha
DOCUMENTARY FILM, with Paul Rotha, Sinclair Road

THE MOVIE STARS

BY RICHARD GRIFFITH

Doubleday and Company, Inc.
Garden City, New York

Library of Congress Catalog Card Number 72-126382
Copyright © 1970 by T. G. Scully as Administrator
of the Estate of Richard Griffith
All Rights Reserved
Printed in the United States of America

ISBN: 0-385-02353-7

PHOTOGRAPH CREDITS

Page 22   DEAD HEAT ON A MERRY-GO-ROUND, copyright © 1966 Columbia Pictures Corporation
Page 23   THE PROFESSIONAL, copyright © 1967 Columbia Pictures Corporation
Page 245   IT HAPPENED ONE NIGHT, copyright © 1934 Columbia Pictures Corporation
Page 257   THE AWFUL TRUTH, copyright © 1937 Columbia Pictures of California, Ltd.
Page 268   IN A LONELY PLACE, copyright © 1950 Santana Pictures
Page 297   TO SIR WITH LOVE, copyright © 1967 Columbia Pictures Corporation
Page 298   THE WILD ANGELS, copyright © 1966 American International Pictures
Page 323   CALL OF THE ROCKIES, copyright © 1938 Columbia Pictures of California, Ltd.
Page 323   SHADOW RANCH, copyright © 1930 Columbia Pictures Corporation
Page 325   BORN YESTERDAY, copyright © 1950 Columbia Pictures Corporation
Page 344   BEFORE I HANG, copyright © 1940 Columbia Pictures Corporation
Page 344   THE RETURN OF THE VAMPIRE © 1943 Columbia Pictures Corporation
Page 350   THE WILD ONE, copyright © 1953 Columbia Pictures Corporation
Page 356   POLLYANNA, copyright © Walt Disney Productions
Page 366   CASINO ROYALE, copyright © 1967 Columbia Pictures Corporation
Page 366   JEANNE EAGELS, copyright © 1957 Columbia Pictures Corporation
Page 394   YESTERDAY, TODAY AND TOMORROW, photograph courtesy of Avco Embassy Pictures Corp.
Page 400   CASINO ROYALE, copyright © 1967 Columbia Pictures Corporation
Page 416   GEORGY GIRL, copyright © 1967 Columbia Pictures Corporation
Page 432   JEANNE EAGELS, copyright © 1957 Columbia Pictures Corporation
Page 438   BRIDGE ON THE RIVER KWAI, copyright © 1965 Columbia Pictures Corporation
Page 443   THE GAME IS OVER, copyright © 1966 Columbia Pictures Corporation
Page 443   IT SHOULD HAPPEN TO YOU, copyright © 1953 Columbia Pictures Corporation
Page 438   GUESS WHO'S COMING TO DINNER, copyright © 1968 Columbia Pictures Corporation
Page 470   THE TAMING OF THE SHREW, copyright © 1967 Columbia Pictures Corporation

ACKNOWLEDGMENTS

The author wishes to express his appreciation to the Museum of Modern Art for the special arrangement which has made it possible to reproduce from the original stills in their Film Library.

Grateful acknowledgment is given to the following companies for permission to use stills from their movies:
American International Pictures, Inc.   Avco Embassy Pictures Corporation   Columbia Pictures Corporation
M-G-M Merchandising Corp.   National Telefilm Associates, Inc.   Paramount Pictures   RKO Radio Pictures
Twentieth Century-Fox Film Corporation   United Artists Corporation   Universal Pictures Company
Walt Disney Productions   Warner Bros.-Seven Arts, Inc.

Grateful acknowledgment is made to the following for permission to reprint their material:

Excerpt from "Sonnet CXXXI" from *Collected Poems* by Edna St. Vincent Millay. Published by Harper & Row, Publishers. Copyright © 1939, 1967 by Edna St. Vincent Millay and Norma Millay Ellis. Reprinted by permission of Norma Millay Ellis.

Excerpt from "Provide, Provide" from *Complete Poems of Robert Frost*. Copyright 1936 by Robert Frost. Copyright © 1964 by Lesley Frost Ballantine. Reprinted by permission of Holt, Rinehart and Winston, Inc. and Laurence Pollinger Limited.

Excerpt from *Image*. Reprinted by permission of *Image* magazine.

From Iris Barry's note on "Monsieur Beaucaire" in The Museum of Modern Art's publication *Film Notes* edited by Eileen Bowser. Copyright © 1969 by The Museum of Modern Art, New York. Reprinted by permission of the publisher.

Excerpt from *Memoirs of a Professional Cad* by George Sanders. Copyright © 1960 by George Sanders. Reprinted by permission of G. P. Putnam's Sons and Hamish Hamilton Ltd.

Excerpt from "Danse Macabre," copyright 1940 by W. H. Auden. Excerpt from "Many Happy Returns," copyright 1945 by W. H. Auden. Both from *Collected Shorter Poems 1927-1957* by W. H. Auden. Reprinted by permission of Random House, Inc. and Faber and Faber Ltd.

Excerpts from *Sunshine and Shadow* by Mary Pickford. Copyright © 1955 by Mary Pickford Rogers. Copyright 1954 by McCall Corporation. English version published by William Heinemann Ltd. Reprinted by permission of Mary Pickford Rogers.

Excerpt from *The Last Tycoon* by F. Scott Fitzgerald. Reprinted by permission of Charles Scribner's Sons and Bodley Head.

Designed by Robert Aulicino

TO ARTHUR L. MAYER

Thus some who have the Stars surveyed
   Are ignorantly led
To think these glorious Lamps were made
   To light *Tom Fool* to bed.

               Nicholas Rowe—
        "Song on a Fine Woman
         Who Had a Dull Husband"

TABLE OF CONTENTS

ACKNOWLEDGMENTS

Arthur Mayer and I began this book together, continuing a collaboration which now has lasted twenty-five years, on and off. Illness forced me to withdraw from the project, and it was consigned to limbo for several years. By the time I was able to resume, my collaborator was no longer available. He had not the time for it. True, Mr. Mayer had retired from the bloody arena of the film industry, but only to enter, in his eighth decade, a scene of equal carnage—the college campus. Today he shuttles annually between Dartmouth and U.S.C., with side trips to New York University, Columbia, and Leland Stanford. Clearly such a schedule could leave no room for collaborative work, and it has fallen to me to write this book.

He has read the manuscript. I wish the conventions of publishing allowed me to reproduce his comments in their original form. Such of his suggestions as we managed to agree on have been incorporated into the book; the remainder rest in yet another bloody arena, that of our mutual disputations, which I hope will last forever. But there is more of Mr. Mayer here than meets the eye. Ever since I met him I have been compelled, for my sins and often against my will, to look at the movies as he looks at them. That means, so far as I can express it at all, a view of the situation which postulates that the willful progress of this medium to date has taken place primarily as part of the progress of the audience, and only secondarily as a result of the efforts of others concerned, including those who have made their millions out of the movies. To be sure, he is fond of saying, "Nobody ever lost money underestimating the taste of the public," but this is camouflage. The bulk of his career has consisted of a series of efforts to disprove it. I make, of course, the usual disclaimer: Mr. Mayer is in no way responsible for the opinions expressed here. I couldn't sleep nights if I didn't make it, nor would I be permitted to. His students will know what I mean.

I have also to thank, for help in securing the stills reproduced here: my former colleagues at the Museum of Modern Art, Willard Van Dyke, Eileen Bowser, Marilyn Golden, and Mary Yushak; the Museum itself; Mrs. Samuel Goldwyn; Daniel and Jeffrey Selznick; Darryl F. Zanuck and Jonas Rosenfield of 20th Century-Fox; Lillian Gerard; and Philip Gerard and Eric Naumann of Universal.

Betty Comden and Adolph Green have allowed me to reproduce the immortal Revuers sketch "We Love Joan Crawford," a privilege for which I'm deeply grateful.

This book literally owes its existence to Samuel S. Vaughan of Doubleday. During tribulations touched on above, it often seemed best to abandon the project altogether. Mr. Vaughan simply wouldn't let go, and he left me bereft of excuses by continually smoothing the path ahead. I am also grateful to his assistants, Karen Van Westering and Sally Gately, for reasons they know themselves.

R. G.

FOREWORD

It is always assumed that every boy under ten wants to be President; and he goes along with the assumption, because to dispute it would be to attack the nature of things, which at that stage in his life he is not yet prepared to do. Later, in "maturity," he may openly thank his stars that this ungrateful and agonizing job, or role, has proved unattainable. All of us, with the exception of Norman Mailer, are grateful that this cup has passed from us and that we may with decency, honor, and legitimate sloth devote ourselves to the attainable goal of becoming a corporation *vice*-president, a major of marines in the Mekong delta, a mechanic—not an astronaut—at Cape Kennedy, or an advocate of black militancy on TV. In these roles we many reasonably hope to perform as expected, and if we know in our hearts that our performance in them is more an act of impersonation than a deed done for its own sake, the world will not necessarily expose us. It can hardly be bothered; it has its own problems, nearly identical with ours. It will let us alone, secure in our modest pretense that we are what we seem to be, and that we aspire to be no more than that.

But actors, like the very rich, are not like us. They exist only to impersonate other people, and what they may be in themselves is nothing to our purpose, or so we maintain. We do not call upon them to produce evidence that they actually possess the character or personality, or even the intellect or passion, which they simulate so convincingly. To us, their believability is all, and if they have the skill to make us believe in something which does not actually exist, so much the better. That art we admire—admire and envy. Not that our envy is altogether open. In spite of his material success, there is still among us the ghost of a prejudice against the actor, left over from an earlier conception of what is virile and what isn't. Walter Kerr has drawn attention to a passage from Pauline Kael's *Kiss Kiss Bang Bang* in which Miss Kael is interviewing Sidney Lumet as he directs *The Group:* "I had asked him during one of our first talks why he had given up acting and he had begun a long explanation about how acting is as a faggot's career and how he knew that if he was ever going to give a woman a real human relationship, etc., and I had simply jotted down 'too short for an actor.'" Women, of course, can afford this sort of exposure of the emperor's nakedness. Even today, nobody really assumes that women aspire to be President—nor ever will aspire, until they can expect to be addressed by some more attractive honorific than Madam President. It was for so long the part of women to be all things to all men than nobody thought to inquire what they might be in themselves—it could prove to be inconvenient to find out, as indeed the event showed. It was easier to take the position that they were essential chameleons, natural-born actresses—and that acting, despite much box-office evidence to the contrary, was primarily a woman's racket, with all that the term implies. Making believe you are what you're not is just not manly; better to carry pretense a step further and insist that you always are exactly what you seem. Let the mask be a single one; to change it too often is admitting too much.

But this set of human reactions to the acting profession contains within it the seed of a paradox. The pinnacle of success in acting is to become a star, and a star does not change. A star is "fixed," in both the old and the new senses of the word. For an actor, to become a star is to be elected President—to be elevated to the purple—to be assumed into heaven, like the Virgin Mary. A star must *be* what actors only seem, and be that being almost from the start. People say that men grow in the presidency, that the weight of the office calls forth powers which otherwise would have slept unknown in them all their lives. But among the varieties of the great, great stars are mostly born great; rarely do they achieve greatness, still more rarely is it thrust upon them. Sometimes in praising them we pause to admire their skill or artistry or flair, but it is not these things that we love or worship or desire to possess. It is *them*.

It was not always thus. The evolution of the star has been part of the evolution of man. The earliest discussions of actors and acting of which we have record took place in ancient Greece, and in the Theater of Dionysus there were no stars. The visible *persona* of the Greek actor consisted almost entirely of a literal mask, a mask fabricated by other hands than his, according to other ideas. All that he was in himself was a disembodied voice, and it was by the quality of his voice and the skill of his use of it that he was judged. Range, power, modulation, sensitivity, brought him his rewards or punishments; he was always a craftsman and sometimes an artist, but he disappeared into the great parts he played, and it was they, not he, which had emotional and intellectual meaning to his auditors. In both Greece and Rome, the actor was condemned and banished with the advent of Christianity. In the presence of Him to whom all hearts are open, from whom no secrets are hid, seeming was held to be unseemly. When the actor reappeared, he did so as a member of a rigidly defined social class: "a vagabond, lascivious and vulgar, a mountebank, a comedian, whose sole function was to entertain"—to relieve the tedium of medieval life. As such he might possess great skill, but his skills were divorced from the projection of feeling, the skills of the contortionist, the juggler, the con artist. Feeling crept back only when the actor became again the instrument of the playwright, the mouth of his words.

The Elizabethan theater in which he regained his stature as craftsman and artist differed from the Greek. It was much smaller, the audience was much closer, more intimately connected with the stage, and felt very differently about the people on it.

These, no matter how heroic they might be, were no longer hieratic figures in a cosmic drama but human beings who shared the common huan lot. It was as such, no longer as gods or heroes, that they came to fascinate. As the theater audience slowly grew, it called for players who were ever more like what they played. Women could no longer be acted by boys; the tangible lure of actual feminity had to felt across the footlights. And now the mystery and magic of acting itself became apparent. Even Shakespeare marveled that "this player here but in a fiction, in a dream of passion could force his soul so to his own conceit that fro mher working all his visage wann'd." By the time of David Garrick, it could be said that he "raised the character of his profession to the rank of a liberal art."

Garrick and his contemporaries and successors so took the public by the throat that they soon literally and automatically occupied stage center. They were always given the great roles in the great plays—and if nothing really suitable for them was conveniently to hand, something, anything, was thrown together to enable them to appear. They become first a major and then *the* major reason for theater attendance. They became stars. Just when the word passed into use is unknown, but by the nineteenth century it was commonplace. Stars were still supposed to be actors first, great actors born with the gift, whom it was the public's pleasure to elevate because of their outstanding merit, or what seemed their merit in the taste of the time. But such prodigies were rare, and as the theater grew into a business, business enterprise was impatient at their rarity. Impresarios began to think it a main part of their trade to find stars, to "introduce" them, if necessary to create them by fiat. Seeking players endowed with the divine afflatus, they were constrained by demand to find this where it only doubtfully existed, and to substitute for it qualities only peripherally related to it—beauty, charm, eccentricity, even actual deformity, whatever caught the roving and increasingly sated eye. They looked far outside the theater for human "values," often very primitive ones, which could be transmuted into theatrical star attractions. Gladiators had been the favorite entertainers of ancient Rome; originally idolized by the mob for their prowess and courage, they became inevitably the sexual favorites of the Roman great, of both sexes. The same sort of thing began to happen in the modern theater, once the star became the key to the box office. The mountebanks and vagabonds, the jugglers and contortionists, crept back in politer guise, and boxer John L. Sullivan was only the most pre-eminent of many sports idols who were taught the rudiments of acting and exhibited as stars. Even in opera, for a time the favorite urban form of theater, and which might be thought of as the impregnable fortress of artistry, since it required, all at once, natural gifts, long training, and exquisite skill—even in opera, the appeal of basic sensation gradually transcended that of feeling and intellect. In that shrewd old play *Tonight or Never,* the aged ex-diva quotes her former lover the King of Portugal: "'Bianca darling,' he said to me, 'You're not singing with your voice, you're singing with your—well, never mind what it was he thought I was singing with.'" Under these conditions the dramatist, hitherto thought of as the onlie begetter of the theater, was reduced to something like carpentry; it became the principal task of most of them to produce "star vehicles," designed entirely to show off the assets of the stars and, as important, to conceal their numerous deficiencies.

Not only playwrights but actors wedded to the older theatrical traditions sought to stem this tide by any means they could. Actors who were also stars tried to combine the best of both worlds by becoming actor-managers. Actors who clearly had no chance of ever becoming stars formed repertory companies whose members all played on equal terms and achieved memorable heights of theatrical artistry. Neither expedient succeeded in attracting a dependable audience—has not to this day. By 1900, in spite of Ibsen, Chekhov, Shaw, and Barrie, the theater throughout the Western world was star-dominated. Charles Frohman "created" four dozen stars between 1883 and 1915, and gloried in the fact. "A star has a unique value in a play," he said. "It concentrates interest. In some respects a play is like a dinner. To be a success, no matter how splendidly served, the menu should always have one unique and striking dish that, despite its elaborate gastronomic surroundings, must long be remembered. This is one reason why you need a star in a play." No doubt he could have cited others. But Mr. Frohman, peace be to him, was no crass commercial tyrant bent on crushing art. He was simply talking about what he had learned from his audiences.

The arrival of the movies hugely speeded up a process already far advanced. The silent screen instantly deprived the actor of his vital organ, his voice, on whose natural qualities and skillful use rested all his hopes for recognition and success. At one stroke, he was placed on an equal footing with amateurs. In place of the voice, the movies soon produced their own characteristic expressive device, the close-up—and in the close-up the trained actor was not only on a level with amateurs but at an actual disadvantage compared to them. The close-set camera revealed the stage actor's hallowed technique as a box of tricks which obscured his humanity, while the "human raw material" which the movies quickly drew to them stood forth unobscured, luminously dramatized by the frame of the screen and the play of black-and-white light and shade across it. The silent camera naturally drew attention away from the speaking mouth and focused it on the eyes, and it was in the use of their eyes that the difference between the old and the new actors showed most quickly. Stage actors were trained in the "use" of the eye, yes indeed, but when they brought what they had learned to the screen, "eye rolling" became a term of abuse equal to "scenery chewing." Mary Pickford had only to stand still and look through the camera at the audience to communicate thoughts too deep for tears.

So the people of the movies came before us first of all as people, and only secondarily as actors—artists—if at all. An acting art of the silent screen did develop, based on the powers of the camera and only remotely related to its stage antecedents in mime and dance. It was often piercingly beautiful and moving and, though irretrievably lost now, it may be one of the typical art expressions of the twentieth century. But it was not by their skill in this art that we judged the people we met in the dark, it was by the look of them and by the way they behaved, and especially in their unconscious behavior—the actions which Freud called "symptomatic." To these things we reacted instantly, in love or hate, and those we loved enough or hated enough we made into stars of a magnitude and incandescence unknown in the theater's two thousand years of history. The immense new world audience, comprising almost all humanity, was bound together in a new way by its feelings toward these creatures—creatures of the camera and of our own imagining. And those feelings themselves, the feelings we harbor toward the stars, propound the problem of our lives and times, the problem of identity.

Actors originally pretended to be gods and heroes, very much larger than life but commensurately two-dimensional in their actions and passions. Their audiences eventually bade them scale themselves down to some more human level, where they could feel with them both more deeply and more comfortably. The twentieth century, characteristically, demands both things at once from its stars. In Greta Garbo's first years on the screen, while the American public gawked at her mysterious image and speculated—was she an actress or a beauty or a camera fluke or just some kind of nut—the Germans coined the perfectly appropriate phrase for her, *die göttliche Garbo*. That, goddesslike, through all her incarnations she remained, and it is that which sets her apart. All the others have had to do double duty. From Mary and Doug and Lillian, through Pola and Gloria and Rudy, Jean and Clark and Jeanette, down to Marilyn and Marlon and Liz and Richard, they have all been constrained by their public to be bona fide gods and goddesses with actual feet of clay. Tonight we may succumb to Julie Andrews' screen magic and be borne with her on perilous seas in faery lands forlorn, but tomorrow morning we expect and demand to see her on a TV panel show in which she dispenses cooking hints, exchanges Broadway banter with show-wise comedians, and retails whatever new news she can squeeze out about the state of her divorce and her plans for her children. It is not that Miss Andrews and her sister stars are no longer "allowed" a private life. It is that they know and accept the fact that their private lives are among the wares they offer for sale, and if they haven't got a marketable one they had better manufacture it quick. That has become as much a part of the business of stardom as the technical trickeries employed to manufacture the stellar illusion on the screen—trickeries which now replace acting, and which are performed by directors, editors, sound mixers, and other technicians so obscure that a star may never meet them in the course of a long career. The pettiness, tawdriness, and tedium of all this needs no emphasis. It has become a problem of the day, like the problem of how to dispose of radioactive waste. But the horrors of the contemporary star system are no fault of the stars. They derive from ourselves, from our implacable, insatiable demand for glorified images of ourselves, however factitious, however meretricious. We perhaps need not blame ourselves overmuch. By and large, we continually accept shoddy substitutes because the real thing is so rare, and cannot be manufactured. In our defense it can be said that when it does appear, we always know it. Marilyn Monroe had no qualifications for success but herself, but we loved her on sight. It has happened that way many times. It can happen tomorrow. It will.

Richard Griffith

New York, May 1968

I
EARLY
FANFARE

The studio caption says "Mystery stars in the Solution Room." This does not mean that Sidney Bracey, Marguerite Snow, and Florence LaBadie are about to dissolve. They were the stars of a weekly serial whose audiences were urged to write in their own "solutions," the winning one being then hastily filmed and released as the last episode. Here, we are asked to believe, the stars themselves mull resulting mountains of mail in the Solution Room.

1 THE NAMELESS

The little people who appeared in pictures between 1896 and 1912 hardly thought of themselves as actors, much less stars. That they were not quite sure exactly what it was they were doing is shown by the fact that they often referred to their work as "posing" for the camera. Some of them, like Mabel Normand and Norma Talmadge, had actually been artists' or photographers' models, chosen for photographable pulchritude. Most of the rest of them were veterans of medicine shows and circuses, or journeyman actors in touring stock companies who turned up in New York once a year, not with the hope of getting into the big time but simply to line up their next tour. Now they found this new kind of work, much less tiring than travelling from town to town, and payday every Saturday made the studios the only Eden they had known since childhood. They hoped the "movie craze" would last as long as possible and let it go at that. In the steady guerilla warfare among the early movie companies there were occasional raids which resulted in the transfer of some players from one film-manufacturing plant to another, but these favored ones found the change made small difference in their pay and working conditions. They were artisans helping to turn out a product, not actors practicing their art.

Such art as they did practice consisted of pantomine, and it was not pantomine of their own invention. The rather nebulous "directors" (sometimes called managers) who supervised film-making based their direction on stage gesture, grossly exaggerated to compensate for the silent screen's lack of words. Often these gesticulations resembled acting less than they did the kind of dumb show which people who speak different languages resort to in their effort to communicate. It was all pretty bad, and for the early movie public there was little basis for preference of one actor over another. But choose the public did. Almost from the beginning, moviegoers felt, and tried to express, a liking for certain players. It was liking based not on skill but on humanity—on a "something about them."

(At left) The first movie stars, stars on film, at any rate, were public personages. People at last could see and admire, in all but the flesh, the men and women at the top of the human pyramid whom previously they had only read about. Queen Victoria's progress through Ireland in the last year of her life revealed to the world that she was indeed as Noël Coward said, "a very little lady." (Above) Sixteen-year-old Lillian Gish, left, was the heroine of this early D. W. Griffith film, *The Musketeers of Pig Alley.* But Griffith's camera in this scene happened to focus on the unforgettable face of the nameless girl in the center of the shot— and a murmurous wave swept audiences at this point in the film whenever it was shown. No one knows what became of this particular extra, but such raw material, and such camera accidents, became the stuff of stardom later on.

2 THE FIRST STARS

Movies of the nickelodeon days had no professional critics, no publicity men and no fan press; it was the film public who picked the first stars—they and nobody else. The pioneer producers were far from eager to do so. They looked upon their wares as so much "product"—even D. W. Griffith spoke of early movie-making as "grinding out hamburgers" and their principal concern was that the product's ingredients, including the actors, should be kept as inexpensive as possible. Some producers despised the human herd who were enriching them, the slum crowds who thronged the store shows of the cities, the poor farmers who drove their produce to town on Saturday and stayed to see the nickel show. But the herd refused to be cattle. Just because the movie was the only diversion they could afford, everything about it fascinated them and inevitably, like all fans before and since, they became connoisseurs. They learned from experience that they liked the films labeled "Biograph" better than the more pretentious ones labeled "Kleine." They gradually became aware that the jolly fat man who, in spite of his monstrous obesity, was so much like you and me worked for the Vitagraph company, and so did the sad-eyed, tall brunette and the vivid ingenue who sometimes also played villainesses. They distinguished between the two Biograph blondes, the one with the large, curving nose and the other so-beautiful one whose golden hair fell in long ringlets—how they loved her! Indeed, they loved them all, and as they saw them again and again and talked them over after the show, they wanted to know more about these people on the screen, so godlike in their beauty but so warm too, and in spite of their silence so much closer than "stage players" had ever been. Soon letters, misspelled and blotted, began to trickle into the studios, asking about the anonymous players—who they were, whether they were married or single, where they had been born, and what their next pictures would be.

Even when the trickle of letters became a stream, producers ignored them. It wouldn't do to let these camera-hogs think they were anybody, or worth anything. After all, all of them could easily be replaced; there were plenty of hungry actors waiting at the studio doors. The word was "no names given out" and the policy was rigidly adhered to for five years, an extraordinarily long time considering the constant increase in the popularity of the movies and the spread of what a European observer called the *virus cinematica*. Then one of the producers broke ranks. When Florence Lawrence, known only to the fans as "the Biograph Girl," moved over to Carl Laemmle's Imp company, he wanted to make sure that her popularity moved with her. So he publicly rechristened her "The Imp Girl," faked what was undoubtedly the first movie publicity stunt by denying that she had been killed in a (non-existent) streetcar accident, revealed her name, and spoke in an advertisement of her "career." That fatal word symbolized the transformation which almost immediately swept over motion pictures. From 1908 onward, the humble screen players had names, publics, and "careers" which were no longer solely dependent on the favor of the movie overlords. The audience now had a vote in the process of film-making, and could maintain its favorites in the spotlight indefinitely—and just as quickly vote them out.

Florence Lawrence. Looking at her pictures and her films today, it is difficult to see *why* Florence Lawrence was the first star, but in terms of billing she was. G. M. Anderson, who preceded her in favor, was hidden behind the mythic identity of "Broncho Billy."

(Opposite page) Francis X. Bushman. This profile belongs to the best remembered of the first matinee idols. When he appeared in person in Chicago, he caused a riot comparable to the political Convention riots of 1968.

(Left) Maurice Costello. This stage Englishman was a slightly uncharacteristic role for one of the earliest movie matinee idols. His magnetism was overlaid by a haggardness which his young fans took for a sign of dissipation and therefore of wordly experience. Today he is remembered as the father of Dolores and Helene Costello— by those who remember *them*.

(Below) Broncho Billy Anderson. This prettified and rather saintly-looking gentleman was without doubt the first star made by motion pictures, the first perennial screen character, and, as he genially admitted, the first movie phony. Known throughout the world simply as "Broncho Billy," the absolute prototype of the heroic, acrobatic, equestrian star, he was born Max Aronson in Little Rock, Arkansas, he hated riding horses, and faked as many of his stunts as he could get away with. A lover of soft living, he allowed his career to die with the death of two-reelers, but by that time he had permanently fixed the pattern of the Western film.

3 THE MOVIE CRAZE

The *virus cinematica* spread fast. The movies were beginning to be talked about in a big way, and even if most of those who did the talking were far below the salt, those above it could not ignore the craze, and soon movie talk had become table talk in every walk of life. As is apt to happen, somebody thought up a way to make money out of all this conversation. Less than two years after Miss Lawrence was launched on her "career," the fan magazines appeared. *Motion Picture Magazine* was founded in 1910, and was swiftly followed by *Photoplay, Picture Play, Screenland, Motion Picture Classic,* and a host of others now forgotten. (The magazines named are still being published, half a century later.) These publications fed the movie craze by speeding up the process of identification of the players, answered the questions implicit in fan letters about who they were and where they came from, and gloated over their sensible and modest reactions to the fame and fortune which were suddenly theirs. That was about all, at first. There wasn't a great deal to be said about the humble origins of these budding stars, or their present activities either. Splendor was still around the corner. But even so, the pablum thus dished out fed certain new thoughts in the minds of the younger men and more energetic fans. When they learned that only yesterday Mabel Normand had been a photographer's model, and Mae Marsh a ribbon clerk, they reasoned, not unnaturally: They were nobodies, just like me, but they made it. Who's to say I can't make it too?

4 FAMOUS PLAYERS IN FAMOUS PLAYS

"Florence Hackett belonged to the theatrical underworld. While her sons Raymond and Albert flourished as boy actors in the openness of the stage, she was working—it wasn't called acting but *working*—in motion pictures." The terminology used by Norbert Lusk in describing this small tragedy well illumines the attitude of the "real" theater, toward its new rival. The stage people had long since made up their minds about the movies and the "actors" who appeared in them. It was considered work little above posing for pornographic pictures (in some movies made by fly-by-night companies, it was actually that). Any "legitimate" player so down on his luck that he had to work in pictures because he needed the money tried to make sure nobody saw him sneaking into the studios. Subsequently he could hope none of his friends would see him on the screen, which they were unlikely to do since going to the movies, as well as appearing in them, carried a social stigma.

Against this background it remains all the more surprising that Adolph Zukor got, and clung to, his idea of luring famous stars from the theater into being filmed in their best-known stage vehicles. It seemed to everyone in 1912 unlikely, indeed unthinkable, that the great personalities of Broadway would listen to Zukor the little exhibitor with a few nickelodeons and vaudeville houses. But if Zukor himself had no prestige, he knew where he could get it. He could import it. In Europe, they felt very differently about the movies. The great European favorites saw in the camera a chance for immortality—a slim chance, to be sure, but still the possibility that their appearance and gestures, if not their golden voices, would go down to posterity. Sarah Bernhardt, greatest of them all, had filmed the duel scene from *Hamlet* (in which she played the title role) as early as 1900, and by 1911 was making pictures regularly. When Zukor learned that her French producer was having trouble finding money to finish her *Queen Elizabeth,* he saw and seized his opportunity. In return for an advance of $40,000 (the exact price is disputed), he secured the American rights to *Queen Elizabeth* and opened it on Broadway under the auspices of his respected theater friend, Daniel Frohman. To this first of all movie premieres came the cream of New York and especially the cream of the theater.

Queen Elizabeth holds only historical interest when seen today, and it is possible that even in 1912 it seemed static and uninspiring to movie audiences reared on the melodrama of D. W. Griffith and Thomas H. Ince and the slapstick of Mack Sennett. But because of Bernhardt's fame, people felt they had to go to see it, and if they did not much like what they saw, they kept quiet about it. The fact that this hollow success garnered reams of press space and made a good deal of money misled everybody, including not only Zukor but the barons of Broadway as well. It seemed perfectly clear that the future of the movies lay in transferring stage plays with their casts bodily from stage to screen. Producers began to dream happily—they still do—of turning all their old successes (and their failures as well) into profitable films. Stars looked forward to lucrative stints before the camera in the summertime when they were "between engagements." Playwrights ransacked trunks and attics for their old plays, which, though unsalable in the theater, would be plenty good enough for the movies. It was an amazing reversal of field. But most people will eat a lot of words for money, and in movies there seemed to be plenty for all, or all who could get into them quickly enough. For Zukor had the ball and was running with it. Before *Queen Elizabeth* ended its Broadway run, he had signed James K. Hackett, James O' Neill, and other stage favorites, and was acquiring starring vehicles for them as rapidly as possible. His competitors were quick to follow suit. From 1912 to 1915, the big news in each week's issue of *The Dramatic Mirror* or *The Moving Picture World* was which new luminary of the stage (or vaudeville or even opera) had been signed for pictures at what astronomical salary, climaxed by Cecil B. De Mille's engagement of Geraldine Farrar at $10,000 a week for ten weeks' work.

Stills are not an entirely reliable guide to the character or quality of motion pictures, but these pictures very reliably tell, and at a glance, what happened to the idols of the stage who let themselves be lured to California. The said idols were too old and too heavy for the motion picture camera. Their magic was a matter of stage illusion, of make-up and lighting and of gestures and actions governed by and attuned to vocal phrasing. Above all, and it can't be repeated too often, they were too old. A stage actress might have to serve an apprenticeship of a quarter of a century before she was qualified to play fifteen-year-old Ophelia, and then her qualifications consisted mainly of how deeply and with what musical meaning she could utter the line "I was the more deceiv'd." As for Ophelia's youthful appeal, that was described in words by the master playwright—words he put into the mouth of Polonius. For the camera, youth had to be embodied by youth, even extreme youth; as D. W. Griffith had already discovered, the hard light of early movie days aged the looks of even comparatively young men and women, and *his* Ophelias and Hamlets had to be portrayed by girls and boys just past puberty, if their mothers were to be believed. The great movie public, of course, did not pause to tease out these distinctions. Barred from the theater by their poverty, they owed no allegiance to the theater's traditions, and felt no deeper emotion about its famous executants than curiosity. That satisfied, and the resulting disappointment quickly swallowed, they turned back to something they already knew they liked better—the lovely and quickening image of Mary Pickford, and those of her many and enchanting colleagues and rivals.

(Top) Lily Langtry was for thirty years the most celebrated international beauty of her age. Minus any acting qualifications, she had only to appear on a stage to inspire floods of adulation and therefore floods of cash. But she had been the "Jersey Lily" far too long by the time she faced the unemotional camera.

(Above) Enrico Caruso was the king of opera by virtue of possessing the greatest voice of his time, which made him acceptable in romantic roles in spite of his obvious devotion to spaghetti. But his first film, *My Cousin,* was so great a flop that his second was never even released.

(Left) Constance Collier's Melisande, her Duchess of Towers in *Peter Ibbetson,* had embodied the dreams of a generation of theatergoers on two continents. She must have been astonished when asked to pose with a prop parrot as a publicity gag for her first film, especially when the film was an elegant version of *Macbeth* in which she starred with Sir Herbert Beerbohm Tree in 1916. Miss Collier had to wait a long time to find her movie niche, first as a voice coach for silent stars in early talkie days, and later as a valued character actress.

5 FAVORITES OF THE FANS

Mary Pickford too was a theater veteran, but that wasn't why the movie fans singled her out as the favorite of favorites. When she was a secondary Belasco actress, Zukor signed her for his "Famous Players" in a subsidiary position to such names as James O'Neill and Frances Starr, on whose greater fame he hoped to capitalize more quickly. But the fans already knew Mary from her earlier movie appearances, and her genuine popularity quickly gained her more fans than any of the suddenly fusty-seeming stage celebrities had ever known in their long careers.

Charlie Chaplin also was characterized as being "of" the theater though when Mack Sennett learned that his New York partners had signed this obscure English variety artist—not even a star—he wondered how far toward absurdity the vogue for bringing stage folk to the screen could be carried. But Charlie quickly discarded his vaudeville tricks, as quickly adopted Sennett's improvisatory style, and within a year had created the screen character of Charlie the Tramp. Indeed, it was The Tramp and Little Mary, not Charles S. Chaplin and Miss Pickford, whom the world came to adore.

Not out of trouping skill, but out of their own *personae,* they created "screen characters"—archetypal figures whose deep appeal lay below the level of consciousness. The camera's ability to fashion such figures out of human raw material, as exemplified by this supreme pair, held the key to success or failure for all future screen players. Those Broadwayites who did manage to survive trial by camera owed their almost accidental success to what they were like and not to what they had done. Anita Loos manufactured the character of the athletic optimist out of Douglas Fairbanks' private personality, not his professional one. Alla Nazimova's stage reputation as a cerebral interpretress of Ibsen and Chekhov meant nothing in the nickelodeon but they took to her for the highly physical reason that she looked like an even vampier vamp than their Theda Bara. Pauline Frederick, it is true, had on screen as well as on stage the old traditional virtues of versatility and technical skill, but she held her public through a long series of conventional heroines, vamps, weary demimondaines, and even mother roles because what was inside her handsome skull shone forth through her enormous eyes and even expressed itself in the proud set of her back. People said of her that she "made thought visible." T. S. Eliot might have called what she offered "the objective correlative," and pop anthropologists today would probably name it charisma. The fans were later taught by their mentors, the press agents, to call it "It" or, subsequently, "Oomph." By 1916 it was clear to the movie bosses and to the once proud, now humbled overlords of the stage that all who came before the camera, professional or amateur, did so on roughly equal terms. Theatrical experience and even theatrical fame in themselves meant nothing. Many of the stars of the teens pictured here had some background, in theater but it gave them little advantage over a photographer's model like Norma Talmadge, over the giant Maciste, a furniture mover whose appearance in *Cabiria* made him a star in his native Italy, or even over a mere movie-struck girl like Mae Marsh. What gave an eager aspirant his first chance before the camera were youth, beauty, and a definitely "sympathetic" (or definitely unsympathetic) quality. What thereafter carried him or her to heights was, usually, strongly-marked, idiosyncratic traits which could be captured in visual terms. Behind the fashions of the teens (a particularly trying period of fashion) it is possible to see from these faces what made them stars to whom a world audience responded.

Ruth Roland gained top popularity as the tomboy heroine of countless serials, mostly Westerns. Her vogue waned in the twenties, but by that time Miss Roland had made and saved enough money to finance her own pictures. The added expense of the talkies put an end to such ventures and Miss Roland retreated to Hollywood drawing rooms, where the silent star was always ready to oblige with a song, whether anybody asked her to sing or not.

(Above) The 1914 Italian spectacle *Cabiria* introduced to movie fans who were bored with "Famous Players in Famous Plays" a favorite who was not only innocent of theatrical experience but who could hardly write his own name. Maciste was a common laborer—a Milan furniture mover—until his role as the giant in this film shot him to international fame and to a ten-year stardom in elemental but popular Italian films.

(Left above) The epitome of the clean-cut or, as it was known then, the "Arrow collar" look, Wallace Reid rose from a bit in *The Birth of a Nation* to spectacular stardom as a flapper's dream. Everyone thought him the ideal young American, virile, aggressive, gay, imaginative, and handsome as Apollo. None could foresee his agonized death from drug addiction ten years later.

(Left below) Geraldine Farrar was brought to films as a "Famous Player," to be exploited for her name as an internationally known opera star, and it was thought that she was doomed to failure like the rest of the stage importations. But Miss Farrar took one look at the silent, action-filled, pantomimic medium, discarded her operatic technique, and made herself over into a movie actress of skill, effectiveness, and glamour. Here she shows what lengths she was willing to go to in *The World and Its Woman.*

(Right) Alla Nazimova survived the other casualties of the stage invasion because her looks enabled her to outdo Theda Bara as the vampiest of vamps. Here she gives the full treatment to Oscar Wilde's sexless *Salome* (1922).

(Above right) Classical beauty, magnetism, and dynamic acting genius made Pauline Frederick a great and uniquely respected star of stage, screen, and vaudeville for thirty years, and her voice on the radio reflected the same qualities in the last stage of her long career. Another voice on the air today answers to the name of Pauline Frederick, and, though the two are in no way related, the new voice bears the same patrician characteristics as the old.

(Opposite page, left) Norma Talmadge's was a perfect example of the movie face in profile. Her curving nose lent individuality to her beauty, and her sparkling, liquid eyes "registered" as well from the side as from the front. (Right) Viola Dana had the kind of "full face" that early cameramen loved. Her rounded cheeks gave her face symmetry without appearing plump, and her enormous eyes, the *sine qua non* of the first stars, at once dominated and balanced the facial pattern. (Above) Pola Negri's mouth was too small for conventional beauty, and her face and head had too many sharp angles to meet the classical standard. But these seeming defects gave her camera appearance a vividness which matched the temperamental spirit within.

THE MOVIE FACE 6

"Those dough-faced movie actresses!" was a favorite epithet of middle-class ladies whose unspoken thought was clearly: If those movie girls can make it looking like that, why can't I? Such doughfaces did indeed exist in great numbers on the early screen, young girls with an irritating almost-prettiness whose featureless faces were made moonier by unskillfully-applied make-up and flat lighting. But they dwindled in number as time rushed on and the necessities of the camera and of pantomine made themselves felt. By 1920 a sort of typical movie face had emerged, recognizable at a glance to audiences everywhere. Symmetry was the first requirement of such a face, but within symmetry it was well that individual features should be strongly marked—firm chin, long upper lip, strong nose, and classic brow. Especially it was important that the eyes be large and liquid. Such faces not only represented ideal beauty to the untutored; they made vivid, and therefore easy to follow, the instantaneous "registering" of basic passions which the silence of the screen required. A good director of the early days could do almost anything with such a face, even if its possessor was next door to idiocy. To this extent, the cynicism of the middle-class ladies was justified. Oddly enough, such faces seemed to go with a specific and not altogether attractive physical type. The actresses who possessed them were usually short of stature, with a head too large for symmetry.

A movie face was an almost certain guarantee of a camera test, which, if successfully passed, led automatically to a contract and, with luck, long service as a leading lady or leading man. But these fortunates often had cause to wonder why they got no further, why they were stuck in a rut of temperate success. The great stars, when they came along, seemed to be the exception that proved the rule. The Hollywood experience gradually revealed that, short of a glass eye or a wooden leg (and Herbert Marshall even had that) you could suffer under great physiognomic handicaps and still go straight to the top if you had "star quality." But what was that?

Phyllis Honer in *Chicago*

Constance Talmadge in *The Duchess of Buffalo*

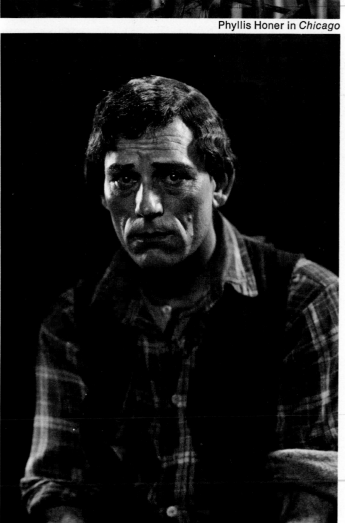

Lon Chaney in *Wolf Breed*

Lillian Gish in *La Bohème*

SELECTED
SHORT
SUBJECTS I

Blanche Sweet

Erich von Stroheim in *The Wedding March*

II
THE
HEYDAY OF
THE STARS

Mae West

James Coburn

Robert Young

Janet Gaynor

Tala Birell

James Mason

WHAT MAKES A STAR? 1

The author hereby disclaims in advance any intent in the following pages to provide a handy guide to stardom for would-be stars, or a key to the discovery of stars for would-be discoverers. I am privy to neither secret; if I were, I would own all the studios—and be deeply involved in litigation with the Department of Justice under the anti-trust laws. Once I sat with Douglas Fairbanks, Jr. through one of the more flatulent of the old Rudolph Valentino vehicles—a film which as a piece of craftsmanship obviously offended Fairbanks as a film-maker and also bored him silly. But at the end he said, "Yes, Valentino had star quality—whatever that is."

Whatever that is. Ask the next person you meet why his favorite is his favorite and you are likely to get either a gush of words or silence. The current of attraction between star and audience, the emotional and body chemistry involved lie far below the level of words. A star cannot come into his stardom until his image has been printed on film and shown to an audience, and to bring this about the movies have had to develop an elaborate machinery, the components of which are usually called Discovery, Grooming, and Launching. This machinery will shortly be described because it gives form to what is called the star system. But no machinery ever of itself and by itself made a star. That takes place in the depths of the collective unconscious. Where the mystique of stardom is concerned, the eager seeker after truth may as well look within himself as read further. On these two pages appear the photographs of eight players, all stars, near-stars or one-time stars. I have chosen two female and two male stars whom I admire for reasons unknown to myself, and also two stars of each sex whom I have, in the eloquent English phrase, "took against," also for unknown reasons. The reader may guess which is which. The only clue offered is that these particular photographs have been chosen to illustrate aspects of the author's liking and disliking. No answers are given in the back of the book, and no prizes will be awarded. This is essentially a Rorschach test. The object of the exercise is to stimulate self-searching, and to provide evidence of the fact that stars are made by elective affinities. The only voting that counts is done at the box office.

Lee Marvin

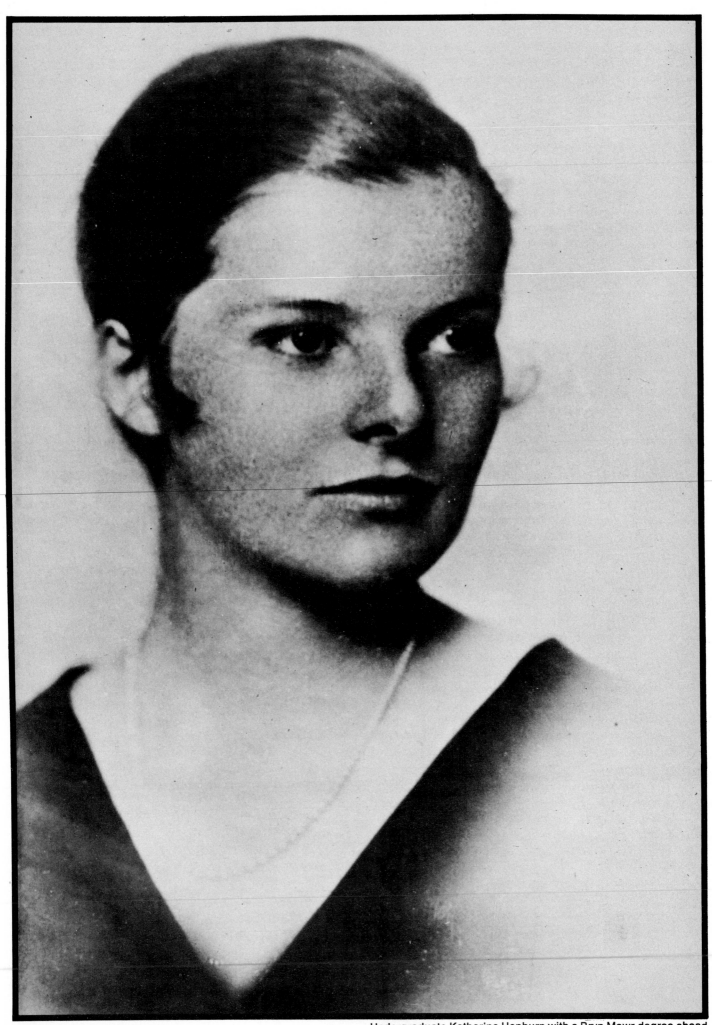
Undergraduate Katharine Hepburn with a Bryn Mawr degree ahead.

WHERE DO THEY COME FROM?

"God makes the stars," said Samuel Goldwyn. "It's up to the producers to find them." But where to look? The answer has for a long time been, *everywhere* in the civilized and uncivilized world. As has been shown, the first movie stars got their chance to get in front of the cameras almost by accident, and a large proportion of them came from the lower income groups. These two facts made a profound impression on Hollywood and the masters of the movies. The studios do the obvious, of course. Their search for new faces begins with the theater and all its related professions, where talent and ambition and performance have already singled out likely aspirants. Almost anyone who has ever faced the public from a stage, a skating rink, a sawdust ring, or even a flying trapeze can sooner or later induce somebody in pictures to give him a test on the chance that the camera and microphone will fall in love with his "specialty," and with him. But the studios do not stop at the obvious. If Robert Flaherty can find a Sabu in the jungles of India, if an ugly college professor named Louis Wolheim turns out to be a superb actor, if an Ava Gardner emerges from the barbarous backwoods of North Carolina, or a Mervyn LeRoy stumbles on a Lana Turner under the noses of all Hollywood—why, then, who knows where digging what ditch, under what lamppost, or even under what stone, the next great sensation may be found? Nobody. The gamble implicit in every aspect of picture-making is nowhere better exemplified than in the search for talent.

Who does the looking? Traditionally, the talent scout, that legendary figure more conspicuous in the plots of movies about show biz than in the actual operation of studio policy. They exist, of course, and in boom times in considerable numbers, turning up in thin disguise at amateur theatricals, and eying college graduating classes as if they were corporation recruiters in search of executive material. But in a box-office slump they are among the first employees to be laid off. They are a luxury for the studios and in a sense a superfluity, since talent-scouting is the second occupation of everybody connected with motion pictures, from producer to office boy. D. W. Griffith, the granddaddy of star-finders, was often in danger of being picked up for suspicious loitering; he followed odd-looking persons for blocks, and sometimes scraped acquaintances with them. If report be true, the career and public image of George Hamilton have been largely shaped on the advice of two veterans, Gloria Swanson and the late Mae Murray. Every casting department expects to have its time wasted by fellow employees extolling "discoveries" whose principal qualification for stardom proves to be that they are relatives or girl friends. Emotion and ego play important parts in the hit-or-miss process. Mary Astor is one of many players whom Lillian Gish tried to help get started. Through her, Miss Astor achieved a screen test at the Griffith studio, but nothing came of it. Years later, Miss Gish elucidated "Mr. Griffith is peculiar. He likes to make his own discoveries, and I think I pushed you too hard."

Almost anybody can "discover" obvious beauty or talent, but to spot potential star quality in apparently unpromising raw material takes a penetrating and exquisitely experienced eye—an eye that knows from practice and from many errors what light can do, what makeup and costume can accentuate or hide, and most particularly how an actor's or actress's unconscious self-image, hidden even from himself, can be brought to the surface and developed, like a positive print from a negative. Nobody at M-G-M could

Sabu with Kola Nogo in Robert Flaherty's *Elephant Boy*   Gary Cooper with paint brush.   Burt Lancaster with Gina Lollobrigida and Tony Curtis in *Trapeze*

Ann Harding with Jasper Deeter at the Hedgerow Theatre

understand from early photographs of an insipid-looking Lucille Le Sueur why Harry Rapf had spotted her in the chorus of *Innocent Eyes,* why he had gone back to the show a second time with fellow executive Robert Rubin, or why he signed her to a contract, even a six-month contract at $75 a week. Neither did the future Joan Crawford understand it. When, at the height of her stardom, she finally ventured to ask Mr. Rapf what on earth made him single her out, he replied with weary succinctness, "Structure and vitality."

AN OLD SOURCE– STAGE MOTHERS

When stage mothers first appeared is mercifully unknown, but the species is probably at least as old as the Theater of Dionysus. Doubtless they constitute a cadet branch of that long line of meddling mamas who from time immemorial have put their daughters on the auction block, as the old melodramas used to say, for sale into marriage or into some less reputable profession. Traditionally, the stage mother's motives have not been entirely mercenary; ego as well as greed has played a major part in her calculations, ego and the obvious need to fulfill through her daughter dreams frustrated in her own life. However that may be, stage mothers have to be conspicuously mentioned among important sources of grist for the mills of the gods, and a fruitful one. The road to stardom is long and tough. Somebody has to provide the energy and determination to follow it to its golden end. Surprisingly often it has been Mama, for reasons of her own.

The motives of the first *screen* mothers were considerably more prosiac. When I asked Lillian Gish why her gently bred mother sought acting jobs for herself and her two fragile little girls at the turn of the century, she answered, "Necessity!" The Gishes were one of those theatrical families so curiously common around the turn of the century who were in the theater not through family tradition, as with the Barrymores and the Drews, but because they had lost their breadwinner through death or abandonment. The mothers of these families, mostly untrained and often uneducated, took to acting because it was the only reasonably respectable profession in which they and their offspring could make a living. If the mother could act at all, or was passably good to look at, she and her brood were welcome in the touring troupes and big-city stock companies because the plays of those days, being family entertainment, had many more parts for children than is now the case.

The Smith family of Toronto, consisting of the widowed Mrs. Charlotte Smith and her children Gladys, Lottie, and Jack, became professionals by accident through a sudden need for a little girl actress to appear in a Toronto production of *The Silver King.* Gladys Smith, who got this part, soon was metamorphosed into Mary Pickford, and her mother, as Mrs. Charlotte Pickford, became the screen mother par excellence. Mighty studio moguls blanched when she approached their offices. She had only one object: to see to it that her daughter's salary increased by geometrical rather than arithmetical progression. Mrs. Pickford's financial manipulations became an industry legend. But the most interesting of these early queen mothers, and the most likeable, was Peg

Talmadge. After her husband deserted her, she led a hard life trying to raise her three daughters, Norma, Constance, and Natalie, and it was she who not only pushed them into pictures but kept them there. The girls thought it was lots of fun at first to be in the movies, but once the novelty wore off, they were perfectly willing to find their fun elsewhere. The movies were, after all, work, and to a Talmadge it made no sense to work if you didn't have to. Mrs. Talmadge perfectly agreed with this worldly, inartistic view of movie stardom, but until her financial goals, in the form of a series of trust funds, were realized, she insisted that the lazy Norma and the excitement-loving Constance continue to "work." The Talmadge sisters are the only stars on record who had to be bullied into continuing their stardom after the first blush of success. At the time of Mama's death, mourned by the entire movie industry, they decided that they were rich enough to satisfy even her, and retired without ceremony and without regrets.

Formidable though they were, the Mesdames Pickford and Talmadge in their single-minded concentration on family security seem rather innocent compared to the tall and somewhat sinister tales of later moms and their manipulation of talented offspring. Actresses who never quite made it themselves seem particularly determined to enjoy fame and adoration through their children. Witness the burlesque queen Belle Paget, mother of Debra Paget (who also never quite made it, at least to the top stardom), and leading woman Sara Warmbrodt, who pushed first her son (who finally eluded her) and then her very young daughter, the eminent Elizabeth Taylor, into the studio hurly-burly at an age when most mothers would have been worrying whether their teeth would come in straight. Miss Taylor's subsequent illnesses, physical as well as emotional, have been authoritatively diagnosed as stemming from the strain of having to live an emotional life for two, herself and her mother, and some of Judy Garland's problems could have derived from a similar source. Lillian Roth has publicly attributed her alcoholism to her mother's constant pressure.

There have been stage fathers too, though on the record Dad has usually had less compelling reasons to exploit his children than Mom. But Lucille Langehanke's megalomaniac father deliberately pushed her toward Mary Astordom, kept control of her immense earnings long after she was a grown woman, and dissipated them in business ventures for which he had no other qualification than that he was the father of a beautiful girl. The great musical comedy star Marilyn Miller had a father who treated her like the Prussian martinet he was. From babyhood she was drilled in every branch of theatrical art; she literally knew nothing else. Before the public, Miss Miller was a vision of peaches-and-cream delight. Outside the theater, she was a colorless nobody. Natalie and Lana Wood, Sandra Dee, Tuesday Weld, Debbie Reynolds—the list is a long one, and runs through every period of pushing parents and pushed children in film history.

All this adds up to a sob story of a kind which has always delighted fans, who are not entirely displeased to learn that life is not all beer and skittles for the lovely and fortunate creatures of the screen. There is another, more agreeable side to the story, one not often dramatized by gossip columnists or in other fiction. Rita Hayworth was lucky enough to be born into the Dancing Cansinos, a large theatrical family, every member of which was talented and at home in the life of show business. Rita just happened to be the one who made it big, and she served a long apprenticeship before she outstripped her sib-

(Above) Sara Warmbrodt, a failed actress, sublimated her frustrations in promoting the career of her daughter, Elizabeth Taylor, and also in trying to live every moment of her life for her. Here she supervises the very young Elizabeth's choice of lingerie—lingerie which must somehow combine child appeal with sex appeal.

(Left) Mickey Rooney was the son of vaudevillians who put him in the movies as soon as he could toddle. Here he is dancing with his mother during his heyday as an adolescent star.

(Below) After his daughter rose to fame and wealth, and lifted him from obscurity and poverty, Robert Bow spent most of his time writing to fan magazine editors complaining about the lousy publicity she got. He signed such letters "R. Bow," validating his signature in parentheses with "Father of Clara Bow."

lings. As for Shelley Winters, born Shirley Schrifft, her mother had been a lyric soprano in a minor way, but it was Shelley, not her mom, who insisted that the entire family uproot itself from St. Louis and move to Brooklyn in order to be near Broadway, and who provided the self-starting drive which took her through long years as a garment center model and a Catskill waitress to her present eminence and excellence. Miss Winters would be the last to claim that her subsequent professional and amorous difficulties were the result of family pressure, and she would no doubt add that they are not, after all, altogether unbearable.

A NEW SOURCE– THE SECOND GENERATION

In her enormously entertaining *A Girl Like I,* Anita Loos says of the 1920s: "By this time the stars were moving out of the Hollywood Hotel and beginning to live in their own private houses with servants, most of whom were their peers in everything but sex appeal—which pinpoints the reason for the film capital's mass misbehavior. To place in the limelight a great number of people who ordinarily would be chambermaids and chauffeurs, give them unlimited power and instant wealth, is bound to produce a lively and diverting result." Those who survived the results of their own divertissements, the standard five-year cycle of stellar popularity, and the acid test of the talkies, found themselves substantial citizens of Beverly Hills, the San Bernadino valley, and even conservative Pasadena. They acquired local business interests, learned how to deal with that peer group, their servants, and spent fortunes giving their children the traditional advantages which they had so conspicuously lacked. The results were, naturally, mixed. The children of any professional group find it hard to grow up straight in the shadow of brilliant, magnetic, or glamorous fathers and mothers. The misadventures of Edward G. Robinson, Jr., John Barrymore, Jr., and Lana Turner's daughter Cheryl Crane have saddened parents everywhere as well as their own. In other stellar children, the instinct of self-preservation has told them to get as far away from the scene of their childhood and of their parents' overwhelming success as they reasonably could. Ralph Blum, son of the versatile actress Carmel Myers, emerged from his elaborate education as a full-fledged highbrow, the range of whose interests decidedly did not include Hollywood and the shallow glories of stardom. He was embarrassed to be identified as the son of Carmel Myers, and amazed to discover that his older intellectual friends remembered her silent vamping with delight. His excellent novel, *The Foreigner,* about the Allied invasion of Sicily in 1943, was the more remarkable in that at the time of the invasion he was approximately ten years old and had never been out of California.

Others took easier and more obvious routes away from the shadow of their parents through marriage or business careers, and no son or daughter of a great star has yet

Mr. and Mrs. Maurice Costello with Helene and Dolores Costello

Constance and Richard Bennett in *Bought*, with Ben Lyon

31

himself or herself become a *great* star. But an increasing number, especially in recent years, have felt impelled to meet the obvious challenge to show that they possess something more than the ghost of their parents' ability and fame, something of their own. Granted the initial impulsion, they have certain advantages. In large measure they are without illusions. The starry-eyed dreams which bring the thousands to Hollywood are not for them, nor the inevitable disenchantment. They don't have to learn how to play the angles, they were born playing them, and all around them are object lessons illustrating how you can make your own luck or throw it away. They do not expect to be signed forthwith to a seven-year contract by M-G-M after a phone call from Papa or Mama. Knowing some of their trade from birth, they know they must learn more, and they mostly head for summer stock, seek a footing in the television assembly line, or if they are particularly farseeing, show up at the Actors Studio in New York. There the remarkable family of actor-teachers headed by Lee Strasberg can be counted upon to give them the most exacting training in every branch of their profession or—just as valuably—tell them from the start that they have nothing to offer and are only headed for grief if they continue to try to capitalize on secondhand fame. The increase in the number of these second-generation fledglings is really a manifestation of the fact that, even as the profession becomes more far-flung, more global in the extent of its operations, it also grows more tightly knit, more dynastic. These children of show business have a better chance than outsiders because their elders know they are better equipped to meet ever higher technical standards, while they are still young and fresh enough to satisfy the old primeval dreams.

IS IT BEAUTY?

Does beauty make a star? Certainly not. Not a single Miss America, or even a Miss Universe, has ever come near being a great star, though many have been signed to contracts, from Fay Lamphier, Miss America of 1926, on. Zsa Zsa Gabor's beauty has ensnared the rich and great of every continent she has visited, but in spite of her countless film and TV appearances, nobody has ever thought seriously of trying to star her; her acting is too obviously hopeless. The even more celebrated international beauty, Lady Diana Manners, got nowhere in her frequent and fruitless attempts to make a place for herself on stage and screen—although it was possibly Lady Diana's lack of manners, rather than her lack of talent, which did her in. Her rudeness may have been *au fait* among the British aristocracy but it was too much for free and easy show business. "I saw you in *Private Lives,"* she said to Noël Coward on first meeting him. "Not very funny." Mr. Coward, God bless him, replied: "And I saw you, Lady Diana, as the nun in *The Miracle.* Very, very funny."

Sometimes ravishing beauty fails to register with the camera for technical reasons which escape the layman. Frances Howard Goldwyn, for the last forty years the distinguished wife of the distinguished Samuel Goldwyn, dazzled Broadway when she first appeared there as the heroine of Ferenc Molnar's *The Swan,* and was signed by Paramount to repeat her role in the screen version (1924). But the black-and-white screen gave her patrician features a pinched and frigid look which caused movie fans to ask what all the shouting was about. Being the intelligent and farseeing woman she is,

Difficulty in pronouncing her first name was no handicap to Gwili Andre in the eyes of RKO, who were convinced that this New York fashion model had everything it took to out-Dietrich Marlene. But her skeletal beauty, though typical of the early thirties, did nothing for such elemental action films as *Roar of the Dragon* and *Secrets of the French Police*, in which she was revealed as a lovely cipher.

Kathryn Sergava

(Above right) A lady first, Florence Vidor's genteel beauty and repressed manner kept her going for years, while more vibrant stars were eclipsed by newcomers. (Above left) Haled before a juvenile court, Barbara La Marr was dubbed by its judge "too beautiful for her own good." That juridical puff was all the studios needed to induce them to give Miss La Marr, first of the La Marr dynasty of Hollywood, the full treatment. Before her early death, she had made the transition from slinky villainess to sympathetic star, an achievement matched by none.

Olga Cronk's mousy prettiness got her nowhere during four years of bit parts in pictures. Then she lent herself to a press agent's hoax which billed her as "Charlie Chaplin's fiancée," found "kidnapped and dying" on a Hollywood hillside. Mr. Chaplin was amused, so was the press, and producers decided there must be more spark in this little girl than they had supposed. Blondined and bobbed into a twenties ideal of typical beauty, aristocratically rechristened Claire Windsor, she reigned as a star for five years, which was considerable mileage to get out of a Cronk.

Mrs. Goldwyn promptly abandoned her career and devoted herself to making Mr. Goldwyn the happy man *he* is.

But if beauty is not the *sine qua non* of success, it is the most immediately and strikingly obvious qualification for stardom. Every showman is on the lookout for it, and when he finds it allows himself dreams of glory. And throughout the history of the films there have been stars who, whatever their other attributes, we remember primarily for their unbelievable perfection of face and form. In pioneer movie days, Corinne Griffith was a hard-working actress who could give an effective performance in either drama or comedy, and her other attainments in addition to her beauty are amply demonstrated by the success she achieved as financier and author after she abandoned her acting career. But with the progress of motion picture photography, her gorgeous looks increasingly dominated her films, to the point where they were all that mattered. Directors could not resist studding the films with lingering close-ups of the star, even if this left the story somewhat at sea. Critics might lament, "Corinne Griffith's talents are wasted on another mediocre production," but the public was content as long as it could feast on Miss Griffith's face and catch an occasional glimpse of her magnificent legs. Vilma Banky was another whose beauty alone put across her rather empty films. Her public might have been happy to watch them even longer than it did, in spite of the guttural Hungarian speech which the talkies revealed, were it not for the fact that, as the afore-mentioned Mrs. Goldwyn warned her husband, Miss Banky's real interest was in the pork chops Budapest which she secretly cooked in her dressing room in spite of his dietary ukases. Hedy Lamarr at her height was so breath-taking that people fell silent when she entered a room. Miss Lamarr complained that nobody ever listened to anything she said; they were too bemused by the entrancing curve of her speaking mouth to hear what came out of it.

Manly beauty has never been as important to the camera as female loveliness, in which the screen roughly reflects the situation in real life. Perfect features and fine physiques are of course sought by the scouts, officially and unofficially and at the beginning of the movies they were generally believed to be essential for leading-manship. The beaux ideals were represented by Francis X. Bushman and Wallace Reid, while the almost pathological devotion of Ramon Novarro's female fans maintained his stardom for six years after the talkies, and his increasing jowliness, had made him a casting problem. But even in the early days, the balding Maurice Costello and the aging Lewis Stone and Conway Tearle sparked feminine response, while Gary Cooper, beautiful in his youth, actually gained in popularity as the years etched lines in his face. As for Clark Gable and Jimmy Cagney, anybody who accused *them* of being beautiful would most likely have got a sock in the jaw, an obvious fact which made them popular with men as well as women. In the matriarchy that is said to be America, rugged masculinity still offers primary appeal. With the notable and extreme exception of Cary Grant, actors whose chief characteristics are polish and suavity are condemned to secondary roles; in other cultures, George Sanders and Basil Rathbone would have been stars, not villains, but not in ours. The fine delicacy of Marlon Brando's acting, the gazellelike spontaneity with which he projects feeling, might have made him a doubtful subject for feminine adoration. But he was fortunate. His tendency toward beauty is rendered irregular by a broken nose. Even luckier, he first appeared among us as the brutal Stanley Kowalski, who gave an appropriate comeuppance to a fake-genteel Blanche DuBois. Mr. Brando has been able to develop and preserve his almost feminine artistry because he physically fits the he-man stereotype. Numerous imitators aped his appearance and his Method successfully enough, but theirs is shadow, not substance. They miss the combination of sensitivity and maleness which sets him apart.

Long ago the veteran French film director Marcel l'Herbier fouled his own nest in a film called *Le Bonheur* (not to be confused with a more recent release of that name) by making Charles Boyer deliver a diatribe against beauty on the screen. It was wrong, he said, to give us beauty secondhand, because it promised us a happiness we could never have. The common sense of common men knows better. Beauty is much to be sought and seldom to be discovered, and only a few have ever laid hands on it to have and to hold. But it was a thousand ships that Helen launched, not one, and who shall be debarred from the hope? To sit in the dark and behold a beauty that embodies all the dreams of men since time began is something new under the sun, and wonderful. If the movie camera needed justification, perhaps this is it.

IS "IT" IT?

Is "It" it? No more than beauty, if the term is reduced to essentials. Elinor Glyn coined the word in 1925, and explained it interminably, with many references to karma and the the Dance of Life. But what emerged from her froth of words was simply good old sex appeal, which everybody in the world already knew about without gloss from Glyn. And sex appeal is a more variable and indefinite term than beauty. Wallace Beery had sex appeal for many women, and Lon Chaney could project it at will through his self-inflicted bodily deformations. Clara Bow, christened the "It" girl by Madame Glyn, is remembered as the epitome of the sexy flapper, but also for a good many rarer qualities. She was a spangled dart of pure light, a sort of gift from heaven of female vitality and enjoyment of life. She was also a considerable actress. "It" was a good spotlight-getter for its creatress, and it survived in the language long after Madame Glyn was forgotten, but as the golden key to stardom it proved to be a sphinx without a secret.

Sex appeal, taken by itself, has a way of thinning out to the vanishing point. To galvanize both men and women, it usually requires a good many psychological associations—memories of mother, the protective instinct, the destructive instinct, the mounting modern need for comfort and reassurance in an indifferent world, risk. None of which has prevented ever hopeful showmen from trying to capitalize on it. If they want to sleep with a girl or, in some cases, alas, with a man, they naturally figure everybody else will want to too, and sing hey for a career ahead. They have at times overlooked a number of factors, including the fact that the girl who attracts you very strongly in the casting office may not attract you or anybody else when seen on the screen, and that the reverse is just as definitely the case. There is no statement on which more people will agree than just Clark Gable had all the It there was. But his wife, Carole Lombard, remarked to a friend, "You know how much I love Pappy, but to tell you the honest truth, he isn't such a hell of a good lay." The ability to project the come-hither quality at a camera is more important for stardom than its casual, unconscious possession in everyday life. Marlene Dietrich had both, but as forty years of fame have proved, there is only one Dietrich.

Miss Lamarr arrived in Hollywood as a sort of prefabricated sex symbol. Because she had appeared nude in a European film in repressed 1933, it was automatically, or at least hopefully, assumed that she would knock us all cold by her mere appearance on the American screen. Her employers, M-G-M, however had some doubts. When they loaned her to Walter Wanger for *Algiers* she did indeed create the expected sensation. But where to go from there? So doubtful was M-G-M of the answer that they remade her first film for them rather than let such a potentially valuable property go out in a weak film (the remake turned out to be even weaker). Their technical wizards could, and did, greatly enhance her photographic beauty. They taught her to act—some. The fact that her accent compelled her to play only foreign charmers was no insuperable obstacle; it had not prevented Garbo and Dietrich from becoming the stars they were. The trouble was, the M-G-M experts could not find anything in Miss Lamarr, her sex appeal, and her reputation out of which to create the kind of individual and prototypical female screen character which had made Garbo and Dietrich great. Miss Lamarr's official stardom continued for ten years, but increasingly she was cast as a sort of straight woman opposite comedians like Bob Hope, her reputation as an irresistible charmer being more important to the plot of the picture than anything she actively contributed in it. When at the end of her career Cecil B. De Mille cast her in his *Samson and Delilah,* he was obliquely acknowledging the fact that he could not find a newcomer who could live up to the expectations aroused by the mere name Delilah, and had better settle for the shadow since he could not deliver the substance.

Jean Harlow to a considerable degree reversed the Lamarr history. Unheralded, Miss Harlow literally burned up the screen in that odd mélange, *Hell's Angels.* She seemed fated to embody sex and nothing else but, and that was exactly what she did for two years in which she slid from starring to supporting roles, until Irving Thalberg of M-G-M decided he could create a piquant contrast between her sultry appearance and reputation and the hesitant, rather wistful person he sensed within the lush body. Miss Harlow surprised even Thalberg by developing into an expert and delicious comedienne as well, but it was the warm and sympathetic quality which he brought out that inspired the love, not the lust, of countless fans until her death. When Ben Lyon saw Marilyn Monroe in the 20th Century-Fox casting office he burst out, "It's Jean Harlow all over again!" and the industry agreed, but the public hastened the process this time. It saw from the first in this eminently layable dream girl a little girl lost, and followed the rest of her career with striking sympathy and an even more striking absence of that malice which conceals envy. In spite of all that was written and said about her, people sensed that there was little in her life to envy. Contrast these two endearing women with Jayne Mansfield. Miss Mansfield's equipment seemingly made her a natural for the age of breast fetishism, but it is not too harsh to say that her lame gestures toward stardom were based 100 per cent on publicity.

No romantic star has ever achieved the upper regions without being able to suggest sex to some degree and in some form. But what the veteran producer-director Mervyn LeRoy had said about beauty as an avenue to stardom applies equally well to sex appeal: "The reason they want pretty-pretty girls on contract lists is that the men who interview them are trying to please executives who have no heart. They are businessmen. They see only beauty; they don't see depth. When I'm hunting for talent, I look below the surface.

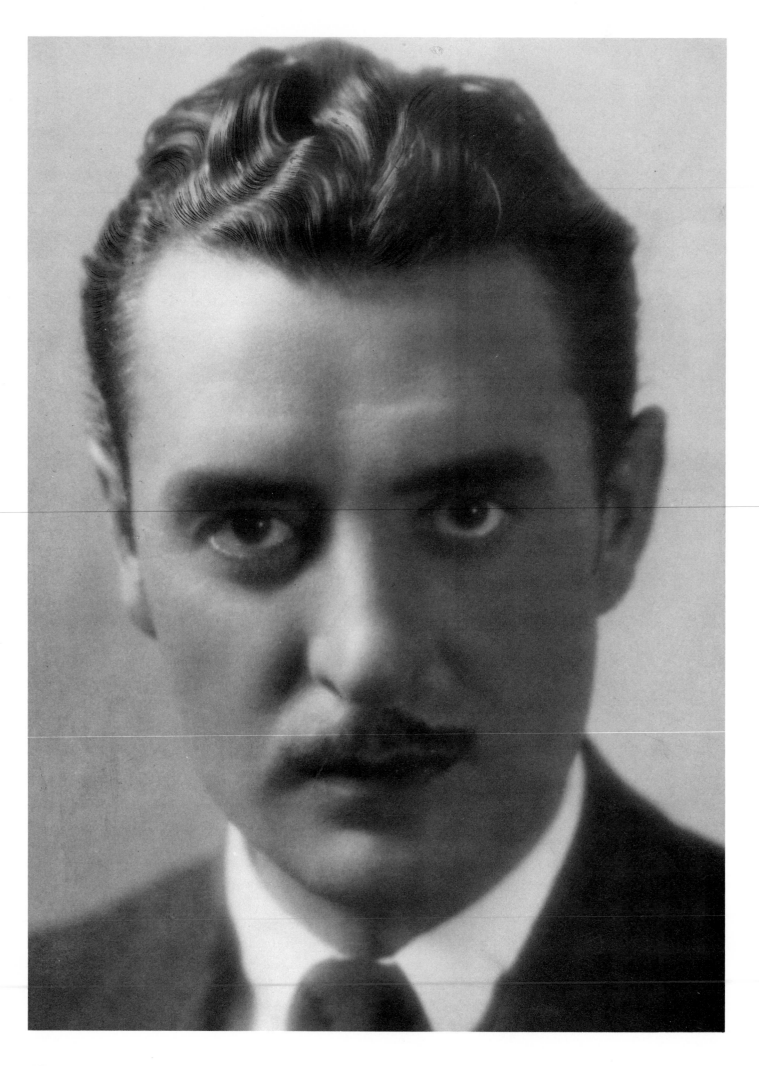

(Above right) Hedy Lamarr had both beauty and "It," and she eventually learned to act too.

(Left) John Gilbert had "It" in silence but not in sound.

(Right) Nita Naldi had too much "It" for sympathetic roles in the twenties.

(Above) Both Marilyn Monroe and Jane Russell had "It," but Marilyn was a real star and Jane a forced one.

(Below) This still of Ann Sheridan, seen with James Cagney, Andy Devine, and Pat O'Brien on location for *Torrid Zone*, gives a pretty good idea why the Warner publicity dubbed Ann the "Oomph Girl". What Miss Sheridan thought of this gimmick she made clear in her own words: "Oomph is the sound that a fat man makes when he leans over to tie his shoelaces in a telephone booth".

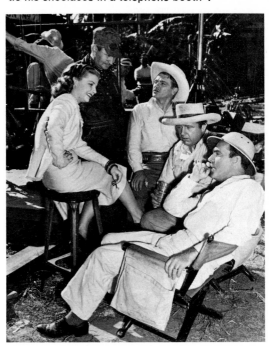

39

I don't care whether the girl looks like a crow; if she has exceptional talent, that's what I want. In Hollywood there are ways to manufacture beauty; you can't manufacture talent." But what then is talent?

IS IT DISCOVERY?

Some years ago Joseph L. Mankiewicz was surprised, and perhaps entertained, to learn that he was being sued for plagiarism. A Brooklyn housewife contended that his *The Barefoot Contessa* was based without credit on her unpublished autobiography, which dealt with her career as a theatrical press agent. Specifically, Mr. Mankiewicz was accused of copying the story of Reri, the half-caste beauty whom Robert Flaherty and F. W. Murnau discovered in Tahiti and used as the heroine of their poetic *Tabu*. Reri was brought to New York for the *Ziegfeld Follies* of 1931, and became "a star overnight." No doubt Mr. Mankiewicz could easily have settled out of court, but he chose to fight the case, probably in the hope that the decision would establish guidelines which would protect the industry from similar misguided harassment in the future. The plaintiff, a comfortable matron, was quite evidently sincere and far from money-mad; with her it was the principle of the thing, no theft without compensation. An interesting battle ensued.

The Mankiewicz forces began by demolishing the argument that Reri was ever "a star overnight," or indeed a star at all. The lovely Tahitian did her shimmy in the *Follies* for a season, pandered to the European love for the exotic primitive in Continental night clubs for a few years, and returned to Tahiti, where she lived out her life much as she might have done had she never met Flaherty and Murnau. Not content with this, Mr. Mankiewicz argued that Ava Gardner's dizzy rise in *The Barefoot Contessa* was pure fiction for the reason that there was no such thing as an overnight star, and never had been. This attack on cherished folklore brought aggressive rebuttal. What about Katharine Hepburn? No, said Mankiewicz, Miss Hepburn was indeed unknown to the movie public before they took her to their hearts in *A Bill of Divorcement*, but she was far from unknown in the profession. She had worked in stock companies and been featured on Broadway in *The Warrior's Husband* by the time David Selznick brought her to Hollywood. Mae West? Her name was strange to the unwashed millions when she made a hit in a minor role in her first film, *Night After Night,* and was starred in her second, *She Done Him Wrong,* 1933. But Miss West and her lubricities had been all too familiar to the big-time vaudeville and theatrical circuits since she made her debut as "the Brinkley Girl" as far back as 1912. Here was a pretty point for the lawyers. Legally speaking, what *was* an overnight sensation? The argument grew technical as it advanced, and bogged down completely over the complicated case of Jane Russell. An expert witness outlined her story. She was discovered by Howard Hughes and starred by him in *The Outlaw,* but Mr. Hughes for his customary impenetrable reasons delayed the release of the film for four years, during most of which Miss Russell languished as a nominal movie player whom the public had never seen. Meanwhile, stills from *The Outlaw* were distributed throughout the world, and Miss Russell, unknown though she was, became the favorite pin-up girl of the World War II GIs, outstripping even the supreme Betty Grable. To capitalize on this fungoid fame, Hunt Stromberg persuaded

Hughes to lend him Miss Russell for the starring role in a wartime topical drama called *Young Widow*. This weak picture died the death, and both critics and public decided that Pin-Up Russell was a pin-up, period. Not until 1946, when she was finally seen crawling into bed with Jack Beutel in *The Outlaw,* did Miss Russell come into her own. Ah, replied the plaintiffs, but *then* she became a real star! "If you like," returned the witness. "Hughes continued to push her for a while, and other studios used her when the plots of their pictures called for a sex symbol, but she never really endeared herself to any large section of the public. I consider her stardom forced." The judge threw up his hands: "These expert witnesses and their opinions!" "If the court please," said the witness, "the box office isn't an opinion, it's a fact."

Miss Hepburn, Miss West, and after a strange fashion Miss Russell were in only one sense overnight sensations. When effectively showcased, they attracted audiences. But the point that Mr. Mankiewicz wanted to make was that it doesn't happen by magic. The public discovers its own stars, and its verdict is final. But before that verdict can be rendered, things have to happen. There must be preparation—experience. Granted there is talent, it must be showcased, and *effectively* showcased, as Mae West's long probation on the fringes proved. For staying power, there must be in the initial talent something which can be developed, given variety and highlight—otherwise the player remains a Reri, a flash in the pan, a non-professional. And there must be the wherewithal to develop it—the machinery.

IS IT THE MACHINERY?

Can a star be manufactured? Can the studio machinery, operating unaided, fabricate a popular idol? It happened only once, and very long ago. In 1914, the journeyman actor Frank J. Powell found himself suddenly a powerful motion picture director faced with the problem of turning a stage hit of the day, *A Fool There Was,* into a movie. In his old age, fingering the medallion given him by Ellen Terry when he was a member of her company, Powell loved to tell the story. "Those were the days when we were importing stage stars by the carload, and the studios were beginning to feel the financial strain. I thought, 'I wonder if I could make a big star, all by myself.' There was an extra girl around the Fort Lee studios that I'd spotted. She was angling for bigger parts, but halfheartedly, in fact everything she did was halfhearted. She had a sort of negative personality. But she had a body, and she had big dark eyes that I thought we could make even bigger with the heavy kohl eye make-up we used then. I called her to see me, the big, stern, mysterious director, and said, 'I've got work for you, and a future for you, but you've got to do exactly what I tell you. Here's some money. Go find yourself a little apartment in the Bronx and stay there and don't see anybody or talk to anybody you know until you hear from me.' We started production with this little girl in the part of the Vampire, and she photographed just like I thought she would. There was hardly any advance publicity for pictures then, and we got away with the whole thing without anybody knowing what was going on. Then I got going. I announced that in *A Fool There Was* we had a new star, Theda Bara (the girl's real name was Theodosia Goodman) who the boob

(Right) The lovely Reri of F. W. Murnau's *Tabu,* 1931, was considered a great "discovery" by everybody except the picture-wise. They knew that Murnau had simply used her as a figure in the pattern of his great film, and then discarded the half-caste French-Polynesian girl. But she had assets, shown above, which induced Florenz Ziegfeld to import her for one of his *Follies.* Soon after, she returned to Tahiti to live much the same life she would have lived un-"discovered." She never made another film. (Left) The extreme novelty, on the screen, of Mae West's sexual frankness made her a genuine "discovery" of picture audiences in 1932. Few of them knew that she had been peddling the same line of goods in vaudeville and musical comedy for the preceding twenty years. (Bottom) Katharine Hepburn's debut as John Barrymore's daugther in *A Bill of Divorcement,* 1932, made her literally "a star overnight"; she was the official as well as the actual star of her next picture, and indeed the only reason for its being. But this overnight star was actually a well-known veteran of show business. Miss Hepburn had pursued an arduous road from Bryn Mawr college dramatics through summer and winter stock and two Broadway plays before David Selznick "discovered" her for pictures. (Bottom right) Miss Russell was "discovered" in slow motion. Featured by Howard Hughes in *The Outlaw,* 1942—47, she had to wait four years for Mr. Hughes to make up his mind to release the picture before Jane could take her place as even a nominal star in the Hollywood pantheon. (Below) Jean Seberg, a youngster from Iowa, was cast, rather noisily after a well-publicized talent hunt, in Otto Preminger's *Saint Joan,* was quickly criticized into non-stardom by the critics, and was cast, rather quietly, aside. But Miss Seberg, an exile in the land of St. Joan, became an estimable figure in French and American "New Wave" movies.

American public had never heard of but who was famous all over the civilized world. She was born in Egypt, half-French and half-Arab, she was not only an actress, she was also a sort of witch who could hypnotize people into doing things they oughtn't to do, and most important of all, she was going to knock the pants off all the men in the world, civilized and uncivilized. It worked, too. They not only swallowed it, they loved it."

The Vamp, *A Fool There Was,* and Theda Bara are a well-aired part of movie history, a cliché trotted out whenever somebody wants to illustrate what the early days were like. The stentorian bushwa put out about Miss Bara, of which the above is a restrained sample, was the prototype of all subsequent publicity "campaigns," and, as noted, people ate it up; the will to believe was stronger than the cold facts which newsmen eventually dug up about little Miss Goodman. Theda Bara was a gold mine, a gusher. But Powell and his studio boss William Fox knew that though against all odds they had created a classical movie image and legend, they couldn't stop there. Even the bemused and enamored public (boobs, boobs, Powell repeated) would not forever welcome one carbon copy of *A Fool There Was* after another. It was a problem. Seated in her white limousine, smothered in furs and trumpery jewels, Theda Bara was still the girl Powell had found in Fort Lee, Theodosia Goodman, passive, cowlike, negative. What could be done with her? Could she perhaps act? They tried her as Juliet, as Carmen, even, somewhat more logically, as Concha Perez in a series of expensive films. But the public which thrilled to the deviltry of her synthetic personality simply was not interested in her acting, one way or another. William Fox made a final attempt to solve the problem; of all legendary femmes fatales, Cleopatra was thought most closely to approximate Theda Bara, and he launched a gigantic production intended to rival D. W. Griffith and the Italian spectaculars of the day. But Miss Bara as Cleopatra was simply the mixture as before, and Fox prepared to quit; he had made plenty of money out of Frank Powell's invention, and enough was enough. Miss Bara might well have followed suit. Through forty films in four years, her salary had risen to $4,000 a week, and she was a saving type. But, like many subsequent stars, Theodosia Goodman had come to believe her own flamboyant publicity, and she wanted to go on. She did not seem to realize that all she had to offer any more was the shopworn image of the Vamp of Vamps. For that there was a buyer, the theatrical producer A. H. Woods, expert then and later at capitalizing on threadbare reputations. In 1919 he presented her with great razzle-dazzle in a Broadway play, *The Blue Flame.* But a Broadway theater was not the Bijou Dream in Big Tussle, Mont. At the rise of the curtain, Miss Bara was discovered bizarrely dressed in a typical Bara drawing room. As an actor entered to her, she spoke the first line of the evening: "Have you brought the cocaine?" In the wake of the laughter which followed, the whole vampire mystique, slated anyway for demolition in the air of post-war sophistication, shattered to fragments.

The creation and exploitation of Theda Bara was a commercial enterprise conducted under primitive conditions—which may have redounded to its advantage. The making of something from nothing has been tried subsequently—but never with comparable success. Even boobs learn, if you teach them often enough. Later attempts to use the machinery of star-making to force a star on the public have been actuated by less mercenary, and possibly far more sensible, motives. The character of the second wife of John Foster Kane in *Citizen Kane* was concocted by Orson Welles out of the histories of two well-known American ladies, Marion Davies and Hope Hampton. What they were known for is no secret and can be got over quickly: Miss Davies was the mistress of William Randolph Hearst and Miss Hampton first the mistress and then the wife of Eastman Kodak tycoon Jules Brulatour. The men, and especially the motives, behind the careers of these two stars are regrettably more interesting than the stars themselves. With the first, it was simple: What Hearst wants, Hearst gets. What Hearst wanted, among so many other things, was to be a motion picture producer. This was all right with the industry, as long as he financed his somewhat uneven Cosmopolitan Productions with his own money. But when he concentrated all his picture-making efforts on his inamorata, and when the ramifications of California politics brought him into close alliance with Louis B. Mayer, the situation became sticky. Marion Davies soon found herself shining among the brightest of Metro-Goldwyn-Mayer stars, in publicity at least, and appearing in a series of colossally expensive films which no one wanted to see unless he was at a loose end on a dull evening. Such naked forcing of doubtful talent might have inspired hatred in Hollywood if it had not been for the personality of Miss Davies herself, a good-time girl who couldn't care less about her career or her fame, and whose wit endeared her to the whole movie colony. She invariably introduced Mary Pickford as "my illegitimate daughter by Calvin Coolidge." But there *was* a branch of the industry which hated the sound of her name, the theater owners who were forced to book her films if they wanted also to book the pictures of Lillian Gish, John Gilbert, Greta Garbo, and other powerful M-G-M box-office magnets. They protested vigorously, and Mr. Mayer often found himself between the devil and William Randolph Hearst. A lot of tricks were tried to ease the conflict. Whenever he could arrange it, Mr. Hearst liked to have his Marion cast opposite the latest M-G-M male find, in the hope that some of the latter's popularity would rub off on her. This was not pleasing to the studio which saw a good potential box-office draw dragged down by Miss Davies. When she was co-starred with the glowing-hot Clark Gable, the executives pulled a fast one. As contracts specified, the picture was advertised in twenty-four sheets as MARION DAVIES AND CLARK GABLE IN POLLY OF THE CIRCUS, but while Gable's name was limned in crimson, that of Miss Davies was in a blue so pale that it could not be seen at twenty feet. Anticipating wrath, the head of the advertising department hastened to tell Mr. Hearst that this blue was a special blue created for the occasion and dubbed "Marion Blue." The great man was not deceived. He was very angry indeed, and attributed the poor financial returns on Miss Davies' films to the fact that she received inadequate promotion.

Besides the blond good looks which ensnared Mr. Hearst, Miss Davies did have one useable asset. She was a wizard mimic (her films were full of bits burlesquing other stars) and she developed a pretty comic talent—her Dulcy in *Not So Dumb,* 1930, was nearly brilliant. The public liked her in pictures like this, but Mr. Hearst did not; he refused to allow her to be smacked in the face by a custard pie, though that was the logical climax of her *Show People,* 1928, and King Vidor had to substitute a stream from a seltzer bottle. Why this was more dignified is hard to say, though it seemed to satisfy. But Marion Davies on the screen was not a star but a projection of Mr. Hearst's dreams, and he wanted to see her in roles which would feed his garish historical imagination. In the early thirties, M-G-M managed to secure the film rights to *The Barretts of*

(Above) Thanks to Jules Brulatour's power to give or to withhold credit for film stock to Universal, the tottering company was forced to sponsor the ''return'' of Hope Hampton, fifteen years after the public had rejected her as a screen attraction. But *The Road to Reno,* 1937, with Randolph Scott, revealed a Hampton more hopeless than ever.

(Right) ''Hopeless'' Hampton, as she was known in Hollywood, in one of her early ingenue roles, circa 1920.

(Left) The first, and perhaps the only, successfully machine-made star. This grinning presentment of evil, ludicrous though it appears today, convinced millions that Theodosia Goodman of Chillicothe, Ohio, was really Theda Bara, a blood-sucking vampire who drained men of their vital essence just by looking at them. Miss Bara immortalized herself by giving the word ''vamp'' to the language, and she was undoubtedly the first ancestress of all the screen *femmes fatales* from her own day right down to Modesty Blaise and Jeanne Moreau's *Mademoiselle.* All this had little to do with Miss Bara herself; it was the synthetic, cold-blooded fabrication of director Frank Powell and producer William Fox. The real Theodosia Goodman married a director, became a leader in Los Angeles charities, and in later years entertained at Hollywood parties by burlesquing her former screen self.

(Right) When Marion Davies met William Randolph Hearst, she was a freshly pretty chorus girl from Brooklyn. By the time his beauty experts finished with her, she was an exhibit worthy of Mme. Tussaud.

Wimpole Street, in which Katharine Cornell had made herself the most beloved stage actress of her generation, and Hearst insisted that his protégeé play the part. The casting of "a prominent whore of a prominent son of a bitch," as Dorothy Parker described Miss Davies, in such a role as Elizabeth Barrett Browning was perhaps not without theatrical precedent, but Irving Thalberg, second-in-command at M-G-M, had already earmarked the part for his wife, Norma Shearer, a considerably more rational choice, and he won the ensuing bloody scrimmage. Enraged, Mr. Hearst severed relations with Metro and moved his production unit bag and baggage to Warner Brothers, to the relief of all except L. B. Mayer and the personnel of the Warner studio. Miss Davies by this time had had it; picture-making was interfering with her pleasures, and besides, she frankly said, she was getting on. Her protector would have none of this. Bolstered by all the beauty experts could do, she was forced to continue in films aimed at a younger generation which was mightily puzzled at the idol offered them. Finally, mercifully, Warners refused to distribute any more Davies films, no matter who footed the bills. The world was not wagging Mr. Hearst's way. Roosevelt was in the White House in spite of all Hearst could do; the nations, against his advice, were about to go to war again; and the public was less willing than ever to accept a now aging cocotte in films called *Cain and Mabel* and *Page Miss Glory.* He didn't like it at all.

Jules Brulatour had a potent weapon with which to promote Hope Hampton. His position in the Eastman Kodak complex enabled him to extend or withhold credit to the movie companies for the raw film stock without which they could not turn a camera. How and when he met Hope Hampton is lost in the mists of antiquity, but round about 1920 she became a silent-picture star for no discernible reason. She was a pretty blonde, but not a very appealing one, and the *raison d'être* for her stardom was so obscure that *Photoplay* magazine was impelled to publish an article called "Who *is* Hope Hampton?" After a few years the Brulatours gave up the struggle, or rather shifted it to another arena. At the end of the twenties, to general incredulity, Hope Hampton emerged as a star of the opera. The Chicago Opera Company, its coffers bulging but its face red, presented her in a series of productions, none of which was as disastrous as Dorothy Comingore's similar adventure in *Citizen Kane.* Miss Hampton's musical career was short. She was not defeated, however. Unlike Marion Davies, she was as determined as her husband to make a place for herself among the gifted, and she waited for her chance. It came in 1936, when the company now known as Universal was in deep financial trouble. Just ahead of bankruptcy, it found itself with a hit on its hands, Deanna Durbin's *One Hundred Men and a Girl,* but without sufficient ready cash to pay for the prints to send to theaters eagerly awaiting it. The company appealed to Mr. Brulatour. He was willing to extend credit, but at a price. His wife, the great star Hope Hampton, must "return" to the talking screen. There was nothing to do but comply, and soon Universal was flooding the fan magazines with photographs of the "new star" Hope Hampton, whose artificial blondeur and conspicuously artificial teeth gave her the appearance of an embalmed doll. The question "Who is Hope Hampton?" was now repeated in dead earnest in Hollywood, and only the oldest inhabitants could answer. Tipped off by them, actors at Universal began to plead flux, syncope, and brain fever to avoid appearing opposite Miss Hampton; Randolph Scott was finally tagged to bell the cat. When the resulting film opened on Broadway the author rushed to see it, knowing that such an opportunity might never occur again and that this one might be only briefly available. *The Road to Reno* was worth the struggle to get to the Criterion Theater at nine o'clock in the morning. Its story was not easy to follow, chiefly because Miss Hampton interrupted it to sing eight songs, long songs. Mr. Scott was discernible, but the camera was chiefly occupied in photographing the star over his shoulders. Strengthened somewhat by *One Hundred Men and a Girl,* Universal refused further experiments and Hope Hampton left Hollywood for the last time. She did not, however vanish into obscurity. She kept a press agent on her husband's payroll and her name was ever-present in gossip-column reporting of café society for the next quarter century. When Jules Brulatour died, his widow gave out that from henceforth she did not want to be known as Mrs. Brulatour, but always, and only, as Hope Hampton.

Pictures today are too expensive, and megalomaniacs fortunately too few, for such fantasies to be repeated. The world, not one man, must love a star if stardom is to have substance, though the machinery of production and promotion, and even of distribution and exhibition, can be manipulated to keep nominal stardom going as long as the money holds out. In the case of Marion Davies and of Hope Hampton, the world was led to water, but it declined to drink. The question now remaining in this survey of rocks and shoals is not only what makes a star, but what within a star himself keeps a star starring.

"NECESSITY"

Prudence and candor combine to restrain the wisest impresarios from generalizing about what makes a star. They know that though they know, they don't know. Actors are even more reticent on this parlous subject—with a beguiling exception. George Sanders, as devastatingly outspoken in life as he is in character, reflects in his *Memoirs of a Professional Cad* on the stellar heights he has never quite attained:

"When I try to discover what is the indispensable quality, one which I obviously lack, that is necessary to become a star I come to the conclusion that it is the *desire* to be a star. Even those who profess most strenuously that they loathe all the vulgar curiosity which they attract would, I am sure, be perfectly miserable without it. . . . What made me sure that Marilyn [Monroe] would eventually make it was that she so obviously *needed* to be a star; in these matters needs count for more than intrinsic talent. There are many highly talented people in all walks of life who never reach the pinnacle of their profession while less talented people do. The people who do get there usually have some deep psychological need to be on top, and this will make them exert themselves beyond their natural capacities. . . . To a girl with Marilyn's background and foreground to be a film star meant to be universally loved. Clearly it is no accident that an unloved girl from an orphanage should become the outstanding Love Symbol of her day, but part of the psychological scheme of things.

"Perhaps the greatest fulfillment in acting, is not just the satisfaction involved in the opportunity for the extrovert to exhibit himself but more the opportunity to act out that part of himself for which he has the imagination and the capacity, but not the heart or the courage.

"Sometimes people are all of a piece—Rubinstein, Douglas Fairbanks, Sr., Gloria Swanson, and John McCormack are some of those who showed the same assurance and

(Above) Though the title of her film was *Happiness Ahead*, Colleen Moore's tears in this scene were real and agonizing.

(Left) Perhaps Darryl Zanuck let the youthful Marilyn Monroe's contract lapse because she looked so much like Shirley Temple. But MM pushed on to stardom because she needed love.

(Below) Lillian Gish in *A Trip to Bountiful*.

exhibited the same zest and talent in life as they did in their performances on the screen and the concert platform. But they are among the exceptions. One thinks of Danny Kaye, so warm, so free and funny on stage, and in person filled with melancholy, somber, confused and suspicious. . . . Jean Harlow, the *femme fatale* of her day, in life full of apprehensions, shy and puzzled. Cary Grant, witty, sophisticated and infinitely debonair, in life a prey to theosophical charlatans, socially insecure, and inclined to isolation. . . . Theda Bara, who became synonymous with women at their most lethal, led a life of exemplary tranquillity and marital probity off the screen. Unlike Joan Fontaine, whose pure profile, austere hair-do and impeccable bearing on screen are in fine contrast to a private life of considerable vitality and color.

"I mention all of the foregoing examples merely in order to make it easier for you to understand that whereas on the screen I am invariably a sonofabitch, in life I am a dear, dear boy."

Mr. Sanders displays a wisdom which his writers have never written into his parts, perhaps on purpose. "Necessity!" cried Lillian Gish when we asked her why her gentle mother had subjected herself and her daughters to the hard life of the theater of those days. But it wasn't the necessity of physical privation which led Lillian and Dorothy on to their admired achievements. It was a deeper need. Colleen Moore once described to me her teen-age days, when the movie craze had just struck America and flappers were discovering that life held more exciting possibilities than any offered by their families or small-town boy friends. " 'Oh, if only *I* was a star!', the girls used to say. I never said that. I said, '*When* I'm a star.' " She was pressed by no financial need; hers was a prosperous Florida family. It wasn't nice, then, for a girl of her sort to go into show business, and no transmission belt of Argus-eyed talent scouts, auditions, and screen tests yet existed. Miss Moore wangled an introduction to D. W. Griffith through an uncle who knew him, and got herself shipped to Hollywood. The rest she did herself, out of herself. A few years later she had a crying scene to do. She would have none of the glycerin tears the women in pictures all used; she was going to *cry*. While the shot was being set up, she stole off behind a tree, willing herself to cry. Onto the scene strode Samuel Goldwyn, and saw her tear-stained face. "Little girl, what are they doing to you to make you so unhappy? Wait till I get my hands on that SOB." Miss Moore's anger was aimed, not at the director, but at Mr. Goldwyn for breaking her mood. "I did cry, though. And not because of any of those tricks they play on you, like telling you your mother is dying. I cried because I had to make the people out front believe me."

In 1925, a girl recently renamed Joan Crawford wandered the M-G-M lot disconsolate, a minor contract player without an assignment. She was a dancer, dancing was all she knew, and every night she would go to the Montmartre or the Cocoanut Grove and monotonously win the nightly Charleston contest. Dancing there at the center of things Hollywood, she attracted the notice, and the lust, of important men around the studios, who earmarked her for future use. But the new Joan Crawford somehow realized that this was not the way forward. Idle, she haunted the sets of the great women stars of the day, particularly Mae Murray's, and watched the way Miss Murray, a dancer like herself, controlled and used every muscle in her body to make the simplest walk across the floor visible and dramatic, a contribution to a scene instead of a mere getting from here to there. When finally she began to be cast as sweet ingénues, she at first got little help from her directors, whose job was to make the male stars whom she played opposite look good. But even from them she learned—by observation, by deduction, by self-compulsion. From Lon Chaney she learned how to concentrate, how to shut out everything but the role and the moment of the role that the camera was about to record. "When he worked, it was like God working, he was so concentrated." From John Gilbert she absorbed the lesson of building and sustaining vitality, how to turn it on just before the cameras turned, how to keep it at the same pitch throughout the shot, how to relax at the end, and then to recapture just the right amount of verve when the next scene began. To everything about the business of becoming a star she gave the same fixed attention—publicity, what is euphemistically called "co-operation," salary, diplomacy, not neglecting studio politics, and the right manner with the right people. Miss Crawford knew little private happiness until her last marriage, but it was not for want of working at it; she said that she felt she owed it to her fans to be a happy woman.

Doris Day stands in contrast. Behind Miss Day's strange, dated, "wholesome" appeal to the millions who still love wholesomeness, there lies a steely quality. She too worked like a beaver at every aspect of her career, particularly the contractual aspects, but as far as her private life is concerned, the public could be, well not damned exactly, but it could go fly a kite or chase some more flamboyant star. She seems to have got away with it too. Perhaps she knows that today the public no longer believe what they read about stars in the gossip columns unless the front pages validate gossip with cold fact. And Miss Day avoids the front pages.

A close friend said of Mabel Normand, "She had the wisdom and foolishness of genius, the strength and weakness of genius, and that strange urge to exhaust the incandescence which set her apart from the ordinary." Some who from deep need have clawed their way to stardom have found that that is all there is for them, that in achieving it they have exhausted life's possibilities. It need not be so. And here we may revert to Lillian Gish. Miss Gish has lived her private life in privacy, but she has brought to her public life the same farsighted, modulated artistry which has made her one of the great actresses of the century. In youth, acclaimed as the Duse of the screen, she must have longed to demonstrate her versatility, but her knowledge of camera values told her that her physical type limited her to the sort of role in which Griffith had made her famous. When that type waned in popularity, Miss Gish anticipated its decline, and quietly moved her sphere of operations to the stage, where different sight lines gave her a far wider range of parts, and where her acquired knowledge of every aspect of the performing arts (including the aspect represented by the people she calls "exhi-bite-ors") made her welcome behind as well as before the footlights. She will do anything for the cause of the theater if she believes in what she is asked to do, and nothing if she does not, publicity or no publicity. She has directed plays and operas as well as a film and written more lines than many playwrights. Every new development has engaged her enthusiasm and her expertise. When television came along, someone asked her in my presence what she did on TV. She laughed, "Oh, I play old ladies." But the old woman in *A Trip to Bountiful* was a master achievement, a moving human creation and a testimony to a life in art. One wished that Griffith could have seen it. The special reverence which actors seem to feel for Miss Gish has its sadder aspects. One senses that some of them contrast their messy and meaningless careers with the beautiful thing that she has made of being an actress. "Necessity!" can lead to rich fulfillment.

Mae Murray in *Fascination*, 1922.

John Barrymore and Helen Hayes in *Night Flight*.

Joan Crawford and Wallace Beery in *Grand Hotel*.

Jeanette MacDonald, Sally Blane and Joyce Compton in *The Affairs of Annabelle*.

Al Jolson in *The Singing Fool*.

2 THE STAR-MAKERS

Among would-be star-makers, those with the best opportunities are directors, with their skill in molding players, and producers, with the longer-term and perhaps more exacting task of bringing a discovery along, presenting him to ever greater advantage, and in general turning him, to put it bluntly, into an asset of a corporation. The nine champions discussed here would never have used such terms to describe their flair for finding and making stars. They were conscious of the romance of the thing, of the public's awareness of the excitement in the gamble, and they never allowed star-making to descend into a routine. That was one thing that gave them an edge over their competitors. Of the nine, all were in some sense producers, but two were also pre-eminent directors, and two others were instinctive loners, whose goals and purposes were their own, not a studio's, and who were as likely as not to spin off a discovered star, after he had served his immediate purpose, for future exploitation by others. The remaining five were typed as businessmen in the public eye, but they were no remote New York tycoons; they were close at all times to the glamour of making pictures, and even under its spell, even when they lifted the phone to argue with the home office about budgets, expansion, the high cost of long contract lists. Business and pleasure were the yang and yin of their lives, and there was never a resolving of the paradox. Showmen at all times, they yet knew that there were moments when, behind closed doors, the bright star-wagon must be described in terms both prosaic and grim.

Take an incident in the life of Adolph Zukor, not named among the nine, but who might well have been. In the third year of the Depression, the great Paramount company was besieged by troubles, the result of an ill-advised expansion campaign in the rash twenties, and it looked very much as if Zukor, its founder and directing intelligence, might be ousted by creditors hungry to seize his empire. One of the latter, a man innocent of picture experience, appeared in Zukor's office metaphorically waving stock certificates, and announced simply, "I'm taking over."

"Very well." Zukor answered. "No doubt you would like to sit and observe for a while before you begin. Unfortunately there are decisions that won't wait, that must be made today. For example, Gary Cooper's contract, which is up for renewal. I have it here on my desk. It runs into six figures annually. But there are factors involved which can't immediately be reduced to dollars and cents. Cooper is past the first blush of popularity, and the novelty of his presence on the screen is behind him. Will his youthful fans stick, as they and he grow older? Has he come along fast enough as an actor to tackle stronger roles and win a new following? Can we get another seven years' mileage out of him, or had his new contract better be reduced to five? Will he accept such a reduction? You and your fellow creditors are, if I may be frank, out to plunder the assets of this corporation. Gary Cooper is one of those assets. As such, he must be preserved or liquidated as of even date. Sam Goldwyn wants him, Cooper is tempted, and we must decide here and now whether we will meet Goldwyn's figure and the other terms he offers. The decision, and the responsibility, are all yours."

Zukor's opponent fled the Paramount sanctum, never to return. Zukor is still there.

D. W. GRIFFITH

David Wark Griffith's shadow falls aslant of every aspect of film-making, in Hollywood and everywhere else. Even today, people in pictures justify wanting to do something in a certain way because "that's the way Griffith did it."

Oddly enough, hardly anybody ever does anything the way Griffith did it, largely for the reason that their objectives differ from his. Mr. Griffith was interested in making movies. Though he was without doubt the granddaddy of all star-makers, he was not until the close of his career really much concerned about the making of stars. A movie to him was a succession of brief images arranged in certain dramatic patterns. Actors, like furniture, sets, sheep, Niagara Falls, the Empire State Express, and campfires in the night, were simply raw materials for the images, *his* images, and he treated them as such. He did not perhaps go so far as Alfred Hitchcock, who, when questioned on the matter, replied "Actors?—Cattle," but his players often felt that that was his general attitude. He insisted that outsiders, and the press, treat his actors as artists, and an unusual formality prevailed in his studio, especially in manner of address. But in front of the camera, they were there to do as they were told, and between takes to get lost.

When he left the Biograph Company, Griffith took with him a group of the anonymous players who had served as his puppets through countless one- and two-reelers. Through the years of *The Birth of a Nation, Intolerance,* and *Hearts of the World,* he shaped them into what became known as "the Griffith stock company," something approximating a repertory troupe; trained to his ways, they got all the juicy parts in his pictures, leaving slim pickings for other actors or for any newcomers except the few he chose to discover and exalt. For the older actors, his company was a haven after storm. They became stock figures, always welcomed by audiences, going through their paces year after year with little effort and no insecurity: Kate Bruce, gentle mother figure of a score of films; Spottiswoode Aiken, the sinister uncle of *The Tell-Tale Heart* and the broken father in *The Birth of a Nation;* the imposing Josephine Crowell, equally effective as the mother in *The Birth of a Nation* and as Catherine de' Medici in *Intolerance.* The junior members, the real candidates for stardom, were treated as apprentices. Griffith never used a script, and "wrote" his films by moving groups of players about during rehearsal, until he found the visual patterns he thought the camera would dramatize most effectively. During this drudgery, the younger actors played all the parts while their elders watched; when Griffith was ready, these latter took up their already assigned roles and shooting began. But it was the youngsters, of course, with whom audiences fell in love, and before whom other producers trailed their lures. It was impossible to blame them for defecting, nor did Griffith do so. Had they stayed with him, they could hope for nothing but continued semianonymity. No player was ever billed above the title in a Griffith production. The opening credit always said D. W. Griffith's *Intolerance* or *Way Down East* or *Orphans of the Storm.* This was followed by a list of players, all in the same size type, and it was up to the audience to figure out who was important and who was not. It wasn't supposed to matter. These were *Griffith* films.

Mae Marsh and Blanche Sweet were the first to be casually let go, Miss Sweet to go to Paramount, Mae Marsh to Goldwyn. Constance Talmadge fell in with the Schencks. Henry Walthall and Richard Barthelmess were considered important enough to have special companies formed to exploit them. Griffith told them to go with God; he could always find more raw material. And they went, taking with them not only their own

Mary Pickford began her long supremacy in Griffith's delicate early masterpiece, *The New York Hat,* 1912. Her success in it was so great that she never worked for Griffith again.

Lillian Gish, Griffith's dream woman, in *Hearts of the World,* 1918. The emotion he most frequently evoked from his virginal heroines was terror, and in this Miss Gish was supreme.

Another Gish registers terror: Lucille La Verne and Dorothy Gish in *Orphans of the Storm,* 1922.

(Left) This genial, cryptic photograph appeared, full-page but without identification, in every film trade annual from 1918 to 1931. No caption was needed: All moviedom knew that this was David Wark Griffith, the Master, the man who knew what the people loved and who kept the audience coming. The picture was a comforting hieroglyph of success; it turned into sad mockery in the years of his decline.

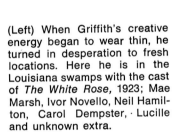

(Left) When Griffith's creative energy began to wear thin, he turned in desperation to fresh locations. Here he is in the Louisiana swamps with the cast of *The White Rose,* 1923; Mae Marsh, Ivor Novello, Neil Hamilton, Carol Dempster, · Lucille and unknown extra.

(Above left) Lya de Putti in Griffith's would-be potboiler but actual box office disaster, *The Sorrows of Satan,* 1926.

(Above right) D. W. Griffith's last silent film, *Lady of the Pavements,* 1929, featured a Fairbanks discovery, Lupe Velez, and an ex-De Mille star, Jetta Goudal.

(Right) When Griffith returned to United Artists for *Drums of Love,* 1927, he tried to regain his onetime mastery, but he also took out box office insurance—the wrong kind. Here are Lionel Barrymore, whom Griffith had introduced to films in Biograph days; Mary Philbin, an artificial star borrowed from Universal; and Don Alvarado, last and least of the Latin lovers.

youth and vitality but also something invaluable to the films of their day, the Griffith technique. They had learned from him to act with eye and underlip, to let their faces be whipped by emotions as if by vagrant breezes at a whispered word from their director. For years the Griffith fledglings enriched the star ranks, and theirs are among the enduring names in screen history.

Only Lillian and Dorothy Gish remained, Dorothy less out of her devotion to Griffith, or his to her, than out of attachment to her sister. She was starred in a series of comedies, supervised by Griffith but directed by others. But Lillian remained the central figure in the design of the great Griffith masterworks. Never could he find, before or later, an actress who came so close to embodying his strange feminine ideal, the blond girl-woman, virginal, wistful, elfin. And nowhere could she have found, in that white-hot moment of the movies' burgeoning, a teacher who invented what he taught even as he taught her. Pliant she was, totally responsive to his control, but she differed from his other protégées in that she was also as absorbent as cotton, soaking up knowledge of all film crafts as well as her own, and grasping too the editorial engineering which made them add up to a whole. Their rapport was perfect, if oddly distant in keeping with his image of her. With the legerdemain of artists, they kept that frail image in front of the public, but behind the scenes Miss Gish was Griffith's brisk assistant, struggling with budgets, with publicity, with costuming and props and sets. Once when he was about to sail for the Bahamas carrying with him a ton of technical paraphernalia, she reminded him that he still owed one Dorothy Gish comedy to his distributor, and that there was no one left behind to direct it. "You direct it," he said. She did, in a studio denuded of equipment, on Fifth Avenue where her mere appearance stopped traffic. What Griffith thought of *Remodeling a Husband* is not on record, and Miss Gish won't tell, but contemporary reviewers thought it her sister's best picture. Performing these tasks in addition to her acting, Miss Gish continued to receive the modest salary of a featured player while her compeers and inferiors in public esteem were earning incredible sums as the stars of films in which everything was subordinated to them and their names.

After the triumph of *Orphans of the Storm*, and ten years after she first came to work for him, Griffith told Lillian Gish to go. Perhaps he knew that she had become an obsession, and one that was beginning to seem monotonous to audiences. He told her that they would have to part if both were still to grow. Miss Gish signed with Metro-Goldwyn-Mayer at $7,000 a week, and Griffith turned back to a studio empty of her presence. No doubt too much could be made of the undeniable fact that her departure coincided almost exactly with the beginning of his decline. But it was just then he began to seem to repeat himself, to offer the mixture as before, as if nothing any longer stimulated his originality, his inventiveness. He seems to have thought that in Carol Dempster he had found a second Lillian Gish. Miss Dempster was a puppet all right, as much of one as his heart could have desired, but the performances that came out on the screen were puppet-like, controlled by strings. Miss Dempster in person was so uninteresting that interviewers complained that they could never "get a story" and less was printed about her in the fan magazines than about any other prominent personality. Griffith did not seem to realize that he could strike no spark from her, only tell her what to do. His persistence in featuring her involved him in difficulties with his distributors, and his eventual reward was less than nothing; she married out of the profession and vanished from the screen.

It is significant that she never made a picture under any other director.

By that time, his fortunes were sinking. He had lost his independence, failed to make a go of it as a glorified wage slave at Paramount, and returned to United Artists, still officially one of its owners, but in reality a closely supervised big-shot director, watched apprehensively by his partners. He tried to rally. This star-making flair he had, which people thought so much of, perhaps he could make something of it now. But Ivan Lebedeff proved to be more suited to cheap villain parts than to stardom, and Don Alvarado, though beautiful, was just one more Latin lover, and a mild one. None of his later discoveries made it to stardom, or anywhere near it. As his energies flagged, so did his vision of what makes people like people. In 1930, his obsession—the very young girl whose virginity is the most important thing about her—flared up, and he cast sweet Evelyn Baldwin in a small role in his last film, *The Struggle*. Its failure took all the fight out of Griffith, and he did nothing further to make Miss Baldwin a star. In 1936, to general astonishment, he made her his wife. They parted soon and sadly. The long-pursued ideal of the golden-haired innocent could not survive the close quarters of married life. In his last years Lillian Gish, her celebrity her own now instead of his, was virtually his only friend.

CECIL B. DeMILLE

As Griffith's were Griffith's, Cecil B. De Mille's films were De Mille productions first, last, and always, and the stars in them were primarily stars in his crown. But his attitude toward star-making really differed radically from Griffith's, and only seemed to coincide with it, for one period, for reasons of strategic necessity. De Mille's father, the Reverend Henry C. De Mille, was a playwright, so was his brother William, and his mother was a dramatic teacher and play agent; from infancy, he knew the importance and the value of stars in any form of entertainment. As a young old stager fresh come to the movies, he directed some of the stage luminaries of the day—Geraldine Farrar, Blanche Bates, Fannie Ward, and others now forgotten. But in 1917 he along with everyone else in motion pictures faced a crisis. The star system had gotten out of hand. Mary Pickford was worth double her weight in gold, but her salary had risen to such a height that the profits on her films were purely nominal, however much money they earned. All her sister and brother stars were following her lead as fast as they could, and it began to look as if they, and not the studio overlords, owned the movies. What to do? The star craze was at its peak. The public loved stars, would not, it was believed, go to see films which lacked them. So, cursing their luck, producers continued to bid against each other for them, and wondered when the debacle would begin. For some of them, it already had.

When this situation developed, De Mille took the bull by the horns. He proposed to his partners in Paramount, Adolph Zukor and Jesse L. Lasky, that he produce a series of modest-budget films which would be billed as "all-star" as a matter of course, but which would actually contain no stars at all, only newcomers so eager for a foothold in films that they would work for next to nothing. Part of the money saved on star salaries would be spent on luxurious settings, gorgeous clothes, a dash—only a dash—of spectacle, and plenty of synthetic sin. As for the new young players, after a few De Mille films those who showed promise could be signed by Paramount at comparatively low salaries and built toward stardom. When they reached it, they would no doubt demand the moon like their predecessors, but until they did, the company might hope to make some money out of them. And if their demands grew excessive, they could always be replaced by still newer De Mille finds.

It was a neat scheme. It worked. With box-office titles like *Don't Change Your Husband, Why Change Your Wife?, Male and Female, The Golden Bed,* and *Manslaughter,* De Mille swept the field, set new fashions, and opened up a new way of picking and developing stars. The most important of the youngsters he thus fed into the Paramount hopper was Gloria Swanson. Miss Swanson had served her film novitiate by the time he found her. She had been an extra for Essanay in Chicago, played rough-and-tumble for Mack Sennett, and became a minor leading woman in minor, and pallid, Triangle dramas, where she might have remained for all the public excitement she had so far caused. Then De Mille saw her in a Sennett comedy, leaning against a door. Like many men from the stage, De Mille keenly felt the lack of words in silent pictures. But unlike his colleagues, he did not try to force words into pictures in the form of subtitles; he sought their visual equivalent. In Gloria Swanson's posture in a doorway, he saw dramatic instinct which was literally part of her body, of every move she made. Their five-year relationship began. In the billing of his pictures, Miss Swanson was merely one of several featured players. But he saw to it that she got the meatiest parts, was photographed to best advantage, wore clothes beyond the wildest dreams of Paris, or, more important, beyond those of Winnie Woolworth. Miss Swanson, for her part, did as she was told, learned all she could, and waited. Came the day they had both undoubtedly anticipated, and perhaps rehearsed for: "I've taught you all I know, Youngfellow," De Mille said, using his nickname for her. "Go and be a star." The star she became might well have called down Paramount's blessing on both director and actress. That the blessing was not forthcoming was part of his later history, and hers.

More than half of Paramount's big stars of the 1920s came initially from De Mille's cast lists. He turned Thomas Meighan from a conventional he-man lead into a matinee idol. Bebe Daniels he rescued from knockabout comedy and gave her roles in drama and comedies of manners—only to have her revert to type when she reached stardom, as an athletic comedienne. Wallace Reid's faultless good looks he shaped into the image of the all-American fella, a younger and slicker Fairbanks. The uncertain Richard Dix he jelled into another breezy type, the sports-loving kind. But in spite of this saga of sunny success, all was not easy at Paramount. De Mille found it increasingly hard to get along with his partners. Their tastes, their bents, their business judgment differed from his. De Mille had a weakness for costly historical spectacle; Zukor and Lasky could not understand why he was not content to go on with the successful "society" pictures which he had pioneered and in which he excelled. A particular bone of contention was the "special unit" De Mille insisted upon maintaining, apart from the general Paramount roster, with his favorite technicians and players attached to it and idle between his pictures. Neither side would yield on this, and differing views became an open split. De Mille departed to form his own company, taking with him those of his protégés who were at that moment hovering on the verge of stardom—Leatrice Joy, Rod La Rocque, Jetta Goudal, William Boyd, Vera Reymonds. In the new dispensation, they were immediately starred in minor pictures directed by his associates. Such films were intended as the meat and potatoes of

Cecil B. De Mille fingers the curls of Claudette Colbert, whom he lured into the title role in his version of *Cleopatra*, 1934, by asking her: "How would you like to be the wickedest woman in history?"

Cecil Blount De Mille

a varied program centered around his own chefs-d'oeuvre, in which he would presumably unearth new finds. But *The Road to Yesterday* and *The Volga Boatman* featured his familiar regulars, *The King of Kings* offered romantic opportunities to no one, and the "finds" of *The Godless Girl,* Lina Basquette and George Duryea, never amounted to much. The talkies convinced De Mille to end his independent venture, a highly inconclusive one which had been marred by dissension with his backers, financiers from outside the industry. He moved gorgeously to M-G-M, where with no difficulty at all he was accorded the special unit which Paramount had so begrudged him. There he launched Charles Bickford and tried in vain to launch Kay Johnson, whose intellectual face and adult speech and manner ill fitted her for a two-dimensional De Mille heroine.

Then, unbelievably, disaster struck him. His third talkie was a flop—a flop foreseen in advance; Nicholas Schenck of M-G-M asked him if he could not cancel the production of *The Squaw Man* midway, but too much money had already been spent on it. This third remake of an ancient play was badly received. The Great Depression had spread over the land, and everyone in pictures felt himself at sea. De Mille seemed to be drowning. As he bitterly says in his autobiography, he, the founder of Hollywood, "could not get a job in Hollywood." He had offers. Anyone of his eminence and proven capacity always has offers, even on the way down. But they were not offers he could accept and preserve the identity of Cecil B. De Mille, and for years he was on the outside looking in. Then, surprisingly, he returned to Paramount in a shaky one-picture deal which had a decidedly probationary air. His onetime subordinate, Emanuel Cohen, said to him pertly, "Remember, Cecil, you are on trial with this picture." Mr. De Mille did not like that kind of talk. He had not liked being an outsider. Clearly he decided to be prudent, to play along, to reduce the odds. The leads in *The Sign of the Cross,* Claudette Colbert, Fredric March, and Charles Laughton, were not De Mille finds but flourishing Paramount contract players. Elissa Landi he borrowed from Fox, but she too was an established star. From then till the end of his career, that remained his policy. Loretta Young, Gary Cooper, Jean Arthur, Barbara Stanwyck, Ray Milland, Paulette Goddard, Victor Mature, Hedy Lamarr, Betty Hutton, Cornel Wilde, Yul Brynner—his later casts consisted of prime talent, skimmed from the cream of any season's box-office crop. Only once more did he really try to push a find, the stalwart Henry Wilcoxon, whom he featured in *Cleopatra* and *The Crusades* in spite of yawning fan indifference. Then Wilcoxon was demoted to secondary roles, where his lack of appeal didn't matter and his acting did. Later he became De Mille's assistant and associate producer. Professional friendships of this sort meant much to Mr. De Mille. Victor Varconi, whose career as a romatic De Mille star was halted by the talkies and his incomprehensible accent, always found parts in later De Mille films, though the dialogue he was given was sparse; he mostly played Indians. As for Julia Faye, she became a sort of Hollywood legend. She began in featured roles and sank to small parts, then to bits, but she was in every De Mille film from 1918 to 1957. She was also his confidante, his expert on Hollywood politics, his secret agent. The inevitable passing of the passing show saddened De Mille somewhat. How he felt came through in the expression of his face and voice in his memorable scenes in *Sunset Boulevard.* "Put that light back where it belongs," he calls to an electrician who has momentarily turned it on the has-been Gloria Swanson. He knew it belonged on youth and novelty, and always would, but he wished it didn't have to be that way.

To a lesser extent than Griffith, but to an extent, Cecil De Mille was divided against himself. No one was more commercial, no one man made more money for the industry, or anything like as much. Making stars was part of showmanship, and he went at it with a will. But part of him turned to a kind of picture in which players and performances were of secondary importance—the part of him he called Champion Driver, a fantasy figure he dreamed up in boyhood. He has said that all the pictures he really liked making were made by the Champion Driver. And it would not surprise this observer at least if the Champion Driver would not have preferred that every Cecil B. De Mille production be cast entirely from unknowns.

THE ORGANIZATION MEN:
LASKY
AND SCHULBERG

Griffith and De Mille were individualists, however much they compromised with commerce, however wily they believed their compromises to be. To develop the star system as a year-in, year-out going concern, another type of mentality was needed: the man who thought in terms not of one great film but of a studio "product" of some hundred pictures a year; whose loyalty is to a corporation; whose success symbol is stockholder dividends, not so much for the sake of the money but as an earnest of the goods delivered, the job well done: the kind of man we call today the organization man. Jesse L. Lasky was, like Griffith and De Mille, a movie pioneer, and before that a versatile showman, but the place he made for himself in motion pictures was very different from theirs. In concert with Adolph Zukor, he set out to make the great Paramount company the largest motion picture organization in the world, with the most important and most profitable stars in the world.

His and Zukor's policy was based on a hard view of the movie market at its flash point, the theaters, eighteen thousand of them in this country and an unknown but much larger number elsewhere. It was Zukor's drive to control as many of these theaters as possible and Lasky's function to provide a glittering film program which would attract them into Paramount's orbit. That meant big "specials" like the superb *The Covered Wagon,* the spectacular *The Ten Commandments,* and the unfortunate *Old Ironsides.* It meant also occasional "novelties" like the documentaries *Grass and Chang* and the semi-documentary *Stark Love.* These were films which tried to explore both the possibilities of the movie medium and the limits of popular taste, but they accounted for less than a third of any year's "product." The remaining two thirds sold to theaters primarily or exclusively on the basis of star names.

This method of selling derived from several sources, but chiefly from the practice once infamous as "block booking." As Mr. Lasky genially put it, his and Zukor's policy was based on "the solicitous desire to spare exhibitors who changed bills twice a week from the inconvenience of booking any but Paramount pictures. The product was sold to exhibitors in blocks, at a fixed price, sight unseen before it was made. This was mass production with a vengeance, and need I mention that if we had been fabricating aircraft, some of them would have been a menace to life and limb." The only known factor in these presold unknown quantities was the star, and even if exhibitors wanted to think in other terms, they had no choice but to try to assess the appeal of a particular player to their particular audience, and, if he assayed high, hope that his vehicles would not stink up the theater too much. Under this dispensation, the acid test of star quality became, how many bad pictures could he survive and still keep his audience appeal? Measured thus, Gloria Swanson was without doubt the Paramount champion. To get one of the four to six pictures she made annually, an exhibitor would have to book at least six other Paramounts, and for the most part he didn't particularly care which six. Her hold on both metropolitan and small-town audiences was so strong that seemingly she could star in any kind of script, or no script at all, and still fill the movie houses to their rafters. Nobody else, not even Mary Pickford, not even Garbo, more thoroughly demonstrated the money value of star glamour, or the viability of the block booking system. But there was one person at the Paramount studio who was not entirely sure that this agreeable situation would continue forever, and that was Miss Swanson herself. She was privy to, and beneficiary of, Cecil De Mille's scheme for creating new stars in his all-star no-star productions and then delivering them to Lasky's tender mercies for all-out exploitation in a multiplicity of nondescript films. She was aware too that this scheme would end abruptly at the precise moment when Adolph Zukor, suddenly revealed as a flinty-hearted bookkeeper instead of a paternal corporation head, would open his books to her and prove that her pictures were not doing the business they once did. She was thought to be arrogant, and she was of course not unaffected by her intoxicating success and the worldwide adulation that went with it. But she had unintoxicated moments when she knew that her only hope of prolonging her success was to make fewer and better pictures which could be sold individually on their merits, and not have to drag with them into the theaters half the Paramount clinkers of the year. That meant accepting United Artist's invitation to join its select company of star-producers, who worked without salary but kept all the profits of their films. So, when Mr. Lasky offered to double her $6500 weekly salary if she would renew her contract to make four pictures—any old pictures—a year, she thoughtfully declined. When he raised his offer to $18,000 a week, she remained adamantine. This provoked a continental crisis, with Mr. Zukor in New York on the phone to Mr. Lasky in Hollywood, irascibly demanding to know what the woman wanted anyway. Nobody had ever turned down that much money before. She wanted fewer pictures, control of stories? That was unthinkable—it wasn't block booking, and therefore not cricket. In desperation the two titans offered her a flat million dollars a year if she would continue working for them for two more years.

She didn't turn a hair, but this third offer must have given her pause. The chance to become an automatic millionairess, with none of the risks involved in independent production, was not be tossed aside—especially when you consider that Miss Swanson's millions, unlike those proffered Elizabeth Taylor for the distasteful chore of working in *Cleopatra,* years later, would be subject only to minimal income tax. On the other

Jesse L. Lasky, fireman, and Adolph Zukor, engineer, in the cab of the crack express known as Paramount Pictures. Translated from publicity symbolism, this meant that Lasky as studio head fed the fires of production while Zukor as president kept the train on the rails—until it ran head on into the Great Depression.

hand, this two-year contract happened to coincide exactly with the two years which her advisers, and her own heart, forecast as the extreme limit of the time she could expect to hold her fans if she continued to star in vehicles which were vehicles and nothing more. She decided that life was a gamble and she might as well take the risk of independence. In doing so she prolonged her starring career by eight years. That, at its finish, she ended up nearly broke may perhaps have given the Messrs. Lasky and Zukor some satisfaction.

Her departure left Mr. Lasky in something of a hole. He had no one strong enough to replace her. He had thought he had, but he hadn't. Unlike most European importations, Pola Negri was already an American box-office sensation when she arrived at the Paramount studio. Her German silent films, *Passion, Gypsy Blood,* and *One Arabian Night,* had broken down the audience prejudice against foreign pictures, largely because of her contribution to them. Nobody had ever seen a movie actress quite like her before. She was sort of a vamp, but a careless sort, lacking the implacable menace of Theda Bara and others with whom we were familiar. She seemed concerned about nothing but her own pleasure, and the pleasure of the moment at that. What she stood for is illustrated by the fact that American fathers took their sons to see Miss Negri as a sort of first initiation into the facts of life and womanhood. In her German films she was indifferent both to appearances and manners, and obviously unvisited by the thought that she should try to please others. She was, someone said at that time "sexually irresistible—and you had the feeling that the back of her neck was dirty." That she was devastatingly beautiful made her disregard of hygiene all the more piquant.

But Paramount could not see that much of her attraction derived from the fact that she was descended from Polish gypsies and still one of them at heart. Mr. Lasky summoned the studio magic-makers and set them the task of cleaning up Miss Negri's neck. He cleaned up her roles too, injecting generous amounts of "sympathy" which accorded oddly with her previous image of a woman who was a savage just beneath the surface. Nobody could quite understand why the synthetic Paramount Pola, luminously photographed and gorgeously gowned, did not carry the same charge as the girl, clad often in tatters, who moved through the murkily lit early German films. Unfortunately, Miss Negri didn't understand it either. She cooperated enthusiastically with the studio's efforts to streamline her into a standardized movie star, and most of the time apparently forgot that she was, besides a star, also an actress of imagination and power. Nothing in her American films approached the moment in *Passion* when she meets the King of France for the first time—and immediately kisses him on the mouth. That was the sort of thing which had electrified her original fans, and which they sought in vain in the studied attitudes of stylized acting in her Hollywood films. By the time Gloria Swanson left Paramount, her onetime rival, Miss Negri, was not only no asset to the block booking system but a positive liability. Theaters could not be lured by her name into booking unwanted films; it was *her* films that were unwanted, and exhibitors, when forced to rent them, showed their feelings by removing her name from the marquees and substituting that of her leading man, even when he was an unknown. An $8,000-a-week star who was also a box-office repellent was no help to block booking at all.

Lasky seemed to have an affinity for this kind of trouble—stars who began with brilliant promise but who before their contracts expired had for one reason or another turned into full-fledged problems. As a problem child, Rudolph Valentino was a self-starter. He fell into Lasky's hands by an incredible stroke of luck. He scored a bull's-eye in the great hit *The Four Horsemen of the Apocalypse*, and the entire industry assumed as a matter of course that he would remain with the old Metro company, which produced that bonanza. But Valentino had quarreled with Rex Ingram, director of the *Four Horsemen*, and Richard Rowland, the head of Metro, was so involved in negotiations for selling the company to Loew's, Inc. that he forgot to secure this new stellar asset by putting him under contract. There Valentino hung, a plum for the plucking, and Lasky plucked. It seemed at first the greatest of coups. *The Shiek* made a profit of a cool million for Paramount, and *Blood and Sand* and *Monsieur Beaucaire* were not far behind that figure. But Valentino refused to be fitted smoothly into the Lasky assembly line. Unlike Gloria Swanson, he did not request story control; he *demanded* it, and when he didn't get it simply stayed off the screen. In vain did the company threaten him with blacklist and litigation; Valentino kept himself in funds through personal appearances and grew ever more intransigent. He simply wouldn't do anything but what he wanted to do, and showed that he meant it by defying not only the front office and the New York office but the courts as well. Very, very doubtfully, Zukor and Lasky departed from cherished precedent and granted his demands for "artistic freedom." The results, *The Young Rajah* and *Cobra*, were disasters from everybody's points of view except Valentino's and one expensive film he insisted upon, *The Hooded Falcon*, was never finished. At this point, Lasky was willing to let him go his own way to the extent of going away entirely, which he did, to that menace, United Artists. Lasky by his own confession was sufficiently piqued at losing the greatest of Latin lovers to try to invent one of his own. Jake Krantz, an Austrian by birth, when renamed Ricardo Cortez proved highly suitable for such pictures as *Argentine Love*.

Betty Bronson proved to be another disappointment. The perfect type for the epicene title role of *Peter Pan*, she was lifted instantly to world fame and stardom by that picture's success. Lasky held the highest hope for her. But the perfect Peter Pan was far from perfect in romantic roles, much less as the saucy flapper of *Ritzy* and *The Cat's Pajamas*. Miss Bronson lasted less than two years as a Paramount star.

And all these setbacks occurred at a time of considerable financial difficulty for the company, a difficulty for which none of its executives was responsible—it was a stroke of fate. The series of events known as the Hollywood Scandals of 1920—23 cost the motion picture industry much public prestige and good will. They cost Paramount a great deal of cold cash. When Fatty Arbuckle's name become mud in the public eye, thanks to a rape charge, Zukor and Lasky allowed themselves to be persuaded not to release the films he had already made, even though more than a million dollars was tied up in them. With Mary Miles Minter exposed as the sweetheart and perhaps the mistress of her murdered director, William Desmond Taylor, her potential as a second-string Mary Pickford was damaged beyond repair. And Wallace Reid's remaining films became a literal drug on the market when he died of drugs.

Strokes of fate are to be borne stoically, but for Lasky they were coming too fast.

(Above right) Kay Francis, Herbert Marshall, and Miriam Hopkins, seen here in *Trouble in Paradise,* 1932, were three of the bright stars whom Lasky fashioned to replace the fading luminaries of the Clara Bow-Pola Negri era.

(Right) Bringing Mae West before movie audiences was Jesse Lasky's boldest feat, and from his point of view the most futile. Before her popularity had a chance to swell Paramount's coffers, Lasky had been ousted from the company.

(Above) Although B. P. Schulberg brought Clara Bow to Paramount, it was Jesse L. Lasky who made her the greatest star of the last mad years of the Jazz Age.

(Left) Josef von Sternberg not only discovered but actually created Marlene Dietrich. But it was Jesse L. Lasky who gave him the opportunity to do so.

Immersed in turning out a continuous flow of pictures like a frozen-custard machine, he began to feel that he couldn't think fast enough to keep pace with events. Perhaps he could feed his picture assembly line ready-made stars from one source. Thus was born the Paramount School of Acting, in which stars of the future were to receive their training, not in obscure apprenticeship, but in the full focus of the public eye. Charles "Buddy" Rogers, Josephine Dunn, Thelma Todd, Jack Luden, Lane Chandler, and Louise Brooks were made famous before they ever appeared in a picture, and then were unveiled in a minor one, *Fascinating Youth*. Only one graduate of this "West Point of the film industry," Buddy Rogers, ever made it to Paramount stardom, but Mr. Lasky, for better or for worse, must be given credit for inventing what is now familiar as the "starlet" build-up. In the meantime, under pressure, Lasky took measures to delegate some of his responsibilities. He had need to. Paramount was now the only picture company to maintain a studio on both coasts. He put Walter Wanger in charge of the one on Long Island—something of a white elephant—and brought into the Hollywood one as his second-in-command his old associate of early Paramount days, B. P. Schulberg.

This proved to be an inspiration. Schulberg had been a minor independent producer since he broke with Zukor and Lasky, and his years on the outside looking in had sharpened his appetite and touch. He galvanized what, at opulent Paramount, was in danger of becoming a somewhat Byzantine method of operation. No one else saw a potential star in beefy, tough-looking George Bancroft, but he did, and with the help of Ben Hecht, Josef von Sternberg, and *Underworld* he created a new screen character, the hero-villain, prototype of all the romanticized gangsters who have fascinated a certain section of the public ever since. Most important, Schulberg brought with him Clara Bow. This Brooklyn-born girl was probably the most undereducated aspirant to stardom ever to make the grade, Marilyn Monroe not excepted. What she had that canceled out all her minuses was a blazing vitality which brooked no control. Her early directors had recognized the vividness she contributed to their pictures in minor roles, but they couldn't see how to shape her. She threw the script aside; she bounded all over the set; she did, not what she was told, but whatever came into her head, and you had to be fast with the footwork even to keep her in camera range. She disconcerted routinist film-makers, and her career, after a flashy start, had been at something of a standstill for four years when Schulberg, her producer, moved to Paramount. He sold her contract to the company for $25,000. It proved to be an incredibly valuable investment.

What Clara had needed to realize her full potential was, simply, to become a star. She was in fact a star of stars. You couldn't put her in too many scenes—she gave a lift and a punch to them all. Lasky as well as Schulberg quickly perceived this. He had a motive—block booking again. For here at last was the real successor to Gloria Swanson, a star who could sell not only her own pictures but his others as well. And it seemed exactly the right moment. Gloria and Rudy had departed, Pola was fading—and a new day had dawned. The vogue of the flapper, which had begun seven years earlier, now had reached its peak. The country, two years before the stock market crash of 1929, was pleasure-mad. It wanted to think only about pleasure (and money, of course), and it seemed to want a sort of implicit cinematic validation. You had only to watch Clara Bow on the screen for a few minutes to decide that having fun was the most important thing in life. So Clara Bow became the "It" girl, the embodiment of Madame Elinor Glyn's distillation of sex, and inevitably appeared in a picture of that name. *It* was probably one of the flimsiest films ever made, but everybody went to see it. While it lasted, Clara's popularity was as intense as that of any personality the screen has produced.

Her popularity was at its peak when the talkies arrived. Lasky, like all veterans of the silent era, was hard pressed at first, but luck was with him. The new medium provided him with far more and far better stars than the Paramount School of Acting ever could. True, Clara Bow was unhappy in the constricted sets and with the wordy dialogue of early sound films, and Emil Jannings and Olga Baclanova were lost to the company because of unintelligible accents. But Gary Cooper's pretty boy personality gained body and bite from his speech, and William Powell was literally a revelation. Dead eyes, weak chin, hooked nose, a generally oily appearance—what further handicaps to romantic stardom could this actor possibly have had, short of actual deformity? In his silent career restricted to gigolos and petty thieves, nobody, not even Powell himself, would have denied the logic of such casting. Speech made him a new man, and a potent one. His voice, and vocal manners, suggested deep knowledge of women, long intimacy with a variety of them, and invited more.

As for the Broadway newcomers who flooded Hollywood, Paramount had better luck than most studios—sometimes by accident, a force which rules the art of starmaking as inexorably as it rules the art of war. Ruth Chatterton was in Hollywood in 1928, but not as an aspirant. She had known stage fame for years as a youthful star, but it had faded. Now she had come to the Coast to be near her young husband, Ralph Forbes, whose fabulous blond good looks M-G-M was sure would make him one of their shining male stars. Idle, seeing little future for herself as anything but a wife, but willing to take a chance, Ruth Chatterton made a silent test at Paramount, a test which no one took seriously; this fortyish ex-ingénue had a nerve, using her prestige and her contacts to try to muscle into a field where only youth was at play. But Emil Jannings, looking for a middle-aged actress for the predatory wife in one of his last silent films, *Sins of the Fathers,* saw the test and thought she was physically the type. Miss Chatterton was striking in this part, as all Hollywood acknowledged. But what a laugh, Ruth Chatterton in a silent picture! Then Lasky, who had held back, saw that he had to take the plunge into talkies, and quickly, if Paramount was not to be dangerously left behind. Seeking to get something, anything, recorded on sound film, he discovered that he owned the rights to Sir James M. Barrie's play *Half an Hour,* the principal feature of which was the fact that it was exactly as long as its title. That would do for an inexpensive experiment with an equally inexpensive cast. Miss Chatterton was among those cheaply available. She proceeded to make her fellow players in the film, and all others who so far had attempted talking pictures, look like amateurs. Moreover, the movie public, which did not know the Broadway star of *Come Out of the Kitchen* and *La Tendresse* wanted to know who she was, and they wanted more of her. Ruth Chatterton was suddenly a movie star in the front rank, thanks to her vivid and expert speech, while her much younger husband, Mr. Forbes, as suddenly found himself headed for secondary roles. His London stockbroker's voice punctured the illusion created by his Viking handsomeness. It was an odd and unprecedented situation. Miss Chatterton's retroussé nose was funny-looking on the screen. She solved that by wrinkling it up all the time, a too cute mannerism which nevertheless fetched the fans, who were somewhat bored with the marmoreal smoothness of the faces of other female stars. Then too, there was the undeniable fact that she was, put it how you like, not really young any more. She took to chewing gum on the set; even ex-waitresses and ex-shopgirls among the stars knew better. When her employers looked askance, she pointed out that at her age she had to do it to keep her chin line. In spite of her freak hit she knew that her time as a star was limited, and she intended to make her pile while the making was good. Within a year of her talkie debut, the cheap actress of *Half an Hour*—mysteriously retitled *The Doctor's Secret* on release—demanded and got a salary of just under half a million a year. "I want to live happily ever after," she explained.

Maurice Chevalier panned out equally well. For years Adolph Zukor, who had seen and met Chevalier in Paris on his annual trip to Europe, had discussed with Lasky the enormous potential of this attractive, inventive purveyor of Parisian "in" humor. But Lasky was doubtful. Remembering the sad fate of Will Rogers in silent films, he feared that the public would see in a voiceless Chevalier nothing but an overgesticulatory and unphotogenic frog. Talkies, he was now willing to concede, might make a difference, but how to translate the Chevalier act into something moviegoers might respond to? The problem was given to Ernst Lubitsch. He had been around Hollywood long enough to know, or believe, that American audiences would accept European performers only in terms of American notions of what Europeans were like. Accordingly, this world-weary boulevardier was transformed into a veritable Gallic chanticleer, whose outthrust lip, tilted straw hat, and exaggerated accent could draw any woman to him for the purpose of being putty in his hands. This worked out fine with every section of the audience except that very small one who knew Chevalier's French work, or remembered his one pre-Lubitsch film, *Innocents of Paris,* in which a much more modest, and much more interesting, performer had been seen. This of course mattered not at all. Interviewers might sense Chevalier's contempt for the caricature of himself which Paramount was exploiting—but he went along with it and with its success, and it is still an elderly version of the Lubitsch Chevalier that we see today, except for those rare one-night stands he gives in New York and Paris, when the broad wink is displaced by subtly mocking, open-eyed stare.

Josef von Sternberg, not Jesse L. Lasky, discovered Marlene Dietrich in Germany and sold her to Paramount, but Lasky was only too willing to be sold. He recognized in her that long-sought non-pareil, a "second Garbo" who might also have her own line of goods to run. First under Sternberg and then under her own power, she ran them with a will, molding herself into the female who still enchants us forty years later. And Lasky and Schulberg were perceptive in those stage invaders of Hollywood whom they chose to lead toward stardom. Kay Francis, Claudette Colbert, Nancy Carroll, Miriam Hopkins, and Fredric March were one and all obvious assets to the Paramount-Publix corporation, as it was now known, and if Tallulah Bankhead's particular brand of decadence did not seem to fetch the public, perhaps it would later (it never quite did). As for the Marx Brothers, the screen was made to order for them; it enabled them to disrupt the entire universe, not just the Broadway stage. Star-making in the new era of the talkies seemed very agreeable indeed. And yet something was wrong. The twenties had already shown Lasky the hard way that one flaw in the theory behind block booking was that it conceived of picture-making as essentially a mechanical process. The trouble was that the stars were not machines but people. They got drunk, raped girls, took to drugs, concealed unsavory or criminal pasts which were eventually exposed, or, worst of all, with a cold and unbecoming concern, left the company just when it needed them most. Nineteen thirty-one and 1932 revealed to him another short-coming. The success of block booking had been based not only on a popular hunger for entertainment but also on a prosperous audience. Depressed by the Depression, people were no longer content with attractive stars in empty vehicles. They shopped around for pictures strong enough to drag their minds away from their own troubles. Mr. Lasky and his system simply could not provide enough pictures with that much pulling power. By his own count, more than one thousand films were made under his supervision between 1913 and 1932.

Yet another crack in the system opened up in the early thirties. The basic objective of Paramount's block booking had been to enable Adolph Zukor to gain control of as many theaters as possible. Zukor had succeeded in buying so large a number as to alarm his competitors. But he bought them on credit—and when the flow of profits from production dried up, his creditors moved in and tried to take over. Zukor was tough enough and wily enough to hang on. The creditors then turned to Mr. Lasky. They revered him; was he not only a co-founder of Paramount, but also the man who had actually to make the product the company had sold all these years? Think of those thousand pictures! He must be tired, very tired. He needed, they thought, at least a brief vacation. It proved to be a vacation with an open end.

Perhaps some part of him sighed with relief. No longer did he carry the whole burden. Now perhaps he could make fewer and, by virtue of being fewer, better pictures. Quality, not mass production, was to be his target. But the eighteen pictures he made for Fox over three years—a fraction of his former output—were not that much better. Some of them, like *Berkeley Square, I Am Suzanne!,* and *The Power and the Glory,* introduced story material and values new to the screen, but none of them hit the exact center of any bull's-eye, critical or popular. Where stars were concerned, he couldn't develop any new ones of his own because he had to use Fox contract players who were eating their heads off on an overloaded payroll. Nor was his venture as Mary Pickford's partner in producing two films for United Artists any more conclusive. *One Rainy Afternoon* and *The Gay Desperado* were tasteful trifles, and Nino Martini, whom he had tried to promote to stardom once before, still struck the public as a man with a very good voice and a not very good screen personality. With a hint of desperation Lasky turned to RKO and a new project in showmanship—at least it was publicized as new. It was called The Gateway to Hollywood, and it used radio to uncover, unveil, and promote potential new stars. It yielded exactly one; Rhonda Fleming, not negligible in her time, but not a great star either.

Mr Lasky was beginning to discover how tough it is to be an organization man without an organization behind you. More and more in these years his pattern became that of a man living on past associations, past favors done, peddling bright new story ideas from studio to studio in the hope of slipping back into the inner circle. Sometimes those previous associations from his days of glory were not so favorable to his present plans and hopes. For years he tried to interest the companies in the story of Alvin York, the World War I one-man army. He was handicapped by York's own reluctance to have his story told on the screen. But in 1940, with America pausing doubtfully on the brink of another war, the old man consented, and Warner Brothers decided that there might just be a public for this particular story at that particular moment. The hitch was that everybody agreed that Gary Cooper should play the part; York himself wanted him to. And Gary Cooper belonged to Samuel Goldwyn. Mr. Goldwyn was an old associate, yes indeed: together they had founded the Jesse L. Lasky Feature Play Company in 1913, and had been amicable partners, and brothers-in-law, for three years. But when they joined forces with Adolph Zukor, and Zukor and Goldwyn clashed, Lasky had sided with Zukor and Goldwyn was forced out of the company. Neither of them had forgotten that, and Mr. Lasky was extremely reluctant to ask his ex-relative what was, from any point of view, a very sizable favor indeed. But he nerved himself to the hurdle and took it. To his surprise, Mr. Goldwyn was both amiable and accommodating. He entirely agreed that nobody but Gary Cooper should play in *Sergeant York,* and would be happy to lend him for that purpose. That seemed to be jubilantly that. But then Jack Warner appeared in Lasky's office with fire in both eye and voice. When contract negotiations began, Goldwyn had revealed that the price of lending Cooper to Warners was the loan of Bette Davis to Goldwyn. Since she was a Warner, not a Lasky star, Mr. Warner had the undesirable feeling that something was being put over on him. Fortunately, Miss Davis wanted very much to play in the picture Goldwyn had in mind for her, *The Little Foxes,* and the deal was rockily consummated. But Mr. Lasky had learned all over again how little influence or bargaining power he had, how he had to beg for chips to stay in the game.

Sergeant York made a good deal of money, but most of it somehow stuck to the pockets of Warner Brothers rather than Lasky's own. Much the same thing happened when he sold the package of *The Great Caruso* and Mario Lanza to Louis B. Mayer, much against the latter's better judgment. Metro-Goldwyn-Mayer made large sums out of *Caruso* and Lanza, but all that Lasky had when the studio gates closed behind him was his comparatively small salary as producer. Bravely, with the infectious enthusiasm which had always been his great asset, he started out to peddle yet another offbeat idea, a story about the nation's high school bands, which may have been the ancestor of *The Music Man.* The only studio which showed any interest was Paramount. There another old associate, Cecil B. De Mille, interceded for Lasky. Perhaps Mr. De Mille remembered when he too had been on probation. Paramount granted a small budget for the picture and found a small office for the old man, somewhere in the rabbit warren of offices over which he had once presided as supreme overlord. Before he could begin this long-dreamed-of picture, Jesse L. Lasky died.

As for B. P. Schulberg, he had survived Lasky at Paramount, but not for long. He too hit the trail of independent production, with even less success than Lasky. In the 1950s all his friends were shocked by the appearance in *The Hollywood Reporter* of a full-page ad signed B. P. Schulberg. In it, he pleaded for a job in the industry, any job.

He reminded his former associates what a wealth of experience he had in every department of the production and merchandising of motion pictures. He concluded by saying, in effect: Don't wake up some morning and kick yourself in the pants because you read in the paper that I have died forgotten in some hotel room. A wave of remorse swept over the picture men on both coasts. People not only thought but said, there but for the grace of God go I. Many lunches and cocktails were consumed while amateur philosophers dilated on how wasteful of seasoned ability the movie companies are. But so far as is known, nobody ever did offer Schulberg a job before he died.

THE ORGANIZATION MEN:
MAYER AND THALBERG

In 1923, three producing companies, Metro Pictures, Goldwyn Pictures, and the L. B. Mayer Corporation, merged. It was a day of mergers. Robertson-Cole, Triangle-Kay-Bee, Associated, and a host of other combinations now forgotten represented the desperate effort of the smaller movie-makers to survive in the face of the increasing control of production, distribution, and exhibition by the majors, led by mighty Paramount. The union of Metro, Goldwyn, and Mayer, however, was of more than passing interest to industry observers. Metro, though small, was the producing arm of the chain of movie and vaudeville theatres controlled by Marcus Loew. Goldwyn, through rudderless and drifting since Samuel Goldwyn had been ejected from its leadership by stockholder vote, possessed a magnificently equipped studio the equal of any in Hollywood. Together these two elements might form a powerful combination. But Mayer? Where did he fit in? Louis B. Mayer had been an exhibitor and distributor in Massachusetts. Almost incidental to his other operations, he had formed a small producing company whose productions could not possibly be remembered today by any but the fanatical scholars. Virtually the only asset he brought to the new three-ring circus was the once top, now dimming star Anita Stewart. He seemed exactly the kind of small-timer who was slated to be squeezed out in this era of consolidation. Now it was announced that he would head the production program of the new company. Why? Nobody in the industry could understand it.

He turned out to be the keystone of the arch. Louis B. Mayer's gifts were as numerous as the sins with which his name is still blackened by those who still have the energy to hate him. As an executive he proved to have the ability, almost unique among studio overlords, of selecting subordinates whom he could trust, and backing them to the hilt. As a studio program planner, he thought (because he himself felt) that values must remain elemental, but, taking his cue from Lasky and Paramount, he knew too that however hoary, they must always be dressed up as the last word. And as a showman he instinctively believed that when the chips were down, people were most interested in people—personalities—stars. For them ideas must be sought, around them stories must be shaped. Before Metro-Goldwyn-Mayer's first year was out, it had

Irving Thalberg at twenty-five. By that time he had risen from secretary to Carl Laemmle, the head of Universal, to Laemmle's assistant, to production chief of the Universal studio. When this picture was taken he had just been appointed executive assistant to Louis B. Mayer at the recently formed Metro-Goldwyn-Mayer studios. A year later he was in charge of production at the new company. A youth who could persuade two such egoists as Laemmle and Mayer to turn over so much power to him held a special place in Hollywood values; Thalberg was dubbed a "boy genius," and the awesome legend has grown with the years. Perhaps it was based on fact.

F-2400

(Above) A gloat. Louis B. Mayer gleefully signs the contract he has wrung from a reluctant David Selznick, giving M-G-M distribution rights to *Gone With the Wind* in return for the loan of Clark Gable to play Rhett Butler. Besides Mayer, Gable, and Selznick, the picture includes Eddie Mannix and Al Lichtman, two of Mayer's staunchest myrmidons. For the benefit of the curious, the dictionary definition of that term is: "A subordinate who executes orders without protest or pity." (Above right) The triumvirs of M-G-M. Louis B. Mayer, Norma Shearer, and Irving Thalberg at the premiere of her *Strangers May Kiss,* 1931. Already a star before she married Thalberg, Miss Shearer used her position as his wife to secure the pick of M-G-M parts and stories, but so discreetly that her sister stars never had cause to complain—openly. (Below) Thalberg's ideals for the uplift of the screen are well exemplified by his importation of Lynn Fontanne and Alfred Lunt to re-enact their original roles in *The Guardsman,* 1931, a replica of the Theatre Guild production of Ferenc Molnar's stage success. Moviegoers were puzzled by the camera appearance of this mannered pair, and the Lunts prudently reneged on further screen experiments, despite Thalberg's enticements.

adopted as its motto, what was also its credo and goal, "More Stars Than There Are in Heaven."

He began with what he had. Anita Stewart soon departed the studio, her bolt shot. But Goldwyn's Aileen Pringle, Claire Windsor, Eleanor Boardman, and Renée Adorée would do well enough to go on with, and so would Metro's Viola Dana and Alice Terry, while Mae Murray and Ramon Novarro were genuinely valuable "hot properties" of the moment. Miss Murray's career was about to peak and then to slide, largely, if we are to believe her own story, because of failure to keep faith with Mayer. Novarro remained an M-G-M star for another 12 years, his career carefully nurtured by Mayer and the actor himself. But two big money-makers were not enough if the new company was to realize its self-proclaimed importance, and it needed lead-time in which to develop its own stars. What could fill the gap? The answer was provided by Irving Thalberg, the famed "boy wonder" who was lured away from Universal, or lured himself away, to join Mayer in the new, unknown enterprise of M-G-M almost from its outset.

The strange relationship between this very young man and the considerably older Mayer is best described in Bosley Crowther's *Hollywood Rajah*. Bitterly and meanly they quarreled over money through the years, but over nothing else. If they had differences about studio policy, they kept them to themselves and presented to everybody else a unanimity so consistent as to give them the constant strategic advantage of surprise. Their secret may have been as simple as the secret of why Mary Pickford clung to Adolph Zukor so long when her immediate financial interests dictated that she go elsewhere: "I always liked his ideas." However that may be, Thalberg thought he saw the answer to M-G-M's immediate dilemma, an answer that remained part of his bag of tricks. He saw the pool of potential talent as consisting not only of stage people, professional and amateur, beauty queens and athletes, and "unknowns," but also of the talent already discovered and developed by other studios. Star "raids" had been known before his time, but he was the first, and possibly the last, to give them functional purpose in long-term planning.

Right at the start, he urged the signing of Lillian Gish. Miss Gish, recently severed from Griffith, was at that moment thought to be second in popularity only to Mary Pickford, and her terms were tough. She not only wanted important money, she wanted, and got, control over the story, direction, and virtually every other aspect of her films. All companies have always been extremely reluctant to grant such rights to stars, but if M-G-M wanted Lillian Gish they had to give in, for the reason that others were prepared to do so if they were not. The results were not happy either for them or for her. While her first M-G-M films realized the returns expected of them, in 1925 and 1926 the image of the virginal heroine was fading out of favor, and fading in over it was the new image of women like Clara Bow, clearly still a virgin but not for long, and of Pola Negri, whose virginity was obviously long gone and unregretted. Miss Gish, for reasons of her own, refused to budge; she fought against kissing scenes in her films, and her basic drive was toward pictures of intellectual importance but little mass appeal *(The Scarlet Letter, The Enemy, The Wind)*. Her contract was terminated by mutual consent before its completion. But Thalberg's Gish adventure was far from a loss to the studio. Her acquisition at the height of her prestige gave M-G-M a bargaining power not only with the theaters but with the other stars whom Thalberg lost no time in luring into the fold.

The first of these was John Gilbert, for years a featured player for William Fox. (It is tempting to describe him as an obscure star, something of a contradiction in terms. But in the movies, it has long been possible to be featured, even to serve in something of a starring role, and yet remain obscure.) Gilbert seemed fated to repeat the successes of others: *The Count of Monte Cristo, Cameo Kirby, St. Elmo,* and, after Valentino's sheik, *Arabian Love.* Thalberg gave him a double transfusion and transformation by turning him into an American doughboy in an original story, *The Big Parade,* and then by casting him not only as passion's plaything—no novelty— but also as Greta Garbo's, in *Flesh and the Devil.* Gilbert immediately succeeded Valentino as the screen's top male star and remained in that position until the coming of sound.

Next came Lon Chaney. Chaney had hits in deformed roles in *The Miracle Man, The Hunchback of Notre Dame,* and *The Phantom of the Opera,* but between these successes he relapsed into secondary roles, just another familiar character man around the lots. Thalberg sensed that behind the horrid make-ups which were the actor's obsession lay a talent of great range and depth and a personality more appealing than any of the monsters Chaney loved. The tough sergeant in *Tell It to the Marines,* the magnetic and melancholy planter in *Where East Is East* proved him right, while Chaney's most effective makeup proved in the end to be the simple white wig and spectacles of the old lady in *The Unholy Three.* Meanwhile, through behind-the-scenes maneuvering, Mayer and Thalberg had secured the contract of the comedian Buster Keaton, the peer of Chaplin and Lloyd, who happened to be the property of Joseph M. Schenck, who happened to be the brother of the vice-president of M-G-M, Nicholas Schenck. He had also brought forward William Haines, who had been around for quite a while, more through his popularity with Hollywoodites than with fans. Thalberg made him a star by projecting onto the screen his private personality of likeable smart aleck. Marion Davies ineluctably made up the fifth wheel to the coach, and by now a coach it was. The slogan "More Stars Than There Are in Heaven" had enough substance to quench the merriment of those who still wanted to regard Mayer and Thalberg as upstarts.

Louis Mayer's sole identifiable contribution to this constellation was electrifying, its *stella assoluta* in fact. He signed Greta Garbo. The word "signed" is used advisedly. It is all that can be established beyond question. For years the legend prevailed that Garbo was excess baggage in the train of Mauritz Stiller, who would not come to Hollywood unless his ungainly protégé could come too, on a miniature salary. Her subsequent glory thus came as surprise and shock to her American sponsors. Recently a counterlegend has grown up. It portrays Mr. Mayer in a Berlin projection room, viewing Stiller's *The Story of Gosta Berling* while simultaneously dickering to get the great Swede (he was really a Finn) to sign with M-G-M. While Stiller urged, "Watch the direction," Mayer was in reality watching Garbo. Then, with Machiavellian duplicity, he pretended to be interested in Stiller only, while secretly plotting to jettison the director and appropriate Garbo as soon as he got them both safely to Culver City. It is useless to try to unsnarl this tangled skein. The plain fact is that Garbo had already made a marked impression on European audiences in *Gosta Berling,* and was soon to create a sensation in her second appearance, G. W. Pabst's *The Joyless Street.* Once that film was released, it was only a question of months before she was gobbled up by one or another American company. Mr. Mayer was lucky to enter that Berlin projection room at a moment when Garbo was still completing *The Joyless Street.* Miss Garbo's story lies elsewhere in this book, but it should be noted here that it was lucky for her, the public, and the company that she became an M-G-M star, highbrow cavilers to the contrary notwithstanding. The vamp label was slapped on her after her first appearance here, but through his choice of stories Thalberg neatly steamed it off and allowed a far more credible and complicated charmer to appear, a new incarnation of the fatal woman. The M-G-M press agents Howard Dietz and Howard Strickling created with high success a public image agreeable to the actress and new to the fans. Mayer over a long period conducted firm but tactful contractual negotiations with a star whose requirements made Miss Gish's demands seem like a daily request for a box of chocolates. The roster of Mae Murray, Lillian Gish, John Gilbert, Ramon Novarro, Lon Chaney, and Buster Keaton had made M-G-M important; the addition of the unique Miss Garbo made the company itself unique. By 1929, it was generally regarded as the most successful studio in Hollywood.

With lead-time gained, Mayer and Thalberg now proceeded to bring out their own string of promising hopefuls, and a prancing line of fillies it was—Norma Shearer, Sally O'Neil, Joan Crawford, Anita Page, Gwen Lee, Dorothy Sebastian, Gertrude Olmstead. Miss Shearer was the first to take on speed; she achieved formal stardom almost at the exact moment that she married Irving Thalberg. But the public had already approved her before that event, and what marriage to the big boss brought Mrs. Thalberg was something stars long for and seldom are permitted, a chance to demonstrate their versatility, to escape from the stereotype of their initial success. Norma Shearer was allowed to win one public in the sweetness of *Smilin' Through,* quite a different one in the tarnish of *The Divorcee, A Free Soul,* and *Riptide,* and her Elizabeth Browning, Juliet, and Marie Antoinette garnered her official acting laurels, if not the unqualified admiration of the best judges. Sally O'Neil rose to swift stardom and to equally swift eclipse. Joan Crawford's ascent and perennial popularity need not be detailed here; it is a red thread through this volume. Of the new crop, these were the only three who were ever billed above the line, but it is notable that Mayer and Thalberg did not drop the also-rans at option time, as was the general custom. They seemed to believe that anyone in whom they had once seen promise ought to be given second, third, and fourth chances, an indulgence which did not always redound to the benefit of those so favored. Hope deferred maketh the heart sick, and Gwen Lee must indeed have been heartsick when she was let out after six years at Metro-Goldwyn-Mayer. Her wisecracking chorines brightened up many a dull picture, and everyone agreed that she was a natural to play Lorelei Lee in *Gentlemen Prefer Blondes.* But she could play neither that part nor any other lead. She was too tall for romantic roles, and no amount of camera trickery could alter or disguise the fact. Anita Page never repeated her immediate hit in *Our Dancing Daughters,* but she too was allowed to hang on, looking as disheartened on the screen as she must actually have felt. It took the failure of three successive attempts to convince Thalberg that there was nothing in Nils Asther. When the talkies tempo-

Miss MacDonald not as the singing cipher she had been hitherto but as a singing *actress* who had a sharp way with witty dialogue. Her image as such sank into the national consciousness and remained there long after she had left the movies. Years later, she was standing in the wings of a summer theater where her husband, Gene Raymond, was performing, when she was approached by a Helen Hokinson-type lady who gave forth with a line Miss Hokinson herself might have been proud of: "Weren't you Jeanette MacDonald?"

Miss Harlow, Miss Loy, and Miss MacDonald had every reason to be grateful that they fell into Thalberg's hands, but Gloria Swanson, Elissa Landi, and Colleen Moore did not. Miss Moore was generally regarded as an ex-star when M-G-M offered her a new contract. She had been a jazz-baby favorite earning a peak salary of $12,500 a week, fifty-two weeks in the year, with no income tax to speak of. She willingly accepted demotion to $2500 a week because she was as confident as Thalberg himself that he could remold her into a Depression heroine in keeping with the thirties. The trouble was, the remolding never seemed to get started. Thalberg loaned her out to Fox for Preston Sturges' *The Power and the Glory*. That seemed all right; she won professional respect for what she made of a colorless role in a weak picture. But when she returned to M-G-M there was still nothing ready for her, and Mr. Thalberg seemed always too busy to discuss her future. Finally she was offered the female supporting role to Wallace Beery in a story of the wrestling ring, *Flesh*. This was a bit much. Impregnably wealthy, she decided not to risk her remaining prestige on this doubtful enterprise, and canceled her contract while it still had time to run and she money to make from it. The net result of her tour of duty with M-G-M was a blank.

The case of Gloria Swanson was even stranger to industry lookers-on who analyzed Thalberg's every move in the hope of divining his secret. After twenty years of outstanding achievement in early, intermediate, and contemporary films, Miss Swanson's career was at a standstill. Her venture as an independent producer had ended badly, and she was ready, she said bravely, "to begin again." But none of the roles, contracts, or salaries offered her were quite "right," a word frequently used by players though they are seldom able to define what they mean by it. Then came an offer from Metro-Goldwyn-Mayer, than which nothing could be righter. It was not a vague offer either, like that which had defeated Miss Moore. Mr. Thalberg had decided that the time had come, in the circling cycle of public taste, 'to revive the obsolete enticements of Ruritanian sex as embodied in old Elinor Glyn's *Three Weeks,* and that Gloria Swanson would be perfection as the lustful lady who lies on the tiger skin and makes eyes at her English milord. In retrospect it seems an odd decision, from every point of view, and one is led into futile speculation as to what the outcome might have been had the picture actually been made. But this was 1934, the year of revulsion among American movers and shakers against Hollywood sex, the year of the formation of the Legion of Decency, the year which made Will H. Hays absolute dictator over all movie material, from stories to leg art. Mr. Hays categorically forbade *Three Weeks*. That was all right: Thalberg had another idea for retreading Miss Swanson. She would be starred opposite Clark Gable in *RiffRaff,* in which she would play a tough working-girl and thus win back her original fans who had tired of her more recent incarnation as an international sophisticate. Then something else happened. For reasons never made public, Jean Harlow was suddenly substituted for Gloria Swanson in *RiffRaff*, after the latter had been widely publicized as its star, and Miss Swanson's only activity for the remainder of her M-G-M contract was to pose for stills which were striking, as usual, but unrelated to any film. She too had drawn a blank, an idle year and a half at precisely that moment in her career when she could least afford it.

Elissa Landi completes the tally of these illustrious Thalbergian casualties. Miss Landi was not an ex-star, nor an idle one. After a splendid start, she had become the routine heroine of routine melodramas, and the steady standardization of her work was driving this intelligent woman up the wall (in addition to her acting, she was a professional dancer, had composed music and lyrics, and was the author of five novels now forgotten, two of them undeservedly so). Thalberg couldn't agree more; he saw in her possibilities that her initial sponsors had been too blind to notice, and he was the man to bring them out as he had done so often before. Quickly he cast her in two films, *Mad Holiday* (another routine melodrama) and in support of Myrna Loy and William Powell in *After the Thin Man*. Miss Landi in these films benefited by M-G-M's lustrous photography and Adrian's gowns, but what next? Mr. Thalberg said, in effect, just a minute, you're in these little pictures to keep busy while I'm figuring out what form the "new" Elissa Landi should take. While he was figuring, he suddenly died. Since no one else around the lot was interested in Landi, she soon departed. The net result of *her* Metro adventure was that other producers decided that, since she had played support to Loy and Powell, she herself was no longer a star, and not worth bothering about any more. Miss Landi made only one more film, a quickie.

Movie companies in those days often signed starlets by the gross and then forgot they were on the lot, but these three ladies were too important to be treated so cavalierly, and speculation swept Hollywood. What had defeated Thalberg's attempts to restore and increase the popularity of each? The M-G-M "stable" at that time included Greta Garbo, Norma Shearer, Joan Crawford, and Myrna Loy, and it was hinted in the fan magazines that these luminaries viewed with no special favor the addition to their ranks of three stars whose past records proved them formidable potential rivals. More specifically, the gossip columnists all but said that Miss Swanson had wangled her M-G-M contract by alienating Thalberg's affections from Mrs. Thalberg, alias Norma Shearer, and that the latter had used her influence with Louis B. Mayer to see to it that no Swanson film project ever reached the sound stages. Conceivable but unlikely: Mayer and Thalberg were not wont to make business decisions on so personal a basis. As William De Mille had bluntly put it long before, what any movie man wants from an actress is something which will boost his picture, not his phallus. True enough it was that the stable had now grown so large that to keep its stars all on top and moving forward was enough to tax any man's energies, without the additional problem of restoring the standing of former favorites. That was, perhaps, nearer the mark in Thalberg's case—that and what it stood for. For this intense, single-minded man was obsessed with the movies in their every aspect. During ten years, Thalberg, with Mayer behind him, had made M-G-M the foremost Hollywood studio (it was said to be the only one of the major companies which never passed a dividend during the Depression). During most of this period Thalberg had done his level best to produce—literally to *make*— the entire studio product by himself. Twice a day he sat in the projection room, viewing the jumble of rushes from a dozen sets, assessing in few words the quality of brief, unrelated shots and—and this was his gift—weighing and placing their value to the individual films of which they were a part. A process shot might be technically perfect, but if the light in it seemed to him wrong for the mood of the picture as a whole, it had to be done over, hang the expense. If an actress up on the screen seemed too dumb for the lines she was speaking, or too intelligent, back went the scene for rewriting, reshooting, and very possibly recasting. Without himself quite knowing it, this powerful executive producer, who could talk grosses and budgets with the crassest exhibitor or banker, was also a sensitive craftsman and artist. That he was also a splendid teacher Scott Fitzgerald revealed in *The Last Tycoon,* whose hero, Monroe Stahr, was beyond cavil Irving Thalberg. Behold him showing Boxley, an English belle-lettrist, what writing for the screen is all about:

"Movie standards are different," said Boxley, hedging.
"Do you ever go to them?"
"No—almost never."
"Isn't it because people are always duelling and falling down wells?"
"Yes—and wearing strained facial expressions and talking incredible and unnatural dialogue."
"Skip the dialogue for a minute," said Stahr. "Granted your dialogue is more graceful than what these hacks can write—that's why we brought you out here. But let's imagine something that isn't either bad dialogue or jumping down a well. Has your office got a stove in it that lights with a match?"
"I think it has, said Boxley stiffly "—but I never use it."
"Suppose you're in your office. You've been fighting duels or writing all day and you're too tired to fight or write any more. You're sitting there—dull, like we all get sometimes. A pretty stenographer that you've seen before comes into the room and you watch her—idly. She doesn't see you, though you're very close to her. She takes off her gloves, opens her purse, and dumps it out on a table—."
Stahr stood up, tossing his key-ring on his desk.
"She has two dimes and a nickel—and a cardboard match box. She leaves the nickel on the desk, puts the two dimes back into her purse and takes her black gloves to the stove, opens it and puts them inside. There is one match in the match box and she starts to light it kneeling by the stove. You notice that there's a stiff wind blowing in the window—but just then your telephone rings. The girl picks it up, says hello—listens—and says deliberately into the phone, "I've never owned a pair of black gloves in my life." She hangs up, kneels by the stove again, and just as she lights the match, you glance around very suddenly and see there's another man in the office, watching every move the girl makes—"
Stahr paused. He picked up his keys and put them in his pocket.
"Go on," said Boxley smiling. "What happens?"
"I don't know," said Stahr. "I was just making pictures."
Boxley felt he was being put in the wrong.
"It's just melodrama," he said.
"Not necessarily," said Stahr. "In any case, nobody has moved violently or talked cheap dialogue or had any facial expression at all. There was only one bad line, and a writer like you could improve it. But you were interested."
"What was the nickel for?" asked Boxley evasively.
"I don't know," said Stahr. Suddenly he laughed. "Oh, yes—the nickel was for the movies."

. . . Boxley relaxed, leaned back in his chair and laughed.

"What in hell do you pay me for?" he demanded. "I don't understand the damn stuff."

"You will," said Stahr grinning, "or you wouldn't have asked about the nickel."

Star-making, teaching, rewriting, reshooting, re-editing—especially re-editing—it was eventually too much for even this concentrated movie mind. Mayer saw breakdown ahead, and in 1933 he insisted on bringing in David O. Selznick to share some of Thalberg's burden. Thalberg made no demur. Now that success had become familiar, almost automatic, he wanted to see if there was something else he could do, something better, something that would command respect—without, of course, passing any dividends. His productions since sound had commanded little respect from critics; they grudgingly acknowledged the sheen and finish of M-G-M films, and they were even ready to grant that besides their stars there was in most of them always the nickel—the focus of interest that kept you in the seat to the end. But they complained, with reason, that the explanation of the nickel usually trailed off into triviality, or, as in Monroe Stahr's story, there turned out to be no explanation at all. Thalberg decided that movies, even Hollywood movies, ought to have meaning, and like most of his compeers, he judged meaning, substance, value, by the standards of the older arts. The success of his near-masterpiece, *Mutiny on the Bounty,* a real movie, probably gave him no more satisfaction than the quasi-failure of *The Barretts of Wimpole Street* and *Romeo and Juliet,* for these were stage adaptations which gave his wife a chance to show that she could match or nearly match Cornell, Hayes, and Lynn Fontanne. He was planning her apotheosis in a vast production of *Marie Antoinette* when he died—suddenly but not unexpectedly. Hollywood had long wondered how long it could possibly be before this sword outwore its sheath. All had admired his success, the money he made, the money he made for the studio—and most candidly admitted that, granted they had his talent, none of them could have matched his achievement, because they lacked the fire in his belly. For him the motion picture Academy created the Irving G. Thalberg Award, the only one of its kind.

He had no successor. For the remaining fifteen years of his reign at M-G-M, Louis B. Mayer kept the reins firmly in his own hands. There was to be no second Thalberg, for the excellent reason that Mayer couldn't have found a second Thalberg had he looked for one. The result was subtle change in star-finding, star-making, and star-handling at M-G-M, a change representing the personal taste of the studio's supreme overlord. L. B. Mayer's reputation was not that of a Chesterfield in his dealings with men, nor that of a Galahad with women. The late Peter Freuchen told a typical story: "They brought me out to M-G-M to advise on a picture based on one of my books—a picture which turned out to be called *Eskimo.* Soon after I got there I went to a typical Hollywood party, a big, glittering one, and met Jean Harlow. Jean was as small as I am big—I'm six foot six, you know—and she was pretty drunk that night. She reached up to feel my biceps and said, 'Aw, big boy, I'll bet you're not as strong as you look.' I put my hands around her waist and lifted her high to the ceiling. In that moment her skirts flared up high enough to show she had nothing on under them—and inevitably a photographer's flashbulb went off.

"The next morning I got a message to get my ass over to Louis B. Mayer's office on the double. When I went in, I found him sitting at his desk crying. 'How could you do this to me, Peter?' he sobbed. 'Here M-G-M brings you out here at a thousand a week and how do you repay us?' He reached under his blotter and brought out a photograph negative and some prints. They showed Jean in my arms, and they showed all Jean had. 'I've got millions tied up in Harlow's pictures,' Mayer sobbed, 'and they'd all be down the drain if that photographer hadn't been an honest photographer and come over here and sold me the negative before he reported to his paper. At that, you've cost the studio—no, me personally—five thousand dollars.'

"Well of course I apologized and got out of there as quick as I could. That was the first time I ever saw a man cry at ten o'clock in the morning. There was Jean in the anteroom, waiting her turn. She said, 'Did you get it?' I said, 'I got it.' 'Wait here,' Jean said, 'and I'll tell you how I made out.' Then she assumed an expression of penitence worthy of Mary Magdalene and went on in.

"When she came out, the expression of penitence was gone. 'The son of a bitch,' she said, 'the son of a bitch.' 'What happened?' 'Well, Louis went into his crying act, of course. So I went into *my* crying act and offered to pay the studio—no, him personally—for the photograph. I wrote a check to his name for five thousand dollars and handed it to him and he took it and gave me the prints. But when I reached for the negative too he grabbed it away from me. "Oh no you don't." he said, and put it in his drawer and locked it. Now he's got me for life.' "

But this endearing old charmer had a Janus face. The last stars developed by Thalberg had been Luise Rainer and Rosalind Russell, representing Viennese Gemütlichkeit and hard, urban sophistication. But the stars most typical of the new Mayer era were undoubtedly Mickey Rooney and Judy Garland. Mr. Mayer's devotion to his mother's good hot chicken soup is well known; he believed in middle-class solidity, 100 per cent Americanism, "wholesomeness." This was not altogether whim. Mayer believed that, after the cynicism of the Depression years, American audiences, and with them world audiences, wanted to see on the screen personalities and situations closer to their own everyday lives and tastes. His acumen was soon demonstrated. The legendary success of the Andy Hardy series, still remembered today and known even to the youngest generation, made Mickey Rooney a national idol of a new sort. And even after all those years of publicized peccadilloes and suffering, the name of Judy Garland still evokes a sort of distilled essence of sweetness, of innate goodness of heart, of nostalgia for a time when everybody was young and life was not only better but, in particular, somehow *nicer*.

Mr. Mayer sometimes paid a heavy price for his nationalist fervor. He rescued Lew Ayres from near-oblivion by casting him in the Young Dr. Kildare series, and Ayres, a faded star, suddenly found himself in top demand for other roles as well as that of the idealistic young healer. Then Ayres betrayed his benefactor. When war came, he reminded the nation that he had first made his name in the pacifist *All Quiet on the Western Front,* that he still believed in that picture's viewpoint, and that he was a conscientious objector who would not fight. Mayer tried to salvage the Kildare series by replacing Ayres with Van Johnson and other actors, but to no avail. An image had been shattered. What Mayer did with Greer Garson was far more successful, if from some standpoints deplorable. In the first pictures in which she was seen by American audiences, especially *Goodbye, Mr. Chips,* Miss Garson pleased everyone by her patrician gentility combined with a verve and worldliness that was as knowing as a wink, but far more subtle. That she was also an artist was shown by her Elizabeth Bennet in *Pride and Prejudice,* a beautifully modulated performance completely in the spirit of Jane Austen. Then, oh, then, came *Mrs. Miniver.* The vast success of this film and of Miss Garson in it caused Mayer to decree that her future roles be written and directed in accordance, that Greer Garson, the star, be reshaped in the image of her most famous role. What emerged was somehow neither Greer Garson nor Mrs. Miniver but something worse than either—a strange caricature of aristocracy, a sort of servant-girl conception of the ladylike, combined with a nobility of character and a spirit of self-sacrifice which made her intolerable to the minority among her original audiences, while welding to her bosom fans by the million. My wife, perhaps the only female in captivity who could not stand Miss Garson at any price, remembers as at once the most nauseous and most hilarious scene in film history that moment in the sequel to *Mrs. Miniver* (what *was* its name?) when the doctor informs the heroine that she has incurable cancer. Miss Garson turns away from him toward the window. Back to camera, there comes over her shoulder the immortal line: "Ai maind, of course." Need we add that it develops that she does not mind for herself, hardly at all; it's just that her death will be such a shock to the children. Miss Garson went on and on with this sort of thing until all memory of her former distinguished and interesting self was obliterated. That she remained an artist underneath it all she proved years later with her performance as Eleanor Roosevelt in *Sunrise at Campobello,* but it took several reels of that picture before the spectator could forget about Greer Garson and realize that he was looking at an intelligent, sensitive, and strong interpretation of Mrs. Roosevelt.

World War II confronted Mayer with a problem which most of the other studios shared. When Clark Gable, Jimmy Stewart, Robert Taylor, Robert Montgomery, and others put on their uniforms, the M-G-M lot was denuded of masculinity. To fill the gap, as he had to, Mayer brought along ex-chorus boy Van Johnson faster than he might have progressed in other circumstances, and resuscitated Walter Pidgeon, who had been around since the mid-twenties without making much of a dent on any identifiable section of the public. The strategy worked. American women went man-hungry for long years, the movies were their principal solace, and young Johnson soon accumulated a horde of hysterical bobby-sox fans, while Pidgeon consoled their elders, especially when he was cast opposite Miss Garson, their favorite star of the period. The same wartime shortage also benefited the movie careers of another bobby-sox favorite, the then fragile Frank Sinatra, and of Gene Kelly. Sinatra had been deferred from the draft as a working father of four, and though Kelly was in the Navy for part of the war, on his return he developed into what might be called M-G-M's principal asset in the last period of Mayer's long reign. Not only a singing and dancing actor of great charm and skill, he proved also to be a choreographer of genius and a movie director of uncommon ability. In concert with the amiable Arthur Freed, supported by the talents of his friends Betty Comden and Adolph Green, he made for M-G-M a series of remarkable musical films whose popularity lasted well into the fifties, though the musical was supposed to have exhausted its box-office appeal with the end of the war. They were peppered with sharp wit and satiric observation of the American scene, but these qualities were never allowed to disturb the underlying romantic mood which ensured audience identification. Kelly's was a lasting achievement. These delightful films are remembered today when epics and message pictures by the score are forgotten, and they are revived not only on television but in theaters as well.

The wartime boom in moviegoing peaked out in 1947 and was followed by a drop in attendance which, if not as startling as that of the Depression years, held within it even grimmer portents. It was one thing if people didn't go to the movies because they were too poor, it was quite another if they stayed away because they were too rich. The affluent Americans of the late forties and fifties had too many diversions to choose from. Besides the growing menace of television, there was night baseball and bowling—or you just might decide that there was nothing more fun than to spend the long winter evenings readying that shiny new sailboat you had just bought for its spring launching. And people, and especially the press, complained that movies no longer packed the punch they once had—they were slicker than ever, but they were censor-ridden, padded, and insipid to the taste, especially in comparison to the English and Italian films which were creeping into the American market. Perhaps is was not the movies which had changed so much, but audiences. The surfeit of imagery which the twentieth century had showered upon the world's peoples was having its inevitable result, the flattening-out of emotional response to imagery.

Mayer reacted to the new situation with characteristic vigor—but with no apparent insight into the new factors in it. The old system which he had helped create had worked so beautifully, why shouldn't it go on working? There was nothing he could do about the divorcement between production ownership and theater ownership which the Department of Justice now insisted upon in belated enforcement of the antitrust laws, and which resulted in an unstable wobbling of both production and exhibition policy. But if film-making costs rose ever higher, he could try to stem the tide by cutting inflated studio payrolls. If Garbo, Crawford, and Shearer were gone, he could find replacements for them; he always had. He did have the acumen to spot a potential favorite in Ava Gardner who had been around Los Angeles since 1941. Mayer brought her along in minor roles and loan-outs until public response to her was clamorous, then developed her into a genuine box-office attraction. She was an M-G-M stellar personality of the classic type, and then Miss Gardner, through her own acumen, accumulated so much money that she could no longer be bothered to work consistently. But Mayer's remaining discoveries of the period turned out tentative, inconclusive—the infallible instinct was becoming distinctly fallible. He signed Gloria Grahame in 1944 and then apparently forgot about her; when she played for M-G-M at all, she played conventional heroines who were not very interesting. Then Frank Capra spotted quite a different quality in her, and from that moment on Miss Grahame played—for other studios—a succession of non-professional floozies who were very interesting indeed. After Marie McDonald had created her "image" as Marie The Body McDonald, Mayer decided that it would be a dramatic switch to sign her to an M-G-M contract and put clothes on her. Nothing whatever came of this, or of Miss McDonald. In the late forties, Mayer imported from England Deborah Kerr and Stewart Granger, attractive, experienced players, and promoted them in expensive films like *King Solomon's Mines* and *Scaramouche*. The public liked seeing them, but it did not *need* to see them as it once had needed to see Garbo and Gable and Crawford and Shearer. They were just part of the furniture of their films—replaceable parts.

This was increasingly to be the way of the future, but no one was sure of that yet. Back in New York, Nicholas M. Schenck and others of Mayer's long-time associates decided that the old man needed help in meeting the new conditions. There began to be talk of "another Thalberg." Schenck thought he had found one in Dore Schary, but L. B. Mayer could not see the resemblance. Though he had made popular pictures, Schary was an intellectual, conscious of the social responsibilities of the movies, in conservative eyes dangerously close to the political left. But he wanted power with which to realize his dreams, and, when Schenck insisted, eagerly accepted the post of second-in-command at M-G-M, with the area of final authority left undecided and in effect in the hands of Schenck. Mayer and Schary tried to stomach one another but couldn't; they did not speak the same language. As the rift widened, Schenck came to a decision. He would jettison his old partner and back the newcomer. Impotent and fuming, Louis B. Mayer resigned the post he had held for thirty years and left Metro-Goldwyn-Mayer. He was far from finished with motion pictures though, he announced, and to prove it bought for production at a fancy price the Broadway musical *Paint Your Wagon*. But he discovered that he too lusted for the power he had wielded so long. He never produced *Paint Your Wagon*. The last six years of L. B. Mayer's life were spent in behind-the-scenes maneuvering to gather enough stockholder votes to oust both Schenck and Shary from M-G-M and re-establish himself as supreme overlord of the studio he had founded. He did not succeed. Instead, Mr. Schenck joined him in exile.

THE ONE-MAN ORGANIZATION
GOLDWYN

Before he happened into the movies, Samuel Goldwyn was a glove salesman operating out of Gloversville, New York. They were good gloves that he sold, and before Goldwyn got through his sales talk his customers were convinced that they were the best gloves obtainable, because Goldwyn had convinced himself of that in advance. Coming from the most deprived of backgrounds, almost wholly lacking in formal education, it was Goldwyn himself who talked Goldwyn into his lifelong passion for quality in everything.

He would pay anything for the first-rate. It used to be said by his detractors that he "bought" success, an allegation which would be more convincing if others had followed his lead; if success can be bought, it is clearly available to anyone who has the price, and there were those in the various Hollywoods of his long career who were in a better position to pay for it than he. But though it has always carried a certain connotation of lavishness, the "Goldwyn touch" was and remains the sole possession of its sole inventor. It was not primarily money that made the touch; it was Goldwyn's ruling passion for excellence.

At the beginning of his career he did believe that, if you paid enough, you could transfer success in another medium to the medium of the screen, a mistake in which he was not alone. Since Geraldine Farrar's film debut created a sensation, he figured that another opera singer of comparable stature and fame would be equally acceptable to silent screen fans, even though they could not hear her sing. But Mary Garden's acting technique, and she was a fine actress as well as a great singer, evaporated before the camera, or rather, turned into a strange caricature of itself. Similarly, when he hired a group of popular writers of the first rank and imported them to Hollywood under a solemn rubric, the Eminent Authors, the scripts they wrote for him were eminently readable but most of the resulting films were not seeable at all, by anybody, including the Authors themselves. Perhaps at this point Samuel Goldwyn began to learn to trust himself. Overawed at first by reputation, he had learned the hard way that reputation did not guarantee success in the new, largely unknown medium of the screen. And since no one could yet be sure what, in place of reputation, *did* guarantee it, he would have to study it out for himself, to spend all his time studying it. With Arch Selwyn he had founded the great Goldwyn studio, from which he took his name (originally Goldfish), but he found out from experience that, unlike Irving Thalberg, he could not distribute his Goldwynness over fifty or sixty pictures a year. He had to take them one at a time if he was really to stamp each one with his own love of the first-class. When his stockholders, irritated beyond endurance by the constant crises which it was his nature to provoke, ousted him from the leadership of his studio, he did not attempt to muscle in elsewhere or to found yet another big studio of his own. He was determined to make one or two pictures a year which would be Samuel Goldwyn productions in fact as well as name. From that time on, his writers might write, his directors direct, his stars act, but always breathing down their neck was Goldwyn, fighting, cajoling, accepting, rejecting, a living litmus paper which turned blue only when his thirst for "class" was slaked. He never mistook himself for a writer, director, or actor; it was instead his job, guided at first almost wholly by instinct, to bring out the best in these craftsmen, and he labored at it. His favorite writer, Ben Hecht, compared Goldwyn at work to a man shaking a slot machine—shaking it and shaking it until the gold poured forth.

In choosing to operate in this manner, Goldwyn was bucking the tide of the entire motion picture industry as it was running in 1924, when he issued his declaration of independence. Those were days of ever increasing bigness, of the consolidation of production, distribution, and exhibition, of a seemingly irresistible trend toward mass production, not to say assembly-line production, of films. Goldwyn owned no theaters. He could not tie his films to ten or twenty others and sell them en bloc. He had to release them through the big distributors, who had their own fish to fry. In these circumstances, his drive toward independence reinforced his passion for quality: Goldwyn pictures had to be the best, or nobody would ever get a chance to see them. On balance, through the years, from *Stella Dallas* to *The Best Years of Our Lives,* they were the best.

His approach to the making of stars was in theory equally selective and discriminating. But selectivity in Goldwyn was always matched by prodigality, and no more than anyone else in motion pictures could he resist making a "discovery," even when the discovered's future career could benefit him but little. Making so few pictures, it was elementary wisdom on his part to concentrate on an equally small number of stars, around whom stories could be built. He had no need for a contract list of featured players and starlets; they could in fact only be a burden to him. But though he lacked the need, he had the impulse. When at an Equity ball he spotted as potential screen material the second daughter of the stage actor Richard Bennett, he could not resist proclaiming as a

(Above) Merle Oberon, David Niven and Samuel Goldwyn. (Left) According to his wife Frances, Samuel Goldwyn admired his longest-lasting star, Ronald Colman, to the point of obsession. But Colman did not achieve his greatest audience hit in any of the literate and meaningful dramas with which Goldwyn provided him. It occurred instead in the rip-roaring melodrama *Bulldog Drummond*, 1929. In this typical scene from it we see the sixteen-year-old Joan Bennett, Lawrence Grant, Lilyan Tashman, Montagu Love, and Colman. (Above right) Eddie Cantor, Miriam Hopkins and Samuel Goldwyn. (Inset) *The Best Years of Our Lives* is Samuel Goldwyn's undoubted masterpiece. Though Fredric March was then regarded as a has-been star, a box office zero, Goldwyn entrusted him with the leading role of the returning sergeant, with sensational results. To millions of ex-GIs, this mirror scene symbolized the lost wartime years which were to have been the best of their lives. (Below) Vilma Banky, Walter Byron, Samuel Goldwyn, Lili Damita, and Ronald Colman. Having derived a fortune from his famous "love team" of Banky and Colman, Goldwyn decided to double the ante by splitting the famous pair and giving Miss Banky a new leading man, Byron, and Colman a new leading woman, Miss Damita. The experiment didn't work. Neither of the newcomers found favor with the public, though Miss Damita made herself a rich woman by becoming Mrs. Errol Flynn and then exploiting the California community property laws with Machiavellian subtlety and cruelty.

Goldwyn "find" this beautiful young girl who had been under the noses of the entire profession for years. Constance Bennett played strikingly a small part in one Goldwyn film, *Cythera,* which starred the forgotten Alma Rubens; in her long sojourn on the screen thereafter she made a fortune for herself and millions for RKO, but not one penny for her original benefactor. Perhaps he was justified in not attempting to develop her: Miss Bennett did not take her career seriously at its beginning, in fact she deserted it for four years of marriage to a millionaire, until she grew tired of being rich and idle. Much the same thing might be said of his lack of permanent interest in Lois Moran, the lovely, fresh American girl he found in a French film which was never released in the United States, and who became a universal favorite after her portrayal of the beloved Laurel in *Stella Dallas.* Miss Moran worked for several studios during the remaining seven years of her career, but she never became a full-fledged star, nor did this disappoint her. She was, understandably, too preoccupied with her private life and the legion of men from all over the world who besieged her. Gary Cooper was quite another matter. Goldwyn's failure to hang on to him was, the producer says today, the gravest mistake of his career. Cooper was discovered by Mr. Goldwyn himself when he applied for a job as an extra, and rushed into the *The Winning of Barbara Worth,* where director Henry King built up his small part into a major one before the picture was finished. After its release, an old associate of Goldwyn's sought him out to tell him of the murmurous wave which swept through audiences when Cooper made his first appearence in *Barbara Worth,* a phenomenon which recurred in every kind of theater, from picture palace to nabe. "I know, I know," the producer replied somewhat pettishly, "but he's hard to cast." Paramount, which picked him up when Goldwyn dropped him, did not find him so. While he was learning to act, he played bits in Paramount pictures, or starred in the minor Westerns in which he felt at home, until the public demanded that he move on to bigger things. Ten years later, Cooper, with *Lives of a Bengal Lancer* and *Mr. Deeds Goes to Town* behind him, returned to the Goldwyn studio at a six-figure salary. He was worth it by then, but how he might have lined Mr. Goldwyn's pockets in the meantime!

Hard to cast Gary Cooper may well have been at that period, for Goldwyn was preoccupied with the first truly great stars he created, the celebrated "love team" of Ronald Colman and Vilma Banky—and that meant either costume pictures or films with a European background. In these terms *Barbara Worth* was an aberration: the small, spare, intensely British Colman was not convincing as a rugged cowboy, nor was Miss Banky as a sand-blown flower of the American desert. Mr. Goldwyn had found her in Budapest, an obscure actress so ignorant of the world beyond the Hungarian coffeehouses that she hardly knew where Hollywood was, and could not understand why her new benefactor wanted her to accompany him there. She learned fast. Through her own efforts, her salary had risen to $5000 a week by the time the talkies arrived. Her eventual fate has already been referred to (page 35). Colman was, of course, in all respects Mr. Goldwyn's beau ideal of an actor. Everything about him—his look, his voice, his speech, his manner, his clothes—shrieked "class," and his acting by any test was strictly Grade A. Here was quality, fineness, all right, all right, and Goldwyn, having had the luck to find exactly what he was after, was determined to make the most of him. During the ten years of their association, Goldwyn was so preoccupied with Colman—preoccupied, says his wife, to the point of obsession—that he made no attempt to develop new male stars. It was a profitable and farsighted obsession. After the two finally parted company, Colman went on through middle age and old age as the respected and sought-after star of top-flight pictures, ending as a radio and television favorite. But Mr. Goldwyn had had the best years of his life and career.

Goldwyn's second major mistake as a star-maker resulted in his for once forsaking his own taste and judgment and succumbing to the chronic Hollywood malady of imitation. In 1930, Greta Garbo and Marlene Dietrich were the reigning favorites. Their hesitant English presented their studios with a technical problem which writers and directors solved brilliantly. Both were surrounded with an air of mystery, on screen and off, which held an indefinable but limitless promise, and they spoke in Delphic monosyllables of assent or denial into which the dreaming spectator could read his most lurid fantasies. This new image of the femme fatale—it really was an old one refurbished, the immemorial "woman with a past"—excited the movie audience, and studios which lacked Garbo or Dietrich made a desperate clutch for facsimiles. A horde of European sirens were brought in and as promptly sent back, or left to languish, except for the few who, like Tala Birell, proved useful in minor roles. Mr. Goldwyn might not have succumbed to this transient madness had he not happened to see in 1931 the German film *Der Morder Dmitri Karamazov,* in which Dostoyevsky's earthy, gross Grushenka was flawlessly played by Anna Sten. Mr. Goldwyn signed her and was delighted to learn that, in addition to being so superbly photogenic, she was also an experienced professional of reputation in Europe. She had made a name for herself on the Russian stage and screen, and, after she fled the Soviet Union, repeated the process in Berlin. This was a *bonne bouche* for Goldwyn, who loves professionalism. But Miss Sten was unknown to the American public, and it was just as well that her record remained in the background, if she was to wear the mantle of mystery in the Garbo-Dietrich mode. She was brought to the United States in huggermugger (but with sufficient publicity to ensure that everyone knew that another Goldwyn find was on the way) and kept under wraps in Hollywood for a year while she perfected her English and her producer prepared to Goldwynize her. A problem. The "new" Anna Sten must not only be like Garbo and Dietrich, she must of course top them, for was she not to be a Goldwyn star? She had been perfect as Grushenka, and Mr. Goldwyn for a time considered a Hollywood version of *The Brothers Karamazov.* Prudently he decided against this, and looked around for a comparable role in which to introduce his nonpareil. One existed: Emile Zola's Nana came as close to fitting the specifications as anybody could wish. But how was this wanton to be introduced to the heavily censored screen of 1933, on which the newborn Legion of Decency was keeping a militant eye? It couldn't be done and it wasn't, but Mr. Goldwyn gave his all; he went through two directors and a costly remake before he called a halt. The final product was, as Iris Barry said in a one-line review, "Not Manet's Nana, nor Zola's, but Anna Sten's, and quite refined." Miss Sten should not have been blamed. She was not responsible for the synthetic compromises which had her Nana safely wicked for eight reels and nobly self-sacrificial in the ninth. She proved her acting mettle by her sincere, deeply felt performances in tragic roles in the next two Goldwyn Stens, *We Live Again* (Tolstoy's *Resurrection* somewhat more positively retitled), and the original story especially written for her, *The Wedding Night.* But the fact that the roles *were* tragic, had to be tragic, revealed a flaw in Mr. Goldwyn's reasoning which *Variety* finally spotted. Writing of *The Wedding Night,* the paper said: "Miss Sten gives a finely sensitive performance. Her hands supplement her face in conveying her emotion and she lives the role of the simple Polish girl who sees only the glamour of the dashing stranger. She is helped in the creation of an impression by not becoming too intimately involved with her hero. There are times when her quiet methods will fail to bring her popular credit for acting. She is handicapped in a way by the more showy personality of Helen Vinson as the author's wife." Mr. Goldwyn saw the handwriting on the wall. If Miss Sten's artistry was too delicate to register in the public eye, if she was eclipsed by her second lead, if above all a script tailored to her measure had to keep her at a distance from her lover and doom her in the end, Miss Sten was not for the American screen.

The three Sten vehicles were the only Goldwyn productions to lose mentionable money in ten years, and they enabled the malicious to say that Sam Goldwyn would go down in history as the man who ditched Cooper and hung onto Sten. Mr. Goldwyn by now could afford their gibes. Through thick and thin, through laughter at his (publicized) neologisms and wonder at the steady standard of excellence his films maintained, his prestige had grown to the point where he could ignore the ridicule of Hollywood barroom wits. Nor was he left unduly out of pocket through the Sten fiasco. Though Eddie Cantor failed to click in silent pictures, every studio wanted him after Al Jolson's success in the first talkies. Goldwyn offered him the most money, and spent still larger sums on the series of lavish, razzle-dazzle, witless musicals in which Cantor starred for him for a decade. The public adored them, one and all. Goldwyn himself is the authority for the statement that the Cantor profits more than made up for his losses on Anna Sten, and enabled him to finance other experiments as well.

From about 1935, a sea change came over his star policy. Instead of concentrating on discovery, he began to borrow established stars, and also to lure them away from their original studios and sign them himself to long-term contracts. He did not do this as box-office insurance, like his friend Cecil De Mille; in spite of Anna Sten, he had never experienced the shock of failure such as De Mille knew when he found himself outside the studio gates in 1931. Nor did he, like Thalberg, seek to revivify waning reputations. His motive seems to have been the strong feeling that there was more in these screen personalities than their original sponsors had been able to bring out, and that he and he alone was the man to help them realize their potential. After a brilliant start Miriam Hopkins, through a series of miscastings at Paramount and RKO, had forfeited fan fervor, and she was being billed below the line when Goldwyn invited her to replace Miss Sten as his top star. Miss Hopkins justified his faith. Her performances in *These Three* and other Goldwyn films were her strongest contributions to the screen. She became again a bright particular star and might have continued so indefinitely had not her beauty been of that blond type which fades early. She became "impossible to photograph," which meant that the technicians could no longer help her to achieve the illusion of romantic youth. Goldwyn was even more brilliant with Merle Oberon. Because of the slightly Asiatic cast of her features, or rather her bone structure, Miss Oberon had at first been publicized by Alexander Korda as half Hindu (she was actually born in Tasmania, of English parents). As a result, like Myrna Loy before her, she was consigned to a series of exotic, and secondary, roles. Alistair Cooke said, "Merle Oberon fought a losing battle against the adjective 'sloe-eyed' until she was, surprisingly, glamorized into naturalness." Mr. Goldwyn did the glamorizing: he brought to the surface her original personality of healthy English countrywoman. Thereafter Miss Oberon had two strings to her bow. She could be exotic or tweedy as the situation called for, and on her own hook she added a third facet to her screen image, that of the intercontinental sophisticate she was becoming in private life. Her occasional presence on the screen today is testimony to the enduring quality of what Mr. Goldwyn saw in her. He was somewhat less successful with Joel McCrea, who had been a prominent leading man to several female stars, notably Constance Bennett, when Mr. Goldwyn bade him follow to higher things. Higher things he did achieve under the Goldwyn standard, in terms of better billing and bigger salary in more important pictures. But there was an acrid, gritty quality in the acting of this handsome, intelligent fellow which got between him and major popular response and disappointed his producer's hopes. After he left Goldwyn his career continued for many years, chiefly in Westerns in which the quality of his screen presence was more appropriate than it had been in the ambitious roles in which Mr. Goldwyn cast him. (For obscure reasons, the latter usually "saw" Joel McCrea as an architect—witness *These Three, Dead End,* and *Woman Chases Man.*)

Bette Davis, Barbara Stanwyck, and of course, Mr. Cooper were the big stars who lent their luster to the sheen of Goldwyn productions in the late thirties and early forties. It began to seem, then, that the independent-minded Mr. Goldwyn had become part of the Hollywood establishment. Then he pulled a switch. Eddie Cantor in his old age was tiring of slapstick acrobatics, and a replacement had to be found if that fountain of gold, the Goldwyn musicals, was to keep on flowing. Mr. Goldwyn's choice was Danny Kaye. This was considered the most outrageous and ridiculous thing he had ever done. Hollywood professionals jammed the New York night clubs to hear and see Kaye when they were in New York; he was their favorite comic entertainer, but, they were convinced, he could only be *their* favorite. His jokes were derived from and directed at the jet set of those days, and the urbane obscenities which were a large part of his stock in trade could not conceivably be acceptable in Iowa (this, it should be kept in mind, was the long-ago 1940s). Kaye was an "in" comedian, not for children or the unsinful. To these protestations Mr. Goldwyn said nothing. He lured Kaye to the Coast and put him through part of the Hollywoodizing process, blondining the star's hair for photographic contrast—but refusing to bob his nose, as the eager experts urged. Then he showed his uncanny talent for perceiving the fundamentals underneath the trappings. (It was he who told Lillian Hellman that her *Children's Hour* could be got past the Hays Office with certain changes, and urged her to accept those changes on the ground that "your story is about the power, not the nature, of a lie.") He kept the Kaye patter songs, the Kaye falsetto technique, but in providing the star with material of wider appeal, he brought out a gift basically akin to that of the great comedians of film history, Keaton, Lloyd, and, if we can say it without lese majesty, Chaplin—the innocent clowns of the screen and all the other innocent clowns from whom they descended. In adopting this *persona* and making it his own, Danny Kaye lost his original audience—the miniature audience of jaded and fretful pseudosophisticates, but he gained a global one.

Frank Shields, Theresa Wright, Joan Bennett, Jeanmaire, Dan Duryea, John Payne,

Dana Andrews, Anne Shirley, Lili Damita, Walter Byron, Andrea Leeds, Farley Granger —Mr. Goldwyn has made as many mistakes as the other star-makers. All the "discoveries" just listed either came to nothing or had their impact only after they had left his auspices. He was quick to sign newcomers he liked, and as quick to drop them if they did not pretty immediately serve his underlying purpose. What was that purpose? Nobody can deny that Goldwyn, like Griffith and De Mille, was a star-maker, but, also as with them, it is apparent to the long-time observer of his work that the real center of his thoughts lay elsewhere. It is significant that his masterpiece, *The Best Years of Our Lives,* was played by veteran professionals, and that the only "new face" in it was that of the paraplegic non-professional Harold Russell, who by the nature of his case could be used only once. It is equally indicative that, after that film of 1946, his efforts to develop new stars grew more and more perfunctory. In order to bring *Guys and Dolls* before a national audience, he might defy casting convention by using Marlon Brando and Frank Sinatra as Damon Runyon characters, but that was not for the sake of "changing their types" or any other such show-business ploy. It was for the sake of *Guys and Dolls.* He was not, like Griffith, enamoured of cinematic high jinks, nor did he have a Champion Driver in him who drove him toward historic spectacles. His own preoccupation was simpler. He liked to see a story told on the screen, and he was convinced that people everywhere liked that better than anything else, too, whether they knew it or not. They might come to see the stars but they stayed to watch a dramatic narrative unfold.

His stars, like his sets and costumes, had always to be the best, but they were a subordinate best. He might rave over "the great photography" of one sequence or the "production values" in another, but unless such footage really served the underlying purpose of the story, it was likely to end up on the cutting room floor. Small wonder that players, whether established or unknown, fought to work for him—not because they were "bought" ("To get what I want," he has said, "I pay as much as I have to and as little as I can get away with") but because the record showed that they were likely to do their best work for him and that the net result of their Goldwyn adventure (it usually was one) would be a boost to their careers. That he should have preserved his feeling for story in an age of the death of illusion and the flattening-out of emotion puts him, like everything else about him, in a class by himself.

THE ONE-MAN ORGANIZATION
SELZNICK

David O. Selznick and Myron Selznick, who as an agent "made" almost as many stars as his brother, had a unique motive for their star-making. It was revenge. Their father, Lewis J. Selznick, had wheedled and muscled his way into motion pictures past pioneers like Carl Laemmle and Adolph Zukor at just that moment in film history when the door had supposedly been slammed on all but the pioneers themselves and their numerous relations. But the senior Selznick not only slipped through the crack; he lived on the excitement of needling his predecessors. In particular he was a thorn in the side of Adolph Zukor, who, legend says, once offered him a million dollars if he would move to China and stay there for the rest of his life. When Selznick's empire-building footslipped, his competitors came down on him like birds of prey. He was ousted from the picture world for good, and this time the door was locked tight. His sons, who had been making their way through posh preparatory schools on an allowance of $1,000 a month, soon found that as far as their father's former associates were concerned, they were just a couple of punk kids.

The family energy and vitality might well then have sought another outlet. Lewis Selznick did in fact become a real estate promoter in the Florida boom of the twenties, a logical step. But not David. The movie bastards had screwed his father. He would grow up to screw them. He achieved his ambition as well as any of us do in this vale of complexities.

Somehow or other he wangled a job as a producer's assistant at Adolph Zukor's own Paramount, and within a couple of years had worked up to associate producership; even today the trace of his imagination can be seen in such forgotten Paramount films as *Forgotten Faces*. Soon, in spite of his youth and comparative inexperience, he was called to minister to the ills of an ailing studio. RKO was founded from scratch in 1928 because Joseph P. Kennedy advised RCA and the other interests which controlled the patents for sound recording devices not merely to lease their patents to the existing studios but also to acquire one of their own. Because the newborn infant was the child of RCA, it was at first called Radio Pictures, a sort of contradiction in terms. There was no question in anybody's mind that the new producing outfit would be a factor from the start. An overconfident RCA executive boasted, "Radio is too big to enter the motion picture field without dominating it." It didn't quite work out that way. Lacking any stars of its own to begin with, RKO eagerly signed established favorites like Bebe Daniels, Richard Dix, Dorothy Mackaill, Rod La Rocque, and Dolores Del Rio as their old contracts with other studios expired. What nobody seems to have realized is that the favorites had already shot their bolt, else their contracts would have been renewed by their original sponsors. Even the absorption of Pathé, with its stars, didn't seem to help the situation. Nothing did. In the race to latch on to each successive fashion in films, such as the gangster or musical cycles, RKO always climbed aboard the bandwagon just when it had begun to slow down. But with the appointment of Selznick as executive producer, the RKO look changed overnight. He permitted Merian C. Cooper to realize an old dream by making *King Kong,* and thus opened up a gold mine which is still yielding pay dirt today. In the skinny, angular Katharine Hepburn he saw a potential star, and the public agreed; her courageous young modern in *A Bill of Divorcement* put her instantly at the top of the heap. She repeated this role, and her success in it, in her first lone-starring vehicle, *Christopher Strong,* but Selznick helped her to vary the pattern, and to show that she was a real actress, by casting her as a naive aspirant to stardom in *Morning Glory* and as an idealistic Victorian heroine in *Little Women.* He was casting sheep's eyes at Ginger Rogers and Fred Astaire when his father-in-law, Louis B. Mayer, summoned him to M-G-M to bolster Irving Thalberg's waning energies. It is significant that after his departure RKO lapsed into its old bad habits, and Miss Hepburn's popularity waned in the series of stereotyped vehicles in which the studio cast her for the next four years.

This extraordinary and evidently very carefully calculated still exposes much of the motive force behind David Selznick's paramountcy in motion pictures. The man on the wall is Lewis J. Selznick, pioneer movie producer who was expelled from the business through a conspiracy of his fellow-magnates. His son resolved not only to re-establish the Selznick name in motion pictures, but to make it also the biggest of all among box office champions. He succeeded.

(Clockwise) One of the unsolved Selznick mysteries is the fact that, though David Selznick was well aware that directing was the most important creative act in the making of a motion picture, he always refused to direct any of his films himself. Instead he hired the best men in the business and tried to bend them to his will. The smiles on the faces of Selznick and Alfred Hitchcock here doubtless masked a variety of feelings, but whatever the behind-the-scenes fireworks, together they produced a series of memorable hits, beginning with *Rebecca,* 1940; Ingrid Bergman, David Selznick, and Cary Grant register amusement at something in the script of *Notorious,* against the sinister background of a De Chirico painting; Selznick's biggest all-star cast: Back row, Alfred Hitchcock, Louis Jourdan, Selznick, Charles Laughton, Charles Coburn, Gregory Peck. Front row, Joan Tetzel, Ann Todd, Ethel Barrymore. Their combined annual salaries totaled five million dollars. The scene is the set of *The Paradine Case;* "I'm going to make you the worst son of a bitch ever to appear in a movie," said David Selznick to Gregory Peck in describing the character of Lewt which Peck was to play for Selznick in *Duel in the Sun.* The news does not appear to disturb Mr. Peck unduly, and right he was. Lewt's bastardliness only endeared the star to audiences of both sexes; David Selznick with the first of the great stars he made, Constance Bennett, at the time of the filming of *What Price Hollywood?,* 1932.

Except for Freddie Bartholomew, who never became quite a real star, Selznick made no "finds" in the two years he was at M-G-M; he was too busy making use of the glittering stable of Metro stars with whom Thalberg could no longer cope alone. He did give Fred Astaire's movie career the push it needed. After fifteen years of stage success, Astaire had turned to the movies because friends pointed out to him that as he grew older he could not expect to dance every night through long Broadway runs. The movies, with their short takes, were supposed to be the answer to this problem. But nobody in Hollywood could see a camera personality in this cadaverous-looking fellow. Selznick used him as a dancer only in *Dancing Lady,* and what the magnifying and defining eye of the camera did for those flying feet—which, on the stage, were more often than not just a rhythmic blur to the spectator—made him as sought after as previously he had been cold-shouldered. He landed at, of all places, RKO, where the Astaire-Rogers dance poems became the studio's box-office mainstay for the remainder of the thirties.

As stated, Selznick had his hands full with the existing Metro stars, but what he did with them served his own long-term purposes as well as L. B. Mayer's immediate ones. *Dinner at Eight* (Jean Harlow, Lionel Barrymore, Wallace Beery, John Barrymore, Marie Dressler) *Dancing Lady* (Joan Crawford, Clark Gable), *Viva Villa* (Wallace Beery), *Night Flight* (Helen Hayes, Robert Montgomery, Clark Gable, John and Lionel Barrymore, Myrna Loy), and *David Copperfield* (young Bartholomew and an all-star cast) were solid money-making hits which established Selznick's reputation where it counted most—with the bankers in New York and even more important, with theater managers throughout the country. The public might still not know David Selznick's name, but their unelected representatives, the exhibitors, knew who was putting money in their pockets and they expressed their knowledge. In those days the leading trade journal *Motion Picture Herald* conducted a monthly poll of exhibitors, who were asked to vote for that producer (not star, not director, *producer*) whose pictures were worth most to them in cold cash and who was thereupon dubbed a Box-office Champion. Selznick won this title so often that a new one had to be created for him, Champion of Champions (Mr. De Mille must have envied him this, for more reasons than one); he kept it until his official retirement from films in 1949.

What his materialistic success meant to him was credit—and credit was the key to independence. For all along he had intended one day to be as much his own man as Samuel Goldwyn, and with Goldwyn's record before him he knew he could achieve genuine independence only if he got the major part of the financial backing for the production of his own films from outside the motion picture industry. To symbolize his stand on this, he arranged to release his films through United Artists, traditionally the stronghold of the independent producer. His M-G-M success had freed him from his bondage to M-G-M, or to any other member of the closed corporation of major producers.

The chief investors in the new Selznick International studio were Selznick's brother Myron, the agent; John Hay Whitney, with whom Selznick had already had business dealings when Whitney decided to back three-color Technicolor productions and release them through RKO; Whitney's sister, Mrs. Joan Payson; Cornelius Vanderbilt Whitney; the financiers Robert Lehman and John D. Hertz; and, interestingly enough, Mrs. Thalberg, Norma Shearer. Even with all this financial muscle behind him Selznick at first moved cautiously into the fresh air of independence. His beginning venture was a modest black-and-white remake of *Little Lord Fauntleroy,* with Freddie Bartholomew, Dolores Costello, and C. Aubrey Smith, budgeted for a very modest, even for those days, $560,000. It grossed a far from modest $1,700,000 and the industry noted with wonder that a picture made on a "B" budget had earned a larger profit than most "A" pictures of the period did. His pictures for the next three years cost considerably more, and even the Box-office Champion was not above taking out box-office insurance in this delicate transition period. His casts consisted of stars as firmly established as the M-G-M luminaries he had just left behind him—Marlene Dietrich and Charles Boyer in *The Garden of Allah;* Ronald Colman, Madeleine Carroll, and Douglas Fairbanks, Jr., in *The Prisoner of Zenda;* Carole Lombard and Fredric March in *Nothing Sacred;* and Lombard and James Stewart in *Made for Each Other.* He even had his fling, à la Thalberg, at refurbishing a fading reputation when he cast Janet Gaynor in the title role of the first *A Star Is Born,* though about that there are perhaps two opinions: when someone congratulated Miss Gaynor on her comeback, she replied, "What do you mean, comeback? I was always on top." These pictures of the late thirties had an average gross of $2,100,000, sensational for the time, but there was something peculiar about these grosses; they never resulted in a dividend for Selznick's backers. "I don't understand the movie business," Mrs. Payson allowed herself to remark. "Everyone assures me that Mr. Selznick's pictures are the best, and that they make the most money, but I've never received a dollar of return on my investment." Selznick was neither lining his pockets nor padding his payrolls; as profits came in, they were all invested in the next Selznick International production. Whether or not he took his backers into his confidence on this subject, he was building toward a grand climax, and he wanted to build on a solid foundation.

As all the world knows, and indeed has never been allowed to forget, that climax was the picture which *Variety* insisted on calling GWTW—the abbreviation takes longer to say than the original title. The oft told tale of how he bought the book for a song before publication still has point, since after that Selznick had only to sit back and watch its readers accumulate into a ready-made audience which eventually included virtually every literate person in the world. *Gone With the Wind* became the granddaddy of all "presold properties," and an unbelievable fluke it will be if such good fortune ever befalls a producer again. By the time he was ready to begin production, and he took plenty of time over this, the question was no longer whether the film would be successful financially; it couldn't help but be, unless he and everyone else connected with it fell down completely. The question now was, would the film satisfy the fiercely proprietary lovers of the book? This issue focused on who would be chosen to play the by this time legendary and sacrosanct characters—not only Scarlett and Rhett but all the way down the line; for years after the release of the film, Selznick continued to receive letters saying that while Laura Hope Crews was a pretty good choice for Aunt Pittypat, Elizabeth Patterson or Nana Bryant would have been even better. First, who would play Scarlett and Rhett? Selznick faced this daunting dilemma with relish, and milked it for all it was worth. Every star in Hollywood was of course crazy to play Scarlett, and one by one the favorite candidates were trotted out into the publicity spotlight—Miriam Hopkins, Bette Davis, Katharine Hepburn, Margaret Sullivan, Under ordinary conditions Norma Shearer might have been expected to cop the part, by virtue of her position as a Selznick backer, but her partner could point to the undoubted fact that she, like the other famous ladies, failed to "fit"—not the Scarlett of the book, but the notions of her which one or another section of the public had formed. All these and other possibilities were discussed soberly in the nation's press, and acrimoniously by its firesides, but Selznick had known from the beginning that to give satisfaction he must find someone entirely new—either an amateur or unknown professional. He rather hoped it would be the latter, but the publicity values of the hunt for Scarlett could not be wasted. With a straight face, he and George Cukor, scheduled to direct the mighty film, interviewed fourteen hundred amateur candidates from such Southern cities as Atlanta and New Orleans, and actually tested twenty-eight of them, at a cost of $1500 a test. Feeling ran high as the portrait of one Southern charmer after another was trotted out in the press for inspection by the national jury, and Selznick, loving every minute of it, was having a high old time. Then his brother Myron stumbled over Vivien Leigh. Miss Leigh, of London, had been seen by but was unremembered by the American public as a bookshop vamp in Robert Taylor's *A Yank at Oxford* and as an ingénue in Alexander Korda's *Fire over England*. She had come to Hollywood in the train of her lover and later husband, Laurence Olivier, who was about to make *Wuthering Heights* for Goldwyn, and they routinely lunched with Olivier's agent, enabling the latter to turn up that afternoon in David Selznick's office and announce dramatically, "I've found your Scarlett." Miss Leigh passed her screen test entirely to Selznick's satisfaction, whereupon he firmly announced that she was *it,* and that the Scarlett O'Hara case was closed. A little baffled, Margaret Mitchell's public retired within itself to await the picture, rather daring the upstart to make good.

No such razz-ma-tazz talent hunt was necessary, or even possible, to find the man or actor who would play Rhett Butler. With rare unanimity the public had decreed that Clark Gable and Clark Gable alone should be, and indeed *was,* Rhett Butler, and that if Selznick disregarded their wishes in this matter he might expect to face their fury and perhaps their boycott. This was the only fly in Selznick's delicious honey of new-found and arrogant independence. He found himself in the same spot which his mentor Samuel Goldwyn had occupied a few years earlier when he called up L. B. Mayer to announce, "Louis, you and I are both in trouble." "What's the matter, Sam?" Mayer had queried. Mr. Goldwyn's reply was, "I want Clark Gable and you've got him."

Mayer did indeed have him, still had him, and no considerations of "loyalty" to his son-in-law Selznick, nor even the fact that Gable himself was determined to play the part, could move the lord of M-G-M. His interests must be protected, not to mention the emollient to Mayer's feelings of annoyance caused when Selznick left the studio flat some years earlier. He sat back and waited until the public clamor for Gable in the role was conclusive, and then named his price. M-G-M would lend Gable, at a figure far above his normal salary, and would advance $1,250,000 toward the eventual $6,000,000 cost of *Gone With the Wind*. In return, Mayer exacted 35 per cent of the profits and demanded that the picture be distributed by Metro-Mayer-Goldwyn, also at an inflated fee. This was a bitter draught, but Selznick had to swallow it. He took the picture away from its logical distributors, United Artists, much to the anger of his associates there, and met all Mayer's other demands. There could be no more stalling.

aroused his enthusiasm, or even struck his fancy, and nothing could deter him from getting what he wanted. For five years after she became a star of the Swedish screen and stage, Ingrid Bergman refused all Hollywood offers, including Selznick's. Finally he sent his wonderful story editor, Katharine Brown, to Sweden to persuade Miss Bergman that Selznick was not your typical Hollywood ogre, that he was "different." Miss Bergman allowed herself to be persuaded. After he had introduced her to the American public in a moderately costly and modestly successful remake of her Swedish film, *Intermezzo*, Selznick loaned her to M-G-M, Columbia, Paramount, and Warner Brothers for, among other films, *Casablanca, For Whom the Bell Tolls*, and *Gaslight*. Because of these successes her salary had risen to $2000 a week—but Selznick, as the owner of her contract, had received a like sum simply for allowing her to appear in them. Out of the pictures she made in her first decade in Hollywood, only three were Selznick productions, but she was nonetheless one of his most profitable assets. He followed a similar policy with Gregory Peck, whom he seized upon immediately after his screen debut for Columbia, before that or any other studio had time to realize that here was the nearest thing to a successor to Gable that the forties were liable to offer. His own discoveries, such as Louis Jourdan and Alida Valli, never realized his maximum hopes for them, but he made a tidy profit out of lending them to others. Symbolic of his methods was the fact that, toward the end of his career, he "rented" practically his entire contract list, en bloc and for a blanket fee, to Warner Brothers—Gregory Peck, Shirley Temple, Joseph Cotten, Louis Jourdan, Betsy Drake, and Rory Calhoun.

Early in 1949, as he was preparing his new film *Portrait of Jennie* for release, Selznick startled everyone out of his wits by announcing his withdrawal from production. Speculation was as rife as it was futile: He was spending too much; he was completely broke; the bankers were tired of his shenanigans. These comments overlooked the inner development of the man. For all his flamboyant ego, he was when the chips were down a realist. Before any of his competitors, he realized that movie audiences were changing rapidly after World War II. What they apparently wanted was no longer the sympathetic sweetness of a Melanie in a heroine, but the vicious selfishness of a Scarlett. In a determined, and deeply considered, effort to respond to the change he sensed, he had in 1946 poured $6,000,000 into the horrendous *Duel in the Sun*. For it, he transformed Jennifer Jones, hitherto chiefly known as the saintly Bernadette, into a snarling tigress who made Scarlett look like a kitten. As for Gregory Peck—King Vidor, director of *Duel in the Sun*, was amazed to learn from Selznick's script that Peck, as Lewt, the "hero," was to blow up a passenger train, for no particular reason except the fun of it, and then ride off into the sunset singing "I've Been Working on the Railroad." Vidor was so perturbed that he invaded Selznick's bathroom while the latter was shaving, and, sitting on the edge of the tub, expostulated that if this episode were included, Lewt would lose any audience identification, and that Peck would suffer from it. Selznick listened in silence, continued to shave, and finally said, "I'm going to make Lewt the goddamnedest son of a bitch ever to appear in a movie." *Duel in the Sun* made a lot of money, after a stupendous publicity campaign which all but oversold it—as *Variety* said, you couldn't walk down Fifth Avenue without somebody clapping a *Duel in the Sun* sticker on your back—but Selznick was aware that audiences did not *love* his new picture as they had loved GWTW. The old combo of sex and violence was no longer in itself enough. He was aware too of the rising quality of foreign films and of their appeal to sectors of the audience which were not responding positively to Hollywood films. Before the National Board of Review, in 1949, Selznick said, "The other day my son called up from military school to say, 'Dad, the boys all want to see *Henry V*, can you get us a print?' I said, 'You mean the masters want you to see it.' 'No,' Danny said. 'The *boys* want to see it.' Well, when the boys want *Henry V*, it's time for me to get out of Hollywood, see the world, and do some heavy thinking."

He hedged his bets, of course. A *Life* article titled "David Selznick Quits" was hastily changed to "David Selznick Takes Time Out," at the request of its subject—just in case. After all, he did have a lot of blocked funds in Europe and might want to use them to experiment with foreign production. He did just that in collaboration with Sir Alexander Korda, Carol Reed, and Vittorio De Sica; his proud boast that he was the first to initiate co-production on a grand scale was true. His box score on the three films he made in Europe was one to two. *The Wild Heart* and *Terminal Station*, futilely retitled for U.S. release *Indiscretions of an American Wife*, were neither Hollywood nor Europe but something less than either. *The Third Man* made a lot of money, chiefly from its theme song—and had the additional advantage of using the services of such remaining Selznick stars as Joseph Cotten and Valli. After these inconclusive ventures, he lingered on the fringe of the spotlight, trying his hand at television with an expensive show for General Electric, and making Delphic pronouncements: he quoted David Sarnoff as saying, "In a competition between mediocrities, the free one will win." Most of his titanic energies in these years he poured into his Golden Laurel Awards, an ideal to which he remained faithful despite its failure to make much of an impression on the public mind, and to exploiting the subsidiary rights of his old films, which he owned— a carrion process which made considerable money. But he knew he was picking his own bones.

His real interest at the last lay in Jennifer Jones. Perhaps he felt that she was Galatea to his Pygmalion; after he had divorced Irene Mayer, and she the late Robert Walker, they married. Miss Jones was past her prime as a youthful favorite by the early fifties, but he kept engineering comebacks for her with other studios. Few of his former competitors could resist free advice from David Selznick, however mad at him they got. *Love Is a Many-Splendored Thing* did seem to restore Miss Jones, but her faltering career still needed outside impetus, and it was undoubtedly for that reason that, with appropriate fanfare, he "returned to production" in 1957 with a prodigious new version of *A Farewell to Arms*, with Jennifer Jones as Catherine. This vast film had everything —wide-screen spectacle, sex, violence, sadism, and Rock Hudson, whom Selznick wrested from Universal to bolster the box office. Everything but Hemingway's spirit, said its detractors, who were many; the film had a very bad press. It seemed to be making money anyhow when Selznick for once succumbed to panic; midway in its first runs, he sold all his rights in it to his distributors, 20th Century-Fox, thus protecting his investment at the same time that he furthered the interests of his wife. It is significant of his waning interest in film-making per se that, having "set up" a production of *Tender Is the Night*, and having made sure that the now rapidly paling Jennifer would be its star, he sold the whole package to Fox before a camera had turned. He even tried to fit his wife into the new film world of the 1960s, with its rapidly altering personality values. Once he phoned the author from Coast to inquire whether I knew Luis Buñuel. When I said I did, he explained that he had been talking to Henry Miller, *Henry Miller,* who had advised him that Buñuel and Buñuel alone could make Jennifer Jones into a viable star of today, Jeanne Moreau-model. While I was recovering from this intelligence, Selznick added that he had decided that Miller was right and would I be the go-between?

"Since when have you needed a go-between, David?"

"Dick, I don't want him to think that I'm making him an offer—that I want to bring him to Hollywood to direct a Buñuel-Selznick production backed by me. I want Jennifer to work for him as an actress, to learn from him and absorb his viewpoint, and to get into the swim of international production. But I don't want him to think that I'm ready to put money into his pictures—and I don't want to say that in so many words. You'll know how to put it to him."

There was nothing to do but comply, but I was less than successful in clarifying these muddy waters. Buñuel replied that he would be much interested in using Miss Jones as an actress in one of his pictures—when an appropriate part for her arose—but that he would not under any circumstances come to Hollywood to direct for Selznick, nor accept any financial backing from him. Selznick in turn expressed his delight that Buñuel was interested in Jennifer—but wished it *distinctly* understood that he, Selznick, was not offering to invest a single penny in Buñuel's pictures, wherever made. The determined comedy of errors played itself out to no purpose, except Buñuel's sardonic amusement. But it showed conclusively how the balance of power had shifted away from the Hollywood establishment and toward the established rebellion against Hollywood.

Until his death in 1965, Selznick continued to fool himself and much of the world into thinking that he was still, in spite of everything, Mr. Movies. But his real feelings he had expressed to his old friend Ben Hecht as they walked. Sunset Boulevard one Hollywood dawn. "The game's over," he said to Hecht. "It was all the fun in the world while it lasted, but it's up. The audience isn't so much gone as changed, the old pattern's worn out and people are no longer interested in it, there are too many cheap substitutes. The others here won't admit it, of course. They go on making pictures and losing money and renting their studio space and making international deals, but the life's gone out of the whole thing. And I'm not interested in lifelessness, or in repeating what I've done. From now on, I'll stand and watch—unless I can think of something new."

He never did think of anything else which met his standards. But, though the game might be up, while it was going he had won it hands down. If he ever doubted his claim on the heights, he had tangible confirmation of it in an offer which his ego ideal, Samuel Goldwyn, once made him. Through intermediaries, Goldwyn said, "Look, we're the two leading independent producers in the world, everybody knows it, why shouldn't we share studio space and equipment? We'd save a lot of money and reinforce each other's prestige."

After considerable self-examination, Selznick declined. Shortly afterward he looked up from his desk to find Goldwyn in his doorway.

"You're afraid of me, aren't you, David?" said Goldwyn, grinning.

"I guess I am."

"You don't need to be, for goodness' sake. Why, together we'd be unbeatable. And as for any conflict, if my people ever claim a boom or a set that you need, don't give it a second thought. Just come straight to me and I will personally convince you that my needs take priority over yours."

"That's what I'm afraid of," said Selznick.

THE ONE-MAN BAND
ZANUCK

The first star that Darryl Zanuck made was Rin-Tin-Tin. It was always a question whether he made Rin-Tin-Tin or Rin-Tin-Tin made him, but on balance Zanuck probably deserves the credit. There had been dog stars before and there were dog stars after Rin-Tin-Tin, but none whom both city and country audiences took to heart so wholeheartedly. He was known as "the mortgage-lifter," both to theater men and to his and Zanuck's producers, and while nothing really lifted the Warner mortgage until sound enabled them to burn it, the gifted dog did keep them going until the talkies arrived. The Warners well knew this, and they showed their wisdom by elevating Zanuck, the obscure scriptwriter who had promoted the Rin-Tin-Tin formula, to a position second only to their own.

The Darryl Zanuck of the dog days was not only obscure but something of a figure of fun. Even today, those among movie audiences who don't know the Hollywood score (or care about it) smile faintly at his name. They equate him with the Zukors, Schencks, Laemmles, and other possessors of comic and outlandish names whom they automatically ridicule and assume he is cut from the same cloth. But Darryl Zanuck is not Jewish, is not a relative of any of the older lords of the movies, and did not spend his childhood in the sweatshops of New York. Born of a Swiss father and English mother in Wahoo, Nebraska, he enlisted in the U.S. Cavalry while still underage and spent his late teens on the Mexican border and, later, in the AEF.

A late example of the rootless pioneer spirit, he knocked around for a few years after World War I until, in the Jack London tradition, he decided he wanted to be a writer. The first story he sold, "Mad Desire," appeared in *Physical Culture* magazine. It was perhaps characteristic of his box-office instinct, but not of the kind of story material he later came to prefer for his films. It did lead him to the fringes of the movies—to the gold rush which had succeeded the Klondike and the days of '49.

In the early twenties, there existed in wicked Hollywood a girl's club remarkably analogous to the Co-Optimists or the Epworth League, which were then, as they are still, characteristic of Olathe, Kansas, Brattleboro, Vermont, or Lubbock, Texas. Its members consisted of female movie aspirants who had been gently reared, and whose home ties forbade them to indulge in the flamboyant dolce vita which drew most of their contemporaries to the movie capital; one of them, Julawne Johnston, was fined by her fellow members for drinking a cocktail in public with a man. It was to these decorous girls, and not to the more prevalent floozies, that young Zanuck gravitated.

He dated all of the club members at least once—not because he was playing the field, but because once was about all any of them could stomach. When his future wife confessed that she was engaged to him, the other girls greeted the announcement with incredulous merriment. "I know, I know," said Virginia Fox. "But Darryl's got a job now, as a scriptwriter for Warners. And he's promised to get his teeth fixed." She referred to two prominent front teeth which gave him something of the appearance of an early Bugs Bunny, and which undoubtedly account for the fact that he was almost never photographed smiling. Even after his rise to fame and power, the jokes about him continued, and they were more spontaneous, less manufactured than the jokes about Samuel Goldwyn's contests with the English language. He is said to have instructed one of his yes men, "Don't say yes until I've finished talking." The origin of his story ideas was sometimes so nebulous that a wag suggested that his latest picture be credited as: "Based on a remark by Gregory Ratoff." When he formed the habit of holding press conferences on the lawn in front of his studio office, an associate lamented, "Zanuck on the grass, alas."

The flower of these yaks, and probably the only one directed at Zanuck in person, came of differences of opinion between him and Jean Renoir over the treatment of the latter's *Swamp Water,* differences which led to a parting of the ways. "Well, goodbye, Mr. Zanuck," said Renoir. "And let me tell you, it certainly has been a pleasure working at 16th Century-Fox."

Yet it was this same funny-looking, slightly archaic, dictatorial man who made or caused to be made *The Public Enemy, The Oxbow Incident, I Am a Fugitive from a Chain Gang, The Prisoner of Shark Island, Les Miserables, How Green Was My Valley, The Grapes of Wrath, Wilson, Gentlemen's Agreement, Pinky, No Way Out,* and *The Snake Pit,* to name only the most memorable. At least one of these films remains among the screen's enduring masterpieces; all were daring in their day, and their daring was rewarded by popular interest; they exerted profound influence throughout the world on both audiences and film production; and several of them jolted Hollywood out of that rut of comfortable mediocrity in which it has a tendency to sink. It might be inferred from the nature of the films listed that Darryl Zanuck is a social reformer, fired with crusading zeal. That would on the whole be an error. Rather, his pursuit of audience interest has led him to a determined search for what is topical, what is on the tip of everybody's tongue, what is the focus of the public eye. He has the courage and the instinct to anticipate fashion, and by anticipating it, inaugurate it. It is as if, after being so long an outsider, he wanted desperately, once "in," to be more completely "in" than anybody else—up on the latest. It is likely that he was as happy to be the first to satirize TV *(My Blue Heaven)* as he was to rub our noses in *The Grapes of Wrath.* He has made a remarkable career of it, profitable to himself and, say what you will, profitable to the common weal.

This feeling about screen material has deeply dyed his approach to star-making. When in 1930 he was appointed head of production at Warner Brothers, he announced that the studio's films from then on would be based as far as possible on spot news. The stars he wanted were players who were sufficiently in tune with everyday American life to fit this policy or, if they weren't, who could accommodate themselves to it. It happened that just before his take-over of production, Warners had bought the First

(Left) Darryl F. Zanuck, of Wahoo, Nebraska, at the time he ran away from home to enlist in the U.S. Cavalry. (Top) A bumper crop of Oscars: Zanuck with Edmund Gwenn, Loretta Young, Ronald Colman, and Celeste Holm at the 1949 Academy jollification. (Above) Zanuck with his daughter Darrilyn and Shirley Temple. (Right) Zanuck and W. C. Fields.

Simone Simon in *Love and Hisses*.

Al Jolson (at wheel) and Zanuck.

Charles Chaplin, Zanuck, Samuel Goldwyn, Mary Pickford, Joseph Schenck and Douglas Fairbanks Sr.

Tyrone Power and Sonja Henie in *Thin Ice*.   Zanuck with his most improbable star, Carmen Miranda.

National company, acquiring along with its assets some quasi-liabilities, in the form of stars whose contracts had some years to run before they could be dispensed with. So it came about that the then highly aesthetic Douglas Fairbanks, Jr., found himself playing hard-boiled reporters and prizefighters, while the onetime matinee idol Richard Barthelmess, by then on the heavy side, was starred in dire sociological dramas like *The Cabin in the Cotton* (sharecropping), *Heroes for Sale* (unemployment), and *Massacre* (lo, the poor Indian). This turned out lucky; the serious-minded Barthelmess gave an excellent account of himself in these films, and thereby prolonged his career. The stars Zanuck himself "made" at Warners were right on the nose. Gangsters and bootleggers were the hot news of 1930-31, and that meant Edward G. Robinson and Jimmy Cagney, whose lasting fame is to this day firmly based on the impression they made in *Little Caesar* and *The Public Enemy*. When Robinson plays a straight or sympathetic part, it is as if he has reformed. As for the women, even Ruth Chatterton was fitted into the hard-boiled mold in *Female* and *Frisco Jenny*. Zanuck unaccountably overlooked the gutsy potential of Bette Davis; throughout his reign at Warners he cast her as vapid ingénues, and it took, of all studios, RKO to reveal via *Of Human Bondage* where her real talents lay. But Warren William, not what could ordinarily be considered a type for leading roles, lasted a long time because he fitted so well into the Zanuck world of crooked mouthpieces, phony agents, and backstabbing columnists. Zanuck also peopled that world with character players who were as important as the stars in giving it the bite of recognizable reality—Ruth Donnelly, Marjorie Rambeau, Warren Hymer, Guy Kibbee, Frank McHugh, Allen Jenkins, Aline MacMahon. So successful with world audiences was this sharply lit, acidly spoken rendering of the American scene, that Warner Brothers preserved it intact for many years after Zanuck had left their midst to found with Joseph M. Schenck a new company, 20th Century. I once took a visiting French film fan to a roadhouse near Rochester, N.Y. The Frenchman carefully inspected the shinning chromium and black leather, the sporting types at the bar, and pronounced, "Pure Warner Brothers!"

At the new 20th Century Company, which released through United Artists, Zanuck found himself an "independent," personally producing two or three films a year instead of generally supervising the production of fifty or sixty. He immediately changed his style. True, *The Bowery,* with Wallace Beery, George Raft, and Jackie Cooper, did echo the Warner past, and *Les Miserables,* besides giving Charles Laughton and Fredric March their first opportunity for substantial film acting, was a production of weight and merit. But in the two years of 20th Century's independence, Zanuck developed no new stars of his own; instead he borrowed the already mighty to guarantee the success of his few, glittery, and expensive productions. Constance Bennett in *Moulin Rouge* and *The Affairs of Cellini,* Maurice Chevalier and Merle Oberon (the slant-eyed version) in *Folies Bergere de Páris* might have been made at M-G-M, though their style was a bit more virile, less schmaltzy, than Thalberg's. But it is significant of his true interests that the one star he brought with him from Warners was George Arliss. This surprised many, since Arliss's theatrical simulacra of Disraeli, Alexander, Hamilton, Voltaire, and Richelieu were chiefly applauded by the old ladies who attended matinees, an audience moiety to whom Zanuck had hitherto paid little mind. But Arliss stood for History and Biography, which stood second only to the Current Scene in Zanuck's estimation—even if, as someone said, he saw history as a collection of front-page stories. There are worse ways of presenting history to a mass audience, and duller ones. After he moved to Fox, historical and biographical films became a dominant motif in his variegated program. And if as a result the public came to think that Don Ameche invented the telephone, if *Suez, Lloyds of London,* and *In Old Chicago* did not tell all there was to tell about canal-building, insurance, and the destruction and rebirth of a Midwestern metropolis, they engaged the imaginations of the young with these topics more vividly than the schools had ever been able to do, as the survivors of the thirties and forties will testify. The Zanuck historical biographies and biographical histories represented a certain stage in the growing-up of the screen—and perhaps of the U.S.A. And *Young Mr. Lincoln* was a masterpiece, a conduit to the primitive America of a hundred years ago as it really looked, sounded, and, almost, smelled.

In 1935, the ailing Fox Film Corporation besought Zanuck and Schenck to merge their flourishing small company with the debt-ridden Fox behemoth, and 20th Century-Fox was born. Zanuck was now supreme overlord of a huge studio, not a deputy for Jack and Harry Warner; the genial Schenck was happy to leave all production decisions to him and preside from on high as chairman of the board of directors. Before indulging his own predilections, Zanuck began by conscientiously putting his corporate house in order. The first item of business was what to do with the stars he had inherited from Fox. Janet Gaynor, queen of the lot for the preceding decade, he thought was slipping; or not earning enough to justify her high salary; or too imperious in exercising her contractual right to a voice in her stories and directors. At any rate he determined to be rid of her, and began a sniping campaign. He loaned her to M-G-M, in exchange for the sizzling-hot Robert Taylor, for what turned out to be a minor film, *Small Town Girl.* He cast her in an all-star production, *Ladies in Love,* in which she had to share honors equally with Loretta Young, Constance Bennett, and Simone Simon. Finally, bluntly, he told her that she had lost her draw and that he was demoting her to featured roles. Miss Gaynor, imperious as ever, was not having any of that. She canceled her contract, moved over to Selznick long enough to prove that her draw was as strong as ever in *A Star Is Born*—and then disappeared from films. Perhaps Zanuck had divined before she did that she had really lost interest in stardom. His divination was less accurate in the case of Shirley Temple, who had succeeded Janet Gaynor as the studio's gold mine. One of the nicest things about Shirley was that her pictures, besides being extremely profitable, were also comparatively cheap to make. He reasoned as other producers have done that if he spent more on them their earnings would increase commensurately, apparently overlooking the fact that Shirley already had all the fans she could possibly get, meaning virtually the entire movie audience. Unfortunately, such super-Shirley's as *Wee Willie Winkie, Susannah of the Mounties,* and *The Blue Bird* coincided with the waning of little Miss Temple's baby cuteness, and the consequent loss of a good deal of that audience. Shirley, from being the studio's chief asset, became under Zanuck its white elephant. But the business of unloading exhausted stars, while hanging onto those who still have mileage in them, is a tightrope trick, and Zanuck's record was on the whole a creditable one, here as earlier at Warners-First National. After examining Warner Baxter's expensive but watertight contract, he quietly allowed it to run its course without tangling with the irascible star; he hung onto Alice Faye, whom his predecessors had been prepared to let go; and he recaptured Henry Fonda, whom Fox had allowed to slip away to Walter Wanger, by baiting his trap with John Ford. The actor has said, "I do what John Ford tells me to do," and since Zanuck consistently offered the director the subjects he liked, he got both Ford and Fonda. The long association of this threesome was rewarding to them and most agreeable to the public.

And then he set out to develop his own stars—to develop them in profusion, almost in bulk. If M-G-M boasted More Stars Here Than Up There, Zanuck could claim with better justice that his were as the sands of the sea. Can any of them claim a place among the screen's immortals? Hardly. The one nearest to that sublime category is undoubtedly Betty Grable, and for her fame and image Zanuck can take credit. Miss Grable had adorned numerous minor Paramount and RKO films before the master of 20th Century-Fox turned her into the most durable pin-up girl of them all. Zanuck was not out to create screen immortals. Stars so designated are apt to develop strong wills of their own, and this particular emperor of ice cream meant to exercise his sway unopposed. The sheer number of stars he made suggests that Zanuck did not really think in terms of stars at all, but of the kinds of pictures he must make now that he was responsible for the profitable operation of a mass-production studio. Musicals were a staple: In them, he offered Faye and Grable, brought in Don Ameche from radio and Dan Dailey from Broadway musicals, and gave the musical pattern a fillip of novelty through the skating star Sonja Henie and the professional spitfire, Latin-American division, Carmen Miranda. The demand was constant for girls so beautiful that it didn't much matter what else they had to offer: Zanuck filled the bill bountifully with Gene Tierney, Linda Darnell, Carole Landis, Maureen O'Hara, Constance Smith, Jeanne Crain, Lynn Bari, Annabella. Comedy was needed to leaven the serious and rather dangerous pictures in which he delighted, *How Green Was My Valley* and *The Grapes of Wrath*. So he seized upon the Ritz Brothers, and deflected Clifton Webb from the smooth villainies of *Laura* and *The Dark Corner* into Mr. Belvedere, a folk character who may well survive when everything else the producer and the star have done is dust.

And, like every star-maker of the first rank, he was quick to take advantage of accident. When Richard Widmark made an unexpected hit as the laughing sadist of *Kiss of Death,* Zanuck realized that Widmark could not profitably go on laughing his way through psychotic, violence indefinitely, and, in a determined piece of reverse casting, made him the hero of military, naval, and cowboy adventures in milieux which were a far cry from the urban slums, prisons, and brothels appropriate to the original version of his screen personality. Similarly, when Paul Douglas registered positively in his first appearance, it would have been the decision of most casting directors, because of his age, to use him henceforward in character roles as a secondary asset to a picture— which would usually have meant using him to bolster a succession of weak pictures which could only lead him downward. Zanuck decided that this gruff fraud, or fraudulent gruff, had enough links with everybody's everyday experience to make him star material, or at least co-star material, and his writers and directors, unexpectedly given an opportunity to depart from the beaten track of "sympathetic" star characters, created for Douglas one who was maybe a heel, maybe a great guy, you couldn't decide which, but you liked him anyway. That such a character could please a public still thought of as passively demanding black-and-white stereotypes destroyed a good many Hollywood shibboleths.

Zanuck duly cast the standard specialized categories, such as comedies and musicals, but since his primary interest was in pictures, rather than players as such, he really liked best those rare players who could fit in anywhere. The most versatile actor he ever found came to him in unexpected guise. "Tyrone Power, Jr.," as he was originally known, was to start with just a slender young matinee idol, Zanucks' "answer" to M-G-M's beautiful Robert Taylor, and as such he was entirely satisfactory to his fans—that 1930s generation of teen-agers between flappers and bobby-soxers for whom no name was ever coined. He might have gone on successfully on that level; the young Power was easy going, worldly, and seemingly devoid of artistic ambition. But behind Tyrone Power, Jr., was Tyrone Power, Sr., a long theatrical tradition, and a set of reflexes which automatically responded to any acting problem put before him. His *Jesse James* lives in the memory of the perceptive as a master performance; he made human truth out of thin and preposterous legend. *Nightmare Alley,* produced at his own insistence, enabled Power to introduce his perhaps unwilling admirers to a set of pathological horrors which later would be much in fashion. But he was equally at home in costume romance, adventure films, or anything else Mr. Zanuck needed him for. Routine repetition of such roles eventually wore out the interest of admirers of his acting, but his twenty-one-year stardom lasted until his early death.

Like all his peers, Zanuck as star-maker perpetrated some beauts. His efforts to induce the public to accept the writer Irvin S. Cobb as a substitute for their cherished favorite Will Rogers after the latter's death (largely, one gathers, because Cobb was even uglier than Will) resulting in nothing, as did his attempt to make Lawrence Tibbett a movie favorite, an enterprise in which Thalberg had failed some years before. The most lamentable of his failures, or at least the most lamented among a certain small section of the audience, was Simone Simon. Those U.S. filmgoers who saw her in the 1933 French film *Lac aux Dames* had their breath taken away. Her character was what would today be called a nymphet, but she seemed then to offer more than provocative puberty; hers was the spirit of questing, idealistic youth, reaching out for experience but governed in its reaction to experience by a strict code of its own, put together out of the intuitions of childhood. Whether this illusion was created by the direction of Marc Allegret, or by Vicki Baum in her novel, cannot now be decided, but it was the illusion that Zanuck bought and imported to these shores. Where, alas, it did not survive. "Sea-moan Sea-moan," as extensive advertising bade us call her, despite her casting in Janet Gaynor's role in the remake of *Seventh Heaven,* emerged on 20th Century-Fox's screens as an insolent, baby-faced tart whose babyishness was rapidly being obliterated by her tartish bag of tricks. It was shattering to those who had invested a good deal of their dream capital in the original illusion. That Zanuck cannot be blamed entirely—he had, after all, recognized her qualities—was amply demonstrated by her subsequent appearances in RKO films and in her native France. As Gloria Swanson once said, "These things happen in the profession."

The decline of the box office in the late 1940s and early 1950s found Zanuck with no better panaceas than those offered by other leaders of the industry; all revived the ancient chestnut, "There's nothing wrong with this business that good pictures won't cure." Disagreement over what constituted a good picture was complete. But as an inveterate wooer of the zeitgeist, Zanuck adjusted more easily to change than the older moguls. So as early as 1948 he shocked the industry by saying in public what everybody had been thinking in private, that the only way the big studios could survive their financial crisis was to rent their sound stages and their know-how to television. Then, the arrival of the big screen was just the bandwagon he needed to jump on. The original wide-screen processes were introduced primarily to give an effect of three dimensions, but they were a long way from perfect, and when his associate, Spyros Skouras, came forth with a workable compromise in CinemaScope, Zanuck irascibly announced: "Depth, we don't need depth! What we need is just one thing, a screen as big as the TV screen is small." That meant spectacle, hardly a Zanuck speciality in the past, and after the spectacular gross of the first CinemaScope film, *The Robe,* it meant the ancient world in all its California splendor. In almost forgotten orgies of violence and gaudiness —*Demetrius and the Gladiators, Prince Valiant, The Egyptian*—players seemed less important than ever to Zanuck, especially since the system of building them to stardom through long-term contracts was being generally abandoned. The superfilms could be used as tryout grounds on a one-picture basis for promising newcomers like Jean Simmons and Robert Wagner, while fading Fox players like Victor Mature and Gene Tierney, still bound to the studio by obsolete contracts, could be used to fill out background roles. Those who are under the impression that Richard Burton as a screen star sprang full-panoplied from *Cleopatra* should look back. All through the fifties he was a figure in a Zanuckian tapestry of antiquity, playing centurions, Christian martyrs, and galley slaves to no discernible public acclaim. Young and handsome then, he was just another good-looking fellow with flawless English speech, and even his earnest solo-starring performance as Edwin Booth in *Prince of Players* got him little notice. Neither Zanuck nor the public discovered him; he had to wait until Elizabeth Taylor did.

In his preoccupation with bigness, Zanuck almost overlooked the sensation of the fifties—MM herself. He had her under contract but let her go, only to call her back at several times her original salary when the public and indeed all Hollywood told him how purblind he had been. He was not pleased about that. But back she came and up she went, and it was undoubtedly her prairie-fire popularity that produced box-office bonanza in Fox's first clumsy experiments with big-screen musicals, *Gentlemen Prefer Blondes* and *How to Marry a Millionaire.* Through the ensuing din of publicity could be faintly heard the sound of hostile exchanges between producer and star. Zanuck could not forget that *he* had not discovered her, and Miss Monroe could not forgive him that he was the last to appreciate her. Perhaps his fundamental mistake was to try to bring her along slowly in the old manner in unimportant films like *Niagara* and *River of No Return,* a procedure which bucked the tide of the times. Soon she decamped for New York and, evidently deciding that an executive-vice-president-in-charge-of-production was less important than a president of a film company, announced that from then on she would head her own company for which alone she would make films, and to hell with 20th Century-Fox. The resulting stalemate lasted more than a year, a long time in the career of a screen actress. It might have lasted even longer had not Buddy Adler, Zanuck's successor, persuaded Marilyn that the two of them could get along well enough to make the remaining pictures on her old contract while she simultaneously pursued her own destiny as an independent producer.

Zanuck's successor! Could such things be? Had Fox's stock dipped that low on Wall Street? The rumors were many, the puzzlement genuine. Certainly Zanuck had not been summarily fired from his post, as Dore Schary of M-G-M was to be before the end of the same year, 1956. Instead, Spyros Skouras diplomatically announced that Zanuck was taking a "four months' leave of absence" from the executive producership, adding rather paradoxically that during the four months the two would work out a deal by which Zanuck would make his own productions for Fox release. The decision was Zanuck's. He made no secret of his annoyance that mere actors like Kirk Douglas and Frank Sinatra were giving themselves the airs of producers, and Miss Monroe's own declaration of independence doubtless added fuel to the flames. The clincher in his decision was the fact that as his own producer he could keep most of his profits, without the crippling inroads of income tax. As *Time* put it, "Fox's loss is capital gains."

He was sort of on the spot. He had ruled so long, as studio head, then independent, then studio head again, omnipotent, arrogant, in his own estimation always just ahead of events. How would he fare in the not particularly brave new world of mid-century one-shot film-making? The spotlight was on him and the knife was out. The actual record of his six independent productions between 1956 and 1962 is curiously inconclusive—a standoff—in which respect it was typical of the times and of the record of other independents. The interracial *Island in the Sun* sounded in advance like one of the old hard-hitting Zanuck social films, in the particular tradition of *Pinky* and *No Way Out;* it sounded dangerous, and Southern exhibitors were indignant. The picture itself turned out to be a fruity sex mishmash which even Harry Belafonte panned—and which made an immense amount of money for Zanuck and for Fox. *The Sun Also Rises* and *The Roots of Heaven*—the latter was more fun to make than to see—were big, conventional, all-star, old-star productions, barely profitable. *The Crack in the Mirror* and *The Big Gamble* were at least in the current vogue of avant-garde incomprehensibility in that no one could figure out what they were all about, but they were both expensive and unprofitable. It seemed that the old veteran's attempt to get in step with the present, to achieve a position of leadership in independent productions, was instead making him seem rather ridiculous. Then he bought *The Longest Day,* wrote much of the screenplay himself, and launched a vast, De Mille-like production which someone called "the most expensive military operation in history." To most industry observers this seemed a step backward, an attempt to recoup prestige by reverting to the historic-topical pattern which had been his stand-by in the distant thirties. The critics said *The Longest Day* was not the distinguished film it should have been, and that its huge array of male stars might just as well have been unknowns, they were seen so briefly and often in such heavy disguise. In the initial reception of this passionately made picture there was a tinge of the negative, as there was to everything Zanuck did in these lonesome latter years, including his star-making—though there perhaps the old Adam was to blame. Accused of wasting fortunes in the fruitless attempt to make stars of Juliette Greco and Bella Darvi, he frankly admitted it. "When you're stuck on a girl, you can do a lot of stupid things. Believe me, it's the last time I'm doing it." Even without the sex factor, finding stars in the strange sixties presented problems he had never encountered before. Ridiculed for casting singers Tommy Sands, Paul Anka, and Fabian as World War II GIs in *The*

Longest Day, he asked, "Do you know any other young guys?" It is a good question.

A standoff his independent adventure seemed. What might have come next will never be known because of what might be called Zanuck's ascension into heaven. The financial debacle which almost swamped 20th Century-Fox in the wake of the production debacle of *Cleopatra* was forcing Spyros Skouras out of the presidency of the company which he had held so long. When Skouras proposed Zanuck as his successor, the board of directors rebelled: Here was the old guard trying to perpetuate itself. At this juncture the book-keepers reported that *The Longest Day* had in its first year of release grossed $17,000,000, more than enough to save the day. That gross did more than save Fox's immediate bacon. In choosing to dramatize an event of emotional meaning to every American over thirty, Zanuck had again touched a national nerve in his once accustomed manner—and demonstrated that, in spite of fashion, the largest audience of all is still the old, un-avant-garde, fuddy-duddy audience—a fact underscored two years later by the success of *The Sound of Music*. After some carnage, Zanuck was elected president of 20th Century-Fox and has remained triumphantly in the saddle ever since. The domestic gross alone of *The Longest Day* is at this writing $17,600,000, with plenty more to come, and the general operation of the company under Zanuck's helmsmanship has made it the envy of the industry.

But Darryl Zanuck, president, is no longer Darryl Zanuck, picture-maker. He is too busy with finances and housekeeping to make the production decisions which once were his twenty-four hours a day. When he made his son Richard Zanuck executive producer of the studio, there was much outcry against such naked nepotism. But the employees of 20th Century-Fox have reason today to be glad of the Zanuck paternal pride and confidence. One voice and one voice only can be heard above the fiscal din of his days. "I don't care how important it is, Mr. Zanuck is too busy to talk. Who's calling?" "His son." *That* gets through.

What were they after, these makers of stars? Power and money is an easy answer. It is not enough. When Adolph Zukor offered Lewis Selznick that million dollars to go to China and stay there, he did not accept. Had he done so, someone said at the time, he would have been Emperor of China within five years. But he preferred to stay where he was and make Zukor miserable. He enjoyed the cut and thrust and parry too much to abandon it, even if he had to cry *touché* at the end. There is a family resemblance in the methods of these men. All of them found stars, made stars, brought back stars, borrowed and loaned stars, and abandoned stars to oblivion. The consistent factor in their several policies is that they *used* stars as counters in a complicated game they played with each other. Griffith and De Mille aside, they recognized a common bond, the brotherhood of frustrated creators. They did not like it when Sidney Howard compared a producer to the Australian kiwi bird, which has wings but can't fly. They were all of them mortally affronted when Irving Thalberg said to Gregory La Cava, "I don't like the way you handled that scene," and the director replied, "Okay, you direct it." Mr. La Cava had to become a producer as well as a director after hurling that defy, and even so his jobs were few. The star-makers had to maintain a tough businessman front because they were vulnerable. They had something to hide. Stars were their surrogates in stirring the emotion they were powerless to evoke. None but De Mille put it into words, but they were one and all would-be Champion Drivers.

SELECTED
SHORT
SUBJECTS III

William Gould as Marshall Kragg and Buster Crabbe as Buck Rogers.

Errol Flynn in *The Prince and the Pauper*.

Robert Preston and Dorothy Lamour in *Typhoon*.

Elissa Landi in *The White Dragon*.

3 THE GREATEST STARS OF ALL TIME

The greatest stars of all time. Who has the temerity to choose them?

We have said earlier that the making of a star takes place in the depths of the collective unconscious, and this is still the most important factor in the process and the least ponderable. Yet there are certain objective facts which bear importantly on the process, and if they cannot be exactly weighed and measured, they can at least be described. The first of these might at casual glance seem to be controlling. If a player continues to please the public year in and year out, through every conceivable change of fashion, surely he has earned his place among the immortals? If that and that alone were the case, Mary Astor would have to be handed the palm as the screen idol supreme. Except for Chaplin, who is many things besides a star, Miss Astor has been with us longer than anyone. She began in 1921 as a sweet ingénue, rose to leading woman, then star, was demoted to leading womanship, then to second leads, and finally to the character parts she plays so superbly today. But the period of her actual stardom was more official than real, and had a forced quality to it. She never had a cult and never created a legend, even when the publication of her diary during divorce proceedings revealed a different and perhaps more interesting side to her character than the screen had shown. We all love Miss Astor, and the sight of her name in the screen credits always leads to the pleasurable anticipation that the picture we are about to see will be enjoyable at least in part, however lousy the rest of it. But somehow she never impaled our hearts on a thorn.

Screen durability is as likely to depend on factors such as general utility, influence where influence counts, or capital power (the money to produce one's own pictures) as it does on the ability to continue to roll up big grosses. The following chart of the length of certain prominent screen careers may surprise those who think they know who's who and what's what and why. It is based on the continuous year-in year-out activity of certain stars and near-stars and it does not include erratic "comebacks" such as Gloria Swanson makes every eight or nine years.

Charles Chaplin	56 years	1913-69
Mary Astor	48 years	1921-69
Joan Crawford	44 years	1925-69
Edward G. Robinson	40 years	1929-69
Marlene Dietrich	39 years	1930-69
John Wayne	39 years	1930-69
Bette Davis	38 years	1931-69
Cary Grant	36 years	1933-69
Ronald Colman	33 years	1920-53
Clark Gable	30 years	1930-60
Gary Cooper	35 years	1925-60
Bob Hope	32 years	1937-69
William Powell	29 years	1929-58
Bing Crosby	28 years	1932-60
Mary Pickford	24 years	1909-33
Elizabeth Taylor	25 years	1944-69
Irene Dunne	21 years	1930-51
Gloria Swanson	20 years	1914-34

Harold Lloyd	20 years	1914-34
Norma Shearer	20 years	1922-42
Norma Talmadge	19 years	1911-30
Douglas Fairbanks	19 years	1915-34
Greta Garbo	18 years	1925-41
Marlon Brando	19 years	1950-69
Will Rogers	16 years	1919-35
W. S. Hart	14 years	1912-26
Carole Lombard	14 years	1927-41
Clara Bow	12 years	1922-34
Mae West	9 years	1932-41
Rudolph Valentino	7 years	1919-26
Marilyn Monroe	8 years	1950-58
Jean Harlow	6 years	1930-36
Marie Dressler	4 years	1930-34

If screen longevity can at least to an extent be measured, intensity of fan worship cannot. Grosses at the box office do not tell the whole tale, neither does publicity lineage. Moreover, fame of a sort may linger long after fans begin to tire of an idol. Death or illness may intervene, as they have more than once, before it is possible to tell for sure whether a new favorite who seems to have everything has also the power to hold the public through the years. No one will ever know whether Mae West, who for two years certainly was the focus of the public eye, might have lasted in public favor had not censorship, the Legion of Decency, and Will H. Hays intervened to tone down her line of goods. They were indeed hilarious, but monotonous also, as her previous career in vaudeville and on the stage had proved.

But Mae leaves a legend behind her, as did others whose money-making power dwindled, and this we think the third essential element in star quality. This myth-making power, the power to become a permanent figure or symbol in the national consciousness, is essential to screen immortality, and even death cannot erase it, as Valentino proved, and even more so, James Dean, whose legend is a posthumous phenomenon created out of the mood of a generation rather than out of the three pictures he made and the reality of the young man who made them.

Longevity on the screen, intensity of fan feeling—the feeling of worship and love—and the power to create a lasting legend are, we believe, the three pillars on which screen greatness is founded. Any star who is lucky enough to possess two of them will surely find his place among the gods and demigods. As for the few—count them on less than the fingers of one hand—who possess all three, they must be numbered among the bounties of nature, like the sun and the stars.

MARY PICKFORD

In 1914 there appeared on the marquee of a small movie theater in San Francisco the advertisement: *Tess of the Storm Country,* with Mary Pickford, "America's Sweetheart." This matchless, and priceless, sobriquet was not the product of any conference of high-salaried directors of advertising and publicity, but of a smalltime exhibitor, "Pop" Grauman, father of the more famous Sid. Some thirty years later, a Hollywood producer, driven by the desperations of show business, brazenly asked Miss Pickford if she would officially give up her title so that it might be bestowed upon a young starlet whom he was promoting. She was long retired from the screen, he pointed out; she didn't need it any more to sell her pictures; with everything else she had to crown her life, she would hardly miss it.

With the mixture of candor and shrewdness which has always characterized her, Miss Pickford replied, "It isn't mine to give." What Pop Grauman invented on the spur of the moment expressed exactly what millions obscurely felt. Mary Pickford had only just become a star in 1914, but already the entire movie audience had taken her to their hearts. They loved her. They loved, it is true, the movies themselves and all the folk connected with them in those days with a love unknown in these, but their love for Mary was a special thing apart; she was in literal fact their sweetheart. In all the words that have been spent upon her in the years since then nothing else has seemed so true and right, though her scholarly fan James Card, of George Eastman House, came close to it when he exclaimed, in an unscholarly but inspired moment, "There was something heavenly about Mary Pickford!"

The pretty blond girl who inspired these all but nameless emotions had led a hard life by the time she became the national sweetheart. Like her lifelong friend Lillian Gish, she came from one of those genteel middle-class families who lost their breadwinner early in life and found that they had nothing to offer a hard world but the not particularly negotiable ability to sit on a cushion and sew a fine seam. The Smith family of Toronto, consisting of the widowed Mrs. Charlotte Smith and her children Gladys, Lottie, and Jack, were in just that position when they stumbled into the theater through a sudden need for a little girl actress to appear in a Torono production of *The Silver King.* Gladys got this part, and thereafter was featured and even starred in the provincial theater as Baby Gladys Smith, but as she grew out of her babyishness she had to step down and take whatever roles she could get, while the other members of the family acted whenever they had the opportunity. The chancy life of the theater often separated them, Mrs. Smith going out with one touring company, one or all of the children with another, their welfare entrusted to the dubious care of stage managers or other actors. It was tough. They ate fairly regularly, but sometimes the meal consisted of a cup of tea, or, if luck was with them, two cups. As for home, that consisted most of the time of the grimy day coaches in which, together or singly, they rode from tank town to tank town across the length and breath of the United States. Years later the fan magazines, hungry for material then as now, periodically quizzed the stars of the day about their loves and hates, though prudently limiting the subjects of their questions to such harmless ones as "favorite jewel," "favorite color," "favorite song," and the like; these juvenile quizzes, perhaps for good reason, strikingly resembled the write-ups of graduating classes in high school year books. Mary Pickford invariably listed crimson as her most detested color. In her autobiography she revealed the reason why. The color reminded her of the red plush seats smelling of coal dust on which she and her family spent hundreds of long, uncomfortable nights while barnstorming the country between 1898 and 1907. Sometimes the ex-Baby Gladys Smith cried herself to sleep to the rhythm of the rails. More often, she lay awake thinking—thinking about money.

A hard life, yes, but by this time the whole family had caught the theatrical infection and eagerly drilled themselves in all its requisite skills. Gladys in particular was determined to become a first-class professional, because, she thought, if she could make enough money, the family could be together all the time. In 1907 she sold herself to David Belasco for a part in his important production of William C. De Mille's *The Warrens of Virginia* and she seemed at last to have achieved her goal. But when the Broadway run and national tour of the play ended after two years, she was, again, just another juvenile actress out of a job. It was at this difficult juncture that Mrs. Smith suggested to her daughter (newly christened Mary Pickford by Belasco) that, since she was "between engagements," she pick up a little money by acting in motion pictures at the Biograph studio, which paid its players the not inconsiderable sum of five dollars a day. Mary knew that "posing for the camera" was anathema to her theater associates. Now that she could proudly call herself a "Belasco actress" she was reluctant to risk her new reputation in shady ventures. But she went. Even at twelve, to Mary Pickford five dollars was five dollars.

When she entered the old brownstone mansion at 11 East Fourteenth Street which housed the Biograph company, she did not know that it was an experimental laboratory. D. W. Griffith had been in charge of production for less than a year, but already he was trying out every innovation he and his pliant cameraman, Billy Bitzer, could think of. That this teen-age girl had more than a decade of stage experience behind her meant far less to Griffith than the fact that her golden curls shimmered under Bitzer's lights, that her large brown eyes sparkled in them, and that the camera seemed somehow to dramatize every move she made. He noticed too that while his other actors used the Delsartean gestures of the "French school of pantomine," or what they fondly believed to be French School, Mary's expressions were restrained, and her gestures small, drawn-out, and for that reason all the more expressive. She moved only when movement was called for, and her stillness otherwise fixed audience attention. This was something new in his experience of movie players, and for the first time he began to discuss with one of them the craft of movie narration as he was beginning to develop it. Miss Pickford's memory of her first close-up is revealing:

I remember it was late in the afternoon when Griffith shouted to Billy Bitzer, "Come on, Billy, let's have some fun! Move the camera up and get closer to Mary."

Now that was a startling departure from the then accepted routine of photography. Obediently Billy moved the camera—an unwieldy contraption which weighed about one hundred pounds and in which Billy sometimes kept his lunch. Meanwhile I broke another precedent and put on a second make-up—one a day had so far sufficed for everybody in the business. Billy took the shot, which was a semi-close-up, cutting me at the waist. I was so excited I couldn't wait to see the results. . . . What a frightening experience when my grotesquely magnified face finally flashed on the screen. The shock of it was like a physical blow. But I was critical enough to notice the make-up.

"Pickford, what do you think?" said Mr. Griffith.

"I think you'll do more of that, Mr. Griffith, maybe even closer."

In *Sparrows*, 1926, Mary Pickford for the umpteenth time succors an orphaned waif, one of many whom she rescues from the clutches of a baby farmer. This vision scene makes explicit the divine patronage which always seemed to hover over her benevolent activities.

134

A tired ex-idol sails away from his abandoned career. Douglas Fairbanks in 1935.

the early 1920s to be rapidly changing, their romance fading into the past. So to the past Fairbanks turned. To the California of the 1850s, to the time of D'Artagnan (he played D'Artagnan three times during his career), to the days when both knights and pirates were bold—to eras offering plenty of scope for the Fairbanks optimism and virility, and for the swinging, singing line of his acrobatics. After 1920, he made only one picture with a contemporary setting.

Besides, he wanted to advance the movies. The world popularity of "Doug" quickly earned him one of the largest fortunes to be made out of motion pictures. He was by 1920 a partner in United Artists, and he was generally recognized as a leader of the motion picture industry, not just a famous and highly paid favorite. He and Miss Pickford, with Griffith and Chaplin, had formed United Artists primarily to secure the major profits from their pictures for themselves, but they also wanted to make it a symbol of quality, of the new and to-be-respected position of the motion picture in the world. In this effort Fairbanks took a vigorous lead. His leadership at first took the form of imitation—imitating a threat. Such German costume melodramas as *Passion, Deception,* and *All for a Woman* were impressing Hollywood and alarming it by their success in the world market. Fairbanks determined to outdo them. He built the largest set in American film history, the castle for *Robin Hood.* He bought world rights to the German film *De Müde Tod,* 1923, for the sole purpose of withholding it from release so that it could not be compared with his own million-dollar production, *The Thief of Bagdad.* He was the first seriously to experiment with color, and made in *The Black Pirate* what is still one of the most beautiful of all early color films, or would be if all color prints had not now disintergrated. Although made in the old two-color Technicolor process, the picture was cunningly designed to use only those colors which could register truly in this extremely limited early process, while firmly eliminating all those which would not—a lesson still unlearned by many users of today's greatly improved color media. Design became a preoccupation with Fairbanks. He wished his films not only to *be* art, but to look unmistakably like art. He imported set designers, costume designers, antique experts from all over the world to help him make his ever more gorgeous productions of *Don Q, The Gaucho, The Iron Mask, The Taming of the Shrew.*

Some of his admirers think that he weakened the impact of his own acrobatic personality in this attempt to elevate the movies, or at least to improve their decor. "Even in *Robin Hood,*" says Alistair Cooke, "the naked line and rhythm of Fairbanks is occasionally shaggy with parades and scenery." But for the generation which grew up in the twenties, the costume Fairbanks was *the* Fairbanks. For them, the image of Doug, the all-American male, had been overlaid by that of a sort of Laughing Cavalier, swinging down the centuries through the treetops of time.

Through both these periods, Douglas Fairbanks reigned unchallenged as King of the Movies. Chaplin was even more popular, but Doug pre-empted the title by virtue of his marriage to the undoubted Queen of the Movies, Mary Pickford. The marriage of this famous and adored pair seemed supremely "right" to the whole wide world, and it seemed equally right that they should reign over Hollywood from their famous home Pickfair (not so named by them, but by an unknown newspaperman). Pickfair was usually referred to as a "mansion" by the press, though an English milord who had once visited it later asked Miss Pickford in London, "Tell me, do you and Mr. Fairbanks still live in that charming little cottage?" What it really was, psychologically speaking, was the Buckingham Palace of Hollywood, the place where all official industry functions and important entertainments took place as a matter of course, and where Mr. and Mrs. Fairbanks extended hospitality to a literally endless stream of house guests, from the Duke of Alba to such truly distinguished celebrities as Albert Einstein and Bernard Shaw. On their days off from the studio (one sometimes wonders how they found time to make pictures at all) they were summoned from one end of the USA to the other to lay cornerstones, cut ribbons, crown festival queens, and march in bond-selling parades. They were, in all but name, unelected officials of the U. S. Government, and they shirked none of it. In the rare intervals between these hectic activities, their home life was a model of placid domesticity, and Pickfair, despite its splendors, was the Typical American Home. After dinner King Doug and Queen Mary, crowns laid aside, sat on a living room sofa with their feet up, munching chocolates and watching a movie.

All this was duly publicized, in the decorous manner in which royalty is photographed and reported. By the middle twenties, American parents were holding up the Fairbankses to their offspring as the sort of ideal marriage to which all should aspire. That such an ideal should have emanated from Hollywood was something of a miracle. It was even more miraculous that this particular aura should have enveloped this particular pair. For Mary Pickford and Douglas Fairbanks, when they fell in love, were both already married, and divorce, in 1917, was still no light matter. It was in fact widely considered something of a dirty business. Both knew that in shedding their spouses in order to come together they risked losing the love of their public and shattering their careers permanently. It is the measure of their need for each other that they decided to take the risk. Their course was fraught with peril. Owen Moore, Miss Pickford's first husband, tried to blackmail her out of a large sum as the price of his acquiescence. He was counterblackmailed by the united leaders of the motion picture industry, who promised him faithfully that he would never get another job in motion pictures unless he shut up and went away. On the sidelines were the professional blackmailers, looking for an opening, and officious officials busily trying to pick legal flaws in Mary's establishment of Nevada residence for divorce purposes. And always, skulking in the bushes and peeping through the windows, there were the vigilant representatives of the press. Any number of incidents in the rocky course of these two divorces could have been blown up into something which looked sufficiently scandalous to hurt Doug and Mary. But the lords of the press, even the yellow press, stayed their hands. Did they do so out of sheer altruism? It can't be proved, but it seems more likely that they realized that any attempt to blacken this beloved pair of lovers would boomerang against the blackeners. If this be true, it is unique in the annals of journalism, and also an index to the new power of the screen and its new position in the world.

Their marriage finally accomplished, Doug and Mary prudently departed on a wedding trip to Europe to wait for the furor to die down and, when it subsided, to see if anything was left of their careers. Then something unprecedented happened. Somehow the public had silently understood and sympathized with what this pair had had to risk and endure to get together, and now it seized the opportunity to express its sympathy and its love for them. In New York, London, Paris, Rome, Germany, crowds turned out to welcome them such as had never appeared to greet any king, emperor, or conquering general. Traffic stopped; communications were jammed; and the police of the cities concerned confronted something with the dimensions of a national emergency. What happened was touching, inspiring, and frightening. Often Doug had to protect her with his muscular body. The mobs only wanted to express their love but Our Mary was in danger of being crushed to death. Their European tour settled with resounding emphasis the question whether their marriage had hurt them professionally. On the contrary it had enthroned, all but canonized, them.

After that there seemed no reason why Mr. and Mrs. Fairbanks should not go on reigning forever in at least their public roles as King and Queen of the Movies, no matter the fortunes of their films. But Douglas Fairbanks was thirty-two years of age when he entered motion pictures. Long hours of massage and exercise kept his body firm and young (Miss Pickford recalls that he had an unconscious habit of smoothing his hips with his hands in loving admiration of their litheness, a trait he shared with Mary Garden), but his rather moon-faced countenance grew moonier as the twenties wore on, and, skillfully though he delayed the passing of youth, he could not but be aware that it *was* passing. Then came the talkies, a new problem. He and everyone else assumed that he would pass the test vocally because of his stage experience. But could his costumed acrobatics be continued in the new medium, with its heightened realism? *The Taming of the Shrew* was an evasion of the issue, since it was Shakespeare and co-starred his beloved wife. *Reaching for the Moon,* 1931, was an awkward attempt to combine old and new. Expensively produced, studded with the "names" of Bebe Daniels, Edward Everett Horton, and Jack Mulhall, and with songs by Irving Berlin (removed before release because the vogue of musicals had temporarily passed), this nevertheless emerged as a routine romantic comedy into which a Fairbanks acrobatic episode had been forcibly inserted. "While one is speculating on the combined ages of the veteran principals," wrote a reviewer, "he is magnetized by a youthful newcomer named June MacCloy." Miss MacCloy married and left the screen before she could capitalize on the fame thus suddenly thrust upon her, but it was she and not the star who attracted the teen-agers of 1931 to *Reaching for the Moon.*

Rather fed up with the talkies, Fairbanks took his old pal Victor Fleming, the director, on a world tour from which emerged *Around the World in 80 Minutes,* a fragmentary sort of travelogue starring Doug in his well-known public role of globe-trotter. This too was an evasion of the question of what kind of star Doug Fairbanks was going to turn out to be in the talkies, and it did not appeal to the Depression-struck audience of 1931–32. Indeed, the image of "Doug," with whom everybody wanted to identify, was being replaced by that of a rich movie producer who seemed to be losing his flair and resiliency. His next attempt, in fact, ended his producing career. *Mr. Robinson Crusoe,* a "modern" version of Defoe, was an effort to give Doug a congenial place in the talkies by placing his stunts against a Polynesian background. It seemed tame, juvenile—even to juveniles—and strangest of all, rather amateurish. The slowly relaxing hand was losing its cunning.

Outwardly, Douglas Fairbanks was still a success story supreme. Why should he care if his starring career was drawing to a close? World-famous, immensely wealthy, one of the owners of United Artists, much involved with banks and stocks, and socially very much in demand, he had plenty to keep him busy the rest of his life. But beneath his assurance, Fairbanks was in a panic. The coincidence of the fading of his popularity with the fading of his youth was too much for him, and it is difficult here to separate cause from effect. The former ebullient disciple of optimism and strength through joy now became moody, erratic, unpredictable. One day this onetime idol of surging mobs said to his wife, "Aw, Mary, nobody cares anything about us any more, let's sell Pickfair and move to Switzerland and just get old." Before Miss Pickford could react to this startling proposal, Fairbanks had left for Europe without her, hopping from city to city, resort to resort. And now this careful builder of a blameless reputation began to get into trouble, public trouble. The scandal and newspaper notoriety surrounding his affair with Lady Sylvia Ashley was replacing the picture of "Doug" with that of an aging roué, and it was perhaps that aspect of so-called showmanship which moved Alexander Korda to invite Fairbanks to star in the British-made *The Private Life of Don Juan* (1934), a thin comedy about the great seducer's declining years. That he accepted this offer shows how badly his judgment had been impaired. Critics said that this Don Juan was no longer the world's greatest lover, and that there was nothing in the picture to suggest that he ever had been: "He seems instead like a tired broker who knows his way around tea tables and drawing rooms better than boudoirs or balconies." The end of the picture had a certain charm and rightness. In the final scene, Fairbanks-Don Juan is shocked at being told that a younger blade has taken his place. Then Fairbanks turns to look directly at the audience, gives us a Fairbanks wink, and says, "Aw, but nobody can take my place."

Which is true enough. Tyrone Power and Errol Flynn remade his old pictures, but they were merely Tyrone Power and Errol Flynn, and as for such phenomena as the Zorro and other series on TV, the weariness of commercially manufactured make-believe is all too apparent. The small fry enjoyed them, but they didn't know Doug, the original Doug, who had no need for make-believe because the vitality and enthusiasm which burst from him almost knocked the camera flat on its back.

CHARLES CHAPLIN

In 1931, on the second of his triumphal returns from Hollywood to the England of his birth and youth, Charles Chaplin decided to visit Manchester, where he had spent several months of his wretched boyhood. Traveling incognito, or as incognito as anyone could whose face was recognized instantly wherever in the world he went, he decided to stop over in Stratford-on-Avon, which he had never visited. After dark he stole out to walk the streets, and though the night was pitch-black he found Shakespeare's cottage. "No doubt," he says in his autobiography, "a kindred spirit had led the way." Next day he was shown over the place, and introduced to the scant memorabilia of the farmer's boy who went to London and became—what? A successful actor-manager, that Chaplin could imagine and believe. But that the country bumpkin could be metamorphosed into the great poet-dramatist was inconceivable to the child of democracy's lower reaches. Chaplin makes clear that he is not concerned whether the poems and plays were written by Bacon, Southampton, Richmond, or someone else; he is only sure that their greatness,

Charles Chaplin at the time he made his first million

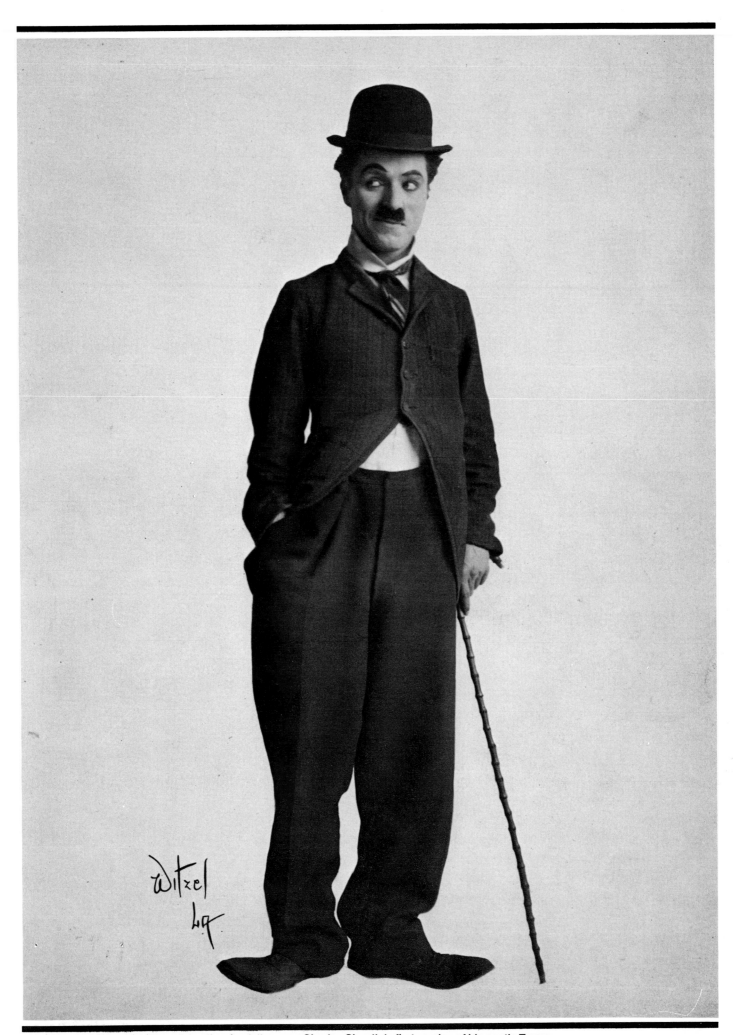

This impudent, almost deliberately offensive fellow was Charles Chaplin's first version of his poetic Tramp.

Under his look of fierce preparedness, Charlie's Cockney soldier hides, and yet expresses, the feelings of modern man about the incalculable immensity of modern war, in Chaplin's most universally popular film, *Shoulder Arms,* 1918.

Charlie grandly prepares to buy a flower from the blind Virginia Cherrill in his best-loved film, *City Lights*, 1931.

their beauty, came from the soul of a man who knew life on its upper levels. The implied paradox is exquisite. "The finest pantomime, the deepest emotion, the richest and most poignant poetry were in Chaplin's work," writes his greatest admirer, James Agee. Yet all of these things Chaplin made out of a handful of dust—out of an experience of life that began with the dregs of urban existence, at a time when that existence was all but subhuman.

This man's story is a paradox from first to last. He was the greatest star of all time—yet to consider him as a star at all is a patent absurdity. Stars as we know them are the creation of their "discoverers," of the production and publicity machines, and of audience response. Chaplin had no discoverer; Mack Sennett simply gave him a chance to show what he could do, somewhat reluctantly at first. The machinery of stardom hardly existed in 1915. Only the factor of audience response, hypertrophied to the nth power, played its part in Charlie's rise: In little more than a year, the peoples of the world made him the most famous man in the world. His attraction for them differed in kind as well as in degree from that of his nearest rivals. Mary Pickford was a youthfully versatile actress *one* of whose characterizations, canonized as Little Mary, was for a time nearly as popular as Charlie's Tramp. But Miss Pickford was the prisoner of her screen character; when the vogue of the child-woman died out, so did her career. The screen Douglas Fairbanks was accidentally struck off from his private personality by Anita Loos, then developed and matured by him, but it too did not survive the passing of the age of innocence. Only Chaplin held the attention, and for the greater part of his career the love, of every audience generation since the salad days of the movies. Only Chaplin is the sole creator of his screen self. And only he, of all stars, has been the sole determinant of the form that self should take and the adventures it should have. From the time he achieved his independence, scarcely five years after he first appeared on a screen, the production money for his films has come, not from studios or banks, but out of his own pocket—where it was put by the audiences of the world.

We identify with the stars, that is the source of their hold on us. In them for a moment we glimpse ourselves as successful, irresistible, at peace with ourselves, good at heart to a degree, and, because of these things, triumphant over life. But Charlie—Charlot—the Tramp—the Little Fellow—lacked all the qualifications for triumph, and triumphed just the same. His very lacks offered us an identification deeper than any the rich, the beautiful, and the strong could provide. Few of us were as poor and hungry as Charlie always was. Few of us were as small in stature, or were as continually confronted by big and menacing men. We mostly had a place to lay our heads at night. If we wanted to smoke a cigarette, that minimum comfort, we didn't have to stoop so low as to pick up a butt off the street. Charlie had almost nothing, he was way below us at the bottom—but he was always rising to the top, and taking us with him. Confronted by the law, he was as abject and placatory as the rest of us, but he had a sharp way of putting down the law before the picture ended. Confronted by wealth and respectability and snobbishness, he strove with them on equal terms and won, in this respect surpassing that naked emperor whose finery had to be supplied by flattery. All the women he wanted were way out of his reach, and he mostly didn't get them—but they didn't ignore him either. They were obviously intrigued by this funny little man, so wholly lacking in the things that women want. They flirted with him and made much of him, and in the complicated give and take between him and them there emerged a sense that for them he had something they weren't getting from the obviously eligible men who, in a normal film, would be the normal objects of their desire and pursuit. And that was funny. With women, as with the law, as with respectability, Charlie turned everything upside down and made you look at it that way. And *that* was funny, funnier than anything you had ever seen, and all done so quickly, with such flickering grace and charm, and piling on top of itself so fast that you couldn't hold still from laughing and for once were glad when the picture ended so you could get your breath. The roar of laughter that went around the world in 1915 and 1916 was heard in the seats of the mighty. In the middle of the first of the world wars, of mass slaughter and mass suffering on a scale hitherto unknown, there was suddenly something important to the world as its warring self.

A little child shall lead them. Children, those natural rebels against the order of things, were the first to discover the little man with the baggy pants. In their literal millions they discovered him, and they dragged their elders to the still questionable movie theaters of the teens to see a movie star who, almost immediately, was universally advertised by a full-figure poster captioned simply "I Am Here Today." The movie craze was in full swing when Chaplin first appeared, and the old nickelodeons and the new picture palaces (there was as yet hardly anything in between) were jammed to the doors almost regardless of what was playing, so that it was a sudden box-office shift *within* that vast new audience which signaled, first to the industy and then to the press and public, that a phenomenon had arrived that was even more startling than the phenomenon of the movies themselves. The shift showed up in a new alignment in family tastes, an alignment most delicately and accurately rendered by James Agee on the first page of his novel *A Death in the Family:*

At supper that night, as many times before, his father said, "Well, spose we go to the picture show."

"Oh, Jay!" his mother said. "That horrid little man!"

"What's wrong with him?" his father asked, not because he didn't know what she would say, but so she would say it.

"He's so *nasty!*" she said, as she always did. "So *vulgar!* With his nasty little cane; hooking up skirts and things, and that nasty little walk!"

His father laughed, as he always did, and Rufus felt that it had become a rather empty joke; but as always the laughter also cheered him; he felt that the laughter enclosed him with his father.

In this division of taste, so casually expressed at the family dinner table, was a portent of much that was to come, many years later, to the sorrow of Charles Chaplin. But for the moment all that it meant was that Chaplin's popularity introduced a strong male element into the movie audience, to balance somewhat that larger female element which worshiped the idealized glamour-stars. Indeed the hordes of Chaplin fans throughout the world seemed to consist of ordinary men and their sons, blue-collar and lower white-collar workers whose chief bought pleasure was to go to see a little man like themselves take revenge for them on a world they could not lick. As that fact became apparent, it immediately attracted the attention of the intellectuals, who on the whole were still repelled by the movies themselves as too "mechanical" to be art, but who could not ignore so conspicuous an archetype of *l'homme moyen sensuel* as this little comedian instantly proved himself to be. Their conflict was assuaged when Mrs. Fiske assured them in the pages of *Harper's Weekly,* so early as 1916, that Chaplin was an "artist." That part of the matter settled, they could devote themselves to what really interested them, which was what Chaplin *meant,* what his unprecedented popularity with the "masses"signified. Scratch an intellectual of the early century and you found an uplifter; the best of them saw in the movies a potential "poor man's university," and they wanted to know what was being taught in those unhallowed halls. When they went to find out, as reluctantly they were forced to do, they discovered that Chaplin meant a good deal. Watching him as an immigrant forced through the degrading sieve of Ellis Island, as an insouciant, asocial, semi-Wobbly knight of the roads, or just as a homeless, hungry city waif afoul of the law and the bosses, they found that he was delivering a great part of their message for them, silently, trenchantly, unblinkably, and undisfigured by that intellectual billingsgate which characterized the bulk of the Marxist attack on capitalism. In the Chaplin films the poor man was being championed not from on high but from down below, on his own level, in terms which didn't seem like championing at all, and to the tune of box-office returns which any capitalist would find more than attractive. And watching all this, the intellectuals found out, among other new things, that they were ordinary men themselves. In the sweaty movie halls, under the boom of belly laughter, some of them discovered for the first time in their lives the human reality of their vaunted brotherhood of man (as well, of course, as its limitations).

It must be said for them that, in spite of preconceptions, in spite of the genteel tradition, the intellectuals responded to Charlie Chaplin with an open heart. He was of course from the first good copy, and they seized upon him as such, as intellectuals will. But the kind and quality of that copy is surprising and warming to read today in the pages of forgotton highbrow journals, sandwiched in between so much dead writing on dead subjects. Chaplin was so new a thing under the sun that he provoked, for once, an honest reaction. The most enthusiastic of his admirers, from the first, Gilbert Seldes, to the latest and best, Agee, responded to the critical challenge implicit in his work in exactly the same way: They simply describe what he did, scene for scene, even minute by minute. Short of poetry—which a few attempted—there simply was no other way to take him off the screen and put him onto the written page. The recognition value of such criticism gave it a flavor of delight which still tastes today. But the general run of commentators, social and aesthetic, were unable to hold themselves to the strict discipline of simple description of what they saw; impelled through long habit to generalize, they resorted to a sort of prose poetry to express their feelings about this "wandering soul, lost in the illimitable crowd," this "child of democracy," son of "many generations of underfed forebears," who seemed to have been "born in a garbage can." As the Chaplin films accumulated and the Chaplin canon built, they grew windier; they saw the Tramp as one who "rebels against laws but submits to fate" and who forever marvels at "the blindness of destiny, man's mystification at the unknown chances of which he is the eternal sport." The more flatulent writers on Chaplin, who by now had become a staple subject of daily journalism, like Babe Ruth or Henry Ford or the President of the United States, began to beg him to rise to the level of real art, to play Hamlet or Peer Gynt or Cyrano or even Napoleon—what a telling contrast to the Tramp! There was a good deal of this sort of thing in the early 1920s, and it was fortunate

Chaplin's millions did not read it; they might have laughed louder at it than they did at Chaplin himself. The standard article on Chaplin oscillated between the poles of Humor and Pathos, and more often than not degenerated into an amateur essay on that most dangerous of subjects, the Nature of Comedy. More farsighted men, who could stand back and see their times in relation to other times, were aware that the Tramp was a creation as great as Hamlet and more significant than Napoleon: "the one universal man of the twentieth century." It was perhaps Waldo Frank who first pointed out that the Tramp was not *merely* a "universal," in the sense that the classic clowns were universals, but a specific character modified by and reacting to the new circumstances of industrial life in which Everyman now had to win his bread and lay him down and, if possible, pray for his soul. Speaking of the "hardness he summons to help him bear his pity," Frank points out that the Tramp "resolves every course with its opposite. This means that he frustrates in himself every impulse of utter giving or utter taking. He remains unpossessed and ultimately unpossessing. But this deep frustration is the key to his profound success. Do not pity him for it. He is no pitiable creature." There is an iron clank to this, a suggestion of the sin of pride, and Frank elsewhere refers to the Tramp as "a kind of fallen angel." Through the fog of thoughtless verbal adulation, there pierced at that time one further portentous remark. It was made by V. I. Lenin: "Chaplin is the one man in the world I want to meet."

What would he have found, if he had met him, before his own death in 1924? A young man in his twenties— a young Cockney—a young millionaire, creating and recreating, by popular demand, a homeless vagabond, and each time creating him with a difference. Incredibly famous, he was sought after and pawed over by the great and pseudo great, and he reacted to it all pretty much as excessively and uncritically as you would suppose such a young man would. But his fundamental mind was on his creation, the creation which had won him everything he had, and his problem, of which he was acutely aware, was what to do with him, how to advance him, how to make him grow. In the five years between the first great Chaplin boom and his final acknowledged supremacy, the pattern of his pictures was often that of one step forward and two steps back— a long, ambitious film which asked to be called a masterpiece, followed by one or two shorter ones which were bedrock slapstick and asked nothing but continuous laughter. That he had much to say, he knew early. In 1916, while he was still with Essanay, he planned and actually embarked on a feature film called, simply, *Life*. This attempt he abandoned as premature, but it shows the early bent of his mind, the decision and determination to give the Tramp adventures that would do more than make us laugh and weep, that would, dangerously, lead us to the brink of thought. The source and base of all his invention was his own life, and this he consistently and amazingly held to, in spite of all the pressures to which he was subjected. Resisting the pressures of the intellectuals was no problem, much to their annoyance; he rather enjoyed resisting them: "I am too tragic by nature to play Hamlet. Only a great comedian can act him." The discipline which ever kept him steady was the certain knowledge that, whatever his soaring ideas, there would come a time before he began work when he must lay them aside and "again come to grips with my implacable, crushing duty to be funny." That duty held him close to his own experience of life, for only from that could he extrapolate and measure the experiences of ordinary men as they caromed off the sharp edges of contemporary events. *Shoulder Arms,* the creation of a rich movie star much criticized as a slacker, was an exact projection of what your ordinary good-for-nothing joe would find funny in army life, dreams of glory and all. Because he was dealing with the American, not the European, experience of the war, Chaplin could treat it as a brief episode, a sort of fantastic irrelevancy to real, earnest, everyday life. What *that* life was like, he had already summed up in the same year, 1918, in what has been called his first masterpiece, *A Dog's Life.* As always with Chaplin, the title and the theme may be general but the action is sharply explicit: A tramp and a dog survive together on the streets of a city; every man's hand is against them, and they have no allies but each other. *A Dog's Life* has a happy ending, with Charlie and his girl ensconced on a neat little farm along with the dog, now the proud mother of puppies. They have bought their way into this miniature Eden on the proceeds of a wallet which Charlie hijacked from thieves who had in their turn stolen it from somebody else. Nobody thought to draw a Marxist moral from this little tale, nor to emphasize the blindness of the blind chance which put the wallet in Charlie's way; everybody was too busy laughing at the sheer wrongheadedness of the manner in which he captured it (a sequence predicting René Clair's *A Nous la Liberté*). But Hannen Swaffer, looking at *A Dog's Life* and other early Chaplin films, wrote: "The whole social fabric is wrong, and Charlie Chaplin knows it. . . . His gospel, screened, is like Mary Pickford's—the hope of a little child."

But where could such a hope lead Charlot? The logic of Miss Pickford's hopes was an adulthood of womanly fulfillment (which, alas, she never reached). The Tramp is always already an adult when we meet him—an adult with two strikes against him. By any ordinary count, you would say that his future is in the past. In this regard, the endings of the Tramp films became more and crucial. The one we hold in memory's focus is that of Charlie's back as he goes off down the road, defeated once again and at first dejected, then kicking up his heels in defiance as he goes off, in his freedom, to encounter another adventure. This is the great image, and it recurs throughout the Tramp's screen life, but after 1918 it became less frequent. In *A Dog's Life* Charlie steals his heaven; in *The Kid,* achieves it accidentally through a piece of operatic plot-machinery which imperials the reality of the Tramp's world; and in *The Gold Rush* the Lone Prospector does indeed strike gold—causing John Grierson to remark with distaste that Chaplin "forgot Charlot the outcast to become a millionaire and marry the girl, like any John Gilbert or Ronald Colman." Finding it "too lonely to be free," our unheroic hero strikes it rich, steals riches, or has riches, if not greatness, thrust upon him. It was a little disturbing to watch these successive departures from the classic Chaplin ending—only a little, because we were so convulsed with laughter at the body of each film that the problematic nature of the last shot was somewhat obscured. Yet we knew vaguely at the time that the creator of the Tramp was in the grip of a dilemma that he could not solve—and, even more vaguely, that the fault was not that of this matchless artist but of ourselves. If the ideal of human freedom which the Tramp held out to us was actually too much for us, too costly to achieve—then the Tramp, like us, would have to settle for what was available at the time. That seemed always to revolve around money, the thing that made our world go round. There was a taste of ashes about these "happy" endings which we did not like to linger over. For the moment, Chaplin solved the problem for us by evading it— he dashed in and out of these endings as quickly as possible, leaving us to savor our enjoyment of what came before. That this was not really satisfactory both Chaplin and his audience knew; his films of the twenties, vastly popular, vastly profitable, cinematically magnificent, did not quite provide that absolute enjoyment, free of any alloy or *arrière-pensée*, with which the early two-reelers had overwhelmed us.

Before he had exhausted these temporary solutions, Chaplin faced a more urgent crisis, the fortuitous crisis of the coming of sound. He knew instantly that, for every reason, Charlot must not enter the world of sound—that he could no more survive in it than he could in the new lighting scheme which was coming into being in Hollywood, "that light which brings a Garbo alive, but in which a Chaplin cannot survive." Commercially, sound would shrink Charlie to the stature of the other stars; humanly, "the one universal man of the twentieth century" must be silent or speak gibberish (as he did in one scene in *Modern Times*). He must either kill Charlie, inter him, and start afresh with an entirely new creation, or preserve him, intact and unchanged, to pursue his now ten-times-more-difficult course of development. When he chose the latter, the immediate consequence was to cut off both Charlie and Chaplin, both creator and creation, from the mainstream of the motion picture. In the silent days, Charlie, both as a creation and as a "star," was at the very least always *primus inter pares,* and also a good deal more by virtue of the fact that Chaplin the director was in the vanguard of cinematic invention and progress. Like Griffith and Eisenstein he was a pacemaker, pulling the rest of the directors and producers after him in his exploration of the possibilities of the medium. Now, by deliberate choice, he stood aside from further exploration and devoted himself for a decade to the reprise and elaboration of an arrested art which was no longer a part of the general evolution of the movies. The most important consequence of this decision was to put a new distance between Charlie and his audience, to make him a less and less viable figure in our dream lives. A prophet would have foreseen this as inevitable; our unprophetic selves merely hoped that it wouldn't be. It took a while to manifest itself, as the intervals between the Chaplin films grew longer and longer. Those intervals signaled Chaplin's own travail as the problem represented by the coming of sound compounded and doubled the still unresolved problem of who Charlie essentially was, what he meant, and what he was to become in a world changing so fast that he was in danger of becoming an archaic irrelevancy. Though released in 1931, *City Lights* was conceived three years earlier, before the Depression. In it Charlie is still only the lost wanderer, battling the impersonal chaos of the city. We know him as of old; we only oddly and fitfully sense that his adventures now belong to a less complicated, *less* impersonal city than the one we are shown. In *Modern Times,* five years later, Charlie is again still the same, but he has acquired a most specific identity as a Worker, driven mad by machinery—so mad that he has a nervous breakdown. The Tramp as a clinical psychoneurotic; it does not seem a very funny idea, nor at all in character, and we are not in fact shown it. We are shown a new, more distant Charlie at a more distant remove from his natural opponents. He is no longer confronted by immediately menacing brawn but by a television image which tells him and ten thousand others exactly what to do and when and how to do it, no exceptions or little idiosyncrasics allowed. When he does face his familiar enemies, the cops, their malice is not their own. They represent and carry out the wishes of the

television images. Worker Charlie and his girl—a streamlined heroine now, Paulette Goddard, very different from Edna Purviance of old—escape from these dehumanized complexities to a Hooverville shack, the 1936 version of the idyllic farm in *A Dog's Life*. Even from this they are ejected, and they end up walking across the familiar horizon. What is beyond that horizon? Another Hooverville shack? Chaplin did not have time to answer, if he had an answer. The gathering malaise of the century, outstripping Charlie's reactions to it, was about to issue in the blind, blunt fact of war. And not a war that could be treated as an episode, like the war of *Shoulder Arms,* but a catastrophe which finally brought out into the open everything that had been swept under the carpet, including the implications, and the incompleteness, of Charlot as a symbol of our times and our selves. What place could Charlot now find in a world which, at best, had had to abandon freedom in order to defend freedom? The answer which emerged provides a fascinating glimpse into the mystery of artistic creation. For this problem of content was solved as though it were a problem of form. After two "silent talkies," Chaplin was deeply disturbed at the continuing necessity of working in an increasingly archaic medium in order to preserve Charlie intact. His difficulties showed up in a small but significant way; it grew harder and harder to cast the lesser roles in his pictures because he could no longer find actors who remembered the silent technique. In 1937 Alexander Korda proposed to Chaplin that he film a Hitler story involving mistaken identity. It was a thin idea, based on no more than the resemblance of the two mustaches, but it unlocked the floodgates of creation. By dividing the Tramp in two, by making one half of him into Adenoid Hynkel, while leaving the other half to remain at least the husk of the old Charlie, Chaplin could solve the problem of talk with a triumphant flourish. Hynkel could indulge in oceans of talk, while the Tramp could remain "more or less silent," in Chaplin's own words. And this formal solution of a technical problem registered with uncanny accuracy the new truth about the Tramp as he could now be seen in relation to our unfolding times. For twentieth-century man is divided against himself, he has a double identity, and Hitler and Chaplin are his natural prototypes. The obverse of Charlie's sweetness was, from the very beginning, his cruelty ("Do not pity him. He is no pitiable creature").

What emerged on the screen inexorably reinforced the justness of this concept. The exquisite eloquence of the silent Charlie gives place to a deafening clamor which is the opposite of eloquence. Hynkel talks on and on, in an almost incomprehensible jargon, but what he says means nothing, or means its opposite. "Democratische geshtuken!" he shrieks, while Garbitsch languidly translates, "Democracy is unsatisfactory." Charlie, on the other hand, what is left of him in the person of the little Jewish barber, hardly speaks at all, and when he does he seems to mumble; he is inarticulate, he cannot "communicate." Moreover, he has lost his resilience. He cannot grasp the violent events in which he has been set down, still less rise above them. Though he is nominally the protector of the girl, Hannah, it is she who seems to propel him forward. But Chaplin is preparing an apotheosis for this ineffectual figure. At the end, substituted for Hynkel by a "miracle," the Tramp speaks out—or rather, Charlie Chaplin, through the mouth of his great creation, spells out in words the meaning of the message he had been silently sending the world for a quarter of a century.

The words of that message rather appalled Chaplin's admirers among the intellectuals of the world. It was so banal, so laden with the old ideas about freedom and brotherhood which now seemed obsolete, or flattened by the irony of events. But another silence was broken at this moment—the silence of the masses. Earlier, when Chaplin and his art and his meaning and his message were endlessly picked to pieces on the upper levels of international life, the millions who loved him down below had remained silent. The only vote they recorded was the vote of the box office, which, picture after picture, year after year, decade after decade, recorded grosses so far above those of other films as to suggest that the making and distribution of the Chaplin films belonged to a separate business enterprise. Now, as *The Great Dictator* reached the theaters, these silent millions at last spoke their minds. Chaplin was flooded with letters from every quarter of the globe. People ill at ease with pen and paper sat down to write to him how glad they were that he had put his feelings into speech. It is too bad these letters have never been collected and published. They were, in effect, the fan mail of a star—but as different from other fan mail as this star is from other stars. One of the fans was Archie L. Mayo, a successful but wholly undistinguished routinist Hollywood director. He asked for and received Chaplin's permission to reprint the final speech from *The Great Dictator* on his Christmas cards, and he prefaced it with these words of his own: "Had I lived at the time of Lincoln, I believe I would have sent you his Gettysburg speech, because it was the greatest inspirational message of his period. Today we face new crises, and another man has spoken from the depths of an earnest and sincere heart. Although I know him but slightly, what he says has moved me deeply. . . . I am inspired to send you the full text of the speech written by Charles Chaplin that you, too, may share the expression of Hope."

That capitalized Hope—"inspirational message"—"earnest and sincere heart"—this is pure corn; so is the speech it prefaces, and it is no wonder that the intellectuals turned from the latter in pained distaste. But its corniness did not dismay Mr. Mayo's fellow fans, any more than they were dismayed by the corn in the Sunday sermons through which the Christian message reached them at church of their attendance. It was the message, not the medium, which counted for them. The operative phase in Mayo's preface, had they read it, would have been "moved me deeply." The letters Chaplin received were the unaccustomed act of people who had always been moved in their depths by the Tramp, and whose emotions had at last been brought to the surface of consciousness by this bald speech put in his mouth. They were an affirmation of faith in the Little Man, in all his aspects, and as such they might well have been taken by Chaplin as his final triumph.

Well, it was a triumph of sorts, but not a very conspicuous one as events were moving in the 1940s, nor could it have been. Even if Chaplin had announced then, as he did not, that *The Great Dictator* was the Tramp's final appearance, you couldn't very well put a laurel wreath on Charlot's impudent brow and embalm him in an Academy; that would have been funnier than anything in any of the Chaplin films. The career of the Tramp might be a completed thing, wrapped round and tied up with the ribbon of the speech, but his creator was still alive and, rather decidedly, kicking. And he was no longer the young man who had created the Tramp and his world out of his own childhood experiences. He was now, he had been for years, the great success of the movies, their rather uncomfortable philosopher-king, whose recent experiences had radically altered his view of life and the human condition. What new image could he now adopt

Critics of Chaplin's *Autobiography* derided him as a celebrity-hound. In fact, it is the celebrities who have hounded him. Bernard Shaw's eager enjoyment of his company is obvious here.

Limelight, 1952. Sitting beneath the symbols of his past glory, while the music of a street band floats through the window to stir his memories, Calvero, old and drunk, prepares to go to sleep and dream of the past.

Rudolf Arnheim characterized Chaplin's Hitler as "the haunted dwarf in the towering palace walls." He is dwarfed here by Jack Oakie as Napaloni in *The Great Dictator,* 1940.

(Right) In *Modern Times,* 1936, Chaplin sought to satirize, and scotch, accusations that he was a Communist by showing Charlie innocently picking up a red flag which has dropped off a truck and being nabbed by the cops as an agitator. But his Neanderthal critics seized on the sequence as proof positive of their suspicions.

for himself to replace the immortal one of the Tramp?

It was a problem of a magnitude which few creators have faced, in this or any century, and it was much complicated by the nature of the said experiences. Chaplin was originally too ignorant of the way of the world, and later too deeply, essentially, non-conformist, to obey "the ancient rule that a prominent man may get away with flamboyant politics or flamboyant sex, but never both." In the early 1940s Chaplin was already under attack for his sexual acrobatics and for a kind of radicalism which was the more annoying to the black-and-white mind because it could not be quite pinned down to anything so specific as Communism. He felt the drag of an ebb tide of respect and love. In these circumstances, he bought and wrote a script for the play *Shadow and Substance,* in which he did not intend to appear himself; like his one earlier dramatic film, *A Woman of Paris,* it was to be a vehicle for a woman, a discovery whom he could mold into a great new star and thereafter manipulate from behind the scenes. This, perhaps, would become the shape of the future for the inventor of the Tramp. But when the discovery, Joan Barry, became the focus of his increasing legal troubles, including her paternity suit and a federal prosecution for Mann Act violation, the dream waned. Instead he turned to an idea Orson Welles had planted in his mind. Welles had suggested that Chaplin play the part of Landru in a documentary which Welles himself would write and direct. It was a proposal calculated to tempt Chaplin at this stage of his journey. Relieved of the burden of sole creation, he could retreat to a simpler level of his vocation and merely act—and thus, perhaps, slowly but honorably withdraw from the arena he had dominated so long. It was not to be. Landru and what he stood for sparked something in him, he bought the idea from Welles, and himself wrote, directed, and starred in what, in the macabre mood into which events had pulled him, he called "a comedy of murders." Thus it came about that, after an absence of seven years, Charlot Chaplin reappeared upon the screens of the world in the guise of Monsieur Verdoux, a mass murderer.

In considering *Monsieur Verdoux,* it becomes clear how meaningless and indeed ludicrous it is to consider Chaplin himself as if he were only a "star." A star could have got away with playing Monsieur Verdoux; it would have been just another role, to be succeeded by still others, one more scalp to hang on his belt, though a bloody one. But coming from the man it did, and in the light of all he had meant to the world, *Verdoux* was a slap in the world's face. Chaplin himself seems to have thought that it would be his most popular film, that in deepening and enlarging his picture of our life, he would carry his audience with him, to a level of understanding which no other popular work of art in our day had even reached for. So much for the illusions which come from years of unbroken success. *Monsieur Verdoux* was not a flop in the ordinary sense—not a merely unpopular film which people didn't think they'd want to see and from which they indifferently turned away, though it was all of that too. In its two releases (Chaplin withdrew the film for a time, while United Artists tried to think of a better way to sell it) it played 3,000 bookings in the United States, less than a quarter of the engagements Chaplin was accustomed to command, and but for the foreign market it would have been a financial disaster. But far from being only that negative thing, a failure, it provoked a howl of rage such as nothing ever recorded on celluloid had evoked from that passive mass we call the movie audience.

The failure and the rage bring into the light, for the first time, that segment of the world movie audience and particularly of the U.S. audience which had through the years not only remained impervious to Chaplin's appeal, but which also, impossible though it seems, had actually hated the Tramp. The largest group within that segment consisted of women—women on all levels of life to some degree, but particularly those women we have come to think of as the American matriarchy. That women were not indifferent to Charlie, even at his most grotesque, anyone who has ever discussed Chaplin with women knows. Certainly the matriarchy were not indifferent; they were actively hostile to "the *nasty* little man," as the mother in Agee's novel called him. But it was not only that he was an enemy of fake gentility, he was worse than that. At the beginning of his career someone shrewdly pointed out that the Tramp would never appeal to the women in the audience because he was not a breadwinner. The Tramp was indeed an embodiment of male anarchic instincts—a call to the plow horse to take off his harness and take to the open road. That of course would never do, and the matriarchy, lips tightly pursed, resisted any appeal Chaplin may have made to their maternal feelings. Whenever his sexual peccadilloes hit the headlines in the twenties and thirties they rose in wrath against him and tried to destroy him, and even the editorial writers of the time sensed that the real target of that wrath was not the dissolute comedian in his Hollywood mansion, but the Tramp on the screen. But he was still too popular; their shafts fell harmless; they had to bide their time. There were other time-biders. Presumably businessmen and bankers joined their fellow males in raucous laughter when Charlie cocked a snook at the feminized world of respectability—but it was a laughter tinged with reservations which, by the date of *Modern Times,* had become rather explicit. As Al Capp characteristically put it, "It had been okay for the comic to make people laugh at a vaguely inhuman Society that generally kicked them around, but it was unfair and unsporting, really, to make people laugh at a specific system of dignified industrial 'efficiency' that robbed them of their dignity." Ernest Callenbach added that *Modern Times* evoked "a brand of hostility . . . which may unconsciously prove the true 'subversiveness' of Chaplin's humor. His underdog comedies stirred the great movie masses with a kind of folk-anarchism. Chaplin was constantly puncturing approved ideas and behaviour. What further reason would powerful men need for a deep hatred of the clown who had made more people laugh than anybody else in history?"

To the matriarchs and the moneymen, with their fingers on the controls of American life, there joined itself, at the time of *Monsieur Verdoux,* a third group, of a different order of puissance, the patriots. Many of these legionnaires and other kinds of war veterans were little men themselves, and responsive in themselves to the unkind things that Chaplin had to say about the upper levels of society. But they were deeply glad and proud to be Americans, and they simply could not understand how this exponent of freedom could go on and on refusing to join himself to the land of the free which was also, as they had proved in two wars, the home of the brave. They understood it less and less as he persisted through the years in remaining a Briton on the ground that he was a citizen of the world. In this case the target of their animosity was decidedly not the Tramp but Chaplin himself, and what is crucial is that Chaplin had the power to deflect the anger of this group any time he chose to do so. He might have chosen the last refuge of the scoundrel and wrapped himself in the flag, and that would have ended the matter.

"But," as A. E. Housman said of Dr. Johnson, "he was an honest man and could not."

That these three sections of opinion—or better, of feeling—had the power to deal a deathblow to *Monsieur Verdoux* all by themselves is very doubtful. Not that they did not have great power; through their organizations they threatened not merely an *ad hoc* but a general boycott of the theaters which showed the film, and, showmen being as vulnerable as they are, the distribution branch of the movie industry caved in under the pressure. But counterpressure could have turned the tide, if it had manifested itself as the jingle of coins in the box office, and that music, for which Chaplin was confidently waiting, he did not hear. In all probability it was not the somewhat tarnished figure of Chaplin alone which the millions of his former fans rejected; it was Monsieur Verdoux himself. That figure, more "controversial" than even his creator, will be debated for many years to come. But he is, whatever else he is, a figure which belongs to a different order of creation from that of popular entertainment. Ever since *City Lights,* the screen Charlie had been putting a distance between himself and his audience. With *Verdoux,* Chaplin seemed also to withdraw, and to look back over his shoulder at his fellow humans with a merciless regard. The realm to which he withdrew is that we associate with old age, an arena which may still be sunlit, but the light is hard and rigorous and impersonal. One thinks of Sophocles. Or of Shaw, who wondered all his life what writing would be like when he got old, and who wrote, in his ninetieth year, a little play about two men who meet on an empty road and say hello and goodbye and that is all—a little play which in its chilling nihilism makes *Waiting for Godot* seem puppyish. Chaplin was no nonagenarian at the time of *Monsieur Verdoux,* but he had begun to make films like one. At any rate, the character he offered as the successor of Charlot contained in its paradoxes nothing that people could simply love, and from it his lovers turned away.

Their withdrawal hurt him far more than all the idiot barbs flung at him by the Yahoos. Did he think at the time, of something he had said in an interview given in the early twenties?: "I am by way of being a student of history. I know the jester always pays, for the king inevitably kicks him downstairs. The most famous court clowns are eventually beheaded, but what happens to the monarch then? In nearly every case, kicking the jester has presaged the fall of the throne." Over the larger implications of this reflection we need not linger; if they are to become true of American society, we will know it soon enough. But one snowbird does not make a winter. Chaplin engendered in himself new hope. He was at long last happy in the last of his marriages, and he was still after all Charlie Chaplin, in full possession of his great talent and of the prestige of achievement over a long period. He would try again to recapture the audience whose affection he now knew he had lost in both the public and private sector. He would bring before them yet a third screen character, a successor to Charlot—and this time he would be more completely than ever before his own self, as he had become.

It is conceivable that that character, the old comedian turned into an old drunk by "my implacable, crushing duty to be funny," might have had for the movie millions the appeal once exerted by Marie Dressler, Will Rogers, or Wallace Beery, and so made of Charlie Chaplin a viable "star" again. It was not to be. Although Chaplin had not committed any public offenses on the political, or if we may be allowed the phrase, on the sexual front since *Monsieur Verdoux,* his enemies turned on him more virulently than even on that occasion. Their by now highly organized, highly vocal boycott prevented *Limelight* from being shown in the United States for a time (it was shown eventually but unsuccessfully) and inhibited the showing of his other films. Only a mighty revolt by press and public could have saved it. Before that had even a chance to take place, the United States Government in all its majesty had forbidden Chaplin to return to the country where for so long he had been a paying and highly profitable guest.

But of course, that was entirely the wrong attitude to take. The Attorney General put things in their right perspective when he said: "He has been *publicly charged* (italics mine) . . . with making statements that would indicate a leering, sneering attitude toward a country whose hospitality has enriched him." As for any revolt, in behalf of either Chaplin or of *Limelight*—"The violation by our government of those principles on which our country was founded," said Louis J. Halle, "was hardly noticed by our press and public. The rest of the world was more shocked, seeing the little tramp, in real life now, being chased by bullying policeman." Everyone at the time, with the likely exception of the Attorney General, must have thought of the end of *The Pilgrim*, with Charlie straddling the Mexican border, menaced from both sides, with nowhere in the world to go.

But of course he did have somewhere to go, to a Europe which fanned his resentment with its own resentment, and which enriched him by making *Limelight*, in spite of the American boycott, by far the most successful of his films. Out of his resentment he made *A King in New York*, which has never had a U.S. showing. This fourth screen character of Charles Chaplin was from all accounts a mere ventriloquist's dummy, a mouthpiece for his bitterness, and it was depressing to read in *The Manchester Guardian* that "to watch a new Chaplin film without once being made helpless with laughter and without shedding a solitary tear—here is food for tears indeed." Since then he has solved his anguish, dispersed his bitterness by an act of self-salvation, and once more come before us, not in his own person, but as the director of Marlon Brando and Sophia Loren—except for a brief flash of himself in which his expression seems to say that the human race does indeed beat all. The critics patronized *A Countess from Hong Kong* as old-fashioned—which it was, including the unfortunately old-fashioned fact that it occasioned more belly laughter than has been heard in many a year.

This old-fashioned *Countess* (he began writing her script in the 1930s) is undoubtedly not the last we shall see and hear of Charles Chaplin, if he remains with us. The profuseness of his invention is incredible. The films (and plays and novels and ballets) he merely planned, the ideas he brushed aside, the scenes he discarded would make a body of work which no film-maker to date could come near matching. The opening sequence of *Shoulder Arms*, photographed but never used, makes Buñuel and the other nightmare artists look unimaginative. The scene with the Armless Wonder which he cut out of *Limelight*—for reasons of length only—made one of the most poignant moments in that poignant film. One would give one's eyeteeth to see the "prologue" which, after one day's preparation, he staged for the premier of *A Woman of Paris*. One can but hope that he will somehow find a way to make the film he planned with Igor Stravinsky, the setting for which was a night club, with the Passion Play as floor show. It is this which sets him apart from all other stars. Stars are made by star-makers, by luck, by machinery and publicity, by, even, a trick of light. Charlie Chaplin is wholly his own creation. As such, we cannot really judge him in his lifetime or in ours. For now, he can only be fully understood by his fellow artists in all fields, who alone know from their own experience where he got what he has brought to us, and exactly how he transformed and transfigured it into Charlot and Verdoux and the old man of *Limelight* who enigmatically beckons us down the last corridors of time. When he was made an honorary member of the Société des Auteurs et Compositeurs Dramatiques, its president, Roger Ferdinand, wrote him:

In truth, real fame is never usurped; it only has a sense, a value and duration when it is turned to a good cause. And your victory is in the fact that you have human generosity and spontaneity that are not inhibited by rules or cleverness but stem from your own sufferings, your joys, hopes and disappointments; all that is understood by those who suffer beyond their strength and ask for pity, and who constantly hope to be comforted, to be made to forget for a moment, by that laughter which does not pretend to cure, but only to console.

One could imagine, even if we did not know it, the price that you have paid for this marvelous gift of being able to make us laugh and then suddenly cry. One can guess or, better still, perceive what sufferings you have yourself undergone to be able to portray in detail all those little things that touch so deeply, and which you have taken from moments of your own life.

For you have a good memory. You are faithful to the memories of your childhood. You have forgotten nothing of its sadness, its bereavements; you have wanted to spare others the harm you have suffered, or at least you have wanted to give everybody reason for hope. You have never betrayed your sad youth, and fame has never had the power to separate you from the past—for, alas, these things happen.

GLORIA SWANSON

Gloria Swanson has made more comebacks in motion pictures than any other star, to say nothing of her many appearances and reappearances on the stage and on television. She is both a living disproof, and a subtle, indirect proof, of the show-business maxim, "They never come back." For Miss Swanson's comebacks do not take in the sense of permanently restoring her to her once high place among the screen immortals. However much interest or curiosity her periodic reappearances provoke, it soon flags. Youth and vitality on the one hand and intensity of fan worship on the other are indissolubly connected, and never the twain shall part. Miss Swanson shows herself the old pro she is by never calling them "comebacks." She speaks instead of "returning" or "going back" to the screen, phrases which suggest a certain temporary quality. But the fact that in the thirty-six years since the end of her official stardom she has been given so many opportunities to "return" shows that in the eyes of the entertainment industry, and indeed of the public, Gloria Swanson was and is a star of stars, born for the camera and the spotlight.

Whether Miss Swanson's tiny body, disproportionately large head, prognathous jaw, huge eyes, dished nose, and enormous white teeth add up to great beauty or not is something the fans have disputed for years. But nobody has ever disputed that here is a woman who looks like drama. When she enters a room, any time, anywhere, every head turns. It amuses her to exploit it. Often she goes to a party in severe black, wearing

The first of Gloria Swanson's five husbands was, of all people, Wallace Beery, later a stellar comedian, villain, and lovable old cuss, but in his youth quite a blade. The wide-eyed young lady here is a far cry from the Swanson known to three generations of audiences. What the dog collar is doing around her neck is anybody's guess. A prisoner of love?

174

(Above) *Zaza,* 1923. Miss Swanson's stagy hauteur toward Rod La Rocque stamped her a great lady in the eyes of her adorers, and her coiffure and costume were further evidence that, in Paramount's proud boast, she was "the best-dressed star in Hollywood." Behind their hands, the dress designers to whom she paid fabulous sums called her the worst-dressed woman in the world.

(Left) *Beyond the Rocks,* 1922. Had Gloria Swanson entered one of the real-life counterparts of her glittering movie drawing rooms she would have created a sensation, but not of the kind she wanted. Her getup here is described as "an orchid satin brocade teagown banded in silver galloon and silver fox with hand-made ornaments of orchid fringe."

(Right) Unsatisfied with her position as queen of the box office, Miss Swanson aspired to higher things, including becoming an accomplished, rather than a nominal, actress. She was on her way to her goal when she made *The Coast of Folly,* 1925, in which she played her own mother and achieved a portrait of that characteristic phenomenon of the period, the flapper grandmother, complete with jeweled dog collar and blondined hair. She is seen here with Alec B. Francis.

an enormous, shadowing hat which she keeps lowered over her face for a time after she arrives. Then she lifts it, and Gloria Swanson is revealed. After that the attention is all hers. No others present, not even the youngest and most curvaceous, need apply.

When Cecil B. De Mille discovered and developed her, he cast her, not as the standard virginal heroine of those days, but as a smart young married woman, lavishly gowned and jeweled, with a look about her of someone to whom things happen. This new kind of heroine did things, went places, and met men who would have been unthinkable for the previous standard breed. The difference excited the public of the budding Jazz Age, and she exploited it to the hilt. So far as the author can discover, not one of the pictures she made between 1920 and 1932, from the dynamic *Manhandled* to the feeble *A Queen's Love Story,* lost money at the box office, while most of them earned fat sums for Paramount and later for Miss Swanson herself. Officially, Mary Pickford was still Queen of the Screen, but even her box office take could fall off when she departed from the only role in which the public wanted to see her. Not Swanson. She was the money magnet of the twenties, and as they wore on, to more and more people her image was the image of the typical movie star.

She lived her role to the hilt. As her salary soared, she gave up bothering about money and simply had her bills sent to Paramount, which paid them, deducted them from her wages, and deposited the remainder, if any, in the bank. When dresses were submitted for her approval—she never went shopping—she was apt, as she reminded Helen Jepson on the air a few years back, to order "a dozen of each in every color." In spite of her earnings, her extravagance kept her always in debt. In 1927 she came to New York to borrow $25,000. then blew more than that on having herself transported back to the West Coast in a private railway car. By her second husband, Herbert Somborn (her first, short-lived marriage was to Wallace Beery) she had a daughter at a time when this was considered the most unwise thing any female star could do. When, after her divorce from Somborn, she adopted a baby brother for little Gloria, the rumor went round that the boy was her own illegitimate son. When this came to her ears, she extracted an affidavit from the Paramount studio crew that she had been on the set and before the cameras at the precise moment when hospital records showed that her adopted son had been born—and published the affidavit.

Her peak moment came in 1925 when she returned from Europe with her French-made film *Madame Sans Gene* under one arm and her third husband, the Marquis de la Falaise de la Coudray, under the other. Her trip across the country was a triumphal tour. Jesse Lasky gave orders that when she arrived in Hollywood, Paramount's employees should turn out en masse in front of the studio for a "strictly spontaneous ovation." A reasonable facsimile of that was managed, but it didn't do Mr. Lasky any good. Almost her first act on arriving in California was to refuse his and Adolph Zukor's offer to renew her contract at a salary of a million dollars a year.

All this her public ate up greedily. What was the use of being a movie queen if you didn't queen it? And Gloria queened it for them in public, more royally and recklessly than any star until the advent of Elizabeth Taylor. Besides, they sensed beneath her surface recklessness a quality which has stood her in good stead all her life—cold courage, including the courage to take a chance when literally everything was at stake. And chance-taking was the popular sport of the late 1920's.

Miss Swanson's refusal of a million dollars a year from Paramount was not altogether the arrogant gesture it seemed. Douglas Fairbanks and Joseph M. Schenck had succeeded in convincing her that if she were to produce her own pictures for United Artists release, she would receive not only all the profits from her own productions but also a generous share of the distribution earnings, since she would be allowed gradually to buy in as a full partner in the company. Then she would indeed be, officially as well as actually, one of the immortals along with Mary and Doug and Charlie. The first of her independent pictures certainly showed her star quality. Since it was Swanson they loved and wanted, she would give them Swanson to the last full measure. In *The Love of Sunya* she played no less than five separate parts. Unfortunately, the picture had little else to recommend it. In 1952, while being photographed presenting the film to the Museum of Modern Art Film Library, Miss Swanson said *sotto voce* to the author, "It was a turkey then and it's still a turkey, but if you want it, be my guest." In spite of its many shortcomings, it was a reasonably profitable picture solely on the basis of its star's box office magnetism. But Gloria was a little shaken by its unfavorable reception in both the ordinary and the trade press. Every picture was now a gamble to win or lose, and she began to realize that as an independent she had to win all the time. Determined to restore her prestige to its peak, and also to demonstrate something hitherto considered debatable, her artistry, she decided to film John Colton's *Rain,* in spite of the fact that Will Hays had forbidden all producers to bring the play to the screen. She got around this edict by the simple expedient of buying the short story on which the play was based, Somerset Maugham's "Miss Thompson," labeling the resulting film *Sadie Thompson,* and blandly denying any connection with *Rain.*

The picture was by far her best, and under Raoul Walsh's direction Miss Swanson and Lionel Barrymore as prostitute and clergyman struck sparks from each other—and *wowed* the public. Seemingly vindicated in her box office judgment, and in her tacit defiance of the Hays Office, Gloria resolved on an even more daring ploy.

Against everyone's advice, she engaged Erich von Stroheim to direct her in his own story, *Queen Kelly.* Like the rest of Hollywood, she was convinced that he could get a great performance out of almost any actress, and she wanted to be next on the list. But at this phase of his career it was Mr. von Stroheim's pleasure to play a sort of cat-and-mouse game with producers. He would sell them stories which they liked and approved, but after he finished directing the film, the story would prove to be quite different from the one they had originally bought. So with *Queen Kelly.* When, after four months of work, Miss Swanson found herself playing the madam of an East African brothel, she realized that even if she finished the picture it couldn't be shown anywhere, so she halted production and shelved the half-completed film at a loss—to herself and to an investor named Joseph Kennedy—of some $800,000.

From this disaster Miss Swanson made a brilliant recovery, going immediately into her first talking picture, *The Trespasser,* which Edmund Goulding directed from his own script. Her voice, singing as well as speaking, proved to be one of the best revealed by the new medium. *The Trespasser* was an outstanding success. But its profits hardly repaid the dead loss of *Queen Kelly,* and both her bankers and United Artists urged her to make another film as quickly as possible to capitalize on the popularity of *The Trespasser. Photoplay,* reviewing the result, *What A Widow!,* said, "Gloria Swanson bit her polished fingernails to the quick trying to find a vehicle as grand as *The Trespasser*. She didn't do it in this broad comedy, with good old Sennett moments." Her next two pictures, *Indiscreet* and *Tonight or Never,* were equally light, and while they made as much money as the average film of 1931-32, their earnings hardly approximated the lush Swanson grosses of the past. Something was happening, and everybody seemed to know it except the star herself. A friend put it in a nutshell: Gloria doesn't understand the difference between fame and popularity." She was of course still a world-famous figure, but the figures she cut in the world, the arrogant, luxurious, exotic actress, loaded with jewels and surrounded by scads of men, no longer sparked the admiration and envy that it had in the twenties. It was at this moment that Miss Swanson chose to marry for a fourth time, this time the European playboy Michael Farmer. Unfortunately her wedding date happened to be 2 months before her divorce from the Marquis de la Falaise was final, and she had to go through the ceremony again to avoid trouble with the law. She got away with it, but there began to be a general feeling among press and public that she was getting away with entirely too much. Apparently unaware of this, Miss Swanson had hastily filmed *Tonight or Never,* in the later scenes of which her pregnancy was rather obvious, then sailed for Europe to "await the stork." The stork arrived six months after her wedding day.

In the meantime she had arranged with United Artists to make her last independent production for them, in England. Out of her element in Elstree, Miss Swanson and the production floundered. She changed directors and scriptwriters, but nothing seemed to cure the weakness of a story which anyhow seemed to belong to the twenties. Thorold Dickinson, the British director who was then a film editor, remembers that he was cutting the picture, called *Perfect Understanding,* when the star-producer put her head in the door of his cutting room and asked, "What's gone wrong today?" He replied, "Nothing, Miss Swanson, for the simple reason that there's nothing left to go wrong. The only thing that could happen now would be for the laboratory to burn down." It did, of course, and the heroic efforts of the cutting-room girls saved the negative of *Perfect Understanding.*

They might have spared themselves the trouble for all the picture meant to Miss Swanson's future. It opened in New York in February 1933, during the grim weeks just before the inauguration of the Roosevelt administration. Poor notices and weak attendance would have justified its closing within a week or less. But Mary Pickford, whose *Secrets* was scheduled to follow it at the Rivoli Theatre, refused to permit her picture to open until the financial crisis had eased. The Rivoli, lacking any other attraction, had no choice but to continue with *Perfect Understanding* and to issue advertising which brightly announced that the picture had been "held over by popular demand" a second, third, and even fourth week, although it played to virtually empty houses. Finally Miss Pickford had to yield, and *Secrets* opened—whereupon, as noted, Roosevelt immediately declared the bank holiday of March 1933! *Secrets,* as well as *Perfect Understanding,* was one of the financial disasters of 1933.

Perhaps the public knew of all this, but the industry was well aware what it meant. Miss Swanson's prestige was badly damaged. Without a contract, and with insufficient capital to continue in independent production, she returned to Hollywood to, as she put it, "begin again." What began for her was an ordeal as subtly demoralizing as any known to civilized man. To be a great star idling in Hollywood, surrounded by colleagues and friends who are in the thick of day-to-day movie-making, is to suffer daily affronts to self-respect and professional pride, whether anyone intends them as affronts or not. Miss Swanson grimly set her jaw and waited for offers. They came. She was asked to play Josephine to Edward G. Robinson's Napoleon in a film that was never made. She was offered the role eventually played by Carole Lombard in *Twentieth Century.* Samuel Goldwyn actually announced her for *Barbary Coast,* which, when it was finally filmed two years later, starred Miriam Hopkins. The trouble was that none of these offers seemed quite "good" enough to Miss Swanson—or quite "right" enough, as they say in the profession. What Miss Swanson meant by "right" was a role and a picture which would restore her at one bound to her former commanding position. That was not very likely in the circumstances, but she could not know that—not after so many years of unrivaled fame and success. She waited some more. The offers grew fewer.

Then, suddenly, everything seemed to right itself. She was offered the contract with Irving Thalberg, the fiasco of which has already been described. With its expiration, Gloria knew herself to be in dire danger. Absent from the screen for more than a year, her last two pictures far from successful, she must have listened apprehensively for the dread phrase "has-been." She didn't hear it. What she would have heard had she eavesdropped was an industry-wide debate on what was called in so many words "the Swanson problem." The problem was circular; Miss Swanson was too proud, and too fearful of another failure, to accept anything less than a top role in a top production, while producers in their turn were fearful that, in spite of her long and remarkable record, she no longer had sufficient box office draw to justify the expenditure and risk involved. Eternally young, beautiful, and magnetic at thirty five she was still very much a part of the Hollywood scene. People knew that under her queenly airs there was a heart, and that it beat in rhythm with reality. Her many marriages, which had begun to tell against her with the public, were to insiders simply proof of her indomitable belief in the possibility of living happily ever after. Arrogant she might be among strangers, in order to maintain her "position," but those in the picture colony who knew her—and they were many, after so long a career—knew her as softhearted, fun-loving, a fair fighter in the clinches—in short, a dead game sport. A tottering queen of her eminence would normally have been a sitting duck for Hollywood snipers, but few took advantage of the opportunities her anomalous position gave them; she was too much respected and too well-liked. She gained by comparison with her fellow divas. Her arrogance was never comparable to that of her rival, Constance Bennett, of whom it was said that her chief characteristic was the ability to put others at a disadvantage. As for Joan Crawford—Alexander Kirkland once said to the author: "Why can't Joan ever forget for a single second that she's Joan Crawford? She doesn't have to remind us all the time—we know. Look at Swanson. Gloria gets drunk when she wants to get drunk and stays sober when she wants to stay sober, and if you don't like what she does you know what *you* can do." Few in pictures had that much courage and poise, and such conduct provoked admiration rather than envy. It also stirred a desire to help before it was too late. Friends urged her to "get back on the screen at any cost" but she still determinedly pursued the will-o'-the wisp of the golden picture which at one stroke would put her back where she had been ten years earlier. It never materialized. Offered a one-picture deal by M-G-M,

(Right) *Her Gilded Cage,* 1922. The dewy Swanson of the teens gave place to a rather tough-looking customer at the beginning of her starring career, but the waitresses and shopgirls who formed the core of her legion of fans thought her just gorgeous and wanted to be exactly like her. The girls in long johns were the acme of arty sex, or sexy art, in 1922.

(Above) One of the great romantic ruins of the twentieth century. Gloria Swanson almost missed the chance to make her wonderful "return" in *Sunset Boulevard,* 1950. Billy Wilder thought he was indulging in straight typecasting when he cast the fifty-one-year-old Miss Swanson as the fifty-year-old Norma Desmond, only to find when she appeared on the set that she looked fifteen years younger than her age. Make-up, lighting, and even diet had to be called on to produce the extraordinary image above.

(Left center) Married to a marquis, at the head of her own company, Gloria Swanson by 1927 had acquired a sort of glazed, *haute* 1920s elegance. But in spite of her continued maturation, this still from her first independent production, *The Love of Sunya,* reveals that, as Allene Talmey said, "the charming and hateful and dignified Marquise de la Falaise de la Coudray is still hard-boiled."

(Left bottom) Her success in the talkies revealed a less plangent Swanson, poised and vibrant yet relaxed, with an excellent speaking and singing voice. On our screen: the temperamental prima donna of *Music in the Air,* 1934, with Joseph Cawthorn.

456-2

she was being fitted for costumes for *Daisy Kenyon* when she suddenly decided that the story was not "right" and walked out. She was posing for publicity pictures for *The Second Mrs. Draper* on the Columbia lot when she learned that in the film she would be playing the mother of a grown daughter. That, of course, would never do. (It is interesting that neither of these stories were subsequently filmed by other players. It would seem that the opportunities which she so emphatically rejected had been tailored to her measure.) Meanwhile Miss Swanson, a star without a salary, dared not reduce her flamboyant standard of living, for that would have cost her both prestige and credit, but carried on as best she could by selling story rights to her old pictures and making radio broadcasts when she could get them. It was at this point that a fan magazine published a story on the unfashionable topic "Do You Want Swanson Back?" Miss Swanson wrote the editor, "It is a warm feeling to have someone fighting for you, and, I must say, rather an odd experience."

The idle years dragged by. One day in 1938 Miss Swanson bumped into a producer friend who began the conversation with an embarrassed explanation that he had nothing "right" for her just now. Since she never asked him for a job, she concluded that the only thing that came into people's minds when they met her was that she was out of work. One thing that everyone will concede Gloria is that she is as proud as she is brave. In her enormous, outmoded Sunset Boulevard mansion, not unlike the one inhabited by Norma Desmond in *Sunset Boulevard,* she gave a cocktail party. There she announced that she was through with Hollywood because Hollywood was through with her. Then she sold everything and left for New York. It was a magnificent, a truly Swansonian gesture.No one else has ever made one like it. The rest cling as long as they can, and then creep away unnoticed.

Through the years people had told her that, had she not been star material, she was intelligent and energetic enough to succeed in any line of work she attempted. She invested the remnant of her millions of earnings, $250,000, in a firm she founded, Multiprises, Inc., which developed and marketed patent inventions. But in spite of intelligence and energy, Miss Swanson lacked sufficient capital power, and the profits from her company went mostly to those who had it, although she still receives royalties from a few inventions. She had in the course of business rescued promising inventors from Nazi-occupied Austria, and they and her other associates in the firm still speak with admiration and sometimes with awe of her grasp of technicalities. But after this experience she knew that she should stick to her last. In the early forties, Miss Swanson hit the sawdust trail of her profession and toured the hinterlands and summer stock in such plays as *Reflected Glory* and *Let Us Be Gay*—old comedies transmogrified to show off her glamour and flair for clothes rather than her ability as an actress. To those who sought out these curiosities when they played the Bronx or Brooklyn, it was notable that her audiences consisted chiefly of women whose graying locks were bobbed in the style of the twenties.

In 1941, while on a visit to her mother on the West Coast, Miss Swanson was suddenly, and rather unaccountably, after a seven-year absence from the screen, invited by RKO to co-star with Adolphe Menjou in *Father Takes a Wife,* a comedy by Dorothy and Herbert Fields. It had a pretty good switcheroo idea in the embarrassment of a wealthy father, Menjou, before his strait-laced son and daughter-in-law when he takes a famous actress, Miss Swanson, to wife. But the Fieldses were unable to take the idea very far, and the result was only mildly entertaining—certainly not that "right" vehicle which she had insisted upon through the thirties, nor the smashing return her still numerous fans had hoped for.

Would it lead to better things? Miss Swanson talked herself out of the role of Mother Gin-Sling in Josef von Sternberg's *The Shanghai Gesture* by offering Sternberg another version of the script which she owned and in which, by strange coincidence, her part was more prominent than in the original. "I need an actress, Miss Swanson, not a writer," said Sternberg in ending negotiations. No other acceptable offers apparently were received, and Gloria shelved any comeback hopes she may have had and returned to her theatrical touring, and to experiments with television when television was young.

Eight years later, in 1949, Charles Brackett and Billy Wilder invited her to California to play what she thought was to be a small part in a new film about Hollywood. It proved, of course, to be *Sunset Boulevard,* in which she created a sensation unparalleled by any other star who has returned to the screen after years of absence. Her subsequent personal appearance tour to sell the picture for Paramount was also a triumph. From shady semi-obscurity, Miss Swanson was back in the spotlight as she had not been since the twenties. Was she also restored to stardom? It seemed so at first. She made another picture, *Three for Bedroom C,* rather a weak one, and enjoyed a highly successful run in the Broadway revival of *Twentieth Century.* Then, in the fall of 1951, Miss Swanson made a bad *gaffe.* Trying out the play *Nina* in Philadelphia, she publicly denounced the director, Gregory Ratoff, for incompetence. When this news reached New York, advance ticket sales rapidly fell off and the play closed after only a few weeks on Broadway. Whether this lapse from the professional code has barred her from further stage stardom in New York—in which at that time she seemed to have a considerable future—no one knows for sure. More probably, if her appearances today on stage, screen, and television are less frequent than her admirers could wish, it is for a quite different reason. She is too indelibly Gloria Swanson. Lillian Gish may play "old ladies," from the haunted, pathetic derelict of *A Trip to Bountiful* to the haughty Mary Todd Lincoln, with a whole spectrum of others in between. But the image of Miss Swanson as the effulgent silent screen-star of *Sunset Boulevard* has been so firmly imprinted on the public mind that directors, in spite of her long experience, versatility, and innate artistry, hesitate to cast her as anything else. She must always play Gloria Swanson—a bit larger than life.

She is content with the role and plays it to the hilt—a glamour queen still in her early seventies, with all the perquisites that ought to go with the object of public idolatry. At the beginning of her career she said, "When I'm a star, I want everyone to know it." Everyone did, and does. She is, like them all, capable of the self-delusions of show business. After the hit of *Sunset Boulevard,* Hedda Hopper and her other friends were trying hard to think of a follow-up that would consolidate Miss Swanson's comeback. Someone suggested that the famous scenarist, Frances Marion, also a friend of Gloria's, be asked to do a treatment of Frances Parkinson Keyes's best-selling *Dinner at Antoine's,* in which the leading role was that of the mother of a grown daughter. "No," snapped Gloria, "that part's too old for me." This may have been understandable back in the days when she refused *The Second Mrs. Draper* for the same reason, but since she had just successfully played a fifty-year-old star desperately trying to recapture her youth, her reaction left her friends and well-wishers somewhat at sea. But beneath such self-delusion is a streak of realism unique to Gloria Swanson. At the time when she refused Paramount's offer of a million dollars a year, she remarked, "I'll bet if I wasn't Gloria Swanson, I not only wouldn't be offered a million a year, I couldn't get a job in this town, not even a bit." That sort of thing is often said by the outwardly successful but inwardly insecure. But more was to come. Shortly there arrived at the Pasadena station, apparently from New York, a chorus girl with blond curls, heavy make-up, and garish clothes. She had the right introductions to the right people, was passed around the studios, and had screen tests at three of them, including Paramount. The results were negative and she was declared hopeless as screen material. Then the chorus cutie threw off her disguise and revealed herself as Gloria Swanson, the most valuable property on the screen. People laughed, of course, but a little grimly. Miss Swanson had introduced a *momento mori* into the Hollywood feast.

NORMA TALMADGE

Norma Talmadge one of the greatest stars of all time? Why? Who *was* Norma Talmadge, anyway? The younger generations ask this question in all sincerity. Miss Talmadge's legend perished with her career, which perished a long time ago. That she *was* one of the great, cold grosses prove. If the young know her not, that is because most of her films have disappeared. They are shown neither in museums nor, even in flashes, on television, because Joseph M. Schenck, who owned the negatives, allowed them to disintegrate; it was the real Norma he loved, not her shadowed simulacrum. So new viewers who know lesser figures like Theda Bara, because they have caught at least a glimpse of them in television reprises of the silent days, know Norma Talmadge if at all only in the form of a faded, greenish rotogravure picture from a fan magazine, with a curved nose and soulful eyes, wrapped in chinchilla, an expensive-looking movie star of the twenties, nothing more.

In a remarkably prophetic article of 1930 called "Will History Remember Them?" a fan writer predicted that Miss Talmadge had less chance of lasting in memory than any of the original movie greats for the singular reason that she was too versatile. Unlike certain other big favorites, she did not establish a single type which caught the public fancy and stick to it through thick and thin. She played everything. It is true that in her last years on the screen she was more often than not an exemplar of Noble Womanhood, but that was chiefly in tactful obeisance to the establishment of the Hays Office and its new code of conduct for screen stars, on as well as off. When she began in 1910 as the leading light of Vitagraph, she played, like Mary Pickford and her other contemporaries, ingénues, children, "adventuresses," polite prostitutes, tough madams, or whatever was dictated by the stark necessity of turning out two films a week fifty-two weeks in the year. As films grew longer, so did her roles, but she did not shoot up to stardom as others of her period and years did. She had been on the screen seven years when short, squat, unprepossessing Joseph M. Schenck met her, fell madly in love with her, married her, and literally did his level best to lay the world at her feet. Since she was a movie star,

Norma Talmadge in 1917. This fresh young beauty was already a movie pioneer when, after nine years on the screen, she simultaneously struck the fancy of producer Joseph M. Schenck and of the new middle-class audience now flooding into the theaters. The combination was a lucky one; the pictures in which Schenck starred her made her an enduring favorite only slightly second to Mary Pickford.

185

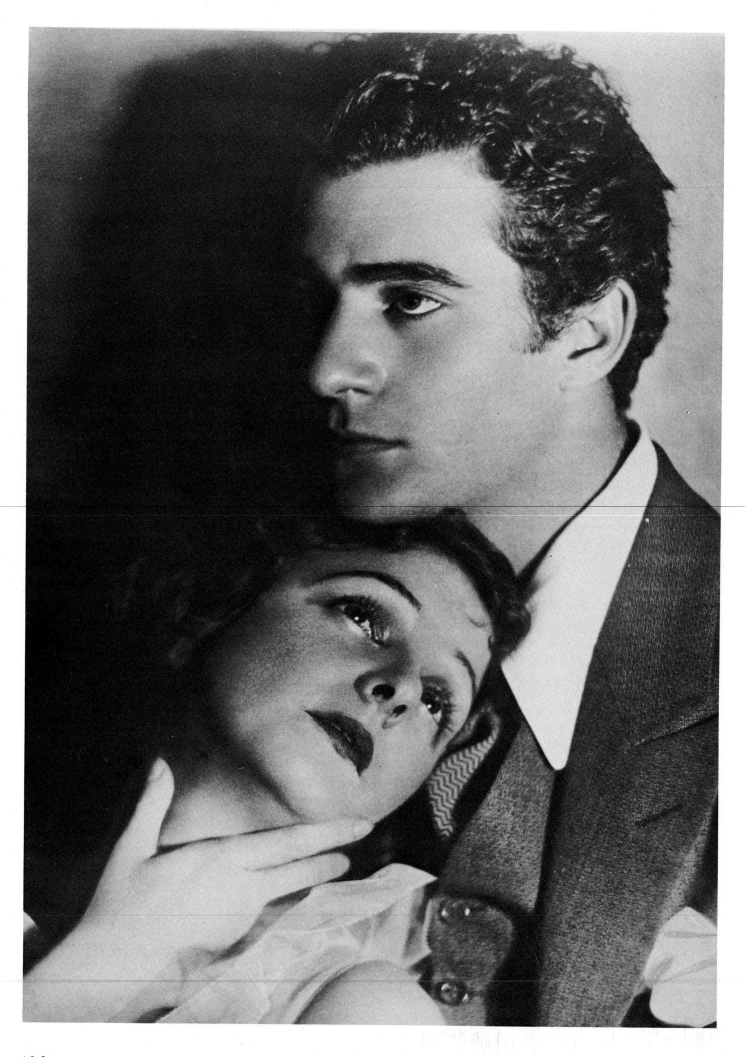

(Above) Though the Norma Talmadge films were star vehicles first, last, and always, they seldom lacked the primitive action which was at once the basic stuff of movies and the starting gun for the star's histrionics. Here the trigger is pulled by an unknown player, Lew Cody is the victim, and Miss Talmadge is clearly about to take off on an emotional bender.

(Above right) *Song of Love,* 1923. "All through her career," wrote Paul Rotha in *The Film Till Now,* "Norma Talmadge achieved success by looking slightly perplexed and muzzy about the eyes. But audiences worshiped her; wrote to her for signed photographs; hung them over their beds and got a thrill out of them; and told their friends how great an actress she was."

(Right) Norma Talmadge with Ronald Colman.

(Left) The very young Gilbert Roland and the veteran Miss Talmadge in their "modern dress" *Camille,* 1927, springboard for their off-screen affair.

(Below) Muzzy they may have looked in many of her films, but the eyes which Norma Talmadge turned to the camera as the old woman in *The Lady,* 1923, were both calculating and pain-tempered. What she gave to the part she had learned from her mother, the dauntless Peg Talmadge. She is seen here with Marc McDermott.

that meant making her the greatest of all stars so far as that lay in his power, and he set about it with everything he had. From that time on, Miss Talmadge had the best directors, stories, sets, costumes, casts, and publicity that Mr. Schenck could provide—and he was in position to provide practically anything. She never made anything approaching a great picture, or even any really very important ones, except for the money they made, which was plenty. But she acquired a world audience of millions of women who would go to see her in anything (the real test of star quality). They might love Mary Pickford and admire and envy Gloria Swanson, but they wanted to *be* Norma Talmadge. Such romantic things happened to her in her pictures!

The highbrows would have none of her. Paul Rotha said, "All through her long career Norma Talmadge has captured and held her fans through nothing more than a slightly muzzy look about the eyes." This was on the whole unjust. It is true that the element in acting known as "characterization" was not her strong point. Costumed as an Algerian slave girl in *The Voice from the Minaret* or as Balzac's Duchesse de Langeais in *The Eternal Flame,* she was still Norma Talmadge—which was what her fans wanted her to be anyhow. But either innate instinct, or her long apprenticeship in early films, had given her a grasp of other essentials of acting which produced performances that linger in the memory. Or rather, fragments of performances, isolated scenes interspersed between action or romance or melodrama. She could be sick, really sick, convincingly, one of the hardest things for any actor or actress to do without the aid of a bandage around the head. And she, the lovely, romantic-looking Norma, could be old, really old. In the best of her films, *The Lady,* we see her at the beginning and the end as a seventy-year-old tough-looking cafe owner in Paris. In between, the flashbacks, she is seen as a London chorus girl, as the wife of a nobleman, and as a demimondaine, and all this is well enough. But it was the old woman who impressed, who became almost a part of one's own experience and understanding of life. She was, as aforesaid, tough, and toughly she goes about solving the melodramatic puzzle the plot sets her, involving the legitimacy and destiny of her son. That was about all that the picture basically required of her, but Miss Talmadge added many grace notes. Her old age was not a matter of white hair and stooped shoulders. She outwits her opponents in the film because she knows more about life than they do, and it shows in her eyes and the set of her head. What shows, too, in her eyes and in the way she approaches people, is a certain fearfulness, a consciousness of time and death, and that however handsome the deck, the cards, for everybody, are stacked: "all things Strike an unhappy balance in the end." It was quite a performance. It is a pity that *The Lady* is one of her lost films. It would show today that Norma Talmadge was, whatever else she also was, an actress who knew what acting is. It was not among her biggest hits, people preferred her in things like *Graustark,* and it is entirely possible that Mr. Rotha is right and it was not Miss Talmadge's acting that made her fans love her, but the slightly muzzy look about the eyes.

About the real Norma Talmadge, the world celebrity, the most famous member of the famous Talmadge dynasty, the wife of the president of United Artists, there are two opinions, difficult to reconcile because the difference in opinion shows up among those who knew her best. In remarking that Constance Talmadge could readily give up movie stardom if something equally amusing could quickly be shoved in its place, Allene Talmey said that, in contrast, "Norma Talmadge loves the movies, needs the movies," that her stardom was the central and most valued fact of her life. But Anita Loos, who certainly knew the Talmadge family as well as anybody, once wrote "Norma Talmadge was a figure of romance all over the world, but I never knew any girl who was less to be envied." According to Miss Loos, Norma Talmadge was bored—bored with everything. She was pushed into stardom, to which she herself was indifferent, by her mother and Joseph Schenck. She was bored by the luxurious life provided by her adoring husband, and as for the ego satisfactions of movie queendom, when people said to her "Aren't you Norma Talmadge?" she replied, "No, I am not that common movie girl" and turned away. It is hard to credit, though Miss Loos ought to know. It is in any case a hard fact that, apparently to rouse herself from torpor, she resorted to ever kickier kicks, including cocaine. It is also a fact that as her career wore on her pictures became fewer and fewer, that she seemed reluctant to begin them, though she became interested and worked hard once production started. The arrival of the talkies seemed to rouse her, to challenge her. She worked hard for a year with voice coaches to eliminate her rather pronounced Brooklyn accent, and the release of her first talkie, *New York Nights,* was so long delayed that her well-wishers feared that she had failed to pass the talkie test entirely. Appropriately cast as the wife of a Tin Pan Alley songwriter, she gave a creditable performance vocally and visually, and the picture was well received. But her second talkie, *Dubarry, Woman of Passion,* was a disaster of historic proportions. This picture survives and should be studied today, though only as a specimen of the difficulties confronted, and the false solutions arrived at, by directors faced in 1929 and 1930 with the problem of reconciling the technique of the silent film with the new elements introduced by sound. *Dubarry* was taken from an old play by David Belasco, the high-flown speeches of which were preserved intact, but interspersed with irrelevant "action" scenes typical of the silent film at its most elementary. Miss Talmadge as Dubarry declaiming to Louis XV "Will you give me the stars to shine in my hair?"; Miss Talmadge receiving from the monarch thousand-dollar gowns for which, the dialogue told us, she gave in return only "saucy smiles"; Miss Talmadge discovered by her lover, Conrad Nagel, bathing nude in a pool apparently situated in a public park in Paris—it was incredible, absurd, interminable.

There was genuine sorrow among the Talmadge fans when *Dubarry* appeared. The downfall of a movie star is usually accompanied by a deafening silence on the part of the public, but Norma's people wrote to the fan magazines to say how sorry they were that she had not made it in the talkies. They made clear, however, that the Talmadge illusion and legend was gone forever. The star herself had three more pictures to make according to her contract, but she canceled them by mutual consent and firmly announced that she was retired. But what next? She was still young, still beautiful, and very, very rich. What should she do with herself? Under the nose of her submissive though far from complaisant husband, she had taken her leading man, Gilbert Roland, as a lover. Now she discarded him and, after the death of her mother, divorced Mr. Schenck. A couple of years later she became the mistress and then the wife of George Jessel, who, to capitalize on her fading fame, arranged a personal appearance tour in which she stood motionless on the stage, a spotlighted, glittering figure, a mere stooge for Jessel's clowning. She tired of Jessel and went to live in Europe for a time. Fitfully she contemplated a comeback, and actually made tests for the role of Pilar in *For Whom the Bell Tolls,* unsuccessful tests. Wracked by severe arthritis, and still addicted to cocaine, she at last married a doctor, who made her last years as comfortable as possible. She died comparatively young in 1957.

The severe disagreement among her intimates as to what Norma Talmadge was really like is strange. After all, she is no remote historic figure, subject to baseless speculation, but a famous woman of the twentieth century who got around, knew people, and in her day was never out of the public eye. One thing is sure: Whether her acting talent gave her little satisfaction, whether or not her private life was dominated by melancholia, she was a Talmadge, first, last, and always, and in full possession of her share of the Talmadge wit. Her marriage to George Jessel ended in a divorce which was anything but amicable; it was acrimonious on both sides. Some years later Miss Talmadge fell severely ill in Florida and was once at the point of death, but she recovered and was on the mend when Mr. Jessel heard for the first time, or pretended to hear for the first time, of her sickness. He phoned from New York to inquire anxiously how she was. Her maid came into Miss Talmadge's sickroom and said, "Mr. Jessel wants to know how you are. I didn't know what you'd want me to tell him, so I didn't tell him anything. He's still on the phone. What shall I say?"

"Tell him," replied the recuperating Miss Talmadge, "that I died and left him all my money."

WILLIAM S. HART

Two-Gun Bill Hart! The phrase had powerful magic. The two-gun tradition still has magic today, but it is a magic worn as thin as the silver spoons handed down by our ancestors, through constant repetition of every detail and variation of the Western drama. Small wonder: The West is the only tradition we have of the wild, active, masculine life, except for the Civil War and, of course, the Revolution, about which, singularly, no successful film has ever been made. The kids of the 1960s still thrill to the gunfight at the OK Corral, but it is a thrill with a difference. They know, because publicity has dinned it into them, that the hero is a law student or garage mechanic singled out by some producer because of his slim hips and wide shoulders; brought to Hollywood and taught to shoot from the hip by experts in firearms; taught such horsemanship as is necessary to today's not-so-hard-riding Westerns; taught how to use his fists effectively for the camera—and how to pull his punches so he won't hurt the villain. Even as the kids of 1916 they may admire and envy Western heroes—but their envy is apt to take the form of wanting to go to Hollywood and be cowboy stars themselves, rather than lead the life the actors simulate.

Bill Hart was a man of the West. Not, of course, the West of Lewis and Clark, or of the days of '49, but the West of that second, uncelebrated, anonymous wave of settlers who came along behind the pioneers and consolidated their gains. His father was a miller who searched for water-power sites and founded mills in Minnesota and Wisconsin in the days when those states were still inhibited chiefly by Blackfeet and Sioux; Bill could speak Sioux before he was six, and as a boy he learned to ride, hunt, trap, protect himself, and survive in a country which was still wild, unknown, and dangerous. When

The loner. William S. Hart fixed for all time the image of the character in Western legend who rides into the town from nowhere, becomes briefly involved in a multitude of human destinies, and strides out again into the night, once more alone. Every subsequent Western hero has partaken of something of this character, but no one since Hart has expressed it so completely by the mere expression on his face. Money, women, booze—all seemed secondary to his profound search for himself.

(Left) Again because of the expression on his face, the gun battles in Hart's films really seemed to be fought for life-and-death stakes.

(Above) The loner in his solitude harbored volcanic passions which must needs find expression. The studio caption for this still from *Branding Broadway* says: "Hart as Bob Sands of the Three Bar Ranch decides to take a town apart in search of excitement and is stopped by the Law and Order League. Then he is shipped out of town."

(Right) Even the great Hart, and even so early as 1916, had to submit to publicity gimmicks like this for *John Petticoats*.

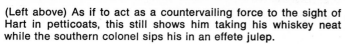

(Left above) As if to act as a countervailing force to the sight of Hart in petticoats, this still shows him taking his whiskey neat while the southern colonel sips his in an effete julep.

(Right) When Hart received requests for autographed pictures from his kid fans, he knew they had to include his horse.

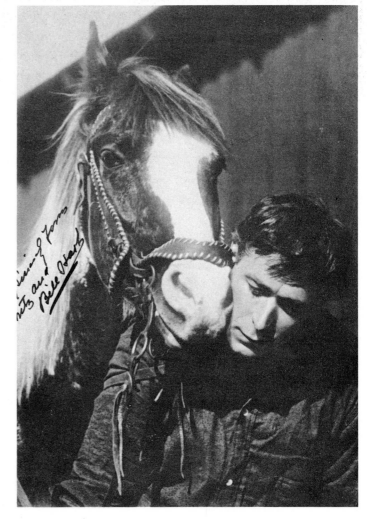

his family moved back East, this hard-bitten young fellow, trained to nothing but an outdoor life, succumbed to an unaccountable urge to become an actor. In the nineties and early 1900s he was leading man to stars like Modjeska and Julia Arthur, played many Shakespearean roles, and was the first Messala in *Ben Hur*. The year he entered the movies, 1912, was by odd coincidence the year of the official closing of the frontier, with the admission of New Mexico to the Union.

The Western tradition was already firmly established on the screen by that time; it had been taken over bodily from the touring wild West shows of earlier days. But the Westerns William S. Hart saw when he joined Thomas H. Ince in California seemed to him ridiculously theatrical and unreal versions of frontier life. He had already starred on the stage in such Western dramas as *The Virginian* and *The Squaw Man* and achieved such verisimilitude as was possible within the limitations of that medium. He now determined to use the unlimited scope of the screen to furnish forth the frontier in all its authentic detail as he himself had known it.

Nobody asked him to do this. He was just another actor brought into the movies on the gamble that he would make a hit with their larger public. It was some urge within himself that made Hart want to make his Westerns realistic rather than romantic or merely melodramatic or violent. Not that he scorned melodrama and violence, for they were as much a part of the real West as of the fake one. As for romance, that was a somewhat different matter. The Western man as he knew him may have been polite, gallant, or shy with a maiden of a respectable family, especially if Papa was around. But the West of his day was short of women, and you took your women where and when you found them, with few of the preliminary niceties. And the women, being the kind of women they were likely to be in that country, knew what it was to be taken casually and even roughly, nor did they expect fidelity ever after. If the Hart films were shown in their entirety today, their sexual aspects would undoubtedly astound the country, even in this period of elaborately self-conscious amorality.

Panning gold, trekking across the plains, hunting outlaws or being hunted yourself— Hart's activities in his Westerns were of a pattern all too familiar to everybody. But he pieced them together in a way that made them seem, not just adventure for the adventurous-minded, but a grim and necessary way of winning a living from a hard world. Perhaps the best of his many excellent films was the early *Hell's Hinges*, 1915. For it and other films, he and Ince "leased" a tribe of Indians from the Government, real Indians to whom Hart had to talk in a version of their own language and in pantomime. And there were still around in California, so soon after the closing of the frontier, plenty of hunters, trappers, gold-panners, and just plain hard-riding hell-raisers glad enough to pick up easy money in movie-making. Only the top roles in his films were cast from professional actors; the rest were men and women of the West. The result had a verisimilitude still highly impressive. The characters stood out from the screen in relief, and they seemed not actors in costume but ordinary people doing just what they did every day of their ordinary lives. As for the central figure in these films, Hart himself, who came to be known as the Good Bad Man (no one seems to know where the phrase came from), he was of course a descendant of the Strong Silent Man, but with a difference in that the Good Bad Man illustrated the complexity of that frontier code of conduct which grew up in the West before the coming of the law. His good-badness was not a moral paradox but a reflection of environmental conditions.

Hart was a figure who fascinated the whole world—and his pictures penetrated into every part of the world. In Sweden he was known as "Billhart," in France as "Rio Jim," in the jungles of the Congo as "William Cowboy." His grim poker face, so seldom broken by a smile, seemed to express every emotion because he was so careful to express none. "That stern yet impassioned figure," the French called him—the French who were the first to understand that his Westerns were not only epic in their background, and epic in the nature of their action, but that the character of Hart himself was an epic one, a Homeric figure whose actions and passions seemed to spring from the deepest wells of life. Small boys adored him and tried to emulate him, just as they adored and emulated Fairbanks. By 1917 he commanded a salary of $17,000 a week, exceeded only by those of Mary Pickford and Charlie Chaplin, and demanded and received complete control over every aspect of his films.

Then something happened. The moral revolution of the early 1920s, resulting in a sort of witch hunt after everything "Victorian," made the Hart films seem suddenly rather naive and old-fashioned. Tom Mix (who had actually preceded Hart on the screen) began to sweep the field with his compeers Ken Maynard and Hoot Gibson in their fancy boots, white sombreros, and even white riding clothes. The contrast between the trick getups of Mix (which it must be admitted did really represent one aspect of the West, the cowboy's love of display) and Hart's grimy clothes—you could almost smell the horse sweat on him—went all to the advantage of Mix in the eyes of a new generation. So did the simple, superficial, shoot-it-out plots of the Mix films in contrast to the orotund moralities of Hart, especially as expressed in his subtitles. Hart himself remained personally popular, but exhibitors began to write in that their audiences found his films out-of-date. Finally, Paramount asked Hart to relinquish control over the story and direction and to appear simply as a star in vehicles made by others.

Hart would not agree. He was aware of the difference between the conventional conception of the West and his own version of it. What Hart failed to realize was that the new audiences of the 1920s were no longer interested in the actualities of the old West. He and Paramount could not agree, and Hart allowed his contract to lapse.

After a year away from the screen he went to United Artists, which he had refused to join when it was originally organized, and made with his own money what proved to be his last film. *Tumbleweeds,* 1926, was a creditable production in typical Hart style, but audiences who went to see it to welcome their hero back to the screen got the shock of their lives. The man was old, and no amount of camera magic could disguise it. He had come to the screen late in his acting career, and time in the meanwhile had not stood still. He simply could not be convincing any more in the physical feats of action pictures. Hart toyed with the idea of making additional films, and when the talkies arrived he took sound tests, but it was obvious that from now on he would be suitable only for character parts, and what was the point of that, after having been William S. Hart? He had saved his money and bought a huge ranch in southwestern California to which he retired and was seldom seen thereafter in Hollywood. His marriage to silent star Dorothy Davenport was short-lived, and after it ended he lived in isolation among his cherished horses and dogs. He lived in apparent contentment. For the Bill Hart of real life, like the Bill Hart of the screen, was fundamentally a loner.

RUDOLPH VALENTINO

Oddly enough, considering the money that might have been made out of them, only three full-scale books about Rudolph Valentino have been published in English. One was the official biography written by his manager, George Ullman, a fine example of innocuous desuetude, which nevertheless earned enough to help Ullman straighten out the tangled financial affairs Valentino left behind him at his death. Another was something sold more or less under the counter. It was called *The Intimate Journal of Rudolph Valentino.* Nobody had ever heard of its publisher and there was no editorial name on its title page. It purported to tell all; it was undoubtedly a fabrication from beginning to end. But it did contain one striking image. Valentino had gone to a Hollywood premiere accompanied by the woman with whom he was currently having a highly publicized affair —a famous, adored, and corrupt woman, a star of the day. The glaring arc lights threw her shadow starkly on the pavement. It reminded him of mud.

Was this what Rudolph Valentino, the most maniacally adored man of the twentieth century, came to think of women at the end of his short life? If any woman alive knows the answer, she is not likely to volunteer it. But Valentino's life and career are the movies' exhibits A and B of an ancient maxim which really needs no further illustration: Things are seldom what they seem.

Of all the great celebrities, Valentino's career was the shortest, shorter even than Marilyn Monroe's. He had come to America in the great wave of Italian immigration early in the century, had found his way into the movies by 1917, and had struggled on for four years as extra and, occasionally, villain, with no one apparently able to "see" any more in him than just another Latin type, a greaser. In 1921 he made his great hit in *The Four Horsemen of the Apocalypse,* followed by his even greater hit in *The Sheik,* and his less successful, but still highly successful, *Blood and Sand* and *Monsieur Beaucaire.* The Valentino craze which then swept the country and the world can be compared in intensity to nothing but the original craze for the movies themselves of 1910-14. Then came his quarrel with Paramount, a series of bad or unfinished pictures, and his move to United Artists. This was supposedly a step upward, but it was already known in the trade, if not elsewhere, that his once unbelievable popularity was already declining. One of the last items to appear in *Variety* about him just before his death in 1926, five years after he became a star, said that unless his last picture, *The Son of the Sheik,* did better for United Artists than its predecessor, *The Eagle,* he would not be asked to make another. "Sounds like he's washed up," the wiseacres said over their lunch tables.

Yet if the creation of a legend is one of the essential qualifications of stardom, this doubtful figure, this almost-flash-in-the-pan, ranks among the greatest. The legend he has left behind is as powerful and long-lived as Garbo's. Its detail are shallow enough. It belongs to an age when there was still one born every minute, and people not only ate up publicity about celebrities as they still do, they also believed it. The frenzied crowds of women at his New York funeral, who injured the police and each other in their determination to weep on the bier. Pola Negri's collapse on the set of *Hotel Imperial* and her determination to interrupt the making of the picture and get to New York to participate in the razzle-dazzle. (When Adolph Zukor heard of this, he wired the studio, "Put a nurse on the train with her— and a publicity man.") Incidentally, Miss Negri did not make it to New York quite in time to secure the last full measure of photography

A Sainted Devil

Monsieur Beaucaire

Monsieur Beaucaire

A Sainted Devil

A Sainted Devil

(Right) The humble barber, Beaucaire, takes impudent liberties while shaving an English milord, secure in the knowledge that he is in reality a prince of France, in *Monsieur Beaucaire,* 1924.

for her tears. Then, the appearance at Valentino's "tomb" on every anniversary of his death of the "mysterious" Woman in Black—or Women in Black, several of them usually show up—for the weary chore of being photographed there by cameramen who have been going through the same motions for the past forty-one years (it is startling to realize that Valentino would be seventy-five today if he had lived). It is a crude sort of legend, not even a particularly gaudy one. Neither P. T. Barnum nor W. C. Fields would have been satisfied with it. But behind its somewhat shabby details lies a maleness that brought out the femaleness in virtually every woman alive.

Valentino never had much of a masculine audience, though he tried to acquire one in his last pictures by adding Fairbanks athletic stunts to his lavalike love-making. The young fellows who a few years earlier would have been called drugstore cowboys did blossom out for a while in sideburns and greased hair, but the average male evidently derived little pleasure, even in his erotic fantasies, in picturing himself as a sheik of the desert, a pampas gaucho, or a smooth-as-satin drawing room ornament. Much their womenfolk cared! *They* wanted all three in their dreams, and something more, the man Valentino behind the actor. Listing this man's assets as seen from this distance does not quite give the measure of what was then the intensity of his facination. As an actor, he was neither here nor there. His performances were sincere enough, especially his performance in *Blood and Sand,* but, seen today, he was entirely too much given to those curling lips, flaring nostrils, traveling eyebrows, and the other signs and symbols of that simplex alphabet of the emotions which, for the untalented or scarcely talented, took the place of the true pantomimic art as it developed in the silent era. Actor or not, that he had *something* on the screen there was no doubt. Hear the voice of Iris Barry, than whom no more devoted lover of the screen existed, but who was also no volatile film fan:

Valentino overnight attained fame and popularity exceeded by no movie actor since. This film *(Monsieur Beaucaire)* with its rather choppy movement, its innumerable subtitles and its general air of dress-up and make-believe is unimportant; it might almost be a documentary of a Hollywood masquerade party. But the lavish lighting, the satiny sheen of the absurd costumes, the dexterity with which the chief character is kept glamorously and sympathetically in the foreground deserve attention and study. For the actor had remarkable screen magnetism. The graceful gestures, the sense of poise and of rhythm he had acquired as an exhibition dancer, gave to his movements a singularly impressive quality, though it was the convincingly sultry style of his love-making which endeared him to thousands of infatuated women all over the world. Even today, the magic of his professional personality in this ornate memento of the movie past has the power to impress and even to excite. This is the epitome of "box office," and through it all Valentino moves, radiantly self-assured and incomparably photogenic.

To this temperate estimate of his professional abilities must be added something of the way Valentino behaved toward women, on and off the screen. Not his "sultry love-making," but the way he handled women in ordinary social intercourse. It was said of him enviously by other males that he knew how to treat a woman in such a way as to make her feel "You're the one." This ability was accompanied by an instinct of finesse which is hard to explain in terms of his background. It was put down at the time as "European politesse," but his upbringing was not particularly aristocratic—it was, in fact, decidedly middle class, and there were plenty of Europeans trying to make their way in the United States who lacked it entirely. Mary Pickford gives an amazing example of how it worked. At the height of her fame she was in a restaurant with her mother. Nearby sat the unknown Valentino, who shortly came over to their table and said, "Mrs. Pickford, you don't know me, but I take it upon me to introduce myself. My name is Rudolph Valentino and I am an actor trying to make his way in motion pictures. They tell me you know more about how to do this than anyone in the industry and I thought you might be kind enough to give me some suggestions as to how to begin." Mrs. Pickford, equal to this as to all occasions, gave him some brief, practical suggestions, and the short interview was ended. Nowhere during its course had Valentino by word or deed acknowledged that seated beside Charlotte Pickford was the most famous young movie star of all time. When Miss Pickford remarked on this many years later, Valentino said, "Oh well, Mary, your mother is a *signora* and I could summon up my courage to address her; I knew she would not mind. But you were a young woman and ·unmarried and we had never been introduced. I could not speak to you."

Women, especially American women, liked that. They responded to these fine distinctions, these filamental indications of *savoir-faire,* particularly if they had known but little *savoir-faire* in their own lives. And there was the challenging, commanding, contrast between all this public politeness and Valentino's behavior, on the screen at least, behind the bedroom door. "Sultry" is hardly a strong enough word for some of his love-making. In *The Sheik* it was brutal, next door to sadistic—and *The Sheik* was by far his most popular picture. What could a woman expect from such a man—what next? To have the inside of your elbow kissed before the kiss of passion on the lips might indeed be "Continental finesse." But to be raped first and then have your hand kissed was something new in the way of a sex thrill; nobody had ever thought of it before.

Why then did his popularity decline, as it did indeed before his death, except among that large minority of the still infatuated whose attics are full to this day of countless scrapbooks filled with pictures of Valentino, often stripped to the waist. It may have had something to do, indeed it almost certainly had something to do with, his relations with the women in his actual life, relations which gradually seeped through into the mainstream of the public consciousness. Women by the scores of thousands would have knelt at his feet, indeed laid down on their back at his beck, but he seems to have taken little advantage of such opportunities. His first wife was the actress Jean Acker, known to film history only *because* she was his first wife. His second was the extraordinary woman Winifred O'Shaughnessy, who became Winifred Hudnut when her mother married into the perfume family and who finally rechristened herself—from Irish to French to Russian—Natacha Rambova. She became chief set and costume designer for Alla Nazimova, and served the star-producer well, so that Adolph Zukor was not entirely displeased when she married his great Paramount star, Valentino; he thought this experienced professional might have a good influence on the somewhat unstable young man who had shot up to such dizzy heights so quickly. He never made a greater error. Miss Rambova literally took over the making of Valentino pictures lock, stock, and barrel. Not alone the sets and costumes, the story, direction, characterization, casting, and even the choice of locations became her decisions and hers alone. Well, perhaps not quite alone. Miss Rambova had supernatural assistance. She was a believer in Madame Blavatsky and other Eastern sages, and Karma, the Cosmic Wheel, the

(Left) *A Sainted Devil.* In visual impact and acting style, Nita Naldi was the perfect Valentino leading woman. But she was too molten-looking to be a heroine; she always had to play the villainess.

(Right) The essence of *photogènie:* Valentino dancing with Helene d'Algy in *A Sainted Devil,* 1924.

(Below) Rudolph Valentino in his first sensational hit in *The Four Horsemen of the Apocalypse,* 1921, with Alice Terry, John St. Polis, and Josef Swickard.

A Sainted Devil

(Right) The apogee of Valentino's excruciating acting technique in *The Sheik*, 1922. Agnes Ayres has the revolver, but he knows he owns a more potent weapon.

(Below) Undressing scenes or torture scenes or both were obligatory in Valentino's pictures. Here he is about to be carved up by Montagu Love in *The Son of the Sheik*, 1926.

Zodiac, astral bodies, and other such phenomena dominated her conversation and began to dot the scripts of the Valentino pictures, production on which could not begin until the stars were in proper conjunction; they also had to stop, no matter what condition they were in, when the stars dictated. In the inevitable knock-down-and-drag-out arguments between Miss Rambova on the one hand and Zukor, Lasky, and the entire Paramount studio on the other, Valentino supported his wife all the way. When his bosses were adamant, he became even more so; he simply left the screen and stayed off it until Mr. Lasky was ready to reach some sort of compromise. That uneasy compromise, consisting of the production of the Valentino pictures by a special unit and their release through Paramount, resulted in two of the worst pictures of the 1920s, *Cobra* and *The Young Rajah*—worst, and, strangely, most amateurish, considering the talent involved. Valentino's box office draw declined dangerously. The Lasky-Rambova-Valentino imbroglios had taken place more or less behind the scenes, but now the public could witness their outcome on the screen, and the press was not slow to explain them. Rudolph Valentino, the menacing, triumphant male, was a henpecked husband.

Miss Rambova was by no means satisfied yet. She wished to produce a picture of her own, without her husband in it. The result was *What Price Beauty?*, the awfulness of which defies description. Then she actually starred in one herself, *When Love Grows Cold*. The title of this had apt relation to the box office and to the headlines, for by now even Valentino had seen the handwriting on the wall. After much backing and filling, he parted from Natacha Rambova, moved from Paramount to United Artists, and began his brief, highly publicized affair with Pola Negri, which was cut short by his death before its outcome could become apparent. But had Miss Rambova consulted her stars on the outcome she would doubtless have predicted disaster, for her successor was as imperious as herself, if not more so. Given the two women he chose as the most important in his life, it appears that Rudolph Valentino, the essence of sex menace, liked best women who would lead him around by the nose.

What would have become of this great idol had he survived his fatal illness in 1926? The increasing knowledge of what his private life was like could only have lessened his popularity among women. As for the talkies, which arrived two years later, he could hardly have survived them. At the height of his fame he made a phonograph record—characteristically, it was "Pale Hands I Loved Beside the Shalimar." This memento of his voice reveals a reedy, fruity tenor which would not have been tolerated in the lowliest opera houses of his native Italy. Had he attempted the talkies, his fate would probably have been sadder than John Gilbert's. How could you produce *The Sheik* in sound? Who would have written the dialogue? Of Rudolph Valentino it might be said, and being of the fatalistic temperament he was he might himself have said, that he was one of the few men who have ever lived who died at exactly the right moment.

GRETA GARBO

"She is a woman who marches to some unstruck music, unheard by the rest of us." The words are those of a writer to whom Greta Garbo gave the last interview she ever granted, in 1929. In his book *Garbo*, John Bainbridge dismissed them as typical fan magazine gush. To the author they seem, on the contrary, the aptest, most accurate, and

1926: *The Torrent.* As a sympathetic vampire in her first American film, with Ricardo Cortez

most suggestive words ever published about Greta Garbo, as woman and artist. To Rudyard Kipling, it might have occurred to call her The Cat Who Walks By Herself. But there is nothing feline about Miss Garbo. Anyone who has ever met her and looked into the almost death-dealing honesty of her ice-blue eyes knows that. She has come as close as anyone in our century to realizing that mythic poetic ideal: "I am the master of my fate/I am the captain of my soul." She will have life on her own terms or none at all.

In her first American films, *The Torrent* and *The Temptress,* 1926, she was—at nineteen—given woman of the world parts to play, in the old vamp tradition, and her directors gave her all the old vampish tricks to play. She went through the motions competently, but with a certain air of indifference and—even at nineteen—a glint of mockery, as if she thought it all, for all its seriousness, rather funny. For those who wanted their vamps to be vamps, built solidly on the old Theda Bara lines, this was unsatisfying and maddening. For other audiences, which included most of the rest of the world, it was unsatisfying—and facinating. What was this young, incredibly beautiful actress—for it was evident that she *was* an actress, not just a beauty—what was she trying to say, what was she after, what was she, perhaps, trying to put over on them? Her next film, *Flesh and the Devil,* the first in which she played opposite John Gilbert, lifted the veil a tiny bit to provide a glimpse—only a glimpse—of the answer. Gilbert meets Garbo for the first time at a ball, dances with her once, and invites her into the garden for a breath of air. He offers her a cigarette, but she blows out the match. Gilbert stares and says in a subtitle: "Don't you know that blowing out the match is an invitation to kiss you?" That was daring for 1926, but Miss Garbo went the title-writer one better. She removes the cigarette from Gilbert's mouth, and with a strange, impatient shake of her head puts her hands on his shoulders and bows her beautiful neck backwards. That was the invitation direct, a piece of love-making business never before screened; Miss Garbo was made by that scene, and no male adolescent who ever saw it will ever forget it. Even today, it startles audiences.

The rest of *Flesh and the Devil* followed the more conventional movie patterns of the day. During Gilbert's absence, Garbo marries his best friend, Lars Hanson, but on his return she resumes her affair with him. When all comes out into the open, our heroine, if such she can be called, perishes by falling through the ice while struggling to reach an island where the two friends are about to fight a duel to the death over her. She had to die, of course, because she was Bad, and, even worse, because she had come between male friends, a rigid convention of the period. But in pictures where she was not really Bad, but more sinned against than sinning, Miss Garbo did survive, and often did no matter what the logic of the plot. Here an explanatory digression is necessary. "Unhappy endings" have never been very much liked by audiences anyplace, any time, but by the middle twenties urban audiences had become reconciled to them when they added to the power of the picture and especially when the story was adapted from a well-known literary classic which ought not to be tampered with. But for rural and small-town theaters, tragic endings were *out,* any picture which included one was doomed to failure, no two ways about it, and why cut your own throat? Before talkies made such a simple solution too complicated, Hollywood had a sure-fire answer to this problem: You made two endings, one for the city and one for the country. Thus in the Gilbert-Garbo version of *Anna Karenina,* called on the screen simply *Love,* in New

York, Washington, and Chicago, Garbo heard the fatal tapping of the track walker and threw herself under the train wheels in a version as faithful to the original as Tolstoy could have wished. In the rural version, Karenina conveniently dies, Vronsky is reclaimed and recaptured, and last scene of all finds Miss Garbo in loving reunion with the young son she had abandoned when Vronsky made her feel that all was for love and the world well lost. It made a curious effect to say the least.

Miss Garbo was beautiful and touching as Anna, but her performance still had a touch of the enigma to it and critics were still undecided about her as an actress. As one of them said, "To date, Miss Garbo has shown no ability to portray any character except the character of a woman of veiled thought and unpredictable mood. To be sure, this is a good deal of a relief, since most of our screen heroines are all too predictable and all too obviously have no thoughts to veil. But what manner of woman and artist lies behind her beautiful mask of a face has yet to be revealed." So thought the bosses of M-G-M as they pondered the problem of what sort of screen character they could develop for what they recognized as a uniquely valuable "property." The day of the supervamp was done, as Miss Garbo's first pictures, late examples of the genre, had already proved. She could not become one of the bobbed-hair, silk-legged flappers who dominated the screen of the late twenties. She obviously, even at twenty, knew too much about life and men and women to be convincing as a jazz baby, nor had she the physical equipment for such roles. But there *was* a contemporary type into which such a woman might be fitted, the neurotic older woman in pursuit of amorous adventure, as epitomized in Michael Arlen's Iris March in his best-selling novel and play, *The Green Hat.* True, Will Hays had forbidden the filming of *The Green Hat,* but M-G-M got around that as smoothly as Gloria Swanson had evaded Mr. Hay's ban on *Rain.* Iris March of the mad Marches simply became Diana Merrick of the mad Merricks, and that was that. Otherwise, all was as Mr. Arlen had written it, including the famous Hispano-Suiza in which the heroine hurls herself to death against a tree. As for the green hat itself, photographed in black and white as a gray cloche, it became Miss Garbo's symbol, and the dominant fashion in millinery until the end of the twenties.

The Green Hat, rechristened for the screen *A Woman of Affairs* (a title one would have thought Mr. Hays would have disliked even more than the original he forbade) set the fashion for Garbo heroines for the remainder of the silent era. In *Wild Orchids, The Single Standard,* and *The Kiss* she was a woman of mature years (throughout this period she played women older than herself) who had cast off the Shackles of Convention in order to find Freedom of Soul and Spirit, which she mostly sought in the beds of a variety of men. To these puerile reflections of "modern" pseudo-philosophy Miss Garbo gave a strange conviction which held audiences of all kinds in a spell of fascination. Whatever the plot was saying, this strange woman did indeed seem to be seeking something, to be listening for that unstruck music, that inner command which bade her live according to her own lights and none other. In *The Single Standard* she provided a moment of acting unsurpassed by herself or anyone else, and which she undoubtedly invented. Having left her husband and son for the man she thought the love of her life, she discovers—in fact, he tells her bluntly—that she is only a passing fancy and a brief one at that. Dazedly Miss Garbo wanders into her bathroom, turns on the faucets, and washes her hands, her face, and then, with increasing frenzy, her hair. It

1928: *The Divine Woman.* The emergence of a screen personality. With Conrad Nagel

1928: *A Woman of Affairs.* The emergence, continued. With Lewis Stone

212

1929: *Wild Orchids.* The emergence of an artist

was as if she sought to cleanse herself, not of anger or betrayal, but of burning shame that she should have compromised her own inner flame for so slight a man. There were more and more such moments in her later silent films, and her acting began to change in other ways. Originally she had been a sphinx, remote, withdrawn, even, one was inclined to suspect, coldhearted. Now she responded to the other players, to reflect their feelings in her eyes, to feel with them. That this mysterious lady, so mythic in her beauty and dignity, should also be a compassionate woman only increased the manic devotion of her fans. By 1929 for the vast majority of women Miss Garbo could do no wrong. And 1929 was that dread year when even the most firmly established favorites had to pass the talkie test or vanish from the screen. Miss Garbo didn't "pass" the talkie test, she ignored it. M-G-M was willing to wait until she had perfected her English and until they had found what they thought the "right" vehicle to introduce her to sound. Meanwhile, long after the silent film had become an anachronism, already quaint to look at, Miss Garbo made three more silent pictures. People still went to see them—that is, to see her.

That phenomenal fact clinched the uniqueness of her position. Only one other star successfully bucked the tide which was running so rapidly to sound, and that star was Charles Chaplin. In retrospect it is clear that 1929, the year of those three anachronistic silent pictures, was the exact peak of her popularity. The original sphinxlike Garbo appealed primarily to men; for several years she was the automatic choice of the average male for the woman he would like to be cast up with on a desert isle. Only when the deepening of her acting made her more "sympathetic" did women join her legion. In 1929 and a few years thereafter she commanded both audiences, male and female. That period, too, confirmed the Garbo legend which remains intact today and is likely to last longer than that of any other entertainer. Press agents and impresarios attempt to create legends about any performer they can, often out of the thinnest of materials. If Miss Garbo's legend has proved so solid and enduring the reason is, we think, that it was not merely based on the facts, it coincided with them exactly. Giving Howard Dietz (studio v.p. in charge of advertising and publicity) due credit for imprinting on the public mind the image of Greta Garbo, The Woman Who Walks Alone, the simple fact was that she *was* the woman who walks alone. For years after she became famous, she lived in a Santa Monica hotel—alone. Her favorite recreation was walking the beach in the rain in trenchcoat and slouch hat—alone. When she finally acquired a house with a high wall around it—rented—she lived there with a Swedish couple as servants, and spent her time sun-bathing beside her swimming pool—alone. When people in the film colony in all innocence tried to make friends with this shy newcomer, she replied bluntly, "I vant to be alone." The phrase passed into the language. The thing was, the thing was true. She *did* want to be alone—with what thoughts for company, no one will ever know.

Her dealings with her employers astounded them. After her hit in *Flesh and the Devil,* she requested a considerable increase in salary. They refused, and threatened to cast her as leading woman in a Western—a threat which had worked well in disciplining Joan Crawford. Very well, she would play it—but for the new salary she demanded. They would demote her to bit parts, to maid parts—these again she would willingly play, but also at the new salary. Then Louis B. Mayer threatened to banish her from Hollywood, to have her American work permit revoked so that she could not work at any other studio, even to have her deported to Sweden by the State Department under the veiled threat of mortal turpitude. Let him do so, said Miss Garbo. Then Mr. Mayer in desperation went into one of his celebrated crying acts. Think, he sobbed, what M-G-M had done for Miss Garbo, how it had lifted her from obscurity to stardom, and what a brilliant future lay ahead if only she would be reasonable. Miss Garbo listened to the Mayer sobs with a heart as soft as a diamond. Having listened long enough, she said, "I think I go home." That did it. Nobody knew whether she meant home to Santa Monica or all the way home to Stockholm, but nobody was taking any chances. The hottest property on the lot was about to walk off it. A salary compromise was reached, and Miss Garbo reported ready for work, ready to do whatever was required of her—on her own terms. For once the ruthless tactics of the studio moguls in bringing a star to heel had failed completely—because Miss Garbo knew her cause was just and refused to settle for anything less than justice. In business matters, as in all others, she remained true to her own voices.

Not only in matters of money, but also in the other essentials, and frills, of stardom, Greta Garbo insisted on backing her own judgment. When she first arrived she was put through the customary leg-art publicity routine, posing with athletes in running pants and the like. She endured this, but said, "Whan I am beeg star like Leellian Geesh, I won't do dot silly stuff." Nor would she, after her first year on the lot, but would pose only for photographers of her own choosing. As for interviews, she gave them as was the custom, but he who turns over the yellowing files will find little to illuminate him; one senses how the interviewers had to sweat to produce any usable copy at all. Every star in Hollywood is misquoted somewhere 365 days in the year and nothing much can be done about it. But when Miss Garbo found words put into her mouth which she had not said, she saw what could be done about it: From 1928 on she refused to see or talk to any member of the press, ever, under any circumstances or for any reason. This somewhat daunted Dietz. With her spontaneous help, he had been busily creating the legend of Garbo, the woman of mystery—but he had to have *something* to work with. From here on in he had nothing but photographs. These she did not seem to consider an empty frill of publicity, but as having something to do with her art, and when she could control the conditions under which they were made, she worked hard at posing for stills—thanks to which we have the lovely ones reproduced here, and a profusion of others from which it was difficult to choose.

In a comparatively short time the Garbo legend, based solidly on the Garbo reality, spread through the land, and on the whole was sympathetically received. Of course there was the minority, vociferous if not large, who called her the "overgrown Swede," ridiculed her for her mannish offscreen clothes and the flat, almost androgyne figure they revealed—and, of course, for her supposed big feet. Her intransigence with her employers, her aloofness, her threats to "go home" were also dismissed as so much publicity bushwa. But the public as a whole, wary as it may have grown of press agentry, was not so sure that this was all an act. They seemed to recognize in Miss Garbo something deep in the American grain, something Bill Hart had also represented, the instinctive loner. Had she been so eccentric a recluse as to rouse doubts about her emotional balance, the case might have been different, but Miss Garbo was not entirely without human contacts. John Gilbert fell passionately in love with her soon after she arrived in America. She can scarcely have been more than twenty when this impetuous, impulsive lover attempted to sweep her off her feet. Joan Crawford records that Gilbert was so infatuated that he could scarcely remember what picture he was playing in, and could hardly wait to finish a scene in order to rush off to her dressing room. Their "romance" was highly publicized, since it happened to coincide with their three pictures together, yet this comparatively inexperienced girl managed to hold the screen's great lover at something of a distance, come what might. She seems to have understood his passion for her, and to have felt liking for the man himself. Once, unconfirmed legend says, she did go so far as to promise to marry him, but characteristically balked at the altar. Still, they remained friends, as subsequent events showed. And she made other friends in Hollywood. The late Lilyan Tashman was one of them. So was Salka Viertel, wife of the German director Berthold Viertel, who wrote many of the screenplays of her later pictures. She shunned, of course, "permeers," and Academy jollifications, nor was she ever seen, much less photographed, at ordinary Hollywood social affairs. She did frequent the homes of members of the small German and Swedish colonies in Hollywood, whether they were stars or nobodies. And, once in a great while, she would turn up a parties given by the Hollywood great, more often than not unannounced or even uninvited. Frequently she brought with her a Swedish phonograph record which consisted of people laughing, every kind of laugh from giggle to belly roar—and nothing else. She would sit and watch the faces of the guests as they listened, then, as often as not, go home. On her trips to Sweden, which grew more and more frequent, she was, for her, almost gregarious, seeking out old friends, mingling with theater and film people, and generally seeming to enjoy herself—largely because no doubt her compatriots, being Swedes, understood her and let her go her own way unmolested. Her behavior in Stockholm was the soundest possible proof that it was the Hollywood and general American hoop-la machine that she detested—not people as people.

The Garbo legend grew and held through her years on the screen; it was too consistent to be doubted any longer. The last holdouts against it were the press themselves. Somehow they could not rid themselves of the suspicion that the whole recluse mystery woman act was a product of the fertile brain of Dietz, and they watched like hawks for some inconsistent gesture, some slip of the mask, which would reveal the whole stunt for what is was. Miss Garbo's annual trips to Sweden became first a sort of annual circus and then an annual bore. Heavily disguised, concealing herself behind the name of "Harriet Brown" or some other pseudonym she would sneak onto the train at Pasadena, sneak into an obscure hotel in New York, and try to sneak onto a Swedish liner, all the time pursued by the newspaper ferrets determined to get something out of her *this* time. All they did get, all they ever got, was a blurred snapshot of a disheveled figure hiding its face behind a handbag or trying to scuttle through a door. In 1935 Miss Garbo decided to put an end to this annual circus bore. When the *Gripsholm* arrived in New York harbor, newsmen flocked down to it, prepared for the usual cat-and-mouse game. Instead they found themselves one and all invited into the captain's lounge and offered champagne and whiskey. Shortly Miss Garbo appeared, beautifully turned out looking like heaven on earth. Addressing her astonished onlookers, she said in effect: Gentlemen, let us put an end to all this nonsense. You are tired of it and so am I. "The

(Above) When Paramount stole Gary Cooper away from Samuel Goldwyn, they thought they had acquired one more beautiful boy, cut to the pattern of the time. Here the young ex-cowboy attempts the emotive technique of 1927 in *Children of Divorce*, with Esther Ralston.

(Left) *Saratoga Trunk*, 1945. In the second half of his career Gary Cooper returned to action roles, but the older Cooper was no "simple" man of action. He had developed a conscience, and it showed in his face.

(Left top) Gary Cooper gave his first fully-matured performance in *A Farewell to Arms,* 1932, but critics ignored the excellence of his work. They were too busy being aghast that Hemingway's masterpiece had been given to Frank Borzage, a "sentimentalist" director. They were wrong. Borzage stripped the false hair from the chest of a highly romantic novel and filmed it straight. Cooper is seen here with Adolphe Menjou.

(Left bottom) *Mr. Deeds Goes to Town,* 1936. Frank Capra's "pixilated sisters" passed immediately into American folklore, and so did Gary Cooper's Longfellow Deeds, the role which made him at long last, after ten years on the screen, a truly great star.

(Left inset) *Love in the Afternoon,* 1958. Billy Wilder's amorous comedy did not find favor with audiences. Gary Cooper was by now too much the father of us all to be acceptable as young Audrey Hepburn's conscienceless elderly seducer.

(Right and below) Every Hollywood lovely wanted to annex Gary's virile handsomeness, and some were professionally powerful enough to do so, on the screen at least, much to the benefit of his career. With Colleen Moore in *Lilac Time,* 1928, and with Tallulah Bankhead in *The Devil and the Deep,* 1932.

devoted themselves to trying to help further public interest in what they considered Gary's true profession and calling, *acting*.

No one else but the three Coopers seemed interested in this subject, certainly not Paramount, which seemed to think that all it had in the young man was another lean, virile, handsome hunk of girl bait, and all they taught him was to paint a cupid's bow mouth on his lips and mascara his eyelashes, to make him look even prettier in the fashion of the day. As for the press, all it seemed interested in was front-paging his flaming love affairs with Clara Bow and Lupe Velez. The elder Coopers did not mind this too much. A young man must sow his wild oats, in Hollywood as in Montana, and while it was a pity their son had to sow his in public and with two such flamboyant movie stars, it seemed to be the custom of the country: when in Rome . . . When a reviewer, and it happened rarely enough, did seem to glimpse something behind Gary's immature good looks, something of thought or feeling, he heard from Judge Cooper and his wife. Not the usual conventional thanks, but thoughtful letters, discussing what the critic had said, asking questions, asking advice. No matter. Gary continued to appear in pictures with titles like *Children of Divorce* and *The Shopworn Angel,* and the only question that interested the industry was how long Gary's vogue with the teeny-flappers would last.

Then came the talkies, *The Virginian,* and the discovery that Gary Cooper was, with Garbo (they were alike in that neither had a theatrical background) the only actor who knew instinctively how to address the microphone. Both realized that they must not project their speeches at it, but treat it as a hovering ear which reproduced their words as if they were thoughts overheard. In life, Gary Cooper's speech was always Western-laconic. He adopted this style as his screen manner too. He spoke, of course, what was written for him, but in his way of doing it he gave the impression that he edited his thoughts before he expressed them, and his pauses and silences often gave or seemed to give more meaning to his lines than was written in them. This was to become the true style of talking-picture speech at its best, but few recognized the fact or Cooper as exemplar of it—not even in Barrie's *The Old Lady Shows Her Medals,* not even in his beautiful, sincere, passionate performance opposite Helen Hayes in *A Farewell to Arms.* The critics had stereotyped him; he was just he-man Coop, trying to make like an actor, a latter-day Strong Silent Bill Hart.

The turning point in critical opinion came when, after long service in routine romantic and action roles, he attempted comedy for the first time. Reviewers were astounded at his success in adding humor to his role in what was essentially a blood-and-thunder epic, *Lives of a Bengal Lancer.* They marveled at his ability to match subtlety to subtlety, toe to toe with Marlene Dietrich in Lubitsch's *Desire.* With Frank Capra's *Mr. Deeds Goes to Town,* his critical reputation was finally made. Here indeed was an actor, a romantic comedian of the highest order, who in his timing was just far ahead enough of his audience to keep them in perpetual surprise and suspense. Not everyone among his admirers was ecstatic over the "new" Gary Cooper. That perhaps very small minority which had all along valued his understated sincerity found these qualities muted or smothered under the acting tricks Lubitsch and Capra had taught him. The scratching behind the ear, the downcast eyes suddenly turned upward in crinkly laughter—they were effective, they got the laughs, but there was lost in them something of that almost telepathic communication between actor and audience which had set him apart even in his early, untried days. Once again, it didn't matter in the least. Gary the Coop was at the flood tide of popularity and acclaim, and to stay there all it seemed he had to do was go on refining the tricks, adding to them, and repeating them again and again. Why not? Audiences loved the tricks and identified them with him. But to the saddened minority who once thought they had found in him the man whose manner of self-expression most perfectly served the qualities of the movie medium, he had become just another competent, show-wise actor, up to any assignment given him—but no longer a very interesting one.

In the meantime, this highly successful young man had seen a good deal of life and of the world. Early in the thirties he deserted Hollywood for almost a year to make a lengthy African safari which obviously served his ingrained instincts well. On the way back, he stopped long enough in Rome to meet the American heiress Countess di Frasso and, of all people, Elsa Maxwell—and they followed him back to Hollywood. There Miss Maxwell undertook to add him to her trophy belt of celebrities and her self-chosen charmed circle of the People Who Really Matter. Since the Countess and Miss Maxwell were something new to the gullible Hollywood of the thirties, his associates were much impressed. Their old pal Coop seemed to have become a sophisticated gentleman, a member of the international smart set. But Mr. Cooper soon tired of Miss Maxwell's unentertaining entertainments, and refused any longer to dance to her tune. He met and married Veronica Balfe, a socialite who had had a brief try at the screen under the name of Sandra Shaw, began to beget children, and settled down to become what he remained ever after, a good citizen of the USA and, incidentally, of Hollywood, California. And his face, and with it his character, seemed to begin to change again. He still used the acting tricks when they were called for, still played what they told him to play, but up from beneath the surface something seemed to be emerging which altered his handsome face and gave it a different meaning. Like a farmer, he began to look pre-maturely old. The deep lines which formed in his cheeks seemed to have come from riding the range in Montana rather than from spending most of his time under the studio arc lights. Perhaps it was the long-dead Judge Cooper coming out in him, as fathers do come out in sons with the passage of the years. At any rate, the image of the later Cooper was that of a man who—again, like Garbo—was in deep harmony with himself, and who aimed to protect that harmony against the world.

Many people do not ordinarily form critical estimates of movie stars, not only for the obvious reasons but also because they first encounter them on the screen when they are too young to be critical, and they take for granted that what they see is what is. The embryo Cooper of *The Winning of Barbara Worth,* the routine handsome hero of the Paramount films, the tricksy comedian of his high-riding years were all merged into, or overlaid by, the final image of Gary Cooper, a figure in the American landscape—troubled by doubts like the rest of us, doubting perhaps to the end, but in the end knowing what he had to do, knowing he had to do it, and doing it. It is without question for this reason that *High Noon* remains his masterpiece and the image of him which all of us still carry. For, besides its other brilliances, this was the drama of a man who had to choose, not between bad and good, but between good and good, to weigh their degrees in the balance and make his final judgment all alone. It is of deep interest that the theme of Quakerism, of the hatred and rejection of violence at all cost and for any reason, never a conspicuous theme in American films, here stands forth as a central issue. (He later made another film about the Quakers, *The Friendly Persuasion*.) In Western tradition, the important thing about the hero was how fast his hand could get to his hip. It was by now taken for granted that in shooting from the hip, Cooper's hand was always quicker than the spectator's eye. But in his last films and in the last incarnation of his screen personality the issue had changed—it now was, should he draw at all? This theme touched a deep dichotomy in the American spirit, and one especially conspicuous now.

He would blink at these words if he were alive to read them, blink, and grin wryly, and read them again, and try to understand them. For to the son of Judge Cooper, the law was the law, if only you could figure out its true meaning and intent, and often that took a lot of figuring. If he gave the impression, in life and on the screen, of being slow of speech, and even slow to act until the flash point came, that was the reason. He was figuring. He died as he had lived, fighting grimly and methodically, not only because he wanted to live, but because he thought he ought to.

JOAN CRAWFORD

"A stray picture called *Paris* might as well have been made in Dubuque, Iowa, for all it has to do with any kind of life the French would recognize, but it does have one thing to arrest the eye: the new young M-G-M player who has just been renamed Joan Crawford. This little girl's mouth is too small for beauty, there are times when she seems afraid of the camera, and she is ludicrously miscast as a girl of the Apaches. She has nevertheless that arresting, appealing dramatic flair that cannot fail. In her scenes with the nominal star, Charles Ray, it is Joan Crawford you look at. She doesn't try to steal them, she probably wouldn't know how. She captures attention simply by being there." So wrote a fan magazine reviewer in 1926 in the course of his routine duties. With some astonishment he received a wire which said CAN NEVER EXPRESS MY GRATITUDE FOR YOUR REVIEW OF PARIS IF AT ANY TIME THERE IS ANYTHING WHATEVER I CAN DO TO HELP YOU YOU KNOW WHERE TO FIND ME SIGNED JOAN CRAWFORD. "Help *me*?" mused the reviewer, a long-time veteran of the movie wars; no star had ever offered to do *that* before, and how could a little ingénue help an established editor-critic? He tossed the wire into the wastebasket along with the other pleasantries of the day. But twenty-five years later she *did* help him, with money and employment, when he was desperate for both. Miss Crawford never forgets, never postpones, and keeps her given word in matters of this kind as if it were her Bible oath.

If Gloria Swanson, Greta Garbo, Mary Pickford, and, say, Marilyn Monroe achieved screen immortality through genius, beauty, or the turn of fortune's wheel, Joan Crawford owes her place beside them to unremitting determination and labor. She has put together her effigy in the temple of all the gods piece by piece, like a restorer of antique furniture or one of those dedicated unfortunates who now seek to restore Florentine art treasures by removing the mud from them by eighths of inches. The figure is perhaps inapt. Joan Crawford did not set out to restore an ancient work of art but to create a

Joan Crawford, 1929

(Above) An Apache girl from Texas. Joan Crawford in her first important role, in *Paris*, 1926.

(Left) In 1930, when Xavier Cugat needed a dynamic young movie star to pose with him in front of the curtain of star caricatures which he had created for Grauman's Chinese Theatre, he unerringly chose Joan Crawford—yesterday's dancing daughter, today's dramatic white hope, perennially the star with an eye to the main chance.

(Right) Miss Crawford gave everything she had learned, and then some, to her first serious dramatic role, Sadie Thompson, in *Rain,* 1932, but her fans did not care for it. They preferred to see her as a rich prostitute rather than a poor one.

new one herself, with no blueprint or sketch to guide her except the vague notion that she wanted to be the best movie star who ever starred, whatever that best might be.

Her efforts to learn her craft and to establish herself at M-G-M have already been described. But her exhaustless energy and ambition did not stop there. As the foregoing anecdote shows, she set out to win over the press to Joan Crawford when even the fan press scarcely knew who Joan Crawford was. No press man, be he the Hollywood correspondent of the Auckland, New Zealand, *Gazette,* was too insignificant to secure her attention if he seemed to want it. Once her foot slipped: She gave the news of her forthcoming divorce from Franchot Tone to a favorite fan writer as an "excloosive," and for many months thereafter she was picking Louella Parsons' buckshot out of her hide. But Miss Crawford set herself fixedly to win back the dean of the Hollywood columnists, and within a few months Miss Parsons was again a Crawford fan. This desire to be liked, to be approved, and to be talked about is no novelty in the profession. It is often a part of the stellar make-up. But Miss Crawford has carried it to lengths unheard of before. She gives her apparently undivided attention not only to the press but to the public as well. Not just the vast, amorphous movie public as a whole, but any identifiable unit of it which seeks her attention.

Fan clubs were a necessary evil of the movies in her beginning days. No player who was lucky enough to garner one could afford to ignore it completely, since it represented the hard core of his admirers whose rooting might do him good with larger sections of the audience and who, if offended, might well do him harm. Yet the members of these clubs by their nature demanded more time, attention, and favors than any star could afford to give them. A delicate balance had to be struck and maintained, often with the aid of press agents and staffs trained to deal with such problems. Not Joan. At the height of her fame and success, she corresponded personally and in her own handwriting with not just the officers of her club, but with every one of its thousands of members, and at Christmas sent each of them gifts, selected and wrapped by herself. Where the inexhaustible energy came from would have to be figured out by an expert on the quantum theory. As for Miss Crawford in person, wherever she could be got at by her fans, she was got at, by her own wish. They thronged Grand Central whenever she visited New York, and followed her literally everywhere she went in the city, again at her own wish—not mere tolerance but *wish.* When she took a cab she always told the taxi drivers (all of whom knew her by her first name) the address she wanted in a voice loud enough to be heard by her fans on the sidewalk, and through some miracle of transportation, there they were waiting for her when she arrived, cheering and calling out her name. And if stopping to chat with them and sign their autograph books made her late for luncheon at Sardi's, Sardi's and whoever was waiting to lunch with her would have to wait; the fans came first. Loud was the derision among the press and the flacks at this relentless currying of popular favor, but Miss Crawford didn't care. Her characteristic reply to wisecracks about her treatment of her fans was, "They've given me everything I've got, I'll give back what I can." There was no *arrière-pensée* in this; she meant it. She knew that cultivation of press and public was good for business, but she also liked it. It made being a star feel *real* to her.

Needless to say, the Joan Crawford Fan Club was the most enthusiastic, not to say virulent, of all the many then prevailing, and the most insistent in pressing the activities of its idol upon national attention. Its shrill proceedings naturally came to the notice of that matchless troupe The Revuers (Betty Comden, Adolph Green, and the late Judy Holliday), who from their eyrie at the Village Vanguard satirized everything that came down the New York pike. Their sketch, reproduced here in its entirety by kind permission, suggests that there was many a crumpled rose leaf in the fan club Eden, even the Joan Crawford one:

"WE LOVE JOAN CRAWFORD"
President: Attention, Crawford Fan Club! We will commence with our morning hymn!
Club: WE LOVE JOAN CRAWFORD!
>
> For she is the epitome
> Of what every girl would like to be,
> And so to pay her fealty
> We formed a Joan Society—
> Through her we're able to elope
> To the land of mink and heliotrope.
> Her pictures are a kind of dope
> That fills our humdrum lives with hope—
> For she is the essence of glamour,
> Why can't all girls be like her?

Member: Damn her!
Club: What's this, mutiny on the Crawford ship?
Member: I'm tired of all that Crawford Lip.
Club: Joan!
Member: Joan, I worshiped at your shrine;
> I was blinded by your shine.

Club: Joan!
Member: Joan, I'm doing all I can
> To keep me a loyal Crawford fan.

Club: Joan!
Member: Joan, I loved your long red hair,
> Joan, I loved the gowns you wear.

Club: Joan!
Member: Joan, you're sleeker than a seal,
> And when Gable kisses you, how that must feel!
> I let my hair grow down to here,
> I painted my mouth from ear to ear,
> I copied all those Adrian clothes,
> And my nails are redder than the rose....

Club: Joan!
Member: Joan, I can't quite make this out.
> Joan, I'm tortured by a doubt.
> Joan, I feel the time is ripe
> For me to emulate a new type....

(Shrieks and moans from the club)
>   I find to my surprise that I would give my last penny
>   To be the lifelong slave and spittin' image of Sonja Henie!

(more shrieks and cries of "Treason!")
>   I want to be fluffy, I want to be blond,
>   My cheeks must be puffy, I want an ice pond,
>   I want to go skating about on a rink,
>   I want a slight lisp and I want to wear pink.
>   I'll cut off this seaweed and wear it in curls,
>   I'll trade in this dress for an outfit that swirls,
>   I'll cultivate dimples, I'll stay home at nights,
>   I'll learn to like snow, and I'll live in Der Schweiss,
>   I'll grow a soft accent, I'll never be bad,
>   I'll learn to start calling Jean Hersholt my dad,
>   I'll learn how to do arabesques on the ice. . . .
>   For I won't be sophisticated,
>   I won't be hollow!
>   To hell with Crawford smartness,
>   In fluff I'll wallow!
>   I want to be the Queen of California,
>   And cut up on the ice like little Sawnia!
>   And cut up on the ice like little Sonia!

President: Oh, you traitor! Fellow members!
Club: WE *LOVE* JOAN CRAWFORD!!!
Member: Sorry, but it's no soap,
>   I found a brand new dope.
Club: Then go!
Member: Oh, I'm through with sin and vice.
Club: Go!
Member: Oh, I'm heading for the ice!
Club: Go!
Member: Oh, I'm free from Crawford's spell;
>   I'm through with Joan. . . .
Club: Then go to Henie!

"Tired of" were the most dreadful words a star could hear from her fans; there was a sort of finality about them. But Miss Crawford was always equal to any such situation as is outlined here. She simply produced a "new" Joan Crawford whenever the old one showed signs of getting frayed around the edges. Long after Sonja Henie had packed her skates and folded up her folding money and gone back to Norway, Miss Crawford was setting the pace for new generations of stars. The focus of her all but manic energy was the fashioning of her screen image itself. At first she was an ingénue, a typical role being that of Rose Marie in the silent version of the operetta of that name. For the rest of the silent era she was simply a Dancing Daughter, due to her success in the film of that name. Then came the dread test of the talkies, dread to all but Miss Crawford—*here* was a challenge worthy of her frenzy to succeed at any price. Her natural voice as recorded was low and pleasing, and if in her first talking pictures it was a bit stilted, that was no doubt because she was being extra careful not to slip into the "he don'ts" and "he ain'ts" of the vernacular of her childhood. Her initial success in the talkies were as shopgirl heroines in films like *Paid* and *Possessed* and *Pretty Sadie McKee,* and it was in these that she won the vast following of fans whom she kept faithful through the tactics described above. But of course Miss Crawford aspired to higher things—dressy roles, high-life roles, *ladylike* roles. This took a bit of doing. There were voice coaches galore to teach her to produce pear-shaped tones, but she was shrewd enough to avoid the pitfall of the la-de-da, a pitfall into which some of her competitors had fallen, especially those from the stage. She must achieve a golden mean, a voice that sounded cultivated yet natural. Voice coaches or no voice coaches, it took some doing. Her uncritical fans of course adored her voice in society roles, as they adored everything about her, but more sophisticated audiences always felt a bit nervous when attending Miss Crawford's version of *Forsaking All Others* or *Susan and God,* which had been played on the stage by actresses like Tallulah Bankhead and Gertrude Lawrence. It was like going to an amateur performance featuring a friend, and sitting on the edge of the seat fearing that sooner or later she would make a *gaffe.* This was absurd; films being films, any *gaffes* Joan Crawford might have made would have been corrected in retakes. Nevertheless, you sighed with relief when the end came, because throughout the film you had sensed her own strain in living up to her ideals of herself as a vocal performer. Her ambitions in this direction were not, by the way, confined to the speaking of dramatic dialogue. She also had hopes for her singing voice. A soft, warm contralto, she had it trained for over a decade by the best teachers she could lure to southern California. She has seldom used it on the screen, but in the process of learning she became something of, if not a musician exactly, at least a musicologist; visitors to her voice studio might hear her singing a part in a Mozart mass. At the beginning of all this, her relentless well-wishers whispered that she would be "ready for grand opera" in two years, or, to put an extrafine point on it, two years and six months. No Hope Hampton, she was not foolish enough to attempt anything of the sort, nor has she ever succumbed to her perpetual temptation to try the stage. Voice culture was simply another aspect of her drive to improve each shining hour until it outshone the sun.

Acting? Was she an actress? Could she become one, not just an expert craftsman, as she had already proved she was, but an *actress*? The answer had to be "of course." But how to become an actress, and show herself to be one, within the strict confines of the screen personality which she and M-G-M had created between them after much trial and error, including a brief period as a blonde? That personality had received the most definite possible stamp of public approval, and it could not be departed from too far in the quest for any such will-o'-the-wisp as "versatility." Adrian had solved the problem of her broad shoulders by designing clothes for her which made them look even broader. The effect was not mannish; it rather emphasized those broad-bosomed qualities associated with the basic female duty of perpetuating the race. It did make the thought of embracing her a rather formidable one, though. The small mouth of which the reviewer of *Paris* complained became huge, so enormous as to evoke laughter from

Joan Crawford and Clark Gable in *Possessed*, 1931

Director Jack Conway and Joan Crawford in *The Understanding Heart*, 1927

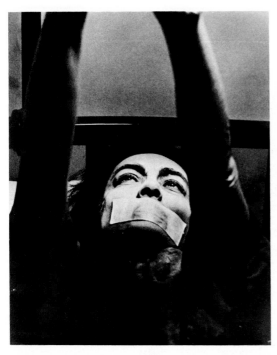

(Above) Joan Crawford's best performance, as the maimed, guilty, and dying star in *What Ever Happened to Baby Jane?*, 1962.

(Right) What the fans of her great period *did* want from Joan Crawford is perfectly exemplified in this still from *Letty Lynton,* 1932, with Nils Asther. A contemporary critic expressed the fear that her lamé gown's high lapel would imperil her jugular vein, and hoped it would not be copied by girls in general, especially in the subway. His hope was in vain.

Joan Crawford, 1933

(Below) Whenever Joan Crawford arrived at Grand Central, as here in 1935, she knew she would instantly be surrounded by teen-age autograph hounds. She knew, because she sent word of her coming in advance.

239

the irreverent, and by slow degrees it grew smaller again. Her large eyes she made even larger by means known only to herself, and she was the first to let her natural eyebrows grow in after the Marlene Dietrich vogue of the pencil-thin, antennaelike eyebrows passed. The general effect of the face was marmoreal, chin up, slightly defiant—a commanding woman of the world who was perhaps not quite so worldly as she seemed. It was a lot of women's ego ideal. But how, within its limits, to "act," to "create a character"? In trying, she not only left no stone unturned, she left none unpolished. When George Cukor, fresh from the stage and uppity about upstart movie stars, was assigned to direct her, she arrived on the set letter-perfect and ready for trial by fire. She got it. After her first scene, a long, hard one, Cukor said, "Miss Crawford, that was very nice, you knew your lines real well and you didn't make a single mistake. Now, let's get down to some *acting.*" Miss Crawford, being Miss Crawford, could well at that point have unloosed the stoppers of Louis B. Mayer's wrath. She chose instead to say, "All right, what do we do next?" and went on to outstrip her martinet mentor in perfectionism and staying power. But alas, it was her job, and Cukor's as well, to produce a typical Crawford picture, and that was all that came of his effort to make her into a "real" actress. It is significant that her one impressive performance in this long period came in the tour de force melodrama *A Woman's Face,* in which the plot required that that idolized face be disfigured through most of the picture by a hideous scar.

Joan Crawford as shopgirl heroine and as a grand lady, Crawford version, had satisfied Louis B. Mayer and his associates; after all, had the millions she made for them not built the Writers' Building? Mayer loved to say so. They showed no inclination to find a new incarnation for her, to adapt to changing fashion and the growing up of picturegoers. More and more she was cast in routine romances. She knew what that meant, she had seen it happen enough to others, and she was not one to sit back and wait and hope. At the age of thirty-six, after fourteen years with M-G-M, she canceled her ironclad contract with the studio, with nothing more solid in view than a one-picture deal with Warner Brothers, from whom she had with difficulty wrung the right to approve the story of that one picture which would obviously decide her future, if she had any. None of the stories submitted to her met with her approval, and she waited a grim year and a half with nothing to do but read scripts, while the usual rumors flew that the Crawford vogue had at long last exhausted itself. Then came *Mildred Pierce,* for which she won her first and last Academy Award; it turned the tide triumphantly. The bitch-goddess Success had momentarily turned against her; very well, she would become the incarnation of the bitch-goddess herself. *Queen Bee, This Woman Is Dangerous, Female on the Beach, The Damned Don't Cry*— the titles of her pictures in the forties and fifties tell the story of the new type she created for herself. Probably its subtlest variation, and her best performance of this period, was *Harriet Craig,* from George Kelly's old *Craig's Wife,* about a woman who cared more about the shining floors of her house and its clipped lawns than about her husband, or indeed anything else. In general, in these pictures she was the hard-bitten, hard-driving woman-who'd-been-around, who'd do anything and take any punishment to get what she wanted. Sometimes she found out at the end that she didn't want it after all—but at least she got it, didn't she? Miss Crawford's forty-five year career, short only of Mary Astor's among women, must be acknowledged the most consistently successful on record. Her pictures of recent years have been profitable, even though they have not rolled up the grosses of the lush M-G-M period. Partly they make money because of package and profit-participation deals and other such Hollywood phenomena of recent years. Partly it is because it doesn't matter any longer how old she is. The young do not need to identify with her. The young like to see power and drive succeed on the screen, and that Miss Crawford gives them, and never mind her years if she still looks like a sexy dame, and that Miss Crawford always does. *What Ever Happened to Baby Jane?* gave a new twist to her bitchiness. After her success as the villainess-victim in that, she abandoned the stiletto of poisoned words in favor of whatever ax or meat cleaver stood by handy. She has, as a screen star, become a specialist in out-and-out mayhem. Films like *Straitjacket, Berserk,* and *I Saw What You Did, I Know Who You Are,* inexpensively produced, continued to make money and keep her name before the public. Miss Crawford makes few films these days; she is too busy with a number of things, but offer her a meaty role and she will move into her studio dressing room for the duration, as has long been her custom, sleep there every night, and emerge on the set in the morning, letter-perfect, every hair in place, ready to knock 'em cold or drop dead before the cameras in the attempt.

If Miss Crawford's private life has been less successful than her public one, it wasn't for want of trying. She worked as hard at it as she did at becoming a star and staying one. Her first two marriages were by-products of the urge for self-improvement. Douglas Fairbanks, Jr., was much smitten with the hey-hey girl he married when very young, and doubtless she with him; they certainly made enough of a public display of their deathless romance. But there was also the fact that young Fairbanks could compel his father and a reluctant Miss Pickford to open the doors of Pickfair to her. She was no longer just a Charleston contest winner but a member by marriage of the movie royal family. In their different ways, young Doug and Joan soon outgrew one another. Then Franchot Tone ambled onto the scene. A scion of the family which controlled carborundum, he took it into his head to become a stage actor, then turned dead serious about the Group Theatre, an organization headed by Lee Strasberg, dedicated to the proposition that it was high time the theater produced aesthetically and socially ambitious plays which, in a nice way, called upon the workers to arise. It has long been said that Strasberg commanded Tone to accept an M-G-M contract when it was offered to him in order to focus the attention of the studios on the Group, and to influence them to buy the film rights to their stage productions for large sums of money. Certainly Mr. Tone seemed to have no other motive in going to Hollywood. Amiable, easygoing, he became a prominent leading man but never a star, in part because he made no really great effort to become one. Then Miss Crawford seized upon him. Here was a husband a cut above a Fairbanks—not a scion of movie royalty but of "old money" and of Broadway Art. As Mrs. Tone, Miss Crawford became even more cultured than she already was, worked harder at her music, her reading, her cultivation of People Who Do Things. They made an attractive pair, but things did not go well between them. Mr. Tone made a discovery. He was not as sophisticated as he thought he was. He had thought he didn't mind being Mr. Joan Crawford because he was Franchot Tone and a serious man of the theater. He discovered that he did mind. Their divorce turned on this issue of differing professional status, as so many others have. Miss Crawford's third marriage was to Phillip Terry, an actor so minor that the question of status was academic.

Miss Crawford remained single for a long time after her third divorce. In keeping with her drive to be a success at everything in human life, she had already adopted four children, Christina, Christopher, Cynthia, and Cathy, and devoted to their upbringing the same fierce energy and blazing determination she gave to everything else. Too fierce, too blazing, perhaps, for the delicate, emotional business of child rearing. At any rate two of the children disappointed her deeply. They grew up rebellious, defied her in public, and told tales out of school. Miss Crawford doubtless suffered heartbreak from the failure of this, the most cherished of all her enterprises, but she stood by her guns. Success, after all, was what ought to be one's goal in life, success was not to be achieved by anarchic behavior, and if you chose to behave that way you had to take the consequences. The issue between her and her children doubtless still hangs in the balance. But in the meantime something happened to Joan Crawford—something nice, something out of key with the tense, unremitting struggle the whole of her life had been. She met and married Al Steele, the Pepsi-Cola executive. Some say the marriage took place overnight, on a bet or impulse. However that may be, they were charmed with one another from start to finish, and it is a pity that this last happy marriage was ended by his death after only four years. Miss Crawford of course energetically, though unobtrusively, helped her husband in every way that the wife of the president of a multimillion-dollar corporation could, and characteristically invented some new ways of her own. Steele's attitude toward her career, on the other hand, seems at first to have been as light as that a nineteenth-century businessman might have taken toward an actress of his fancy. But not after he had spent a couple of nights with her in her studio dressing room, and some days on the set watching her practice her trade. He discovered that being the central figure in an expensive motion picture which must return a large profit could call for as much organized ability and drive as the making and selling of a soft drink. From that time on their respect was mutual, and their enjoyment of one another immense. They both liked to *do things* all the time. It tells a lot that Miss Crawford remained a director of the Pepsi-Cola corporation after his death, and not by courtesy alone.

Will Joan Crawford continue making films until, the image of the old Joan at last forgotten, she can prove consistently in character roles what she has always wanted so desperately to prove, that she is a real actress? Very likely. Will she succeed? Much more doubtful. To be brief about it, she never succeeded in her films in providing that quality of warmth, of softness, tenderness, sympathy which appeals from the experience of the actor to the experience of the audience. She has tried hard, but it never seemed quite real. Small wonder. She has had little enough experience of it in her own life.

CLARK GABLE

If King Douglas Fairbanks held his crown partly by virtue of being the consort of Mary Pickford, his successor Clark Gable was the most democratically chosen monarch ever to achieve The Throne. Gable was elected unanimously by the public. He had no rivals. Any fan magazine writer who strove to stir up interest by weighing him against competitors, actual and potential, would have starved to death. People *liked* him so

Clark Gable as a movie extra in 1925

1931: With Norma Shearer

1934: With Claudette Colbert

1932: With Marion Davies

1931: With Greta Garbo

1934: With Myrna Loy

1942: With Lana Turner   1933: With Jean Harlow

1936: With Jeanette MacDonald

1955: With Jane Russell

1953: With Ava Gardner

1939: With Vivien Leigh, on the set of *Gone With the Wind*

With Rosalind Russell

much. They liked everything about him. He was one of the perfect representatives of the real meaning of the word "star." People went to see his pictures because they knew that no matter how the picture turned out, they were going to enjoy watching him for an hour and a half.

He took a while getting there. A worker in rubber plants and oil fields, a movie extra in the twenties, he finally achieved professional standing in the last days of the legitimate theater as a national institution, when "road companies" still went out for week-long runs, interspersed by one-night stands, through virtually the whole country. He became leading man or second lead in the companies of Alice Brady and Pauline Frederick, and it was an open secret that his duties for them after the third-act curtain were more important than those he performed onstage. Of Miss Frederick, the great Miss Frederick, he once exclaimed, "My God, you'd think she never expected to see another man as long as she lived." However that may be, his association with these ladies made him at last an insider in the profession, and he got parts, good parts, wherever he could be suitably cast in spite of what were thought of as facial deficiencies. Then Lionel Barrymore began to take people to see him in performance after performance of the Los Angeles stage production of *The Last Mile,* in which he was appropriately cast as Killer Mears. Everyone recognized the electricity he generated in this congenial role. But how could it be harnessed and driven for the camera? Could the force of his portrayal of a condemned killer desperate to escape and live be diverted or molded into something more "sympathetic"? We shall not repeat the oft repeated story of how Gable's big ears and other photogenic drawbacks got him turndown after turndown, or bit parts in gangster roles, until Irving Thalberg saw that it didn't matter what he looked like as long as he gave the audience a jolt in every scene in which he appeared, which by that time he had proved that he could do. The story in any case proves no more than that the minds of most people in Hollywood, like the minds of most people everywhere, run along rails. Mayer and Thalberg at first exploited his "sex menace," a new and fashionable phrase in 1931, casting him in underworld parts which gave him a good excuse for treating the women rough. Like Cagney, he slapped them around a good bit—this too was a 1931 fashion—but the real Gable love-making approach, in art and in life, was quite different. He didn't leer at his prey, like Valentino, or steathily up on them and seize them in a steely embrace. He simply signaled with his eyes what his intentions were, and waited. If the girl affected indignation or virginal withdrawal, he just laughed at her—laughed, and made a wisecrack, often a wisecrack unconnected with sex. Whatever their relative social status or momentary relationship, he was a man and she was a woman, and they were alone, and there was only one way for them to end up, horizontally speaking. It was not even necessary to show the horizontal scenes. He knew, and she knew, and the audience knew, that that was what was going to happen. He was that kind of a man.

That kind of a man. Like nearly all the great screen personalities, Gable's impact was immediate. Like Gloria Swanson, he had only to enter a room to command the attention of everybody in it. Nor did he try to pretend to hide what he had. Not for him the dark glasses and hunched shoulders routine. In bachelor days, and during some of his duller marriages, he was much given to solitary trips supposedly devoted to hunting and fishing in the wilds, but often simply explorations of the highways and byways of the western United States. On such escapes from Hollywood he did not stop at the big hotels, but at beaneries, niteries, and motels. If a truck driver seated beside him on a stool in a dog-wagon said, "Ain't you Clark Gable?", his answer was, "Sure." If barmaids and waitresses gave him the eye, as they were sure to do unless paralyzed by astonishment at serving Clark Gable, he made no difficulties about spending the night between their sheets. This is not the way of the gifted, the celebrated, and the rich. Their casual sex affairs are carefully arranged by go-betweens, sometimes at great expense; otherwise the consequences are apt to be dangerous and embarrassing. Gable didn't give a damn, and he never suffered from it. Only once, from far-off England, was an attempt made to extort money from him, but that was arranged by professional blackmailers and was thrown out of court. For the rest, he shared his male wealth with hundreds—maybe thousands—and got only gratitude in return. Carole Lombard's estimate of her husband's sexual prowess has already been quoted, but after all, that was only one girl's opinion, however experienced, and the rest differed sharply. Their attitude seems to have been, "My God, I've had Clark Gable once, and once ought to be enough for any girl." He was, to repeat, that kind of a man.

After his gangster period, Mayer and Thalberg cast him in action parts—as a hell diver, a test pilot, the overseer of a rubber plantation, rough guys who could be expected to take their women where they found them, and that satisfied his public very well. There came a soggy period when they tried him out in conventional hero roles, as a minister of the gospel opposite Marion Davies in *Polly of the Circus* and as a romantic officer with Helen Hayes in the remake of *The White Sister*. The public saw no reason to waste Clark Gable in parts which might as well be played by, say, Ramon Novarro, and the columnists, desperate as ever for copy, began to hint that he was slipping. Frank Capra settled that once and for all in *It Happened One Night,* in which he set the Gable screen personality, as two years later he transformed Gary Cooper's. From here on in, for more than twenty years, Clark Gable continued to play Clark Gable to everybody's satisfaction and pleasure—the adventurer of life who never looked around corners to see what was ahead, relying on his humor, his wits, his fists, and other parts of his anatomy to get him out of any tight spot his recklessness got him into—or, if he didn't get out of it, to take it on the chin with a smile. There were enough variations to be played on this character to make it endlessly entertaining. In *Boomtown,* his doctor tells him he has heart disease, and that he must give up steaks and liquor at once. "I see," Clark replies, "you mean that in order to go on living, I've got to stop living." You knew he wouldn't. Twice in his career perhaps he attempted serious performances, "characterizations." With Greta Garbo, in *Susan Lenox,* he played a man who was tortured by his belief that the only woman for him was a whore—which she eventually became in reaction to his lack of faith in her. Bad picture though it was, no one who saw it will ever forget their final reunion, the last desperate resort of a love that can never be satisfied, that will always be riddled with doubt. *Parnell* was another matter. Gable either could not understand, or could not project, the complexities of a character which made W. B. Yeats write: "Parnell may free all Ireland/And you still break stone." No one perhaps but a born Irishman could understand it—and don't let one ever back you into a corner in order to explain it. Parnell was Gable's one box-office flop. As for Rhett Butler, no comment required. If Miss Mitchell did not consciously write the part for him, her subconscious did.

Gable's amorous life, always of great interest to his public (how could it be otherwise?), was a checkered one, part of it displaying a curiously dissappointed character reminiscent of Valentino's. His first wife, Josephine Dillion, a professional dramatic coach, recognized him a rough diamond of dramatic magnetism and did her best to polish it, but when he drifted away she made no attempt to cling; she knew this potential fireball was not destined to be hers for any length of time. How different Rhea Langham Gable. She was a wealthy Texas widow who married Gable when he was unknown, financed his early Hollywood struggles, and then, when he struck it rich, proceeded to enjoy to the hilt her public position as the wife of the world's most desirable male. She was older than Gable and looked it, especially in photographs, and it was disconcerting to his fans to look at night club photographs of their man seated beside this ample, slightly rattled woman, among the young and gay. Soon it was known that the Gable ménage was largely a marriage of convenience, but Rhea Gable, if this was the best she could get, was perfectly willing to settle for it, so long as she received the honor and deference due her. Gable said and did nothing until he fell in love with Carole Lombard. Then he asked for his freedom. Rhea Gable refused it, emphatically and with finality. Hollywood was divided about this. People liked Rhea Gable, thought her a fine person and an amusing one—but Gable and Lombard were so obviously, as in the picture title, made for each other that it became increasingly difficult to sympathize with the dog-in-the-manger attitude of his present official wife. It took Gable five long years to pry himself loose from Rhea Gable, whereafter she adopted the role of a sort of dowager Mrs. Gable and played it for the rest of her life. Then Clark and Carole proceeded to demonstrate what could be made of the battered institution of marriage; they gave it a shine which must have reinspirited many of the worn of heart throughout the world. Carole liked to do crazy things—not that they were crazy to her, just natural—and Clark sat back and watched it and loved it and eventually went a little crazy himself. They studied each other's likes and adapted to them; luxury-loving Carole became a huntress and fisherman just to please her man—who thought it very funny. Their quarrels were epic but erotic. They were both at their professional peak, and that bugaboo, the conflict of careers and of status, bothered neither of them. They had it made.

Carole Lombard's death in an airplane crash almost crushed Gable. For the first time in his life, he faced a situation he could do nothing about. He went out with his male cronies and tried to follow his old pursuits, but much of his time he spent brooding alone at home, and his studio and his friends worried about him. Fortunately for him, so to speak, World War II had arrived, and it gave him a definite and obvious thing to do with himself: fight. Neither he nor his studio tried to wangle him a deferment on any of the thousand grounds which can be found when a priceless "property" is involved: American morale might have collapsed if Clark Gable had tried to evade war service. Instead he took his training, did his share of the fighting, and came out a major in the Air Force. Evidently this experience helped some. Soon afterward he married the woman generally known as Lady Sylvia Ashley. Her ladyship has given more trouble to editors and typesetters than any other international celebrity. She was a chorus girl when she married one of the oldest titles in England and became Lady Ashley. When she divorced her English husband and married Douglas Fairbanks, she liked to be known both as Mrs. Fairbanks and as Lady Sylvia Ashley. When Fairbanks died and she married Gable, while continuing to call herself Lady Sylvia Ashley, bewilderment became so general that people just gave up and referred to her as "Lady Gable." The marriage was short-lived and she is again known today as Lady Sylvia Ashley when she appears in the public print, which is seldom.

Gable's last marriage was to Kay Spreckels, a popular Hollywood divorcee and non-professional, who devoted herself quietly to making him happy and comfortable. He was getting old now and looked it, even on the screen, and his scenes of action and even of love-making grew shorter, his dialogue scenes longer. The old sparkle was a little diminished. He couldn't bring himself to care much any more. He was continuously in demand by independent producers after he left M-G-M, but he had to be persuaded to accept a role. He deliberately lifted his price so high as to make it almost prohibitive to hire him, and when he made a picture at all it was likely to be as a favor to a friend. Inevitably, inexorably, the legend has grown up that his attempt to repeat his old action feats at the behest of John Huston in *The Misfits* weakened his heart and led directly to his death, and it is on the record that he was highly critical of the unprofessional delays and high jinks which pervaded that ill-fated production. When he died soon after, he was deeply—rather quietly—mourned. It was as if people, inside their heads, turned away and said, "Goodbye, Clark—and thanks." He left behind him a posthumous son by Kay Gable—his first and only child, conceived when he was in his sixties. More than any offspring of the movie great, people will watch to see what John Gable turns out to be like.

CARY GRANT

We come now to three screen immortals who, at any Academy Award dinner for a number of years, might have been contenders for the non-existent Oscar for Stars Least likely to Succeed—Cary Grant, John Wayne, and Humphrey Bogart. Their qualifications for this honor were identical: Even after they had become professionals, they spent more years of their total careers in semiobscurity than in the spotlight of public adulation. Audiences were familiar with all of them, and accepted them for just what they seemed to be, good enough actors doing good enough jobs in pictures where the real interest focused on other players. Then came the magic moment, the turn of Fortune's wheel—one or another of them was cast in a role or roles which made the public see them in an entirely different light, a magnetic, entertaining one. Why? They had nothing more to offer than they always had had, except the extra skill of years of experience. What turned them overnight into sensations? It would be easy to set down as a mystery, an insoluble one. But it has to do with a specific kind of mystery—the mystery of casting; the obduracy of producers in refusing to see what a player really has to offer; and, often, the false images players form of themselves at the expense of their real talents.

When Cary Grant joined Paramount in 1931, the studio press agents could announce that he had been born in Bristol, England, January 8, 1904, that he was a student during World War I, that he had emigrated to the United States in 1921 and for the next ten years appeared in such stage productions as *Golden Dawn, Boom Boom, Wonderful Night, Nikki.* Cast first in small parts in such pictures as *The Blonde Venus,* with Marlene Dietrich, this nice-looking, bright-eyed young man with the deeply cleft chin seemed a definite comer. So thought Paramount, swiftly promoted him to leading man—where he stuck for the next six years in pictures like *Hot Saturday,* with Nancy Carroll, and *Thirty-Day Princess,* with Sylvia Sidney. He was a straight romantic lead, and it must astound the young fans of this blithe star when, chancing upon an old film on TV, they behold him speaking in deadly earnest lines which today he would kid, throw away, or command the director to have rewritten. There he seemed to stick, headed nowhere, and he became the subject of frequent loan-outs to other studios, always a danger sign for any contract player. But one of these loan-outs happened to be *Topper,* in which he and Constance Bennett played a couple of insouciant ghosts who interfere in the affairs of mortals with grace, charm, and a curious sort of human, or inhuman, understanding. That was the turning point for Cary. Riding the crest of the screwball comedy wave, his whole personality changed. His *dégagé* manner, beloved of all, seems to be based on a state of perpetual surprise at the state of the world and its inhabitants. He expects that surprise, because it happens to him constantly. His screen personality suggests that classic dialogue between the surrealist who exclaimed, "Only the marvelous is beautiful," and his critic who replied, "Yes, but since everything is marvelous, everything is beautiful." In such films as *Mr. Blandings Builds His Dream House, I Was a Male War Bride,* and *The Bachelor and the Bobby Soxer,* it became a contest between directors and writers to see which could provide him with the most embarrassing of a series of embarrassing moments which Cary walks and talks his way through with a bland unconcern. Sometimes he is shown harassed by his difficulties, but this is a little off the true Grant note. Nothing, to the Cary of today, is serious enough to take seriously. Long before James Bond achieved world fame as a debonair secret agent, Grant as spy or counterspy in such films as *Notorious* defeated his opponents, not by concealed walkie-talkies or gadgets up his sleeve or in his belt, but by talking his enemies into believing what even the audience knew was not so. It remained for Alfred Hitchcock to devise (he would) the most embarrassing of all Cary's embarrassing moments, in *North by Northwest,* by showing him doing broken-field running in front of a low-flying airplane shooting at him. This was grim enough, in Hitchcock's best underplayed style, and Cary ran for dear life, but the expression on his face as he ran seemed to say, "How did I ever get myself into such a *dull* situation?"

So he goes on at sixty-odd, a boon to the box office, bland and youthful-seeming as ever—though it vicariously winds the author to see him doing a chase scene today. His survival at the very top of the heap is sometimes attributed to the scarcity today of stars with proven audience pull. This can be only part of the story. A visit to any theater where a Grant picture is playing will provide proof that people genuinely enjoy him to the full; they seem proud of his perennial youth, and the whole nation rejoiced when he produced his first child at sixty. If he is interested in his profession as such, he has shown few signs of it, in spite of his splendid performance in Clifford Odets' beautiful, sincere, and devastating *None but the Lonely Heart.* Apparently he goes on making pictures because producers won't let him stop. Beseiged with more offers than he could even find time to discuss, he instructed his agents to give out that he would not even read the script of a film for which he was offered less than a flat million-dollar fee. He found himself with more scripts to read than ever before.

The private life of this vastly successful man has stood in strange contrast to the impression he makes on the screen. George Sanders has already been quoted on this subject: "Cary Grant, witty, sophisticated and infinitely debonair, in life a prey to theosophical charlatans, socially insecure, and inclined to isolation." Mr. Sanders' opinion is doubtless not the last word on the subject, but certain it is that Mr. Grant, in

A young picture of our oldest star. Cary Grant in 1932

(Above) Cary Grant today with Audrey Hepburn; (Right) Cary Grant with Ingrid Bergman and Claude Rains in *Notorious*, 1946, first of the postwar spy dramas; (Left) Elissa Landi, Cary Grant, and Sharon Lynne in *Enter, Madame,* 1934. Paramount had typed Cary at this period as a nominal leading man, stooge for female stars, shy and sort of put-upon; (Below right) Cary Grant astounded Hollywood by fighting to appear in Clifford Odets' version of Richard Llewellyn's *None But the Lonely Heart,* 1943, in which he played on equal terms with Ethel Barrymore and gave an electrifying performance as a cryptic Cockney tough guy, a forerunner of the Teddy Boy. He has never matched, nor even attempted to match, such acting since; (Below) Cary Grant did not hit his box office stride until 1937, with Irene Dunne in *The Awful Truth,* the epitome of the screwball comedies whose style he had made his own.

257

the thick of movie-making all these years, did not stud the columns of Louella and Hedda as a rounder, a partygoer, or a party-giver. He has spent much of his time between pictures in Europe. His marital record is hardly a chronicle of domestic bliss, to wit: Virginia Cherill (seven months); the effable Barbara Hutton (three years); Betsy Drake (three years); and, most recently, the mother of his child, Dyan Cannon. In the publicity put out during his last marriage he was portrayed as a contented man, rejoicing in domestic life and fatherhood, as gay and fun-loving off the screen as on, in spite of his years. But Sanders was right.

JOHN WAYNE

Big John Wayne, known to all as "the Duke," is not listed here among the Greatest Stars of All Time by the author's choice alone. Cold fact dictates his inclusion. Year after year, exhibitors with monotonous unanimity have reported that John Wayne and John Wayne alone can fill seats, with or without benefit of popcorn. His pictures are so similar that it is difficult to recall their names or to distinguish one from another, but he is probably the biggest money-maker in movie annals.

It is passing strange. John Wayne might not only have been nominated for Actor Least Likely To Succeed but also, for almost a decade afterward, the Most Obscure Star of All Time. Marion Michael Morrison played football at the University of Southern California until he found a job as prop boy at the Fox studio. Because of his height, six feet four, director Raoul Walsh singled him out to play the lead in a super-Fox-Western of 1931, *The Big Trail.* In dismissing this piece of misbegotten gigantism, critics pointed out that the hero could not only not read his lines with any conviction but could hardly get his words out at all. Fox tried him once more in a college picture, *Girls Demand Excitement,* but young Wayne was no more at home in the presumably more congenial football atmosphere than he had been as a pioneer scout. That might well have been the end of the Wayne experiment, except that Warners needed some Westerns to fill out its program, and a cheap, very cheap actor to star in them. This need soon passed, and so passed Wayne from the Warner lot. Then he descended to the Gorkian lower depths of the cinema—not to such relatively well-known quickie companies as Republic or Monogram, not to the Producers Releasing Corporation, but to Majestic, Mascot, Lone Star, Fourth Division, and other outfits which the average fan has not only forgotten but never heard of in the first place. For them he "starred" in Westerns which mostly were made in less than a week each, and which consisted of hard riding, hard shooting, and the tersest of dialogue, not only because of the "star's" vocal deficiencies but because it cost money to take a sound truck on location. He was a good-looking fellow, well muscled and with a handsome face, and once in a while one of the major studios would pick him up for a minor role whose physical type he happened to fit. He never stayed for more than one picture. As an actor, he was hopeless, no two ways about it. Probably he thought so too. Quickie Westerns were an easy way of making a modest living; why not let it go at that?

Then John Ford, for reasons he has never explained, decided that John Wayne was the perfect type for the manacled murderer whom the sheriff guards in that long and memorable journey in *Stagecoach.* Immediately thereafter he cast him in *The Long Voy-*

Marion Michael Morrison

(Left) Marion Michael Morrison, the football star turned studio prop-boy who turned actor —and turned off the critics. (Right) The Most Obscure Star of All Time: John Wayne in *Somewhere in Sonora,* one of the series of small-time Westerns in which, for a decade, he "starred" for quickie producers. (Top) The Duke Steps Out: After John Ford used him in *Stagecoach,* John Wayne was suddenly in demand to play opposite the biggest female stars, as here with Marlene Dietrich in *Seven Sinners,* 1940.

(Right) "Very John Wayne" is what the GIs in Vietnam would call this scene from *To the Shores of Iwo Jima.* In the picture, Wayne does not himself raise Old Glory on that famous hill, but he does *hand* the flag to the men who did so. (Bottom) John Wayne with **Sophia** Loren, 1957. (Below) *Hondo,* 1954.

263

age Home, and subsequently in a long series of successful Western dramas. Soon Wayne, his quickie past behind him, was starring for others as well as for Ford, and attracting a steady audience of fans which grew and grew and grew. More articulate than at the beginning of his career, Wayne nowadays earnestly explains what caused the change. "John Ford taught me what to do in front of the movie camera," he says. "He taught me not to *act* but to *react.*" This earth-shaking discovery is of course one of the first principles of movie acting or any other kind of acting, and has been since the days when Greek actors wore masks to project or symbolize feeling. A player who does not react to his fellow actors is an amateur, and the timing of his response to what they say and do is the essence of his technique. But when Ford's advice finally penetrated the brain and nervous system of John Wayne, it did make all the difference. It was perhaps the particular quality of Wayne's "reaction" that so attracted fans. It is slow. He watches and listens impassively to the behavior and speech of others. Then he waits awhile before he responds, either in speech or in action. If you've seen him often enough, you're pretty sure what he's going to say or do, but the fact that he makes you wait for it produces a kind of involuntary suspense which affects the reflexes even as the mind rejects it. Then too there is the fact that the pictures he makes today, handsomely mounted and expensively produced, are at bottom as elementarily intestinal in their appeal as his old quickies —which has much to do with their success. He carries the simplistic virtues of the cowboy into other roles. Further than this the author cannot carry his analysis of the art of John Wayne. It eludes him. But the hard fact of his immense, continuing draw is the monolithic monument of movie life today.

Through the years of his obscurity and his success, John Wayne has done little to help pay the rent of fan writers. He has led an amiable, informal life, in company chiefly with John Ford and other outdoor-lovers. He has been married three times—twice to Mexican girls—and produced six children. He is said to have gambled a good deal in horses and oil, not always brilliantly, but his own film producing company, Batjac Productions, has done very well indeed, especially with *The Alamo,* an expensive, ambitious, unconvincing production which through reissue after reissue continues to make money. He proudly boasts membership in the Hollywood Alliance for the Preservation of American Ideals, an organization which has apparently adapted a maxim of the old West to modern conditions: "The only good Communist is a dead Communist."

HUMPHREY BOGART

Humphrey Bogart is no name for a star. None of the studio geniuses who chose box-office names for the Rock Hudsons or, as Bogart referred to them, "the Tabs and the Lances," would have hit on this one. If you can get yourself to dissociate it from the image it automatically brings to mind, the name may seem to belong in that peculiar category of movie names—the names of minor players or obscure technicians—whose oddness has impressed itself on the mind as we watched the screen credits pass through the years: Van Nest Polglase, Hermes Pan, Farciot Edouart, Orville O. Dull. And that, for a quarter of his screen career, was where the name of Humphrey Bogart was to be found, down among the dead men—he got fifth billing, sixth billing, even, in one picture he made after he had been on the screen three years, tenth billing. The fan magazines,

Humphrey Bogart in *Up the River*, 1930.

Humphrey Bogart with the invaluable Joe Sawyer in *Black Legion*, 1936, which might well be described today as the biography of a Wallaceite.

(Left) *In a Lonely Place*, 1949—the only time Bogart's stiffened, partly paralyzed upper lip was allowed to show in a movie scene.

(Left) When she was Mrs. Bogart, Mayo Methot's drunken fisticuffs with her husband became legendary. Here he is only lighting her cigarette—the studio caption says.

Dark Passage, 1947

Three typical Bogart shots

In *Chain Lightning, 1950,* as Matt Brennan

trying to make copy out of him after their fashion, decided for a brief period to call him "Humph." His reaction to this may be imagined, but he was too unimportant to be appeased.

His fans of today, eating their way through every scrap of material ever printed about him, as relentlessly as they view and review his most ancient films on TV, have yet to come up with any of the customary early proofs of unrecognized genius. There weren't any. He was that maddening kind of actor who stands where he is told to stand, reads the lines he has memorized with the proper inflection, reacts correctly and on cue—and who seems to give absolutely nothing to a part or a picture beyond the bare essentials. That minimum he does deliver, which is why he is on salary at all, but to a director bent on creating mood and exciting feeling in an audience he offers nothing more than the grand piano he leans against or the cocktail glass in his hand. We all know such actors, we even sometimes remember their names.

These players come a dime a dozen, and just as there is no reason for a studio to push them, neither is there any reason to replace them with an identical nullity; as a result, they often last for years in pictures and get automatic raises at option time, through the inertia or absent-mindedness of their bosses. That Bogart did not hang on longer in this anomalous position was due primarily to the fact that his salary, $750 a week, was a bit too high for an actor so negative. In 1930 he had been brought out from New York at that figure, in the first mad talkie days when everybody who had ever crossed a stage was being signed up by the desperate moguls; it is significant that his first assignment was not an acting role but the job of voice coach for the silent star Charles Farrell. By 1932 the

Bogart as the classical Sam Spade, to Mary Astor's Miss Wonderly, in *The Maltese Falcon*, 1941.

With Bette Davis in *Dark Victory*, 1939

madness had passed, the sheep were separated from the goats, and the latter were limping back to a Depression-crushed Broadway which could not absorb them. Bogart could hardly complain that he had not been given a fair trial. He had made eight pictures in two years. When his number came up, the studio decided to drop him on the nominal ground that his stiffened upper lip, partly paralyzed by a World War I wound, was hard to photograph. You could never, the argument went, sell a stiff upper lip to women.

Bogart seemed to have missed the tide, and his youth was behind him. His numerous friends in the theater could do little to help a colorless ex-Hollywood ex-juvenile; they were trying desperately to hang on themselves. His non-professional friends, who thought he was a hell of a guy, wondered how such a fellow had ever decided to be an actor in the first place. He wondered himself when, to keep eating, he demonstrated chess-playing at a dollar a game in the window of a Sixth Avenue "sportsland." Young actors had done sillier things when jobless, but at thirty-five, it seemed he had jumped straight into old age, that the next step would be to join the elderly chess players in Washington Square Park.

Then Leslie Howard picked him to play Duke Mantee in *The Petrified Forest,* and at Howard's insistence a reluctant Warner Brothers brought him back to Hollywood to repeat his role in the film version. It was a curious role to provide so momentous a turning point. In contrast to the snarling violence of the screen gangsters to whom Edward G. Robinson and Jimmy Cagney had accustomed the public, Duke Mantee sat motionless behind a tommy gun for almost the entire picture. Compared to the star's florid lines, his dialogue was sparse. But there he sat, cradling his gun—and for the first time the blankness which had characterized Humphrey Bogart's professional personality focused into meaning. The blankness was a fence, a wall. a duckblind behind which something lurked—but what? What was this nondescript armed cipher going to do with his gun? Who was he? Was he even really there?

The effectiveness of this new kind of gangster type was undoubtedly the doing of Robert E. Sherwood, who knew how to derive suspense from character. It seemed at the time that he had written merely an effective slot to fit a personality which conveyed menace through its very ambiguity. That was the conclusion drawn by Warner Brothers from the undoubted audience impact of Bogart's appearance in this film. They kept him on as a second-string gangster, a backstop for their powerhouse of Cagney, Robinson, and George Raft, and a possible replacement if any of these big shots stepped out of line. Through *Bullets or Ballots, San Quentin, Dead End, Racket Busters, Invisible Stripes,* he was handled as a gangster type, and it was pretty much as such a type that the critics and public of the late thirties accepted him. That he was effective in such roles and an asset in such pictures, no one who went to movies at the time would have denied—and yet there was something odd about the effect he made, something slightly off-center, as if he wasn't quite with what he was given to do. His typecasting as a gangster was somehow off-type casting, just as he had never seemed quite to fit the stage juveniles to which his youth and good looks had anchored him in the twenties, or the roles he played in his first bout with the movies. And, though he was now much more assured and much better known, reviewers who had to try to "place" him in the movie pantheon found themselves in difficulties—difficulties so great that it was an irresistible temptation to dismiss the problem altogether. He was good, yes—but they felt something missing in him, something they thought essential to the make-up of a first-rank movie personality.

What was missing was a conventional approach to hero roles, or villain roles. A key to the meaning of this "lack" is to be found in what the author believes to be the best of his performances, in the 1937 film *Black Legion*. (The version now available on television has been severely cut on story lines alone; what is left is enough to enable the spectator to follow the plot, that and no more. Such cutting would do little damage to most of the forgotten films of the thirties, but in the case of this unique movie it is fatal.) *Black Legion* is the story of a young factory worker who is gulled into joining a worker's organization with Ku Klux trappings, the veiled purpose of which is strikebreaking. The young man is first disgusted and then horrified as he gradually discovers the real purposes of the organization and the higher-ups behind it, but by that time he is in the toils and he is only saved from involvement in murder, and indeed from his own death, by a somewhat fabricated miracle. This plot does not really get under way until the second half of the film. The first half devotes itself, as no other Hollywood film of any era has done, to a leisurely and detailed study of character. It wants to show us just what manner of young factory worker would be attracted to this black-robed outfit with its shrill patriotic credo and its latent hostility to democratic ways. He is a forthright, likable young man, if somewhat low-keyed in manner. His job is just a job to him, the necessary way of bringing home the bacon. He has great camaraderie with his fellow workers, and their mutual concerns, the chief of which are sports active and passive, occupy the foreground of his life. In the background, he is contentedly married, with two children, and it is clear that the life of the family centers around the mass media. His wife listens to radio soap operas and their commercials, and he listens to the late afternoon adventure programs slanted to teenage boys. He reads aloud the sports pages to his children, and the comics as well, and it is obvious that he identifies with Superman as keenly as they do. By this time his vague Middle Western xenophobia is stimulated by the promotion of a "Polack" to a job he thinks he deserves, the audience knows that we deal here with a grown-up child, a nice boy but a boy for all that, and there is nothing in his probable future to carry him forward into maturity. His experience with the Black Legion proves to be a test of maturity, and it is a credit to the maturity of everyone connected with the making of this exceptional film that enough has been shown of his fundamental decency, side by side with his childishness, to make his arrival at manhood convincing.

This does not sound very much like the Humphrey Bogart we know, and it isn't. It is his one purely intellectual feat of acting, a portrait which must have been drawn from observation, since there was nothing in his own upper-class background which could have furnished the details. And yet there is a link between this ordinary joe adrift in industrial civilization and the romanticized Bogart of his great days, the cryptic private eye, the amoral (yet knightly) gunrunner, the Rick of Rick's in Casablanca, the revolutionist who is not serious about revolution, who in fact does not care which revolution he is in as long as something goes up and something else comes down. The adventures of the later Bogart are the daydreams of the Bogart of *Black Legion,* put together and served up with that blend of sophistication and infantilism which is the unique characteristic of the mass arts. They are the might-have-beens of the boy who didn't drop out of high school or join the Marines. What stamps them indelibly as dreams is their mixture of incompatibles. The blankness of the early Bogart screen personality is never abandoned or even much embroidered; there is nothing about his speech, manner, clothes, or visible tastes and preferences to set him apart from any other man you might brush past in the subway. Everything about him links him to the lives of the most ordinary men and women in his audiences. Yet this unidentified and unidentifiable man is, in his confident behavior, at ease in every phase of human life, on every level, anywhere. Trying like so many others to fathom the exact nature of the link between Bogart and his audiences, Alistair Cooke thought: "They were constantly flattered by the revelation that a sudden call to dine with a jewel importer at the Ritz would find him shaved and dapper, handling the silverware properly, unawed by the wine list."

This subtle and dreamlike upgrading of ordinariness was not the whole measure of the Bogart image and legend. There were other, contradictory elements—and, as it proved, the more contradictory the better, since that meant that the composite whole offered the best of several mutually exclusive worlds. As the conventionally scapegrace son of distinguished parents (a doctor and a famous illustrator) he led the Scott Fitzgerald life of the New York 1920s—rigidly conventional, it seems from this distance. He missed none of the clichés of the time, Greenwich Village, Tony's on Fifty-second Street, and, if he did not wade in the Plaza fountain, he and his cronies ran out of gas on the Queensboro Bridge, conned their taxi fare out of cops, and shuttled between speak-easies and Turkish baths in a predictable routine. The most striking characteristic of 1920s wild-oats-sowing seems to have been, in retrospect, that it was supposed to last forever. When the Depression knocked the props out from under the Fitzgerald world, Bogart was in the midst of his own personal depression, the sticky transition between his sleek stage juveniles and his screen gangster personality. But after his performance as Duke Mantee had established him as a Hollywood star of the second rank, he went right back to the old hell-for-leather way of living though most of his former boon companions had turned sober and even solemn, in the left-wing fashion of the day. It was as if he had left something unfinished and was determined to use his new financial security as a means of catching up on the wasted years. That, in the late 1930s, security for a movie star was universally thought to depend on toeing the line, or at least not getting too far out of line, seemed to make no impression on him whatever. That he got away with it was due to his inveterate habit of taking the bull by the horns.

Ignoring or rebuffing most of the mechanics of star-making, he latched onto that single element in it which he would have seemed least likely to cotton to, publicity. Actors have press agents because what they say on their own is mostly either dull or damaging. Somebody has to write dialogue for them that will make them sound like themselves—i.e., their exciting screen selves. Bogart astounded the Warner publicity department by producing, on call and with ease, quotes that sounded more like him than anything the writers of his screenplays had been able to dream up. When the world learned that, in Bogart's opinion, the trouble with the world was that everybody in it was three drinks behind, the world was very pleased, not because it missed those three drinks but because the words were just the right words to come out of that masklike face. When Bogart showed up at "21" and El Morocco he was no longer the young actor about Broadway who had frequented them unnoticed for years; he was the archetypal movie tough guy, and as such, the expense-accounters in the bar just had to knock the chip off his shoulder. The chip wasn't there, but Bogart, out of a sort of sense of professional responsibility, rose to such occasions as if it had been. Whether he socked his tormentor, or got socked, or whether the brawl evaporated as inconclusively as night club brawls do, the way he fielded the event in the press the next day nailed it down as one more for our side. The fisticuffs may have gone against him but the victory was invariably his. He was a master of the calculated anticlimax. When Sherman Billingsley in fury ordered him out of the Stork Club, Bogart glowered: "You mean I'm really and truly barred?"—and many of the patrons left with him.

The picture of himself that he was half-consciously building was helped by his relationship with his third wife, Mayo Methot. Miss Methot was not unknown to moviegoers. A series of underworld films had made her familiar as the oddly named actress who was even better than Isabel Jewell or Gloria Grahame at playing shapely but shopworn dames whose drooping cheeks and dead eyes signaled that they were exactly one inch from throwing in the towel. That Bogart should have chosen this battered babe in preference to any of the lissome lovelies that life in Hollywood offered him carried its own logic to the growing band of admirers who were beginning to be as interested in the offscreen Bogart as in his screen character. Their alcoholic marital battles (the most dangerous of which were screened from the public) took place over a wide expanse, stretching from their house off Sunset Strip to the Warner lot in Burbank and on down to San Pedro harbor, and few representatives of the press or the law in the Los Angeles area were able to remain unaware of them. But the public, reading about them, simply shrugged its shoulders and said, it figures. Bogart and his wife were aware of this. Once when Bogart was being pestered by a night club heckler, his wife, fed up, stepped between them and knocked out the pest with a single punch. Bogart, delighted, held Mayo's arm up and said to all present, "She's marvelous. I wouldn't go anywhere without her." On another occasion, George Frazier reported, the Bogarts were leaving "21" and found themselves surrounded by autograph hounds: "In his anxiety to get away Bogart slammed a taxi door just as his wife was about to step in. The awareness that she was surrounded by a gibbering mob of her husband's admirers increased her anger. 'That cheap little ham actor,' she screamed, going on in such a vein for two or three minutes. The kids listened in awe. Finally one youngster closed his autograph book and turned to his companion to say, in a voice quivering with admiration, 'Gee, she's even tougher than he is.'"

With *The Maltese Falcon*, Bogart moved up to top-flight stardom and out of the gangster stereotypes he had played for six years, into the world, first of the private eye, and then of the wartime adventurer, more often a soldier-of-fortune type rather than any character who could legitimately be mistaken for GI Joe. With emphasis on him as the principal *raison d'être* of his films, the details of the personality he had been developing on screen and off sharpened. The Bogart of *Across the Pacific, Casablanca, To Have and Have Not, Key Largo,* and even of *The African Queen* was, when we first saw him at the beginning of each picture, a man who seemed to have decided *against* a number of things in life. To conventions and manners, social and military usages, all the minutiae of getting through life, he gave a smiling lip service which shatteringly signalled that he had rejected them all. The way he crossed a room, shook hands, removed his hat or didn't, lit a woman's cigarette or pointedly failed to light it revealed his determination to give minimum due to custom and to stop precisely there. His speech and manner of speaking were so patently insincere that when, as sometimes happened in his pictures, he had to express a genuine feeling or conviction, he was immediately in difficulties; he had, so to speak, used up his credit, cried wolf too often. That part of himself which he deeply reserved to himself could only find outlet in action uninflected. That, of course, made him the perfect movie figure he was. What he said was sardonic persiflage; what he thought you could only guess; it was what he did that you watched for. He was his own objective correlative.

Before Salinger, he had created a grown-up, beat-up Holden Caulfield, a man who no matter how you sliced it wasn't having any, except on his own terms, which were tough. Could the terms of this self-alienated man ever be met, by any turn of events? It seemed unlikely. But almost at the moment that his screen character took this final shape, life for Humphrey Bogart took a new and unexpected turn. He extricated himself, not a moment too soon, from his increasingly dangerous marriage to the alcoholic and now schizophrenic Mayo Methot, and at the same time married Lauren Bacall. For such as Bogart, Miss Bacall was simply too good to be true—a dish, a good joe, a professional, a loving woman. When, about the time he turned fifty, she presented him with two children, it seemed he had done what a Bogart-Holden Caulfield-Sam Spade would never do: He had given hostages to fortune. A suspicion of mellowness began to modify the public image of the great romantic toughie. He took good care that it remained only a suspicion. Even as paterfamilias, acknowleged great star, admired and even beloved figure, he must remain, and very obviously, a law unto himself. But his compulsive negativism began to show an obliquely constructive side. He continued his inveterate needling of the great and near-great, and especially of those studio executives whom he considered his inferiors, but he seemed now to needle in favor of something, better pictures, greater latitude for actors beyond the confines of what he considered idiot typecasting, a higher respect for the intelligence of the movie public. He attracted and allowed himself to be surrounded by a mixed bag of distinguished persons who were also admirers and champions: John Huston, Adlai Stevenson, Alistair Cooke, Truman Capote. He no longer snarled when it leaked out that he was a subscriber to the *Harvard Law Review*. Like so many other actors, he began to seek the sea as the one milieu, the one place of repose, in which he did not have to act out for himself the image of himself. His wife said that he loved his yacht, the *Santana,* more than he had ever loved a woman.

When his time came to die, he hated it and fought it and was afraid of it: He obviously felt that most of the really good things in his life had come late, and he wanted more of them than he was going to get. But from this he could not escape to the *Santana;* he had one last time to act out for the benefit of his friends and lovers the part of Humphrey Bogart, laughing every step of the downward path. He was one of the few actors, perhaps the only one, who could and did honestly portray naked physical agony, but for this last acting assignment he chose to keep it covered. The transaction of his own death was his most deeply considered performance.

That this saturnine, unbeautiful figure should have become the movie idol of the youth of the fifties and sixties, the only American movie figure they wholeheartedly accepted, is of a piece. "I don't trust any bastard who doesn't drink," Bogart said. "People who don't drink are afraid of revealing themselves." The operative word here is "trust." Alcohol is very far from "in" with the young, but Bogart's serious commitment to drinking was a sign to them that he was doing his own thing, all the way. A man whose wife said of him, "He is the only man I have ever known who truly and completely belonged to himself," was *their* man, on a level deeper than either he or they would want to put into words.

and she acquired a female as well as a male following, a devoted one which mourned her untimely death. She went Thalberg and everyone else one better by revealing an instinctive or self-taught flair for comedy which lifted her far above the freak sensation and put her on a par with the top professionals in pictures like *Libelled Lady* and *Blonde Bombshell,* the latter a semiautobiographical comedy about the private life of a screen star which told more about that side of Hollywood than most film-makers felt it politic to reveal. It is doubtful, for all her talent, that had she lived she would ever have developed into a Lynn Fontanne or Ina Claire of the silver screen. More likely she would have married William Powell and let the screen get along without her as best it might.

BETTE DAVIS AND MARLENE DIETRICH

1. Davis. Bette Davis wasted five years—through no fault of her own—in playing washed-out ingénues until *Of Human Bondage* proved her an actress of fire and imagination, and with an intellectual grasp of her craft. Thereafter she rivaled and often surpassed Joan Crawford in playing "gutsy" roles, and the public loved it. That she was also an artist of range, depth, and sympathy, she proved in *The Corn Is Green, Now Voyager,* and other films. She was one of the many candidates for the much disputed title of First Lady of the Screen, and for many years Warner Brothers billed her simply as "Wonderful" Bette Davis. But it wasn't her acting the public came to see, it was the spitfire, and the mannerisms in which the fire was expressed—mannerisms so pronounced, so easily imitable, that they overlaid the finer shadings of her work. The arrogant toss of the head, the swish of the skirt, the voice, grating or lightly contemptuous, the eyes, appraising and more often than not dismissing—formidable was our Bette, and formidable she remained long after her vogue and formal starring career were over; her posteresque personality has kept her in demand for pictures through all the years and changes, through age itself. In spite of her many marriages and divorces, and some inevitable attendant publicity, she has managed to keep her private life singularly private.

2. Dietrich. Marlene Dietrich's career has been one of the longest, the legends clustered about her are innumerable, and at first the intensity of her fans' worship of her seemed to rival Garbo's. It was that intensity which died. This insolent woman whose most commonplace words seemed freighted with meaning—it is as if, said a critic, the priestess of the Delphic oracle had stepped down from her pedestal to talk about the weather—proved to be a sphinx without a secret. Neither the personality created for her by Joseph von Sternberg nor any of the later self-created reincarnations ever managed to include the quality of sympathy, of mass movie audience identification. She was gorgeous, fun to watch, luscious to think about going to bed with—but remote; an invisible wall seemed to separate her from the public. Her survival as a screen and night club star through to the years of grandmotherhood is due to the simple fact that Miss Dietrich knows how to put on a show. "Marlene Dietrich is a *professional,*" said Alfred Hitchcock, "—a professional actress, a professional dress designer, a professional cameraman." Whether strip-teasing for the GIs overseas, letting Orson Welles saw her in half, or caressing her audience with

her limited but luring voice, Marlene delivers an evening's entertainment with the gusto of a restauranteur out to give you just a little bit more than your money's worth. Of the legends that have gathered round her through the years, including her relations with von Sternberg and with "Papa" Hemingway, whom she is said to have given that execrable nickname, the most intriguing is that the lighting in her bedroom is so arranged that the floor is flooded with illumination, so the man can find his shoes and socks, but the bed and its occupant are shrouded in darkness.

MARILYN MONROE AND MARLON BRANDO

1. Monroe. The short, tumultous, sad life of MM has become more important in American folklore than her career or her acting. If Grandpa is ever summoned to the equivalent of the chimney corner in the homes of the future to tell the tiny tots all about her, it will be about Marilyn and Di Maggio, Marilyn and Miller, Marilyn and Olivier that they will want to hear, not about her ambition to play Grushenka, or even the parts she actually did play. But screen legends must, somewhere along the line, originate on the screen itself, and perhaps the most memorable shot of the 1950s was Tom Ewell's fixed, incredulous stare as Marilyn walks away from him, with a wiggle that no one before or since has matched. Beyond the wiggle and the mammaries, she did in some of her films—*Bus Stop, The Seven-Year Itch,* and *The Prince and the Showgirl*—achieve something like a screen presence and authority of her own. But for the most part her work was uneven, patchy, and there were signs in her pictures that the director had shot around her, leaving out scenes she wasn't up to or simply failed to show up for. As her phobias increased—the chief of which was fear of the cameras, for all her experience before them—this sort of thing increased, and audiences grew wise to the fact. She could make an out-and-out flop, such as *Let's Make Love.* The public had come to the point where it would rather read about Marilyn's doings than go to see her on the screen, and at thirty-six, after ten years of incredible fame, Marilyn Monroe was definitely on the downgrade as a box-office attraction, a fact of which she was well aware. But the legend of Marilyn will live forever. It was her candor that won us—candor in the face not only of a squalid life to start with but also of her own mistakes. She stuck out her chin and took it on the chin and smiled—until she got tired of smiling.

2. Brando. What would have become of Marlon Brando if Tennessee Williams had never written the part of Stanley Kowalski? Something momentous, to be sure, because Brando was born for the trade of acting. But Kowalski as portrayed by Brando so indelibly imprinted himself on the imaginations of two decades of youth as the archetype of rebellion that it is difficult to imagine what the fifties and sixties would have been like without him, let alone what Brando would have been like without him. The spectator unconsciously carries the Kowalski image with him to see a Brando picture, so that when Marlon interprets a Napoleon or a Marc Antony with flawless integrity, the wonder is all the greater. Brando's initial rebelliousness, he was quick to make known, was all in the cause of art—of honesty and truth and meaning on stage and screen, and above all of

Marilyn Monroe in *Bus Stop*

Marlon Brando in *The Men*, 1950

freedom. His prairie-fire popularity soon achieved him a freedom no actor had ever enjoyed—but what did he do with it? He directed *One-Eyed Jacks*. This Western is indeed beautifully directed, scene by scene, but it goes on forever and winds up nowhere. The disaster resulting from his dictatorship over the production of the second *Mutiny on the Bounty* need not be recapitulated here. Since then he has, to be blunt about it, apparently been content to walk through whatever roles paid him the most money. Marlon Brando's name is one of the few—perhaps one of two—of the star names developed in the post-television era which could be billed alone above a title, with assurance of success and without that rash of "co-starring" and "also starring" and "introducing" by which producers seek to bolster their feelings of insecurity. It is not likely to remain in that high, honored position unless the ageing Mr. Brando can formulate and concretize just what it is he really wants to do on the screen—if he knows.

MARIE DRESSLER AND WILL ROGERS

1. Dressler. Marie Dressler and Will Rogers had to wait until almost the end of their lives before achieving world popularity, otherwise both would be classed among the immortals. Marie Dressler began convulsing audiences as an energetic comedienne in the 1880s, and continued to reign on stage, vaudeville, and screen until, in the 1920s, audiences finally seemed to have tired of her and she was subsisting on bit parts in the movies when she could get them. The shrewd old lady knew that losing face in the theater was as bad as losing face in the Orient, and she was equal to the situation. She went to the manager of the Ritz, an old friend, and said, "Haven't you got something, a maid's room up under the eaves, that you could let me have for what I'd pay at a boarding house on a side street?" He arranged it, and she was thus able to tell friends and new acquaintances, "You can always reach me at the Ritz." After her great hit in *Anna Christie,* and her even greater ones in *Min and Bill* and *Tugboat Annie,* Miss Dressler both impressed and annoyed Hollywood by snubbing studio "society" in favor of the rich and famous friends she had made in her long stage career in Europe and America. But they really *were* her friends, the fruit of a long, vastly enjoyable life in show business, and she saw no reason to turn her back on them and cultivate Hollywood biggies who had been nobodies last year and probably would be so again next year. Miss Dressler used every trick she had learned in fifty years as an entertainer to hold the audience she had snared in her old age, but it was herself that shone through, and which people loved. Probably her best role was her last, in the film version of Sidney Howard's *The Late Christopher Bean,* as an old servant who treasures the paintings her artist lover had given her, not because they had become priceless, but because he had loved her.

2. Rogers. Will Rogers, too, had to wait until late in life to make the movie public his own. A smash hit in the Ziegfeld Follies of the teens, he stood on the stage in cowboy outfit, twirling a lariat, and making wisecracks which brought the house down in continuous laughter. That was all there was to his act, but movie producers of the early days thought there must be some way to bring this sure-fire entertainer before the audi-

Will Rogers

Marie Dressler and Harpo Marx (at party for Thalbergs, 1931)

ences of the silent screen. But though the highbrows liked his silent films, *Jubilo* and *Doubling for Romeo,* and *One Glorious Day* was acclaimed as a masterpiece, the Rogers pictures brought poor returns. Will's wisecracks expressed in the form of subtitles missed fire, and though men liked him, female audiences refused to accept this ungainly creature as a movie star. But the talkies, and dialogue, enabled Rogers to get his arms around the whole audience, men, women, and children. As a Babbitt seeing a fictitious Paris and London for the first time, as a shrewd Yankee getting the best of everybody in verbal horse-trading, he seemed to represent the complete Philistine, but you knew perfectly well he wasn't anything of the sort. To him the human comedy was just that, with himself the best butt of his own best jokes. It was he who said, "The movies are the only place where you can sit in the audience and applaud yourself." Essentially a stand-up comedian, he adapted himself with ease to the stories built around him, and he could act, too, pithily, when occasion demanded it, which it seldom did, as he showed in *State Fair.* He was a great entertainer who was mourned deeply by the average guy because he showed in all his work that he knew what the average guy was up against.

WILLIAM POWELL
AND CAROLE LOMBARD

1. Powell. The unlikely transformation of this snaky, even slimy, villain into a suave star of boudoir and melodrama has already been described. Its unlikelihood still seems extraordinary. Put a photograph of Powell at his height in front of a youngster of today and tell him that this was once a great star, and the response will almost always be "Why?" None but those who have seen him in action can understand. For here was a finely honed acting intelligence, here was underplaying done with facile ease, here was the deliberate, conscious use of every asset he had, the easy concealment or minimizing of all his physical liabilities, which from the point of view of the camera were many. Words were his chosen weapons, but when the time for action came, something happened in the eyes of this slight man which was like the sound of the cocking of a revolver. Mr. Powell might have gone on delighting audiences forever, but, as has been stated, he had been around so long before achieving prominence that his period as a romantic star was limited—though it lasted quite long at that. In old age, Mr. Powell sometimes comes out of retirement to give a lift to pictures which can often use it, such as *The Senator Was Indiscreet, Mr. Roberts,* and *How to Marry a Millionaire.*

2. Lombard. Carole Lombard and William Powell were briefly married, and it seemed like an ideal match; this sophisticated pair complemented each other superbly. This was in the period when Miss Lombard was the glazed, immobile heroine of countless woeful dramas in which she concealed tears behind a tinsel mask. But that, that was not the real Carole Lombard *Twentieth Century* at last revealed. There she reverted to the technique of her Mack Sennett days and soon made herself the queen of screwball comedy in such masterpieces and near-masterpieces as *Nothing Sacred, True Confession,* and *To Be or Not to Be.* Her favorite form of entertaining was a house party, and life and the

William Powell in *Love Crazy*

Carole Lombard

screen to her were simply a fun fair. Her clowning began with her arrival on the set, and the cameras might start turning whenever they would. She taught Clark Gable how to play, something he had long worked at without success, and she taught him something else simple and difficult—that it is more blessed to give then to receive. She said whatever came into her head. When others commiserated with her that, after the deduction of income taxes and other expenses, she kept only 20 per cent of her six-figure salary for herself, she replied, "I don't care. I enjoy this country, and I don't mind paying my share of the freight." President Roosevelt expressed himself as very pleased at this, and nobody else dared express anything else.

ELIZABETH TAYLOR
AND NORMA SHEARER

1. Taylor. Whether Elizabeth Taylor will end up among the immortals is something only the Olympian gods can say, and they have not yet spoken. Perhaps, like us, they have been too busy watching. She began in beauty. Her present claim to fame is her unrivaled notoriety—if such a word and its attendant values have meaning any more. Matrons who "adored" the petaline, wholesome teen-ager of *National Velvet* now huff and puff at her outrageous, flagrant defiance of convention and even of the law (perhaps they would huff and puff less if Miss Taylor's unconventionalities took place behind closed doors, like yours and mine), then rush to the nearest theater to see what kind of iniquitous monster this once adored little girl has turned into. As a performer, Miss Taylor is camera-wise, sometimes sincere, sometimes seemingly indifferent. That she was good in *Suddenly Last Summer,* in *A Place in the Sun,* and in *Butterfield 8,* few would deny. Her Cleopatra is neither here nor there; it is such a miracle that this film got pieced together at all that detailed criticism of its parts is not in order. *Who's Afraid of Virginia Woolf?,* designed to prove her histrionic ability and ease the transition to more mature roles, deserves "A" for effort, and that's about all. Her Martha was competent but monotonous; it failed to suggest all the past that produced the present virago. There is also about it the air of doing as she was told. But it was no inept failure, as her detractors had hoped; it was a good try at a part in which she was fundamentally miscast. Meanwhile there is Rome, the Lido, London, the front pages, the magazines, and Burton, Burton, Burton. Miss Taylor and her husband must have discovered by now what the Bible could have told them long ago, that there is unfortunately no way to invent a new sin.

2. Norma Shearer. Like Elizabeth Taylor, Norma Shearer is a close contender for the top honors. From the soft-eyed Kathy of *The Student Prince* in the silent days, through the calculated and flaunted wickedness of *The Divorcee, Let Us Be Gay, A Free Soul,* and *Riptide,* the momentary return to sweetness and light in *Smilin' Through,* and her final canonization as Elizabeth Barrett Browning and Juliet the women adored her and flocked to her matinees. With Gloria Swanson and Joan Crawford, she was to her female admirers a symbol of what a woman could make of herself. A slightly walleyed ingenue to begin with, she gradually corrected that defect, obliterated the hard Canadian r's from her speech, dressed better, looked better, and acted better as each year passed. Her triumph was *The Women,* in which she firmly held stage center in the key role, despite a cast studded with her peers among female stars, each determined to steal the picture for herself. That she was also Mrs. Irving Thalberg, wife of the overlord of M-G-M, was very nice, of course, but it probably meant little more than that she got what she wanted a little more easily and quickly than some of her competitors—a fact attested by her remaining an M-G-M star for seven years after her husband's death. She more or less drifted out of pictures after making what she later acknowledged was the mistake of mistakes, turning down the title role in *Mrs. Miniver* because she would have had to play the mother of a grown son. Some years later she married a skiing instructor and became adept at the sport. She has from time to time toyed with the idea of coming back, but has devoted herself instead to discovering new potential star material.

288

Elizabeth Taylor in 1944

Norma Shearer, with Herbert Marshall, in *Riptide,* 1934

SELECTED SHORT SUBJECTS IV

Orson Welles in *The Stranger*, 1946

Adolphe Menjou

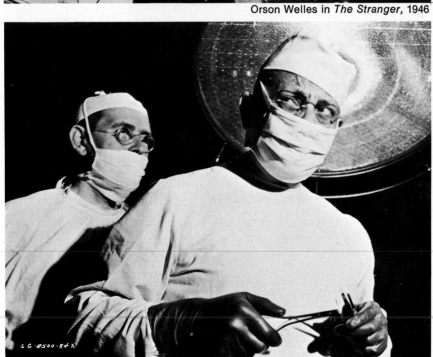

Erich Von Stroheim

Lana Turner and Van Johnson

Lizabeth Scott in *Desert Fury*, 1947

Katharine Hepburn and Spencer Tracy in *Keeper of the Flame*, 1943

5 THE STELLAR PANTHEON

"...But wait till you see her in her new film. A *type!*"

"In France," says Alice, "if you call a person a type it's an insult."

"Well, it isn't in Hollywood—it's a compliment—with a salary tied to its tail."

Alice M. Williamson, whose books were far from worldly, was nevertheless a woman of the world, and her account of a sojourn in Hollywood, *Alice in Movieland,* recorded with delight all the topsy-turvy values to be found if you ventured down the rabbit hole. *Typage,* as the French and Russians called it, was indeed almost a necessity for the mass production of silent films. Because of the lack of words, it was both economical and helped speed the action if the audience recognized on sight the Hero, Heroine, Villain, Vamp, Mother, Whore, even Bookkeeper. Sound modified this system, but essentially it has remained the same. Sooner or later nearly all durable screen players slowly group themselves in categories in which their most striking qualities are shown to best advantage. They may and often do cross the line from one type to another, but by and large each of the immortals has his own niche and sticks to it. The evils inherent in this system are of course many. Strong physical characteristics may cause directors and producers to consistently miscast players whose psychological and temperamental interiors fit them for quite different roles. The constant show-business quest for something new frequently leads to casting a player against his own type ("off-type casting"), a trick which sometimes works beautifully, sometimes disastrously. And many a player must wait long years to outgrow mere handsomeness or beauty to show what he really has, what character trait or mannerism will really fetch the public. In this regard, the metamorphoses of Myrna Loy, Merle Oberon, Jean Harlow, and William Powell have already been described. And then, of course, the miracle sometimes happens, as when Frank Sinatra, the skinny, knobby-kneed swooner-crooner proved himself to be one of the most accomplished, sincere, and effective actors in screen history. Today we witness a new revolution in casting, caused not by the discovery of new values in individual actors, but by a shift in the way the audience looks at them. James Coburn and Lee Marvin began their careers, logically in terms of the old dispensation, as minor tough guys or out-and-out villains. The vogue of the anti-hero has made them, at least temporarily, into stars. They have not changed, nor are they presented in a new light, but what once made them shrinkable-from now makes them attractive.

But by and large the public rests content with its Hollywood pantheon, and he who ventures forth from his niche in aspiration toward that of another does so at some peril. The immense audience satisfaction in seeing an Edward Everett Horton, a Phil Silvers, or an Eve Arden come on as their familiar selves is still solid and constant. Psychiatrists might call it repetition compulsion, but the satisfying of such compulsions is an important function of popular art. The mythmaking qualities of the screen are enhanced by this stereotyping of stars. It makes life seem as simple as most people wish it was. And besides, it saves you the trouble of figuring out which are the Good Guys and which the Bad, which in today's world is an incredible blessing.

292

1928: Esther Ralston and Gary Cooper in *Half a Bride*

(Clockwise)
1925: May McAvoy; 1928: John Westwood and Marion Douglas in *Shepherd of the Hills;* 1926: Leatrice Joy; 1922: For a time Mary Miles Minter was Mary Pickford's principal rival; and, like Miss Pickford, she had a hard time growing up in the public eye. Here she is at the halfway house, with curls still down her back, but wearing a "velvet bathing suit, with ruffles of taffeta, suitable for beach purposes only."

1927: Clara Bow and Buddy Rogers in *Wings*

1928: Sally O'Neil and William Bakewell in D. W. Griffith's *The Battle of the Sexes*

1934: Helen Mack, Lyda Roberti, and Mary Brian, youthful Paramount "stars" of the thirties

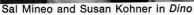
Sal Mineo and Susan Kohner in *Dino*

1967: Lulu in *To Sir with Love*

1930: No youthful star ever made a more immediate hit than Sue Carol, seen here in *The Golden Calf.* "Sweet Sue" was written to signalize her popularity, but those who sing it have forgotten, if they ever knew, that her vogue lasted only two years and that she slid swiftly into what would have been permanent oblivion had she not become, first, a Hollywood agent and then the wife of Alan Ladd.

Jane Fonda   1967: Peter Fonda in *Wild Angels*

1934: Ben Alexander, a child star of the Teens and much later the second lead of *Dragnet,* seen here in the awkward transition stage with Mari Colman and Richard Cromwell in Cecil B. De Mille's misbegotten epic of thirties youth, *This Day and Age.*

Alice Terry

Dolores Costello

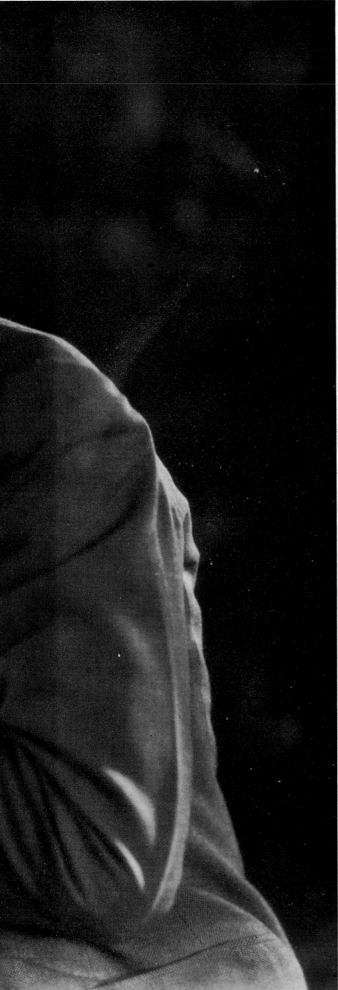

Billie Dove

Dolores Del Rio

Dagmar Godowsky   Madeleine Carroll

Ann Harding   Vilma Banky

302

Katharine Macdonald

LOVE

(Opposite left) 1927: Prolonged passionate embraces were the principal feature of the three silent films which Greta Garbo and John Gilbert made together, but this scene from *Love,* a version of *Anna Karenina,* carries more of the electricity between them than any of their mushy close-ups.

(Below) 1928: Vilma Banky and Ronald Colman in *Two Lovers.* Miss Banky and Colman, Samuel Goldwyn's "love team" of the twenties, were considerably more genteel than Gilbert and Garbo, but equally beautiful to look upon.

(Left) 1931: Janet Gaynor and Charles Farrell in *Merely Mary Ann.* The Gaynor-Farrell team exemplified pure, non-adulterous, spun-sugar love for seven years, to the pain of the discriminating and the delight of the majority.

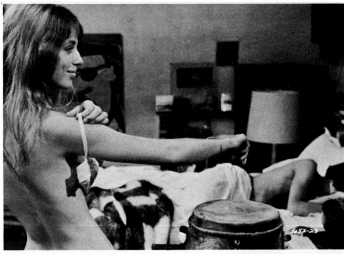

(Left top) Wallace Reid and Lois Wilson succumb to a sudden impulse.

(Left bottom) 1934: Married love, flip, insouciant, and understated, was the novelty which William Powell and Myrna Loy introduced to films in *The Thin Man*. Here Miss Loy watches Powell with tolerant suspicion.

(Above right) 1968: Elizabeth Taylor and Richard Burton in *The Comedians*. Sole survivors of the "love teams" of the past, the open secret of Taylor and Burton's box office is that their love for each other was established in the public mind before they ever appeared on the screen together.

(Above) 1968: Modern movies have little time for "love" as the screen used to understand it. The studio caption for this still from *Lita* says: "Joanna Shimkus dresses before leaving for home after her first love affair. Jose Flatats remains asleep as the young girl returns to her dying Aunt Lita."

(Right) Robert Mitchum and Ava Gardner in *Carriage Entrance*.

Charles Farrell and Dolores Del Rio in *The Red Dance*.

1932: Five years before their marriage, Carole Lombard and Clark Gable struck sparks from each other on the screen in *No Man of Her Own*.

Hobart Bosworth in *The Sea Wolf*

1939: Sam Jaffe, Victor McLaglen, Douglas Fairbanks, Jr., and Cary Grant in *Gunga Din*

310

ACTION STARS

1940: Errol Flynn in *The Sea Hawk*

1940: Clark Gable and Spencer Tracy in *Boomtown*

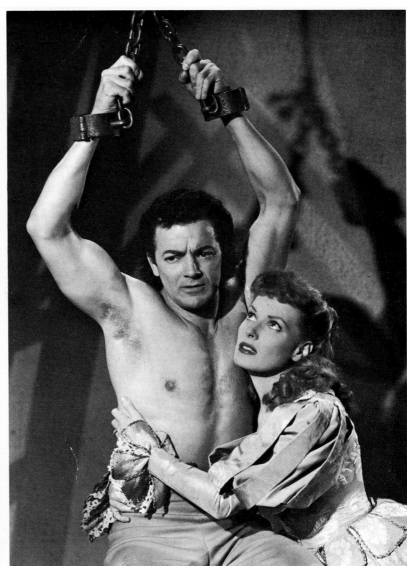

Cornel Wilde and Maureen O'Hara in *Sons of the Musketeers*

1947: Tyrone Power in *The Captain from Castile*

1942: John Wayne and Randolph Scott in *The Spoilers*

1954: Charlton Heston in *The Naked Jungle*

1918: William Farnum

1921: Tom Mix

318

1928: Tim McCoy and Rex Lease

1922: Hoot Gibson

1932: Gene Autry

1930: Bill Boyd

1928: Ken Maynard

1933: Randolph Scott

VC-A-6

1954: Burt Lancaster

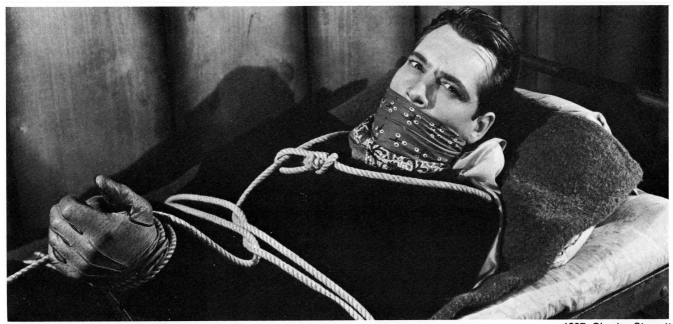

1937: Charles Starrett

1948: The John Ford Western Repertory Company. Left to right, Henry Fonda, John Wayne, the veteran George O'Brien, John Agar, and Ward Bond.

1932: Buck Jones

1927: Chester Conklin

(Left) 1924: A graduate of the Mack Sennett laughing academy, Louise Fazenda survived several movie metamorphoses, including the coming of sound. She was a valued adjunct of film comedy for thirty years. She is shown here with Alan Hale in *Main Street*.

(Below) 1919: Roscoe "Fatty" Arbuckle became a star in the early period when "the pranks of naughty boys, the humors of undress and obesity, physical mishaps of all kinds" were the staple of film comedy. But he developed a peculiarly delicate pantomimic style, as this still illustrates.

COMEDY STARS

(Above) Dick Powell and Joan Blondell in *Gold Diggers of 1937*

(Right) 1916: By common consent, Mabel Normand was the greatest of screen comediennes, at her best the peer of Chaplin, though her work declined in later years through illness and drugs.

(Below) 1951: "You don't come across, I don't come across," says Judy Holliday to Broderick Crawford in a classic definition of their relationship in *Born Yesterday.*

1933: Benito Mussolini once besought Louis B. Mayer to make more pictures with "the fat man and the thin man." Lovers of Laurel and Hardy, seen here in *Pardon Us*, may resent being endorsed by Mussolini, but, their appeal was universal. "You attend to your business and I'll attend to mine" was one of the great comic lines of all time, the point being that neither Laurel nor Hardy ever had any business, separately or together.

1957: Red Skelton plays the part of Rusty Morgan, a happy, likeable, not-too-bright boy who works in a lunchroom, in *Public Pigeon Number One*.

1925: A majority of one. Buster Keaton is not fazed by finding himself alone in a theater because he is always alone everywhere. One of the two greatest movie comedians, he is the least dated of all of them, and today his work seems particularly apposite and modern. But his fervid admirers now might well consider that for long years after the end of his stardom he was forgotten, or remembered only as a square.

1923: *Why Worry?* was the title of this picture, but Harold Lloyd's primary appeal as a comedian was to the worry wart in all of us. Much of his time on the screen was devoted to repetition-compulsions such as this. It made him for many years the richest of all movie stars.

1931: Polly Moran and Jimmy Durante in *The Passionate Plumber*

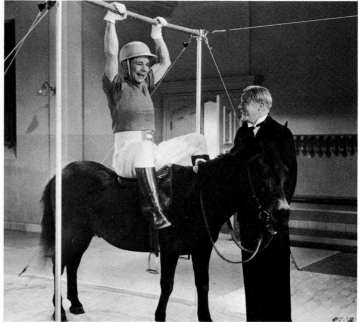

1934: Joe E. Brown in *Polo Joe*

1936: Warren Hull, Hugh Herbert, Patricia Ellis, in *Love Begins at Twenty*

331

(Left top) 1937: Allan Jones, Groucho, Chico, and Harpo Marx, and a certain suspicious-looking suitcase in *A Day at the Races*. Can it be that Groucho is about to depart for—Brazil?

(Left bottom) 1941: Leon Errol and W. C. Fields in *Never Give a Sucker an Even Break*.

(Right) 1960: Alone among present-day comedians, Jack Lemmon has created a screen character which owes little to fashion and much to his knowledge of human quiddity. Here he is in the first stages of a cold in *The Apartment*.

(Below right) 1947: Dorothy Lamour gives Bing Crosby the office, while Bob Hope looks on in Hope dismay: *The Road to Rio*.

(Below left) 1955: Jerry Lewis' detractors consider him the great contemporary example of the subsitution of energy for talent, but his admirers think him the equal of Chaplin, as does Mr. Lewis himself. This typical shot is from *Three Ring Circus*.

(Below) 1954: Lucille Ball was the poor man's Ginger Rogers for ten years of the thirties and forties until television enabled her to exploit her marriage for commercial purposes and, somewhat incidentally, revealed her comic genius. Here she is in her triumphant return to the screen in *The Long, Long Trailer*, in which Lucy, as usual, is about to make Desi do something he knows he better not do.

334

UNDER-WORLD STARS

(Left) Lon Chaney as the master crook and Betty Compson as his outwardly demure confederate in *The Big City*, 1928. Chaney and Miss Compson both made hits in the "great" crook drama of 1919, *The Miracle Man*. He went on to stardom in which he alternated between underworld roles and the deformed characters which were his hallmark. Betty on the contrary essayed "sympathetic" heroines such as Barrie's Lady Babbie in *The Little Minister*. She did not find favor in these, and was sinking from sight when Chaney rescued her by casting her in support of himself here.

(Right) Evelyn Brent achieved fame as the prototype of all gangster's molls, Feathers, in Ben Hecht's and Josef von Sternberg's *Underworld*, 1927. Miss Brent continued to play Feathers with slight variations for the rest of her starring career, as she does here in *Broadway*, 1929. The stereotype she established provoked the following immortal exchange from S. J. Perelman: Feathers: Hello, you two-timing bastard. Tyrone Rukeyser: Why, what's the matter, Feathers? Feathers: Nothing. I always say that when I come into a room.

(Below Priscilla Dean, Gustav von Seyffertitz, and Sidney Bracey bring synthetic expertise to bear on a safe-robbing plan in *Birds of Prey*, 1927, a sort of primitive mock-up for *Rififi*.

(Right) Sooner or later all stars, whatever their normal identification, had to pass through the underworld, though they seldom stayed there. This publicity still from *Ladies of the Mob,* 1928, in which Clara Bow gave a remarkably true and touching performance, tries to exploit all her assets at once.

James Cagney and Edward G. Robinson brought a new feeling of untheatrical reality to the gangster film, as here in *Smart Money,* 1931.

George Raft's menace, sexual and otherwise, was thought to lie in his glazed immobility, and a short career was predicted for him. Then he unaccountably became a good actor. He is still in his inscrutable phase here in *Night After Night,* 1932, with that standard prop of the thirties underworld, Wynne Gibson.

(Top) Those veteran low-lifers James Gleason, George Bancroft, and Wynne Gibson in *Lady and Gent,* 1932.

(Above) Matthew Betz, Wallace Beery, and Chester Morris register their confident intention to escape in *The Big House,* 1930, the most successful and best of all prison dramas.

(Right) Paul Muni as Al Capone in *Scarface,* 1932, showed what he thought of his fellow men by mowing them all down, singly and in bulk. What he thought of women can be seen above.

Victor Mature and Richard Widmark in *Kiss of Death,*
1948, the latter's notable debut as a "laughing killer."

Lee Marvin beserk in the psychedelic nightmare of
Point Blank, 1967.

(Right) Jack Palance and Zero Mostel in *Panic in the
Streets,* 1950. Of all latter-day actors, Palance alone
would have qualified as a crook star in the palmy days
of the underworld film. You know at a glance that he is
one of Nature's un-ennobled.

Laird Cregar, Alan Ladd, and Tully Marshall in *This Gun
for Hire,* 1942. Screen tough guys had always been dark
and swarthy, not to say greasy, but *This Gun for Hire*
ushered in a switch—the Nordic punk, the blond beast
of the city. Whether psychotic and withdrawn like Alan
Ladd, or saturnine like Dan Duryea, or raucous and ruthless like Richard Widmark, these sinister Aryans confirmed the increasing audience feeling that things are
never what they seem.

WHEBÈS WANDÍ

341

HORROR STARS

PD.929

(Right) Horror did not really take shape as a permanent movie genre until the 1930s, but one of its two supreme masters was certainly the twenties star, Lon Chaney, whose genius for distorting make-up was a projection of his personal fascination with crippling, with maiming, with all that makes men into monsters. His death's-head make-up in this classic scene from *The Phantom of the Opera,* with Mary Philbin, is indelibly imprinted—no, scarred—on the memories of all the over-fifties.

(Left) The second great master of horror was a sensitive, artistic, very English actor who chose to be known as Boris Karloff. Raised from bit roles to stardom by the accident of his casting as *Frankenstein,* Karloff dominated the horror movie in every kind of role for forty years. Mary Wollstonecraft Shelley's monster has turned on its creator with a vengeance; Karloff, not her creation, pervaded the horror imagery of the twentieth century.

(Above left) The mechanical man seen here with Boris Karloff in *Before I Hang* is merely an anatomical model, but he and his many counterparts in horror films forecast our present-day fear of computers.

(Above right) Karloff preferred roles which projected psychological horror when they came his way, but he could portray lusty brutality with the best of them, this time as Basil Rathbone's lethal minion, the executioner, in *The Tower of London.*

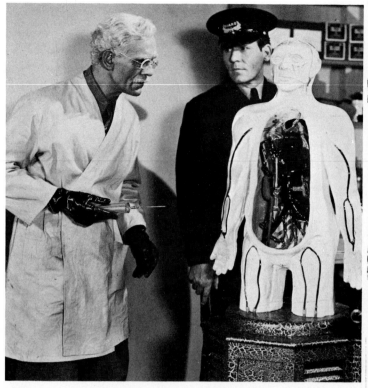

(Above left) Next to the automaton, the *Doppelgänger* was the device most frequently used within the formula of the horror film to give us a glimpse of our double nature. Here Karloff confronts the Second Man five times repeated in *Before I Hang.*

(Above right) Almost the only surviving bona fide horror star is Vincent Price, who plays his horror so floridly straight that it's only gradually you realize that his tongue is firmly in his cheek. Here he is as Poe's Prince Prospero in *The Masque of the Red Death,* complete with falcon on glove.

(Left) A gifted actor in and out of horror films, Bela Lugosi never rivaled Karloff's popularity except in the title role of *Dracula,* an incarnation often repeated. Here he reacts on cue to the one thing the bloodsucker fears, in *The Return of the Vampire,* with Kent Smith.

(Right) Peter Lorre created a world sensation as the psychotic child murderer in Fritz Lang's German film of workaday horror, *M.* When Hollywood tried to shoehorn him into its own kind of conventional horror film, he didn't fit the slot, as with Frances Drake as the demented pianist in *Made Love,* 1935, a long time before Yul Brynner. Lorre eventually made a place for himself in American films by burlesquing cruder bogeymen—with an occasional flash of his own sick menace.

ACTING STARS

(Right) 1929: George Arliss was an actor of ability who early discovered that his public liked personality better than acting. When his *Disraeli* was transferred bodily to the screen, the public decided that his stagy bag of tricks was probably what "great" acting would be like in the talkies. He is seen here in a moment of Hebraic triumph over the simon-pure Anglo-Saxons David Torrence and Ivan Simpson.

(Below) 1931: Helen Hayes as the dying wife in *Arrowsmith*, the most genuine and affecting performance of the comparatively brief screen career which she sandwiched in between her two careers on Broadway.

(Left) 1932: No more unlikely candidate for stardom than Charles Laughton could be imagined in 1932, but he clicked instantly with audiences. He is seen here in his first screen performance as the homicidal householder in *Payment Deferred*, with a young man named Ray Milland.

(Below) 1922: Early in her career Lillian Gish was dubbed "the Duse of the screen," and John Barrymore called her the greatest artist he had ever seen (he later bestowed the same praise on several others, including Garbo). There were those who insisted that Miss Gish owed her seeming mastery to the training and manipulation of D. W. Griffith, and what she owed him can be seen in the composition of this scene from *Orphans of the Storm*. But Miss Gish's long subsequent career on stage and screen revealed her as that rarity, a creative actress.

(Left) 1932: Paul Muni won official acting renown as a crepe-hair character actor, but his soundest work was done without make-up, as here in the memorable *I Am a Fugitive from a Chain Gang*.

1937: Devoid of stage training, the inheritor of Mary Pickford's sweetness and light, Janet Gaynor's instinctive response to the camera escaped the notice of the discriminating, who were put off by the very titles of her vehicles—*Delicious, Adorable, Sunny Side Up*. Not until the end of her starring career, in David Selznick's *A Star Is Born*, did she convince everyone that behind her somewhat insipid façade lay histrionic power, depth, and control. Fredric March shares this scene with her.

1941: Ingrid Bergman made her first impact as an actress rather than a Nordic beauty as the Cockney prostitute in Spencer Tracy's version of *Dr. Jekyll and Mr. Hyde*.

1964: In *Dr. Strangelove*, Peter Sellers carried on the tradition of multiple impersonation which has sometimes been accepted as the high-water mark of acting, but his real talent is for comedy.

(Top) 1961: For a quarter of a century, Spencer Tracy was everybody's ideal screen actor. This is his judge in *Judgment at Nuremberg.*

(Above) 1954: The characteristic look of exaltation in Montgomery Clift's eyes, seen here in *Indiscretion of an American Wife,* may well have been a distant early warning of his ultimate madness and death. A notably gifted actor was lost in him, well before his death.

(Right) 1954: The prototype of all the nihilist rebels of the fifties and sixties, on the screen and life, was the Marlon Brando of *The Wild One.* Brando has exercised his extraordinary versatility in many directions since then, but this is the portrait which will last in the gallery of immortal screen characters.

©D-8080-72

351

SINGING AND DANCING STARS

1929: Maurice Chevalier in *Innocents of Paris*

1916: Vernon and Irene Castle in *The Whirl of Life*

1954: Judy Garland in *A Star Is Born*

1949: Vera-Ellen and Gene Kelly in *On the Town*

1936: Nelson Eddy and Jeanette MacDonald in *Rose Marie*

353

1940: George Murphy and Eleanor Powell in *The Broadway Melody of 1940*

Bing Crosby in *Two for Tonight*

1934: Fred Astaire and Ginger Rogers in *Roberta*

CHILD STARS

Jackie Coogan. Chaplin's great discovery in *The Kid* went on to become a star in his own right, beloved of millions and the maker of millions—for his mother and stepfather, as it turned out, not for himself.

(Top) Farina. This whiteface shot of the only black member of "Our Gang" symbolized in the twenties what it would stigmatize today, the exact position of the "sympathetic" Negro in white society—the lovable scapegoat.

(Above) Hayley Mills in *Pollyanna*. The daughter of the veteran actor John Mills survived this remake of the role which even Mary Pickford hated and went on to become the only child star to achieve greater public favor in adulthood.

(Center left) If there's one thing female stars like better than putting on too much make-up to play wickedness, it's scrubbing off all their make-up to play innocence. Here Ginger Rogers achieves an astonishingly childlike effect in *Kitty Foyle,* with Ernest Cossart.

(Bottom left) Margaret O'Brien, seen here in *Music for Millions,* aroused exactly the same parental feelings in the human breast as had Shirley Temple, but her magic was more evanescent than Shirley's.

(Above left) Jackie Cooper, with Lionel Barrymore, in *Treasure Island,* 1934. When Jackie Coogan reached the awkward age the boy Cooper succeeded him in audience adulation, though with lesser intensity and for a shorter time.

(Right) Spencer Tracy and Mickey Rooney in *Boys' Town.* The expression on young Rooney's face suggests the fine and serious artist who was buried under Andy Hardy. The artistry is still his today, but it no longer embodies a daydream.

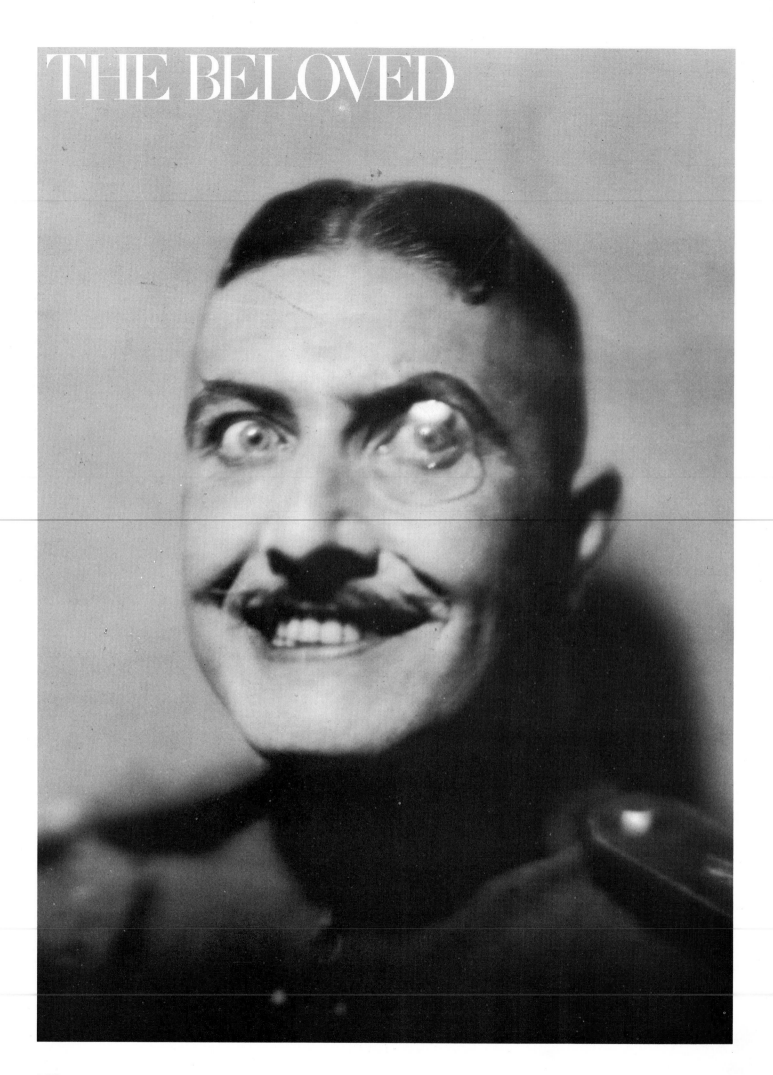

(Right) 1933: As the tragic heroine of Erich von Stroheim's *Greed* and *The Wedding March,* Zasu Pitts gained *reclame* from the aesthetes, but she was prouder of the idiot maids she played in early talkies. The tragic figure was a Stroheim puppet, the comic character her own creation. The absurd, courageous, and only ever so slightly pathetic women she played struck a universal chord. Here she is with Slim Summerville, her co-star in many films, in *They Just Had to Get Married.*

(Center left to right) 1924: Theodore Roberts capped his career as the "grand old man" of the early screen with his portrayal of Moses in Cecil B. De Mille's first version of *The Ten Commandments;* 1948: In her youth, Aline MacMahon played sardonic secretaries to gangsters, movie producers, and racketeering lawyers in a series of vastly popular topical films. Today she is by acclamation the mother of us all. Her finest role was the UNNRA official in her best picture, *The Search;* 1937: May Robson was called "Muzzi May" by the failed starlets and other industry unfortunates whom she mothered in the daily routine of the studios.

On the screen she was more of a grandmother figure, fondly indulgent yet tartly disciplinary when occasion warranted. She is here the proud grandmother of Janet Gaynor in *A Star Is Born.*

(Right) 1931: When Marie Dressler made her great hit in *Anna Christie,* the studios didn't know what to do with a hot box office property who was, after all, an old lady. Cast in *Dark Star* in support for a forgotten ingenue named Dorothy Jordan, she so overwhelmed the picture, and projection-room audiences, that the film was renamed *Min and Bill.* From then until her death three years later Miss Dressler, though aged and ailing, was undoubtedly the most adored star on the screen. Min's Bill, of course, was Wallace Beery.

(Left) 1926: Roy d'Arcy in *Beverly of Graustark.* It may seem odd to class a villain among the Beloved, but silent film audiences loved their louses almost as well as they loved their lovers, and D'Arcy was pre-eminent as "the man you love to hate," surpassing even Erich von Stroheim and Lew Cody.

Shirley Temple, who in this picture might be anybody's little girl photographed in her own back yard, almost deserves a special category of her own, outside the Stellar Pantheon, just as the Academy found it necessary to give her a Special Award. She belongs in too many categories—and she is also in a class by herself. She was, of course, the supreme Child Star. Jackie Coogan matched her in fame and childish histrionic ability, but his afterimage is that of a wronged orphan. Shirley escaped that, and she was born too early to disillusion her fans by turning hippie—though it must be admitted that her recent political incarnation, with its overtones of matriarchy, reaction, and the DAR, is not to the liking of all who once adored her. She might be included among the Greatest Stars of All Time, though her reign was short and her earnings far below the level achieved by others before and since. That she belongs among the Beloved there can be no question. To the world public she was indeed, in the title of one of her pictures, *Our Little Girl*—or would have been in the best of all possible worlds.

(Right) 1941: Another who survived all movie metamorphoses was Adolphe Menjou. Beginning in supporting roles, he rose to silent stardom in comedies modeled after those of Lubitsch. Demoted to character roles by the talkies, he was later re-elevated to romantic featured parts, then back to character roles. He is seen here in slapstick in one of Gloria Swanson's comebacks, *Father Takes a Wife*.

Lewis Stone

C. Aubrey Smith

Beulah Bondi

Monty Woolley

Edward Arnold

Barry Fitzgerald

Charles Coburn

Walter Huston and Mary Astor

Ernest Torrence and John Gilbert

361

FREAK STARS

(Left) Julian Eltinge became a screen star on the strength of his popularity as king (not queen) of the female impersonators—standard fixtures of vaudeville entertainment in the teens and twenties. The cream of the jest in that innocent day was that this expert imitator of women was in reality a very masculine man, as he demonstrates in this off-the-set shot with Donald Crisp and Cecil B. De Mille.

Johnny Weissmuller, the archetypal Tarzan, seen here with Maureen O'Sullivan's Jane, was one of a dozen sports stars metamorphosed into movie stars by the need for muscle men to incarnate Edgar Rice Burroughs' immortal creation.

(Left) Thanks to their vast radio following, the first movie made by Amos and Andy was a box office smash, but their subsequent films died the death. Somehow the illusion created by these folk characters could not survive the ocular evidence that they were actually played by two white actors in blackface, Freeman Gosden, and Charles Correll; (Right) That Charlie McCarthy was made of wood was known to all, but he was far more real to audiences as a screen character than was his creator, Edgar Bergen—thanks to the latter's effortless expertise; (Below) With symbolic logic John Huston chose Audie Murphy and Bill Mauldin to portray the heroes of his study of Civil War bravery and cowardice, *The Red Badge of Courage.* It says something about the relation of art to life that Mauldin, the profound observer and recorder of the GI experience, failed to make it as an actor, while Murphy, the actual protagonist of that experience, made it big and made it stick.

SELECTED SHORT SUBJECTS V

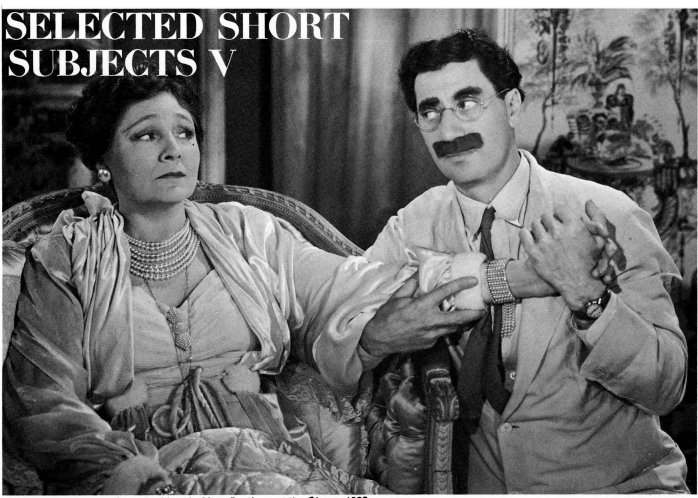

Margaret Dumont and Groucho Marx in *Marx Brothers at the Circus*, 1939

Sue Lyon and James Mason in *Lolita*, 1962

Orson Welles in *Touch of Evil*, 1958

Early Sophia Loren

Paul Newman and Pier Angeli in *Somebody Up There Likes Me*, 1956

Kim Novak

Jayne Mansfield

Barbara Stanwyck

James Dean in *Rebel Without a Cause*, 1955

THE 6
STELLAR LIFE

I shall ride the parade in a platinum car,
My features will shine, my name will be Star,
Day-long and night-long the bells I shall peal,
And down the long street I shall turn the cart-wheel.

W. H. Auden

"I'm goin' to Hollywood—goin' to be dis*cov*uhed," breathily whispered Marilyn Monroe in *Bus Stop*. She was speaking to someone else in the film, but really to herself, lost in an involute daydream, immune to the abrasions of reality. We are meant to laugh at this moment in *Bus Stop*, because the character's qualifications for discovery are so obviously and pitifully few, and we are relieved when she has the good sense to abandon her ambitions, latch on to a handsome hunk of cowboy, and go off to Montana to marry him. But though we laugh, we also sympathize; Marilyn's daydream is ours. In those slack moments when we give ourselves up to it, which we do, our expectations are the same as hers. After the ritual proof of manhood or womanhood which is discovery—itself a bizarre dream—all we expect is fame, glory, a luxurious life in the great world among important people, and, as a pendant for all this, sober admiration for our histrionic genius. Because they try to distill the quintessence of joy, daydreams are monotonous, single-track; nobody has described them better than Auden; whatever he is doing at any given moment, a star ought always to *feel* that he is turning one cartwheel after another.

The reality of the life of a star has been tailored to follow the specifications of the daydream as exactly as is humanly possible. That has been seen to by the people who manage these things. There are reasons for this. Today, the stellar life has become a saleable commodity in itself. Yesterday, in the heyday of the stars, it was thought advisable to dramatize it as one long ecstasy in order to support the illusions of the screen itself. Both involved, and involve, continuous repetitive publicity. We are as familiar with the diurnal details of the life of the stars as we are with our own pedestrian tooth-brush-to-toothbrush routine. The pictorial vignettes which follow are simply prime examples of a regimen as predictable as the Stations of the Cross.

And who can object? Not we—and not the stars, for the most part. The standardized pattern which is supplied them in place of an idiosyncratic life of their own is just too attractive. The life they actually lead within that pattern may turn out as tragic and sordid as Marilyn's own, but it is a glittering tragedy, a sybaritic sordidness. So the pattern triumphs in the end. An Errol Flynn may salve his adventurousness, and his questing conscience, by dabbling in something as controversial as the Spanish Civil War—but we tolerate his divergence from the norm because we have a shrewd sense that he will come back to the fleshpots in the end. They are such attractive fleshpots. A Ramon Novarro may trumpet his aspiration to enter a monastery—a sincere aspiration, no doubt —but at the end of his life, though independently wealthy, he was still clinging to the fringes of show business. Once upon a time the author found himself on a radio panel with Lillian and Dorothy Gish, Aileen Pringle, Leatrice Joy, Lila Lee, and Nita Naldi. The question asked these luminaries and ex-luminaries was: "If you had it all to do over again, would you do the same?" Needless to say, the sisters Gish, whose life was one long success story from sixteen to seventy, said they would do it exactly the same. Three of the other less successful ladies were less definite, but not the forthright Miss Naldi. When asked the question, she gasped, "Oh Gawd, just one more chance."

(Left) When she wasn't being "Miss Flame Thrower," the early Marilyn Monroe was kept busy as "Miss Potato Blossom," in the interests of makework starlet publicity.

(Below right) Rita Cansino was just another dancer, serviceable for second leads to such as Warner Oland in *Charlie Chan in Egypt,* until the removal of her widow's peak by electrolysis helped speed her metamorphosis into Rita Hayworth.

(Above right) This early publicity still of Rudolph Valentino as a spaghetti cook was suppressed by his publicity men when he rose to fame as a primitive lover, more Arabic than Italianate. The result of the suppression was that the photograph was instantly reproduced everywhere in the world.

(Above left) The harassment of autograph hounds was a menace in navigation for some stars, especially frequently tipsy ones like Humphrey Bogart, seen here with Lauren Bacall negotiating the approach to the Brown Derby.

(Clockwise, opposite page)
The candid camera was at first regarded as a menace by stars pampered by expert lighting and photography, and some of them took evasive action, as does Katharine Hepburn here. The only result was pictures that made the stars look even worse than they feared. Second only to the permeer as a tribal ritual was the adolescent pastime of imprinting the stars' handprints and footprints in concrete in front of Sid Grauman's Chinese Theatre in Hollywood. Here Janet Leigh and Victor McLaglen shelter a bearded James Mason from the rain as he goes through the classic motions. With the passing years the sidewalk in front of Grauman's has become so crowded that the prints of forgotten stars have had to be removed in order to make room for those of newcomers, but Mr. Mason's mementos have doubtless not yet suffered that fate; An armored Ingrid Bergman makes a 16mm record of the shooting of her ill-starred blunderbuss, *Joan of Arc;* Louise Brooks.

(Top) Before films were made in their actual settings as a matter of routine, location trips were a drag for most stars. Here Lew Ayres and Jane Wyman express a splendid ennui on location for *Johnny Belinda* at Fort Bragg, California, which did duty for the rockbound coast of Maine.

Radio was at first regarded as a threat to the box office by the studios, then as a valued adjunct of publicity. Some stars enjoyed performing before the microphone—and live audiences—more than they did before the more lucrative camera. Bing Crosby and Frank Sinatra are having a ball.

Louella Parsons aside, Hedda Hopper and "Prince" Mike Romanoff were undoubtedly the two most influential non-professionals in the Hollywood of yesteryear—though Miss Hopper enjoyed a double status because of her long service as an actress before she became a queen of gossip in the press and on the air. But Gary Cooper isn't lighting her cigarette because of nostalgia for the days when she adorned his supporting casts; he's lighting it because of what she may say in her column next day.

Errol Flynn "and friend."

Marilyn Monroe evidently enjoys dancing with Marlon Brando, but he registers his usual anger at being photographed unaware.

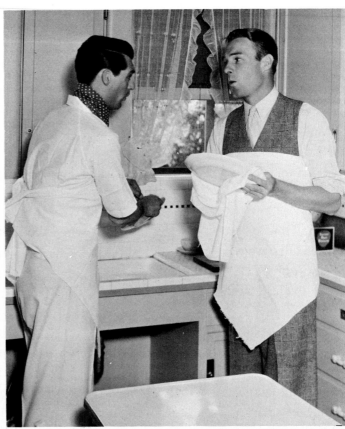

The movie "permeer" was institutionalized by Hollywood as a publicity-getter very early in the game. Here Lois Wilson and Gloria Swanson arrive at the premiere of Norma Talmadge's *Camille* in 1926.

Cary Grant and Randolph Scott

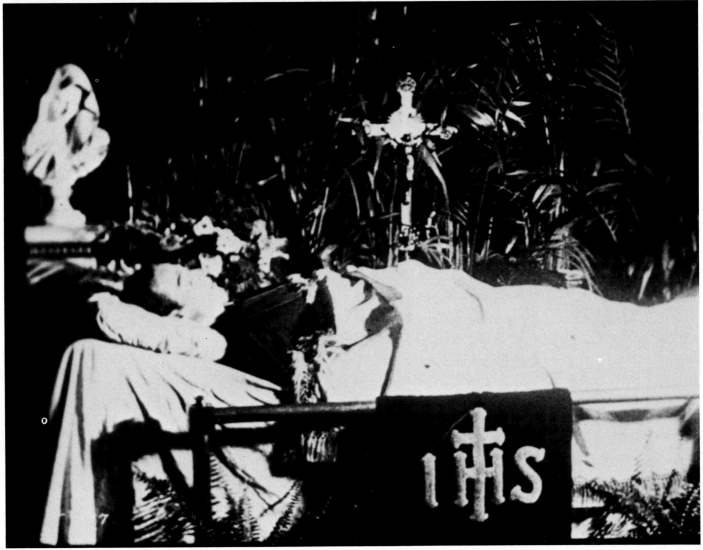

Rudolph Valentino

7 WHAT'S AFTER ECSTASY?

No memory of having starred
Atones for later disregard,
Or keeps the end from being hard.
—Provide, provide!

                    Robert Frost

What's after ecstasy? What happens when the lights go off, when the jangling, intolerable telephone becomes intolerable because it *doesn't* ring, when the *paparazzi* are off in another direction, when producers cannot be reached by phone or through agent, when even "friends" become "unavailable"? What comes next? What do you *do* with yourself then?

It is a little death. But should it, after all, be so hard? You knew it had to come someday; somewhere within yourself you were at least partly prepared for it. Why does it seem like the end of the world? Kay Francis didn't think it would be. Not ego gratification but financial security attracted her to movie stardom, and she had distinct plans of her own for the future, after the conclusion of what she thought of as an interlude in her life. She arrived in Hollywood at just the right moment, when new types and abilities were very much needed, and, fresh from Broadway and Fifth Avenue, she made many of her older rivals look out-of-date. Soon she was a star valuable enough to be "stolen" from Paramount by Warner Brothers in the latter's famous talent raid on the former. Unintoxicated by her success, Miss Francis proceeded according to plan. She rented (not bought) a house, drove herself to the studio in a modest car, and entertained just enough to keep up appearances. It began to be whispered that she saved her money, than which nothing is in worse taste if it gets around and is talked about. As her sleek personality, flair for clothes, and so-so acting outwore the interest of fans, and Warners showed no signs of renewing her contract, Miss Francis exhibited no dismay; her high salary remained the same, and she was perfectly willing to earn it even in the cheap and hastily made films they gave her toward the end. Nor did she wait for starring roles at other studios. She took what came her way, leads or second leads, and even played supporting roles when the salaries were good enough. Then she produced, starred in, and financed two Monogram quickies, one of which, *Allotment Wives,* happened to be about a subject which was very much on the public mind at the end of World War II, and she cleaned up on it. Her Hollywood sojourn finally wrung dry for every penny that was in it, Miss Francis exploited the remnants of her reputation by touring the coutry in flimsy plays which never reached Broadway—one of them was *Windy Hill,* by her fellow ex-star Patsy Ruth Miller—and rounded off her long show-business career in summer stock. So much for so much. Miss Francis had attained exactly what she set out to attain by becoming an actress—money. She had a sizable fortune and the freedom to do whatever she pleased. Yet while she was touring in her last play, she attempted suicide through an overdose of sleeping pills. She was saved in time, and the incident was glossed over. But in her latter years she was said to be saddened that no one recognized her when she entered a room.

The fading-out of a star becomes apparent to him before it happens. Only the self-enchanted, the almost schizophrenic, can ignore the signs and portents—the insistent gossip, the subtle downgrading of deference, the shame of sinking box-office grosses which the trade papers emblazon for all to see. Besides, his nerves are sensitized in advance to all these phenomena. He has ever present in his mind a classic pattern of disintegration, derived from the days when most stars great and small were under contract to the major studios—a pattern which has become a sort of oral tradition, told and retold in Hollywood taprooms in memory of that heyday of the stars which everyone knows will never come again but which everybody wishes he himself had lived through, whatever the outcome. The avatar of that heyday was the contract system. A contract, that mere piece of paper in the studio files, was then a star's most valuable material possession. It was not only a guarantee of stardom and big money; it was, far more importantly, tangible evidence of present and future marketability. The taproom tale, whoever its momentary protagonist, always begins just before the debacle, when a contract star still has two or three pictures to make under his present agreement with his studio. Preparations go forward for their making, but there's no excitement about the process any more. It is obviously just a routine to be got through as quickly as possible. There is a dead-end feel about it all. The studio publicity department will still arrange an interview for the star if a publication requests it, but the unrelenting pressure to be photographed, to talk to newsmen, to go places and be seen has evaporated. What is never mentioned in any circumstances by anyone on the lot is the renewal of his contract. It is as if, in William Saroyan's words, "there's no foundation all along the line." Comes the inevitable day when someone, usually someone delegated by higher authority, tells him as civilly as possible that his contract will in fact *not* be renewed, not on any terms, not at any price, not at all. He cleans out his bungalow dressing room and makes his way off the lot quickly, hoping not to run into any of his fellow stars, and especially any cheery soul who hasn't heard the bad news yet. And now what? He is still a star, dammit, nobody can take that title away from him if he chooses to hang onto it. But how is he to maintain stellar status in the eyes of the industry and the profession? He discovers that there is virtually nothing he personally can do about it. If he hires his own press agent, the latter's singlehanded endeavors seem pretty futile compared to the vast studio publicity apparatus which kept him in the public eye day after day. He may have, while in jeweled bondage to the company, dreamed of negotiating for himself meaty roles in stories which are "worthy" of him, but he soon discovers that, no matter how rich he may be, he cannot possibly compete with the astronomical sums which the majors offer for the latest hot property. He is stalemated.

Here the taproom taleteller usually pauses for breath before delivering the *coup de grâce*—and here his listeners may well intervene with horror stories of their own, many of them contemporary. The star of today, unless he is big enough to own his own company, is apt to be under contract to an agent (or agency) rather than to a studio, and his services are sought on a picture-to-picture basis rather than for a term of years. The evidence of his continued viability as a star is that he is eagerly sought for a new picture before he has finished his current one—or even before he has begun it. When that pressure relaxes, he finds himself in the same situation as the ex-contract star of yesterday—whirled round in a flux of near-stars, once stars, and nominal stars whose common denominator is that no producer of motion pictures thinks he *has* to have them, them and nobody else, for his next project. The star continues to get offers, of course—not very good offers. Almost invariably they are for less desirable roles in inferior pictures at salaries considerably below his high mark. Here is the dimming star's real Hobson's choice. Shall he for the sake of "prestige" hold out for the money and billing he has long enjoyed—and risk remaining off the screen until the public has decided that out of sight is out of mind? Or shall he take what comes his way simply in order to remain in circulation? If he takes the latter course, if he takes a co-starring or an "also starring" role, save the mark, he goes on the set to find that everything has changed. He is deferred to, as befits his record, but with a subtle difference. He is but one contributor to the making of the film, no longer its center and focus. The cameras and lights are not lined up to exploit his assets and conceal his liabilities; they are arranged for the benefit of the real star of the picture. When he sees himself on the screen he looks different. Nobody is sabotaging him, nobody wants him to look bad, but that special sort of attractiveness and magnetism, that sharply defined individuality which once was his, is now blurred, indistinct, even in his own eyes. The public thinks so too and vaguely wonders why, then dismisses the matter and turns to less puzzling favorites. Soon his leading roles become second leads, and unless he happens to fit them so well that he is at least a minor asset to a film, they grow fewer. His next step downward is into the quickies.

A word must be spared for this remarkable phenomenon, which has existed since the beginning of the movies, and which used to be known as Poverty Row. The quickies were made by small companies lacking significant capital, distribution, or exhibition apparatus, at a cost never exceeding $100,000 and frequently amounting to far less. The best known of these companies in their heyday were Columbia, Tiffany-Stahl, Rayart, Principal, Monogram, Republic, and the Producers' Releasing Corporation. Their art, if so it may be described, was to exploit the public's consciousness that movies were expensive by making pictures that looked costly but weren't. So far as possible they were made on location; for interior scenes they rented studio space or shared it with penurious neighbors. Their casts consisted of unknown players, or even amateurs, and of long-gone has-beens, the best known of whom served as star. The films themselves looked like slightly inferior "Grade B" or "program" pictures as produced by the major studios and could compete as such, since they were offered to the market at far lower rentals than the majors charged for their least worthy product. They were booked by small independent theaters in the hinterlands, chiefly because these obscure theaters could not afford the rentals charged by the majors. While production costs were still comparatively low, and before most of the independent theaters were gobbled up by the great chains, this system was comparatively viable. Harry Cohn built his great studio, Columbia, entirely on the basis of such a humble beginning. He developed the method of "bunching" scenes, which enabled him and other quickie producers to avail themselves of players who had genuine claim to stardom. He arranged the script, the shooting schedule, and the construction of sets so that a star could make all his scenes in two or three days and then depart. The star was paid his customary salary, but by the day rather than by the week, so that Cohn could sport an important name on his pictures at a cost of a few thousand dollars. This device made working in quickies not entirely disreputable; even important stars with long-term contracts at the major studios would make one now and then, "between pictures." It was an easy way to pick up a piece of change, especially if you were behind with the mortgage. As for shopworn goods like Claire Windsor or Mae Busch, they survived for years on the minor screens of America in quickies in which they were advertised as if they were still flaming sensations. Betty Compson exploited the situation so ably that she became known as the "Queen of Poverty Row"; she appeared in no fewer than fourteen pictures in a single year, yet gave performances so adroit and effective that they led to an actual, though brief, comeback in the big studios.

The coming of sound inflated costs, and dialogue made the bunching system an impractical one. Quickies are still made today, often by companies which make one picture at a time and then dissolve their corporate identity. But they are no longer a haven for the once great except in small parts or bits. Today's chasers of the fast buck prefer to feature television personalities, or Hollywood beginners who have not yet had a big break, the more so because such little films are for the most part directed at teen-age audiences. Yesterday's great artist is a has-been; today's starlet *might* grow big. The quickies of the 1960s put an extra edge on this distinction. The quickie-makers prefer to employ not the great star of the past nor the hot sensation of the moment (he or she is far too expensive) but what can only be called a teen-age has-been, yesterday afternoon's front-runner, like Fabian or Paul Anka, who has reached the advanced age of twenty without quite making it to the top and who is therefore to all intents and purposes out of the running. In Harry Cohn's early days he watched like a vulture for the contracts of an Alice White or a Dorothy Mackaill to expire, then quickly engaged them for one picture and one picture only, hoping that the public would be deceived into thinking that they were still up there among the elect. Something of the same sort happens now. Independent producers wait for a pop singer's record sales to fall off somewhat, then sign him for a movie in the belief that the fans will not have time to discover that they love him less on January 1 than they did on December 31.

Another resource of the ex-favorite is also diminishing, the personal appearance tour. Once the greatest stars, like Mary Pickford, Douglas Fairbanks, and Charles Chaplin, showed themselves to the public to help sell a picture or float a war bond drive. Such descents from Olympus were truly choice, once-in-a-lifetime treats to the common herd so honored. They served a variety of purposes beyond publicity and money-making. Colleen Moore recalls that her producer-husband, John McCormick, urged her to make as many such appearances between pictures as possible, not so much for the sake of giving the populace a glimpse of her inimitable self in the flesh as to butter up the First National exchange people in the cities where she played and induce them to work harder at selling her pictures than those of her First National rivals, Corinne Griffith and Dorothy Mackaill. But by the middle twenties, many big stars had become a little chary of vouchsafing their public a glimpse of themselves. Without the camera to beglamour them, quite a few had failed to live up to expectations. Thereafter the personal appearance became almost the exclusive perquisite of those on the way down. The announcement that So-and-So was about to embark on a national tour meant to the knowing that So-and-So could get nothing to do in Hollywood. The big-time vaudeville circuits and the large picture houses which featured stage shows in addition to film attractions were willing to pay thousands a week for the use of these slightly tarnished names on their marquees, and theoretically the appearance in the flesh of these stars would stir such enthusiasm in the hearts of fans that they would be swept back to the screen on a wave of popular acclaim. It seldom, it almost never, worked, for the reason that the said stars had nothing to offer in person except the satisfaction of brief curiosity. They stood, spotlighted figures, on the stages of the vaudeville houses, declaiming nervously how great it was to be there and how they loved greeting their fans face to face, sang a song or two if they were capable of it, and that was that. Only two screen personalities ever reversed this all too familiar procedure. Leatrice Joy, when her turn came to hit the sawdust trail, worked up an act that had merit on its own in addition to her mere presence in it, and she also developed that spellbinding, up-and-at-'em technique which made vaudeville top entertainment in its day. Her act was a hit, on a par with the real headliners of the two-a-day, and Hollywood, shaking its head in amazement, summoned her to the Coast for a comeback. She made one more picture, then retired voluntarily. Sound had come in, the old relaxed atmosphere of picture-making had vanished, and her onetime cronies had been replaced by stage newcomers whom she didn't know and didn't want to know. "Hollywood has become like a family of in-laws," was her parting shot. "I liked it better playing out in the sticks."

Evelyn Brent was the only other major star who tried to use the personal appearance phase of her decline to restore her audience and her bargaining power. Miss Brent was enjoying much popularity as a Paramount star when she and Jesse Lasky had a falling-out which evidently decided him to jettison her as quickly as possible. He constantly loaned her out to other studios for roles in inferior pictures, much to her damage. When her contract finally expired, she did a few free-lance roles and a few quickies, but none of them restored her to favor. Aware of this, Miss Brent resorted to personal appearances, but she determined to make them mean something. She did not arrive for an engagement in late afternoon, do her stint, and then catch the midnight choo-choo for her next booking. She came to town with plenty of notice and stayed a week. She made herself available to photographers and press at their convenience, right down to the lowliest high school reporters. She was happy to attend any church social, cornerstone-laying, or ribbon-cutting that might be going locally. If there was already an Evelyn Brent fan club in the community she was visiting, she invited all its members to tea at her hotel; if there was none, she saw to it that one was organized forthwith. She also saw to it, like Miss Joy, that her act was enjoyable in itself and was not a mere bobbing from the stage. When Miss Brent returned to Hollywood after her tour—she devoted a year to it—she left behind her large audiences who thought of her as a friend. Then something unprecedented happened which also has never recurred. A wave of spontaneous mail hit the studios, demanding to know what in the name of time was the matter with the bosses that they let Evelyn Brent languish in idleness while promoting insipid blondes who hadn't a tenth of her beauty or ability, much less her spirit. But all that came of this remarkable phenomenon was that Miss Brent was cast as the heroine of a few Westerns, which got fewer as the thirties wore on. Whatever it was that had landed this lovely lady in the bad books of the studio moguls she stayed there. She had got herself on some sort of blacklist, and not even positive, vocal, tangibly demonstrated popular demand for her, supposedly the key to success, could get her off it. My friend Arthur Mayer says: "Nonsense. Her pictures no longer did business." So, perhaps, she was twice blacklisted—first by a decline in public interest and then by the trade, despite a revival of public interest. There were mysteries aplenty in the old star system.

The grimmest, most tenacious, and in the end most futile struggle to make a comeback via the quickies, the personal appearance route, and every other means she could think of, was waged by Agnes Ayres. Beauty, charm, and shall we say, the personal interest of Jesse L. Lasky had made her a star in the early 1920s, and when she was cast opposite Rudolph Valentino as the ravished heroine of *The Sheik,* she became the envy of every woman in the world. At this, her peak, Miss Ayres decided to retire from the screen and marry Manuel Reachi, the Mexican consul in Los Angeles. She did so, bore a daughter, and, because of her husband's diplomatic post, became a social wheel in both Los Angeles and Hollywood society. In 1926 Valentino and Joseph M. Schenck, preparing to film *The Son of the Sheik,* asked her if she would mind coming over to United Artists for a few days to make some minor scenes for this sequel to her former triumph. She agreed on condition that film be preceded by a full-screen title which read as follows: "Agnes Ayres has graciously consented to return to the screen to resume her original role as the wife of the Sheik, as a favor to Mr. Valentino and this picture." Intoxicated by this whiff of greasepaint, and by her success in exacting from Schenck a credit which even a current top star might envy, Miss Ayres decided her retirement was all a mistake, divorced Reachi, and announced her permanent return to motion pictures. She secured a leading role in one film, *The Awful Truth,* which lived up to its title. There were no further offers. Then Hal Roach decided that it might amuse audiences to see this beautiful creature in short slapstick comedies, and for a year Agnes Ayres was kicked, slapped, tripped, and took pratfalls, none of which she did very well. The Technicolor company, trying to interest the industry in its embryo two-color process, starred her in a series of two-reelers. This, surely, would be the magic key to a comeback; Agnes Ayres in color was bound to knock 'em cold. But neither the color process nor its star aroused interest anywhere. She made the usual personal appearance tour and some quickies so obscure that even her most devoted former fans could hardly find them in the theaters. Sound came, and she squeezed through the talkie test in a minor role in a sort of super-quickie, Frank Capra's *The Donovan Affair*. After that—nothing.

Then, six years after the end of her stardom, Agnes Ayres essayed Broadway. She went on foot from casting office to casting office, reminded booking agents of her screen record, confessed her utter lack of stage experience, and asked for a chance to start at the bottom; she would do anything. Her grit and persistence made her a byword among stage people, but they yielded her not even a walk-on. A few years later a reporter unearthed her working as a saleswoman in a Los Angeles department store and quoted her as saying, "When you see producers spending a million dollars trying to make some peasant into a star, while they ignore people who once had a name and a following, it's awfully hard not to ask 'why?'" That might well have been the last ever heard from or of Miss Ayres, except for one of those phenomena which erupt in show business every now and then. Ten years after the death of Rudolph Valentino, someone got the idea of reissuing his silent *The Sheik* and *The Son of the Sheik* with synchronized musical accompaniment. They did business, at least among curiosity seekers, and because it cost so little to rerelease them were mildly profitable. Miss Ayres was exhumed from by then total obscurity and sent out with the pictures on a personal appearance tour in which she told all as "Rudy's girl friend," which she wasn't. She invested her earnings from this necrophilic enterprise in a chain of grocery markets in Hollywood which proved to be highly successful. Miss Ayres was then in a position to live comfortably on her investment, but the life she chose to lead must have been anything but comfortable. At thirty-nine, she still dreamed of a screen comeback. Through heaven knows what bribery and at heaven knows what cost, she engaged a daily table for both lunch and dinner at Romanoff's—not a table on the fringe of the semicelebrities and ex-celebrities, but one right in among the Zanucks and Mayers and the top stars of the day. There she sat at every meal, smiling at everybody who would smile back and at some who would not. Agnes Ayres mercifully, died young.

This horror tale, though it has typical elements, is not generally typical of the fate of ex-stars. For one thing, the depression and lassitude which afflict most of them are not matched by Miss Ayres' courage and determination. On the negative side, the lady simply was not equipped for the professional role she aspired to play, after the passing of her first brief vogue. The "peasant" she referred to above was Anna Sten, whom Mr. Goldwyn was then trying to promote, and Miss Ayres' comment on her was decidedly out of line. Anna Sten failed to win the American public, but her long stage and screen experience in Kiev and Moscow, and her later fame in Berlin, placed her far above the Agnes Ayres sisterhood of Hollywood, graduates of the beauty contest, the publicity stunt, and the casting couch, who had little to offer either the industry or the public once their first bloom had faded and the novelty of their presence on the screen was behind them. The really trained professionals had a much better chance, especially those who came from the stage and were remembered by its people. When Helen Hayes's ennui with Hollywood life coincided with her box-office slump, she had only to return to Broadway to inspire furious competition for her services. She went on to become the *doyenne* of the American theater, with film roles also at her disposal whenever one turned up that interested her enough to compensate her for the boredom of spending a few months in southern California. Miss Hayes, of course, is in a class by herself, but others with comparable qualifications found a similar welcome when they took the trail back, notably Conrad Nagel and Franchot Tone. Ruth Chatterton would have made it too had she not clung to the shadow of stardom at the expense of the substance of character acting. Ann Harding was so immutably the exemplar of nobly self-sacrificing womanhood, surpassed in this only by Greer Garson, that it seemed she had no future after her stardom ended, but she survived her stereotype to play second leads for a decade. As a member of the famed Lupino family, Ida Lupino inherited generations of British stage tradition, and thanks thereto performed the slight-of-hand feat of passing behind the camera as a director while she was still officially a star—and you felt that this had been what she wanted to do all along, with stardom merely an expedient means to an end. Players like these have resources to sustain them through the psychological shock which comes with the collapse of stardom because they know they have something else to offer. They are qualified all-rounders.

It is possible to be overqualified, especially in the case of players indigenous to the screen. Every fan has wondered why his onetime favorite seems to disappear completely once his term of prominence is ended, and in many cases is literally never seen or heard of again, in spite of his years of fame. The explanation offered by producers and directors for this strange eclipse is a fascinating one. Any actor, they say, who has the making of a screen star is by that very fact almost automatically disqualified from making a subordinate contribution to the values of a film. While star quality can be projected across the footlights by technique alone, in films it takes sensational human raw material to register a comparable effect in the camera's frigid eye. Especially was this true in the silent days. Such blazing magnetism is difficult to key down to the level of secondary roles. Its possessors throw the over-all design of a film out of focus and they place their less experienced and, often, less magnetic juniors at a disadvantage.

This is not a matter of conscious scene-stealing, though that is of course attempted by stupid or compulsive ex-favorites, as we saw in Bette Davis's *The Star*. This sharp-edged film had Miss Davis a former top diva who has at last wangled a bit role through blackmail of a director who was once her lover. She is to play a scrubwoman whom the hero casually encounters as he walks through the corridor of a public building. We have been shown that Miss Davis is perfectly capable of handling this assignment correctly, but she doesn't. She makes herself up to look far too young, and instead of tending to her scrubbing she bats her false eyelashes at the hero in an effort to register gratuitous sex appeal. Inevitably her scene lands on the cutting room floor and with it her hopes of a comeback.

But such egomania is not the core of the problem. It lies, really, in the ex-star's ex-celebrity. In the middle thirties, 20th Century-Fox and Metro-Goldwyn-Mayer awoke to the fact that many of their onetime leading players were hanging around Hollywood jobless—jobless and, in many cases, in want. With uncharacteristic compassion, or perhaps with an eye to the publicity possibilities, they formed what they called stock companies, which re-employed their former employees at a wage varying between $75 and $150 a week, not bad for Depression times. In return for this guaranteed living, the lucky players were required to make themselves available for any part which turned up, from a bit to a second lead. It seemed an intelligent experiment but it didn't pay off, the contrary in fact. In M-G-M's *Wife Versus Secretary,* Aileen Pringle appeared briefly as an anonymous bridge player in a scene which centered attention on Myrna Loy and Jean Harlow. Miss Pringle had only a few words to say, and she did nothing to attract attention to herself, but audiences were so busy murmuring to one another "Isn't that Aileen Pringle?" that they missed the dialogue between the principals and with it the point of the scene. That sort of thing would never do, of course, and the effort to employ ex-stars in an organized way had to be abandoned. Such employment as is now offered luminaries of the past is sporadic—sporadic and cautious. Sad to say, the wise and responsible director who has the balance and proportion of his picture in the forefront of his mind will prefer to use a competent but unfamiliar character player rather than the ex-star he used to pal around with in the days when they were both beginners. Because of her lifelong friendship with John Ford, Mae Marsh was cast in virtually all of his pictures, but even Mr. Ford had to see to it that Miss Marsh was placed well in the background or was seen only in a flash. As for Lillian Gish, every ambitious young director wants to use her because of her personal magic and the magic of her association with Griffith and all the high traditions of the screen. But he soon learns as others have learned before him that Lillian Gish is big medicine, that she will draw off attention from the leading players unless she appears only in a scene or a sequence in which they are not present. True it is that Miss Gish, the complete professional, has the faculty of making herself invisible when the logic of the action requires it, but it doesn't make a great deal of economic sense to pay her thousands a week for the purpose of being invisible, especially if her name in advertising and publicity matter has aroused expectations in older moviegoers which are not fulfilled on the screen.

To be totally cut off from the opportunity of practicing the profession you love is one of the bitterest of human experiences, all the more bitter if you are really good at it. The ex-star reflects that in this respect he is worse off than those of his fellow actors who never achieved stardom at all, and he gloomily remembers the show-business adage about stars: "When they're young they're no good at their job, and by the time they're good at it, they're old. "When he tots up his other assets left over from stardom, he finds that they are shaky and evanescent. Prestige and position are the first to go. Should the contractless celebrity persist in moving among the stars and producers who only yesterday were his accustomed companions, he will find himself tolerated, but only barely and only for awhile. At any moment a friend may lose his temper and remind him that he is a has-been devoid of bargaining power, even social bargaining power. Invitations fall off with an abruptness and finality which anywhere but in Hollywood would be considered rudeness beyond the pale. Should the reader who most of the time manages to preserve the amenities no matter what find this strange, he is reminded that to the denizens of show business the sight of an ex-star is the sight of a death's-head, that the first thought of all of them is "there but for the grace of God . . . ," and that they cannot help wishing he would go away and—not die, exactly, but at least lick his wounds in a proper spirit of humility. The words "slipping," "washed up," "through," and "has-been" themselves are uttered every day and casually enough, but they inspire mortal terror every time they are heard. Fear is a destructive emotion, and fear is what his friends feel when their old pal the ex-star calls them up "just to say hello."

The star who finds his cherished standing gone can always fall back on money—if he has any. It is an excellent second line of defense, none better. As the Provincial Lady once reflected, "It is All Nonsense to say that Wealth wouldn't mean Happiness, because we all know quite well that it *would*." But wealth eludes most of the gifted, in spite of the fact that for the past century they have been among the highest paid of the general population. The only stars who seem to have been successful in saving money are those who enjoy saving for its own sake, from Mary Pickford and Ruth Roland through Colleen Moore and Corinne Griffith down to Kay Francis and, nowadays, Doris Day. A few, a very few, are driven to save against their real inclinations because they are obsessed by the fear or the memory of poverty, as in the case of Chaplin. A lesser few get rich and stay rich because they can't help it. Cary Grant is not known to the public primarily for his financial acumen, but his ever increasing earnings over a period of thirty-five years were just so great that he couldn't get rid of it all, even with alimony deducted; some considerable part of it had to stick to his pockets. He lacked Gloria Swanson's flair for spending, a flair which amounted to genius. From the time she was promoted to stardom in 1923 to her last picture role of the thirties in 1934, Miss Swanson earned around $4,000,000. Her living expenses in this period were reputed to be $10,000 monthly, with the low taxes of that day a negligible addition. She ought to have ended up worth something like $2,500,000, but when she liquidated her assets in the mid-thirties, she was left with $250,000. That is not exactly penury, but neither is it wealth beyond the dreams of avarice, especially if you have to keep up appearances on less than a tenth of your former income.

Many stars with a lesser power for earning money than Miss Swanson's, and a lesser gift for getting rid of it, have found themselves, at the end of their careers, not knowing whether they were rich or poor. Frequently they had entrusted the management of their income to favored relatives or "trusted advisers," some of whom have been known to decamp with all movable assets, as Blanche Sweet and John Barrymore found to their anguish—or the self-styled financial experts have frittered away their employers' earnings in harebrained investments, a favorite form of which used to be the jerrybuilt apartment houses which litter the Los Angeles area. The unfortunate, for which read foolish, ex-star finds himself left with the standard stellar equipment of a mansion in Beverly Hills, a beach house at Malibu, and such appanages of luxurious living as outsize jewels or an outsize yacht. But the mansions and beach houses are found to be covered with mortgages, and to meet the interest payments the yacht must be knocked down for what it will bring and the jewelry sold—secretly, to be replaced by paste. Soon the inevitable forced sale of the real estate and appurtenances brings creditors swooping down en masse, and the debacle is complete. The star may manage to salvage something from these complicated liquidations, but the agony of doing so is further depressing to his spirit, already worn thin by the strain of bearing up under one failure after another. Everything that happens to him in these dour days is on the negative side, and he wonders what hidden flaw in him has turned his luck so sour. He can't help feeling like a pariah, and pretty soon he begins to act like one.

His debilitation shows up markedly in personal relationships, especially the most intimate. When John Gilbert was dethroned by the talkies, he had just signed a contract which guaranteed him half a million dollars a year for three years. That sum was his come weal or woe; whatever else betide, financially he was sitting pretty. But Gilbert was married to Ina Claire, whose Broadway supremacy was based in part on perfect speech, and Miss Claire lost no opportunity to tell her husband, in public as well as in private, to keep his voice low, *low,* and to bring his tones out pear-shaped—thus. The continual reminder that as a great star he was no longer even a good actor made him feel less than a man; his professional downfall literally destroyed him in the end. The fallen star of either sex finds that marriage, far from being a prop to him in his desolation, becomes a mill which grinds his ego to powder. If the spouse is mercenary, he or she decamps without delay, often to the tune of headlines; if loyal, the ex-star experiences the misery of the jobless breadwinner—in spades. Women stars generally have a feeling that if all else fails they can always marry rich, and sure enough they can in the first flush of success and fame; in fact, they constantly do, to the loss of the screen and the public. But a fallen favorite is as much damaged goods in the marriage market as in her profession. If she does succeed in snaring a supersolvent husband, she is likely to discover herself at an unaccustomed disadvantage. When Hedy Lamarr married a Texas zillionaire, it seemed that she was crowning a career of many marriages with the best catch of all. She discovered that her husband and her in-laws evaluated all their possessions in terms of their cash value, and that her status was something like that of a blue-ribbon mare. She was beautiful and famous, which was to her credit on the right side of the ledger, but she wasn't rich in her own right any more, and in the eyes of the Texas society in which she now moved, that meant that she had no standing as an autonomous individual but was simply one of her husband's less negotiable assets. Miss Lamarr did not enjoy that, not after so many years of calling the tune. So, like Agnes Ayres and so many others, she jettisoned her husband, in a more than usually acrimonious divorce suit, took off for Hollywood, and tried to hit the comeback trail.

In nine cases out of ten—no, in ninety-nine out of a hundred—the hope of a comeback is delusory, and it leads to other delusions. In order to support his hopes, the ex-star has to kid himself about the realities he faces every day. The more he is frustrated, the more likely he is to retreat into a world of his own devising, and sometimes he retreats so far that he can't get back. It is notable that the majority of films which deal with the downfall of onetime favorites, from *What Price Hollywood?* to *What Ever Happened to Baby Jane?*, specify actual insanity as the eventual fate of the washed-up star. When she was asked her opinion of *Sunset Boulevard,* Mae Murray replied, "None of us floozies was ever that nuts." What made this statement startling to those in the know was that when she made it Miss Murray had long been as nutty as they come; that she was, in fact, Exhibit A. While she was still capable of filling engagements on a lower level than that of her great days, she gave herself such airs and made such demands that even sympathetic producers dared not engage her. Her appearance eventually became an outlandish caricature of the superstar, rather a dangerous caricature. She would walk down Fifth Avenue with her head bent back as far as it would go, as if she was gazing at the heavens. The concerned observer realized that she was trying to present a youthful chin line to passers-by, and he hoped that she wouldn't fall flat on her face at the next curbstone. At charity balls, which she attended all the time, she would command the orchestra to play the theme tune from *The Merry Widow* and waltz to it solo, compelling the paying customers to withdraw from the dance floor. In her last deluded days, she continually shuttled between New York and Hollywood by transcontinental bus, each time with the hope of a comeback as the reason. At a stopover on the last of these trips, the poor old lady got lost and was picked up wandering the streets of Kansas City; she died soon afterward.

Miss Murray was fortunate in that her friends, and her ex-husbands, saw to it that she did not live in actual want. Less celebrated has-beens are less lucky—a lot less. Unemployable as actors, they are equally unemployable even in menial jobs because of the hallucinations which accompany receding fame. Ex-stars infest Hollywood. They haunt its cheap lodginghouses and its down-at-heel saloons. You can spot them in the crowds of fans who surge around new favorites at the latest gala premier. In not too distant days, you might be approached for a handout on Sunset Boulevard by a faded woman or unshaven man whose hard-luck story was that he used to be So-and-So, and whose humiliation was complete when he had to produce his identity card to prove it. That sort of thing is fortunately gone by. Today, ex-stars, like all indigent movie actors, can find haven at the Motion Picture Country House, which is supported by everyone in the studios. Here they live in surroundings of comfort and beauty, and they are permitted the satisfaction of accepting bit roles or extra work in pictures and TV if any are offered. But even in this good fortune there is irony. The Motion Picture Country House and its activities are never publicized, except in fund-raising drives, and it and its inmates are never photographed, even for that purpose. The ex-celebrities who seek refuge here end their lives in anonymity.

"To be a star is to own the world and all the people in it," says the authoritative Miss Lamarr. "After a taste of stardom, everything else is poverty." The emotional binge of stardom leaves its victims in a state of perpetual hangover. It is a pleasure to conclude what is essentially a sad story with consideration of one of its exceptions. Madeleine Carroll is surely one of the great beauties of the twentieth century. At her peak her loveliness was such as to cause otherwise sensible men to write bad poetry, which tells its own tale. But in addition to her beauty and charm, Miss Carroll is a woman of breeding, education, intelligence, and taste. Her French mother and English father saw to it that in childhood she acquired cultural and worldly values which enabled her to view her stardom with a sense of proportion. When World War II came, she abandoned her career to do what she could to help win it. She was not even morally obligated to do so. The British Government in its wisdom at the outset of the war told its Hollywood children that they could do more for the motherland as movie stars than by fighting or otherwise serving in the ranks. Miss Carroll did not think so. She was determined not to be cut off from what she regarded as the central experience of her generation. She did not go overseas as an entertainer, in which role she might have gained ego satisfaction from the applause of the troops. She enlisted as a nurse, for which she had been trained in youth, she spent three years in a hospital train near the front, and she tried to conceal her identity. When one of her patients saw through her disguise of austere uniform and lack of make-up and asked her, "Aren't you Madeleine Carroll?", she replied, "Don't be silly, what would Madeleine Carroll be doing in a place like this?" At war's end she did not rush back to Hollywood to try to take up where she left off. She lingered in Paris, succoring European friends who had been through the hell of the occupation; starred in a minor French film because she believed in its social message; and herself produced two documentaries, primarily to further the career of their director, the youthful Victor Vicas. At last she went back to the Coast to find out if she was still a star, she reported her experiences there with irony and with a certain indignation. "Well, I got back," she said gleefully. "But I didn't like what I had to do to get there. Producers don't look at you as a man looks at a woman, they look at you as if they were judging a horse." Odious as this must have been, there is something to be said in their defense. Miss Caroll's *blondeur* is unfortunately of the type that fades early, and the studios may be pardoned if, while engaging her for one picture at a time, they were unwilling to sign her to a long-term contract. Miss Carroll herself understood this, and after three postwar starring roles, she decided to beat a strategic retreat which carried within it the possibility of a renewed offensive. She hied herself to Broadway and searched for a play which would be more than a mere vehicle for her name and her glamour, which would have substance of its own. She found it in Fay Kanin's *Goodbye, My Fancy*. But the play, though meritorious, had its shortcomings and Miss Carroll's then husband, Henri Lavorel, suffering from a bad case of first-night jitters, fretted audibly that its weak spots might reflect on its star in the eyes of the critics. "Well," said the lady, laughing and arching her beautiful breasts, "I can't worry about it. Men have always liked me, and the critics are men—I hope." Her instinct was right, as usual. The general critical verdict was reflected in Walter Winchell's "A kiss for MaDOLLeine Carroll—and a pattycake for the script." What she might have made of this initial theatrical success is anybody's guess. She divorced Lavorel during the run of the play, and shortly after it closed fell in love again, married, and bore a daughter. Her happiness unfortunately did not last, but, intrepid as ever, she was not thrown by its evaporation, nor did she, after five years of retirement, attempt to remind her profession and her public that she *used* to be a star. Instead she returned to Europe, to the world of leisure and culture to which her parents had introduced her in childhood, and of which she has been an ornament ever since. Her starring career, and the battles she fought to build and maintain it, must seem far behind her now. Does she ever think of them?

(Opposite page, top) The quickies were a refuge for falling stars, but because of poor photography, they seldom did anything to arrest the downward spiral of a career. Priscilla Dean can hardly have recognized herself in *Klondike,* 1932, with Lyle Talbot.

(Bottom) Neither Technicolor, the role of the Empress Josephine, nor Otto Matiesen as Napoleon did much to further Agnes Ayres's comeback in *The Lady of Victories,* 1928, though she had accepted demotion to short subjects on the theory that the sight of her face on the screen again would bring the fans flocking.

Ruth Chatterton, shown with David Niven, gave her finest performance in *Dodsworth,* but her career ended soon afterward. Though she had scored as the selfish, aging Fran Dodsworth, she tried to insist on continued stardom in youthful romances.

Almost alone among stars, Kay Francis prolonged her career beyond her day of white-hot popularity by accepting lesser roles at a greatly reduced salary—even financing a couple of quickies herself when all else failed. She is shown here at her peak in *Jewel Robbery,* 1932, with William Powell.

(Clockwise) Pola Negri's hopeful trade press ad for her comeback in *A Woman Commands,* 1932, bore no fruit. Her producers made the mistake of presenting her as a "new Dietrich," forgetting that Miss Negri was popular before Miss Dietrich was heard of; Florence Lawrence, among the earliest, perhaps the first, movie star, in Hollywood in 1932; The beautiful Ann Harding had the good sense to allow herself to grow old gracefully in a long series of roles after the end of her stardom, as here in *The North Star,* 1942; Evelyn Brent's highly successful personal appearance tours proved beyond peradventure that she was still popular, but all that they netted her on her return to Hollywood was secondary roles in cheap pictures like *Wrecking Crew,* with two other ex-stars, Chester Morris and Richard Arlen.

(Opposite page) Ida Lupino relinquished stardom without a struggle. She had always wanted to become a director—and did.

pola negri

Returning to the Screen in
"A WOMAN COMMANDS"
An RKO PATHE PICTURE

8 STARS THAT NEVER WERE

(Left) Among the many publicity gimmicks Universal used to exploit Erich von Stroheim's *Foolish Wives* was the name of the leading actress. New to the screen, she was said to be of aristocratic lineage so high that she must never be referred to by her first name but always and only as Miss Dupont. Today such a ploy would prompt intensive newspaper research into her background, but the lady was so dull to look at that nobody could be bothered. Soon she descended to secondary roles, as here with Pola Negri in *Good and Naughty,* still billed as "Miss Dupont," to a deafening lack of public interest.

(Above left) Madge Evans had been a child star of early movies who spent her awkward years on Broadway. When, with that advantageous background, she returned to pictures, she was hailed by all, including the public, as the perfect modern ingenue. She remained just that, in a world where growth and change are vital to survival. It was reported at the time that when Irving Thalberg of M-G-M signed Myrna Loy and decided to fashion her into the "perfect wife," he lost interest in Miss Evans' parallel possibilities. She continued as a perennial leading lady for another decade, until her marriage to the playwright Sidney Kingsley.

(Above right) The obvious honesty behind Karen Morley's acting made her an immediate hit, but it was this same forthrightness which eventually did her in. She could not conceal the fact that she was too intelligent for most of the roles she played, especially in the tortuous sentimentalities of "women's pictures." Nor could she conceal her left-wing political sympathies, and her activities in support of them landed her on a Hollywood blacklist.

(Right) Anna Sten was starred by Samuel Goldwyn in her first American film by virtue of her great European reputation as an actress and a luring screen personality. But Emile Zola's *Nana,* in which she was perfectly cast, had to be denatured before it could reach the censored screen of 1934, and, try though he did, Mr. Goldwyn could never fit her great qualities into any stereotype acceptable to the prejudices of mass audiences. Miss Sten's career was a tragedy of show business.

(Above left to right) James Murray, a King Vidor discovery, Lawrence Tierney, the pugnacious screen incarnation of *Dillinger*, and Sonny Tufts, a scion of wealth who ambled into acting for the fun of it, all shared traits which were summed up in a central one, the love of drinking. Each had the acting instinct, and the charm of the boozer, but no evidence of professional responsibility.

(Left) Richard Cromwell's sensitive performance in the remake of *Tol'able David* promised to make him as great a star as Richard Barthelmess had become by virtue of the original version. But the rigidities of type-casting kept the gifted Cromwell everybody's younger brother for fifteen years. In *Lives of a Bengal Lancer,* he youngerbrothered Gary Cooper and Franchot Tone.

(Right) Toby Wing and Lona Andre in *School For Girls*

(Below) As an undergraduate at Princeton, Philips Holmes stole the first picture in which he was fortuitously cast from its titular star, Buddy Rogers. His classic Greek profile, his obvious intelligence, and his professional inheritance from his father, the Broadway favorite Taylor Holmes, seemed to augur a highly successful career in the newborn talkies. But in spite of all his assets, Philips Holmes lacked self-confidence. Even the role of Clyde Griffiths in *An American Tragedy* failed to re-evoke in him the vital spark to which the public first responded. After Paramount dropped him every major studio gave him a chance, but to no avail; his work grew progressively weaker and more uncertain. He died young. He is seen here in his strongest performance, in *Her Man,* 1930, with Marjorie Rambeau.

SELECTED
SHORT
SUBJECTS VI

Sophia Loren in *Yesterday, Today and Tomorrow*

Richard Burton and Elizabeth Taylor in *The VIP's*   Patty Duke in *Valley of the Dolls*   Janice Rule

George Peppard and Audrey Hepburn in *Breakfast at Tiffany's*   Milton Reed in *Night Creatures*   Paul Newman in *Hud*

Mae West

III
DEATH AND TRANSFIG-URATION

Marilyn Monroe

1 THE STARS GROW OLD

It is passing strange to watch them. It was their beautiful youth which attracted us to them in our own youth, and the extension of that youth on the screen artificially prolonged our own. There came a day when we realized, with or without a sigh, that we ourselves were aging considerably faster than our movie contemporaries. And then a slightly later day when, looking at familiar, well-loved favorites, we saw the bloom go off. They were certainly not old, up there on the screen, but neither were they really young, and the tricks of lighting and camera angle necessary to maintain the illusion of youth were becoming obvious even to us laymen. And that, usually, was that. Five years was the standard stellar term, a ten-year star was a phenomenon, and we had to reach into Latin to describe anybody who lasted longer than that—*rara avis, sui generis*. And on the whole, we in the audience were well content with this state of affairs. Youth, and the passions of youth, were what we wanted from the stars; they existed to serve it up to us. If they could no longer do so, let them step down and join the rest of us as we watched the eternally self-renewing parade.

All that has changed completely. Youth still throngs the screen, as it always will, but the really great stars, every last one of them, are no longer young and hardly make the pretense of being young. With due allowance for the conventions of make-believe, it is no longer really necessary for a writer to torture a script in order to make us accept an obviously mature performer as a heroine, still less a hero, who is just on the threshold of life. For we have seen these particular performers mature with our own eyes. We have watched the laughter lines crinkle up the eyes, watched the furrows deepen, the dewlaps form, even as we have watched the same things happen to our own faces in the mirror. And we do not effectually complain. Every so often a cry goes up for new faces, because that always makes good copy, and because it is a standard show-business panacea when signs of audience restlessness appear. And the new faces duly materialize, and are duly exploited and publicized. But they do not shoulder their elders into oblivion as once they used to do. The starlets appear and disappear; the stars remain.

This is a revolution and a deep one, a foundational shift in taste and emotional need. Europe, we have been told too often and too long—Europe, with its sense of the past, is the place where old favorites last, even unto death. When Sarah Bernhardt, in her sixties, essayed the Maid of Orléans, the most sensational moment in her performance came when one of her judges asked Joan *"Que âge avez-vous?"* and she answered *"Dix-neuf ans."* Bernhardt spoke this line directly to the audience, and it brought her storms of applause. But America is the country of youth, and youth is what it has been selling to the world, via Hollywood, for almost the whole of the present century. How has it come about that American audiences, and the Hollywoodized world audience, now accept as dream images players who, whatever else they offer, do not offer youth, and whose appeal is inevitably intermingled with the passage of the generations, with time and change and even death.

That it *has* come about there is not the slightest doubt. Not everybody realizes, perhaps, just how long John Wayne has been around, nor how many screen incarnations he went through before he became just about the biggest box-office star that ever was. But everybody everywhere *is* aware that Cary Grant first became a father at the age of sixty, and that, the same event coincided with the peak of the demand for his professional services. The men, of course, stand the erosion of the years better than the women. It is comparatively easy to furnish them with parts which present them at just that temples-touched-with-gray border line between youth and middle age when they, or their stunt men, can still convincingly perform the feats of youth, and when the look on their faces says that they have been around long enough to know how to handle a woman—a woman of any age. In one of her periodic indiscretions to the press, Gloria Swanson burst out a few years back: "Glamour! I detest that word. It's like everything else in this town, immature. Only the French know about real glamour. All they care about here is the ghastly American worship of youth, and that's why there is no place for the mature actress on the screen today. Oh, the men are still around, but those aging Romeos are playing opposite *children,* and I think it's nauseating. What adult woman wants to see that? How can she identify with some *child?"* Unfortunately for Miss Swanson and the actresses in her age group, adult women seem to be able to identify even with very young girls—if the men playing opposite them treat them as if they were women. At that, the women are not doing too badly. So long ago as 1960, in an indiscretion equal to Miss Swanson's, Debbie Reynolds told a reporter: "I have to remember that I have only about five workable years left. Once you lose the leading lady face, you're cooked, and I'd rather quit than stay around until they don't want me any more." According to latest evidence, Miss Reynolds shows no sign of quitting. To take a more extreme example, in the middle fifties the Universal producer Ross Hunter decided that there was still a female audience for the oldtime "woman's picture" which other studios had abandoned. In his successful efforts to revive this staple, Hunter latched onto Lana Turner, then rapidly fading from view as a heroine of young romance. He made her carefully photographed, carefully corseted figure the centerpiece of a series of fudge sundaes which proved all over again that *plus ça change . . .* It was a brilliant tactic. Along with her look of a slightly shopworn but still alluring sex bomb, Miss Turner brought to Hunter's films the ambience of her sweater-girl beginnings and of the later scandals in her "private" life, in which she demonstrated that it was still exciting to live dangerously if you could survive physically. For the rest of the decade, thanks to these films, she joined the ranks of her seniors, Rosalind Russell, Joan Crawford, and Barbara Stanwyck, whose names could still be used as collateral in putting togther the capital for a multimillion-dollar production. As a frustrated film creator, Mel Shavelson, put it: "Only a star's name is bankable, even today. They won't rely on talent. They can't read scripts. And so they put their money on the 'chemistry' of star combinations. And they wonder why the critics say that the most original and interesting pictures are being produced abroad."

Interesting to whom? To the critics, and to a new, growing, but still comparatively small audience. But the box office, like the bankers, continues monotonously to say that the biggest audience of all still wants stars, including the old stars, no matter how old they are. The players mentioned above belong to the oldest star generation of all; all of them got started in the thirties, with the exception of Debbie Reynolds, a forties girl, and, of course, Miss Swanson, whose origins are prehistoric. What is most significant is that their juniors, the next generation of established stars, what might be called the "new wave" if it wasn't too ironical, simply cannot be called young any more. Today (1969) Tony Curtis is 44. So is Paul Newman. And Jack Lemmon. Doris Day, so recently the queen of audience hearts, is 45, as are Marlon Brando and Charlton Heston. William Holden is 51. Dean Martin is 52. And, *O tempora, O mores,* Ingrid Bergman is 56.

The new dispensation of middle-aged glamour followed upon a technological revolution, which led to an economic revolution, which led to a revolution in human experi-

Paul Newman

Cary Grant

David Niven

Lana Turner

Marlon Brando

Gloria Swanson

William Holden

Van Johnson and Debbie Reynolds

Mel Ferrer and Ingrid Bergman

Tony Curtis

ence. That is perhaps a little bit too pat. Television has not changed our souls, no matter how much sociologists stress its creeping, subliminal influence. But we are not the same people as those who first succumbed to the magic of the movies—and that includes the survivors of those early audiences. We want different things for ourselves, and so we want different things from our stars. To explore this shift in values, it is well to begin with what has happened to Hollywood, the place and the idea, which for forty golden years seemed so immutable a part of the scene.

2 AH, BRIGHT GHOST!

Ah, bright ghost,
Who shadow all I have and do . . .
Edna St.Vincent Millay

Even death has changed. The deaths, so young, of Marilyn Monroe and James Dean were in the romantic tradition which enfolded the deaths of Rudolph Valentino and Jean Harlow, of Barbara La Marr, and of those early star suicides, Bobby Harron and Olive Thomas. But the circumstances surrounding the deaths of Clark Gable, Humphrey Bogart, and Gary Cooper introduced a new element into the stellar fantasia as we know it in our time. We had followed these three modern heroes almost all their lives, on the screen and in their unprivate private lives as young lovers, young roisterers, great stars, pillars of the motion picture industry, and finally into what can only be called "respected old age." We followed them to the edge of the grave: Medical bulletins gave us every detail of their last illnesses, and on television newscasts we followed the comings and goings of their doctors as we might those of ex-Presidents of the United States. Few ex-Presidents have been so deeply or so widely mourned. And for these three death has not come as the end. In our imaginations they have joined the characters of literature and legend, Don Juan, D'Artagnan, Tom Jones, Ulysses, and share that immortality. As this is written, Rhett Butler can again be seen on the screens of the world, seen by millions who were too young to see the original release of *Gone With the Wind,* or read the book. And every night on the box, Bogie looks out at us from his deep eyes, and Coop rides again, and yet again. Our sons watch them, puzzle over them, and identify with them, and so will our sons' sons.

Montgomery Clift, Marilyn Monroe, and Clark Gable in *The Misfits*

James Dean in *Rebel Without a Cause*

Robert Walker, with Van Johnson, in *Thirty Seconds over Tokyo*

John Garfield dies in *He Ran All the Way*

AFTER THE FALL 3

There used to exist, within the bosom of that venerable institution, the National Board of Review of Motion Pictures, a committee called the Committee on Exceptional Photoplays. This group of critics, poets, novelists, freethinkers, and film fans met once a week to review the cream of the current crop of "photoplays," and to publicize what they considered the best of them by whatever means came to hand. In radio days the committee's deliberations were often put on the air, and when television arrived it seemed both logical and desirable to use the new medium to promote the best products of the older one—especially because it would now be possible to broadcast brief scenes from the pictures discussed—discussed, it should be borne in mind, always in terms of praise. What was envisioned was a highly intelligent preview service via television, one calculated to quicken the box office for the best pictures, and never mind the bad ones.

In order to show scenes from their films, it would of course be necessary to secure the co-operation of the motion picture companies, and the National Board of Review delegated the author of this book to do the job. Despite the superficial desirability of my project. I had some lingering doubts about how it would be received. I decided to take the bull by the horns and tackle first what was notoriously the most cantankerous of the companies, mighty M-G-M. I sought out the genial Howard Dietz, Metro's director of advertising and publicity, who certainly would be alive to the promotional possibilities in an idea such as this if anybody in the industry would be. Mr. Dietz listened to my story with the keenest interest, and at its end burst out laughing. Somewhat affronted, I asked him why.

"Well," he replied, "thank God for Mr. Schenck. Your proposal is just the sort of thing I naturally fall for, and I would have undoubtedly wasted a lot of time trying to sell it to our distributors and exhibitors. Mr. Schenck has saved both of us a lot of futile effort. Just yesterday he sent a memorandum to every department head instructing us, and every employee of Metro-Goldwyn-Mayer, to impede the development of television by every means in our power—great *and* small. I think that's that, don't you?"

It was. The Mr. Schenck referred to was Nicholas M. Schenck, president of M-G-M and Loew's, Inc., and as his long-time associate, J. Robert Rubin, put it: "Whatever Mr. Schenck is in favor of, we are for"; the reverse also held good. His attitude was far from atypical. The movie grandees did not really suppose that they could stop the growth of TV, or even effectually obstruct it; but they wished so hard that it would go away that they were often reduced to pettiness in their efforts to combat its effects. It was giving away free what they were selling, and they were showmen enough to know what that would eventually mean. But the only possible remedy, the creation of a radically new production and distribution system which would include television as one of the outlets for the movies, along with the theaters, was repugnant to them. The old system was *their* system, they had created it, they were identified with it, and for many of them it was their only claim to identity; comparatively few of them had had much directly to do with the creation of the actual movies which were fed through it. So they clung to it and tried to keep it intact and unchanged, and in doing so wrecked it more drastically than need have been the case.

The star system, which was a key element in the old production-distribution system, was predicated on the assumption that each of the eight major studios would have to produce between forty and fifty pictures a year to satisfy the market. Granted that not all the three-hundred-odd pictures so produced required stars, there was need for them in plenty, and also need to have them on call, hence the contract system as an extension of the star system. This led naturally, at least in the thinking of the studio bosses, to a view of the stars as "properties" or "capital assets," and they were actually included as such in the annual inventories of studio assets. The free-lance star, a prominent feature of the star system in early days, had virtually disappeared by the beginning of the sound era. The magnates preferred to "own" their stars, and to "lend" them to one another as need arose, until the last dollar of profit had supposedly been squeezed from each one. Now, with the shrinkage of profits and the concomitant shrinkage in the number of pictures produced, these "assets" suddenly turned into non-liquidatable liabilities. The obvious thing to do was to allow contracts to lapse when they expired, but the studios could not bring themselves to abandon their old methods so completely; they preferred to keep up appearances by re-signing their stars for "non-exclusive" one-picture-a-year deals—only to find that they could not even offer their stars these single pictures, but had to pay them for them just the same. As minimal profits turned to major losses on the companies' books, these pretenses had to be abandoned. The stars were let out as fast as they could be got rid of (considerable arm-twisting went on behind the scenes). This was not all: By 1953 all of the studios had abandoned their "B" production units, the developing ground for new talent, and the machinery for the discovery and training of stars was allowed to fall apart.

This major surgery temporarily reduced production costs, but it in no permanent way improved the situation of the studios; in fact, it opened Pandora's box. Pictures still had to have stars, and with no new ones coming along, the producers had to bargain with their former human chattels on terms completely to the advantage of the latter. The newly liberated stars lost no time in exploiting their unaccustomed bargaining power. They formed their own producing corporations and bestowed upon them the same fanciful and romantic names they had formerly given their yachts: Batjac Productions (John Wayne); Bryna Productions (Kirk Douglas); Pennebaker Productions (Marlon Brando); Melville Productions (Gregory Peck's tribute to the author of *Moby Dick*); Jaguar Productions (Alan Ladd); and Portland Pictures (James Mason). If this sounds a bit like fairyland, it was. The stars now had what they had always dreamed of, their own choice of parts and stories. They secured their production capital from the studios in return for distribution rights. They got to keep three quarters of their pictures' earnings, since the latter were subject to capital gains tax, not income tax. They owned their own pictures in perpetuity. And best of all, they now could tell Jack Warner or Darryl Zanuck exactly where to get off—which they hoped was nowhere.

It was dreams come true, but the dreams had a way of turning sour. It was simple enough to form a corporation, all you had to do was hire a lawyer and draw up the papers. But to reap any sort of return, you had to follow through step by step, and that was not as easy and pleasurable as your persuasive agent had convinced you it would be. Shrewd men like Bing Crosby, Burt Lancaster, and Kirk Douglas, who enjoy business management, are still receiving generous dividends on an investment of time and reputation now many years old. But the average star, if there is such a animal, soon found the vigilance necessary to protect his interests exhausting as well as unfamiliar. He discovered, too, that what with agents, tax accountants, investment advisers, and—

inevitably—relatives on the payroll, the pie had to be divided up as many ways as it did in the days when he earned a guaranteed salary—and that sometimes there was no pie to divide. Under these pressures, the star frequently fell back on the methods of his own profession and approached his role of corporation president as an act of impersonation. Said a Hollywood pressman of the time, "The matinee idol of the Eisenhower era is a man in a gray flannel suit. What he says in a conference can matter more than how he says his lines. He must learn how to pick a story as well as play it, fire an actress on the set as well as set her on fire. And while he is at it, he should learn how to direct the director." He might have added that in these times the star-president, or presidental star, found himself playing his biggest scenes at the bank.

By the mid-fifties, the more responsible agents were steering their clients away from the star company bit, or inducing them to abandon it, in favor of the "participation deal." By this gimmick, the star received 50 per cent (or 30 per cent) of the net (or gross) of a regular studio production in which he appeared. This guaranteed him most of the advantages of producing his own pictures but fewer of the liabilities. He had a voice in the choice of stories, casts, and directors, and he maintained his tax advantage because he was in effect investing his time and reputation in the film in lieu of straight salary, but he was relieved of responsibility for budgets, schedules, and similar worries with which for the most part he was so ill equipped to deal. This dispensation allowed face-saving all round in the now chronic warfare between stars and studios. The companies got their stars back, on a picture-to-picture basis and at heavy cost. The stars could take off their grey flannel suits and get back into blue jeans or wine-colored dinner jackets, as their whimsey took them.

These maneuvers and skirmishes took place against a backdrop of continued slow decline, if not exactly fall. Despite occasional upturns and spasmodic hits, the general level of the motion picture box office continued its gradual slide downward from the peaks of the forties—while production costs continued to climb. Panic became endemic in Hollywood. At first unconscious, then dissembled, finally overt, it became an ordinary condition of existence, something to be lived with, like a low-grade virus infection. The great movie corporations existed on a perennial brink, the name of which was liquidation, since there were many within and without their directorates who thought that the piecemeal sale of their assets would bring in more money than their producing potential. Everybody else, though lapped in luxury, *felt* as though they were living from hand to mouth. In this atmosphere production policy took on a tinge of hysteria. Since nobody could think of anything which would lure the audience back to the theaters, except the same old things, the answer which dictated itself was *more* of the same—to press each button *harder*. So screens grew bigger, wider, and, temporarily, deeper, violence grew more violent, sex sexier, and De Mille more De Millious. It would be pleasant to add that the stars grew starrier, but something like the opposite occurred. Since the picture-makers of the fifties could do nothing to increase the incandescence of individual stars, they simply multiplied their number. In doing so, they gradually ate into the quality and character of stardom itself.

From stardom's beginnings, the essential idea of a star has been that of a solo attraction. To call a film a "star vehicle" was to imply that it was designed exclusively to show off the star doing the things he, or she, did best, and he was expected to ride his vehicle to success with only marginal assistance from other production values. When a star appeared in a film which was not a vehicle, which had merit and importance of its own, he was regarded as simply a pump primer, a lure to start people coming to a picture which would later create its own audience by word of mouth. As for "co-starring" films, except for the love teams like Banky and Colman or Gaynor and Farrell, these were tours de force, a once in a lifetime or once in a careertime event: When Mary Pickford and Douglas Fairbanks at last yielded to the pleas of their loyal legions, there was a touch of the valedictory about their joint appearance in *The Taming of the Shrew*. Beyond that category, the "all-star" production was generally a misnomer which meant that none of the players featured in it had attained genuine stardom or anything like it. Before World War II, the genuine all-star films were exactly four in number: *Grand Hotel,* 1932 (Garbo, Crawford, Beery, John and Lionel Barrymore); *Dinner at Eight,* 1933 (Beery, Harlow, John and Lionel Barrymore, Marie Dressler); *State Fair,* 1933 (Janet Gaynor, Will Rogers, Lew Ayres, Sally Eilers); and *Night Flight,* 1934 (Helen Hayes, Robert Montgomery, Myrna Loy, John and Lionel Barrymore). That spate of spendthrift films derived from the accidental fact of the purchase by the studios, close together in time, of theatrical and literary properties which happened to have more than one or two meaty parts apiece. The fashion soon expended itself, and it was not repeated. After 1935 screen title cards resumed their familiar appearance: Greta Garbo in *Camille;* Barbara Stanwyck in *Internes Can't Take Money,* with Joel McCrea; Fred Astaire and Ginger Rogers in *Carefree; Babes in Arms,* with Mickey Rooney and Judy Garland.

The 1950s reversed what had come to seem the immutable order of things. By the middle of the decade the lone-starring vehicle had virtually disappeared. The co-starring film had a lightweight air, and its credit titles were impoverished-looking, especially when (unlike Astaire and Rogers) the two stars concerned had no particular reason to belong to each other. What emerged as standard and staple was the all-star film which did not have the effrontery to bill itself as such. In every other film, a curious new hierarchy of star values was offered a supposedly panting public. Three and sometimes four genuine star names were billed above the title of the film. Below it, and following the phrase "co-starring," appeared three, four, five, or six well-known players, some of whom, however, had never been starred in their own right. Following *that,* there faded in the names of another three to six actors who we were informed were "also starring" in the picture, perhaps in the sense of also ran. As if this were not God's plenty, the credits droned on that the film "featured" any number of minor lights, some of whose appearances were brief indeed. But hold, we are not through yet. In solitary splendor there would then loom up the name of a single player, usually a vintage one drawn temporarily out of limbo to enact a presumptively difficult or important role—thus: " . . . And Joan Blondell as Maizie." There was another "And" to come. It was "And Introducing." Any model, anybody's mistress, any fresh-faced girl or boy would do to foster the illusion that in addition to its stars, co-stars, also stars, ex-stars, and featured players, the picture was offering us an authentic star of tomorrow whom we could have the delicious pleasure of discovering on our very own. There were still further excesses. After the success of *Around the World in Eighty Days,* film after film was studded with "cameo stars," world celebrities filmed in their native habitats, or brought to Hollywood at vast expense to play what were virtually walk-on parts. Supposedly we sat in our seats chortling over their recognition, but they flitted by so fast as often to go unspotted, and the reaction of the walk-out audience was, "But where *was* Marlene Dietrich?" The cameo star gambit, on top of everything else, led to a further evil; it is from this period that we date the film which begins well before its credits, generates considerable interest and suspense, and then achieves anticlimax as the names of the stars and production personnel obliterate the action.

Such phenomena issued from counsels of despair, or better, theories of despair. The principal theory was highly scientific, in fact chemical. The multistar picture not only tried to overwhelm us with sheer weight of numbers; it was also founded on the "chemistry" of star names. It was firmly believed that certain combinations of stars exerted a catalytic effect on a film (at least in the public mind), galvanizing it into a life which it might not be able to achieve on its own. The shortage of top stars being what it was and is, these laboratory experiments often took the form of a game of musical chairs. Suppose that the plot, or chemistry, of a particular film, scheduled to be shot in Rome, Hollywood, and northeastern Siberia, seems to call for a combination of Frank Sinatra, Doris Day, Sophia Loren, and Cary Grant. Suppose also, which is a lot of supposing, that a bank has been found which is willing to put up the astronomical sums to pay the salaries involved, let alone the cost of location shooting. The game begins. Mr. Sinatra, sent the script, is enchanted with his part and his prospective co-stars, but. But his television, night club, and picture commitments are such that he cannot participate unless production can be postponed until 1973. It can't, and in a process resembling guilt by association, Dean Martin is selected to replace him. Using him will necessitate certain script alterations, and while they are being made word comes from Mr. Grant that his tax situation is such that he really cannot afford to make the picture unless he is given 90 per cent of the television rights in lieu of salary. The bank must be consulted on this, and contracts rewritten to compensate the other stars for Mr. Grant's imperious, and very precise, demands. Meanwhile Miss Loren is not only eager to make the picture, she is ready to begin right now, this very instant. She is at home, at the moment, in Rome; cannot the Roman sequences be shot while these other matters are being ironed out? Miss Day is also involved in the Roman sequences, and Miss Day has not even been approached yet, but to hold Miss Loren certain close-ups and background shots are made at Cinecittà, and production costs begin to be registered on the books. Miss Day now apprises that these days she never makes pictures which she does not own outright, and that the special inducements offered are insufficient to cause her to depart from her rule. However, she happens to know that her friend Shirley MacLaine, who she thinks resembles herself in a second-string sort of way, is available for two weeks in March next year, and also from the end of July to the beginning of November, due to the sudden cancelling of another multistar production. While this is being pondered, the news arrives that the Soviet Government, which had unaccountably given permission for shooting in northeastern Siberia, has changed its mind; there are to be war games in that part of Siberia next year (the Soviets do not of course volunteer this intelligence, but the CIA has obliged). Well, the sequences of *Doctor Zhivago* were convincingly shot in Finland and Spain, and Ava Gardner lives in Spain—Ava Gardner, who is slated to play the "And-As" role—in this case, "AND Ava Gardner as Mrs. Laetitia Pilkington." But now it develops that Ava Gardner has an old contract with Samuel Bronston, not yet lapsed, which absolutely forbids her to appear in any picture which is to be shown on television.

THE REIGNING BEAUTY OF THE SCREEN!

MARLENE DIETRICH in **"THE SCARLET EMPRESS"**

Directed by Josef von Sternberg

A PARAMOUNT PICTURE

Ad for *The Scarlet Empress*, 1934

BEBE DANIELS

"My Past"

The tell-tale autobiography of DORA MACY'S life!

uphone" is the registered trademark of The Vitaphone Corporation.

BEN LYON
LEWIS STONE
JOAN BLONDELL
NATALIE MOORHEAD
Screen adaptation and dialogue
by Charles Kenyon
Directed by ROY DEL RUTH

Beautiful, alluring — surrounded by men, yet always lonely; showered by luxuries, yet unhappy — love and marriage offered her, but always the dark shadow of her past to come between her and happiness! Dora Macy, the girl whose missteps forever echoed to haunt her! You have read her famous story which the authoress dared not sign. Now see it brought to life with the glamorous Bebe Daniels, playing the part of a modern girl whom men remembered — but women can never forget!

WARNER BROS. & VITAPHONE PICTURE

Sold!

"Love would have been such an honest reason.. But you sold yourself."

WARNER BROS. *presents:*

Constance Bennett

in BOUGHT

A beautiful girl who takes but never gives!...loved but not loving! . . . engaged but not married! . . . bought but not paid for! . . . *JACKDAWS STRUT* from which this great production comes has created more talk than any other novel of modern life . . . And Constance Bennett more gorgeously gowned—more emotionally satisfying—more dramatically supreme—makes it the finest picture play of her career . . . Directed by ARCHIE MAYO.

"Vitaphone" is the registered trademark of The Vitaphone Corporation

A WARNER BROS. & VITAPHONE PICTURE

"ICE STATION ZEBRA"...REMEMBER THE NAME— YOUR LIFE MAY DEPEND ON IT!

An American nuclear sub...A sky full of Russian paratroopers... A race for the secret of Ice Station Zebra!

Metro-Goldwyn-Mayer presents Martin Ransohoff's Production of

"Ice Station Zebra"

in CINERAMA

starring
Rock Hudson   Ernest Borgnine   Patrick McGoohan   Jim Brown

co-starring
Tony Bill · Lloyd Nolan · screenplay by Douglas Heyes·screen story by Harry Julian Fink
From the novel by Alistar MacLean · directed by John Sturges · produced by Martin Ransohoff · A Filmways Picture · Super Panavision® and Metrocolor MGM

NOW! DIRECT FROM ITS ROADSHOW ENGAGEMENT

Every Ticket Holder Guaranteed A Seat

NO SEATS RESERVED

STEPHEN BOYD · AVA GARDNER · RICHARD HARRIS
JOHN HUSTON · PETER O'TOOLE · MICHAEL PARKS
GEORGE C. SCOTT

"★★★★ A MASTERPIECE" —N.Y. DAILY NEWS EDITORIAL

20th Century-Fox presents

THE BIBLE ...In The Beginning

"AN AWESOMELY ABSORBING FILM!" —LIFE

Screenplay by CHRISTOPHER FRY · Produced by DINO De LAURENTIIS · Directed by JOHN HUSTON

411

Since television rights are essential to the financing of the film, and also to satisfy Mr. Grant, that is that. It will be necessary to replace her in the "And-As" role with Mary Astor, who can play any part from six to seventy-six without the necessity for script alteration, and who isn't under contract to anybody, even herself. Miss Astor is reported to be ill, but if her trouping record is any guide she will show up in Finland, Spain, Rome, northeastern Siberia, or the Kremlin itself whenever she is needed. On second thought, it might be well to rewrite the script around Miss Astor, using her as a plot link between the stars, whose scenes can then be shot wherever they happen to be, and whenever they have a free moment.

This casting chaos, with its concomitant distortion of story lines and disruption of shooting schedules, made budgets meaningless. Pictures were brought in at two and three times their estimated costs; hope of profits vanished, catastrophic losses became inevitable, and the hapless entrepreneurs who put together these glittering star combinations were left with empty pockets and no prospects for future financing of similar efforts. Hollywood's long-fabled extravagance seemed to have gone hog-wild; pictures were being made for the sake of making pictures, not for that of making money. But the businessmen of Hollywood were still all business. It was just that none of them, twist and turn as they would, could figure out a remedy for the root evil, to wit: that every costly picture had to have still costlier stars; that the shortage of such stars was extreme; and that said stars had grown, not only long in the tooth, but so long in the bank account that they could afford to do exactly as they pleased. And there were no replacements for them, in being or on the horizon. Any young player who attracted interest on the stage or in television got his chance in pictures—but he had to hit the jackpot right away or not at all. There was no one to develop him, to nurse him through the initial stages, to bring him along. To the talent agencies, with their throng of illustrious clients to be served, he was either "hot" or nothing. The star corporations, for obvious reasons, were not interested in promoting the promising. The new independent outfits like Seven Arts or the Mirisch Brothers made their plans on a picture-to-picture basis, using the big stars in being, and it was rare for them to get behind a newcomer. As for the husks of the great studios, having abandoned the contract system for economy reasons, they were unable to figure out any alternative way of making stars, though they knew that only the development of new stars could restore their bargaining power with the old ones. From time to time they made a stab at it.

The ringleader in these sporadic attempts at star-making was Jerry Wald. Mr. Wald was about to make it really big as a writer-producer when the old Hollywood setup crumbled around him. Frustrated just short of the opportunity to climb up there on top where Mayer, Warner, and Goldwyn sat, he became, for the rest of his life, the boy who stood on the burning deck, whence all but him had fled. With might and main, and with considerable imagination, he attempted to breathe life into the production system which had only been viable when movies were the nation's favorite family entertainment, and a family necessity like bread or newspaper. Loyally he made his pictures in Hollywood rather than abroad; made them, where possible, in the studio instead of on location. To his credit, he took advantage of relaxed censorship to introduce new themes and subject matter to the screen, drawn, or perhaps more correctly, drawn-out, from contemporary writers of the first rank such as Faulkner and Lawrence. And he tried to buck the ebbing tide and restore the old system of step-by-step star-making. When Darryl Zanuck decamped as production head of 20th Century-Fox, Wald moved his production unit there, and in addition to his own picture-making, tried to prop up the studio as a whole. He signed up young players as lavishly as if he was operating in the good old days. In 1958 he unveiled *In Love and War,* an all-star no-star production imbued with the spirit of youth and featuring Robert Wagner, Jeffrey Hunter, Bradford Dillman, Dana Wynter, Hope Lange, Sheree North, and France Nuyen. On it *Time* commented: "All of them, as producer Jerry Wald proudly points out, have been carefully nurtured in the Fox talent school as part of what Wald calls the studio 'reforestation program.' A few pictures like this could reduce the whole lot of them to cordwood." Undaunted, Wald continued to produce his youthful jamborees, the most successful of which was *The Best of Everything,* with Hope Lange, Stephen Boyd, Suzy Parker, Diane Baker, Robert Evans, and, to bolster things up, Joan Crawford in the "And-As" role. *The Best of Everything* was a box-office smash, but it didn't make any stars. It couldn't. A gap had widened which no one could jump, the gap between the introduction of a promising newcomer and his metamorphosis into a "bankable" star name. In olden days a studio head could make a star by fiat, and star him in a series of pictures designed to test the exact extent of public response to him; if the mogul had made a mistake, the loss could be absorbed by the studio program as a whole. But with every picture a separate gamble, producers had to offer to their banker backers—or to studio boards of directors and the *other* banks behind them—a pretested name which was as solid a guarantee of audience interest as it was possible to obtain. So far as star values are concerned, major pictures of the fifties and sixties have divided into two categories, the multistar combine designed to satisfy the financial angels, and the all-star no-star film which usually adds the weight of a top director's name or a daring theme to the modest plusses represented by its moderately well-known young players. Such pictures, by their prevalence and continuity, have contributed measurably to the erosion of the idea of the star system itself. They have conditioned the public to the acceptance of movies in which star appeal is subordinate to other kinds of entertainment values.

The public. The x factor. It always had the final say in the making of a star, but its say came as the last step in a long process. Today it must speak first or no one will listen, despite ever more frantic bids for attention by would-be stars from all quarters of the globe. It seems nowadays that almost anybody can get before the cameras—and almost nobody can move upward from there unless he registers an immediate flaming hit. Then he is welcomed into the charmed circle of the bankable, can form his own company, get himself a piece of the action, and join the delectable game of musical chairs.

Here for the moment we leave the old system, trying to preserve itself in the teeth of the storm, and all unconsciously devouring itself. Before considering the effects of the new dictatorship of the public, it will be well to take a jet-plane overview of the new circumstances of mid-century life which have changed, not only the stars, but the need for the stars.

4 HOLLYWOOD INTERNATIONAL

Whether it was the jet plane or the blocked dollar which contributed most to the internationalization of American movie-making is a question for a medieval scholiast. The world wags that way; since the second big war, "diversification" of interest and assets on a global scale has become a necessity for every major industry—and particularly for Hollywood, which has through most of its history drawn over 50 per cent of its revenue from overseas markets. In the past twenty years "American" films have been made in England, Ireland, Scotland, France, Holland, Germany, Norway, Finland, Switzerland, Italy, Yugoslavia, Greece, Turkey, Israel, Spain, Egypt, Kenya, the Congo, Tanzania, Australia, Brazil, Argentina, India, Thailand, the Philippines, and Japan—virtually everywhere except the Communist countries, and talks of co-production deals with the Soviets are so continuous that sooner or later one of them is bound to work out. It is no longer necessary to go to Hollywood to be "discovered." The world has become a movie set, and while it may excite, it surprises no one to learn from his local paper that a location unit is coming to town and that you, too, can be a movie actor—for $15 a day and lunch money.

It was unquestionably blocked currency which first pried the picture-makers loose from their self-circumscription in the sound stages of southern California. After World War II, war-torn and impoverished countries like France, Italy, and Germany hungrily welcomed the Hollywood product from which they had been cut off so long. But they couldn't afford to let Hollywood siphon off any really large proportion of the francs and marks and lire due it without damaging their own precarious economics. So they froze the earnings of American films, and in effect invited Hollywood to make them an offer. In the complicated wheeling and dealing which followed, the expedient most agreeable to both sides was that of using blocked funds to finance the making in European countries of essentially American films, with American stars and skeleton crews, but with equipment and all other production personnel recruited locally. This pattern of international film-making proved so profitable and economical that it became and has remained standard. The consequences have been profound.

In addition to novel and beautiful locations and cheaper labor costs—at first, at any rate—producers suddenly found themselves in a position to draw at will on the acting talent of an entire continent. Since the settings for these films made it logical to cast Europeans, any player from any country west of the iron curtain could be and was considered for all but the top roles if he spoke English. Even if he didn't, he could be used if the part really cried out for him, thanks to the complicated marvel of dubbing. The use of native players gave freshness and reality to films so produced, but it also had a far more important effect. American films produced abroad became forcing-beds for new stars, a substitute for the old studio talent schools and for the contract system itself. This was a genuine and fruitful innovation. In the silent days, when foreign films could obtain national distribution in the United States simply through the translation of their subtitles into English, European stars could become known to American audiences before their importation by Hollywood; Pola Negri and Emil Jannings were already famous when Paramount brought them from Germany in the twenties. But when sound confined foreign-language films to a few large cities, importing, grooming, and introducing a European favorite became a gamble, an expensive one if it failed. Under the new dispensation of internationalized production, prospective stars could be unveiled to the public in secondary roles at the going salary for such parts, and on a one-picture basis. If they failed to make an impression, that was that. If, on the other hand, one of them made a hit, here was a ready-made star whom the happy producer could tuck under his arm and take back to the West Coast—unless someone else was shrewd enough to snap him up before his immediate sponsor realized how the tide was running. Since round about 1950 this has become staple procedure, an almost automatic way of sifting wheat from chaff, and so delightfully inexpensive.

Anna Magnani was the pioneer. Her Italian films were for the most part only shown in American metropolises, but she had achieved a sort of secondhand celebrity as a by-product of the Bergman-Rossellini affair when Hal B. Wallis decided to take the chance everyone in Hollywood wanted to take, to see if this powerhouse of talent—this acting genius—could strike a response in the heart of the Middle West and all that the Middle West stands for in terms of American values. Far from beautiful, further still from youth, she shattered all the stellar conventions; but no one could resist her magnetism, her utter femaleness, her earthiness. It is true that Miss Magnani never became a blazing favorite, never built up an army of fans in the manner of the great stars of old. But under the new dispensation it no longer mattered. She was an asset to American films which were hardly conceivable without her; when no role turned up in Hollywood which fitted her special requirements, she could and did go back to Italy to appear in Italian films and on the Roman stage, until something else turned up here which cried for her presence. It was no longer a question of sink or swim, Hollywood or bust, and no second chances. Miss Magnani could have the best of both worlds, and new worlds besides, as producers all over the globe altered their scripts and their schedules to try to find a way to use her. The example of intercontinental commutation which she set is now followed by everyone. In the case of Simone Signoret, it was unfortunately not set quite early enough. Such of her French films as *Casque d'or* stirred the elite to passionate enthusiasm for the most stunning actress and woman since Garbo, but these films were seen by few. Only when she was cast as the shopworn heroine of the British film *Room at the Top* did mass audiences catch a glimpse of what was already slipping away from them. Mme. Signoret is an international celebrity today, and adds her authority and the remains of her beauty to many international films, but the dream figure she might have become had we seen her in her glowing youth is now only something to dream about. Much the same could be said of Melina Mercouri. For Sophia Loren, it was different, and luckier. As for the present and future, we have the chance nowadays to turn thumbs up or down on Rita Tushingham, Romy Schneider, or Senta Berger while they are still young—often extremely young. Just as in the old contract days—even more than then, perhaps—we are given the opportunity to sample the newest crop of candidates for stardom as soon as they are nubile.

For indigenously American stars, international movie-making had provided enlarged professional opportunities and enlarged lives. Once the ball got rolling, they had a pick of parts and pictures far wider than any Hollywood had ever afforded them, with commensurately increasing bargaining power. And spending a season or two filming in Rome or Paris or London, let alone Tokyo or Hong Kong, did things to them as people. It wised them up. They were around the world capitals long enough to gain permanent entree to the real jet set, the invisible one, of which they had hitherto been

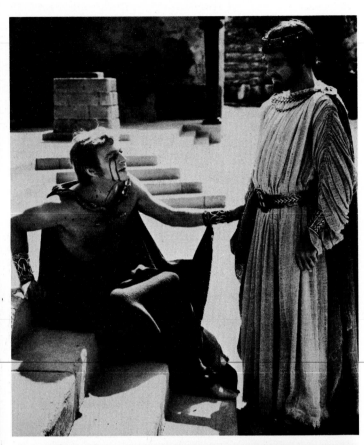

(Clockwise) Christopher Plummer and Richard Johnson in *Oedipus the King,* filmed in Crete; Gregory Peck on the London location for *Arabesque;* The only fat girl ever to become a star, Lynn Redgrave, with James Mason, in *Georgy Girl;* Although the picture was American-financed, Lillian Gish was the only American member of the cast of *The Comedians,* which otherwise starred Elizabeth Taylor, Richard Burton, Peter Ustinov, and Alec Guinness. Because the film was produced in Nice, the camera slate is in French; Anne Heywood and Fred Astaire at St. Mark's in Venice for *The Midas Run*.

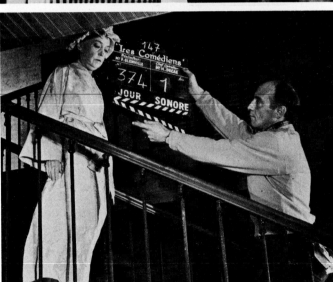

416

(Clockwise) By the mid-fifties, Paris had become a place where Hollywoodites continually ran into their next-door neighbors. Here Henry Fonda and Mel Ferrer visit Audrey Hepburn (Mrs. Ferrer) and Gary Cooper during the making of *Love in the Afternoon;* Sandra Dee and Tony Franciosa inspect a Portuguese swordfish on location for *A Man Could Get Killed* in Sesimbra, Portugal; The universal distribution of *La Dolce Vita* made Marcello Mastroianni and Anita Ekberg familiar screen personalities to American audiences; Gerhard Hersch, Rita Tushingham, and Alec Guinness in *Dr. Zhivago;* Teen-age favorites Bobby Darin and Sandra Dee picnic in the ruins of antique Rome while filming *Come September.*

417

Orson Welles and Peter Sellers in *Casino Royale*

Senta Berger and Max von Sydow in *The Quiller Memorandum*

Room at the Top established the stereotype of Simone Signoret as a faded but magnetic enchantress. Her international fans of today are unaware of her earlier incarnation as a freshly youthful beauty in films shown exclusively in France. She is seen here with Laurence Harvey.

Geraldine Chaplin and Sir Ralph Richardson in *Dr. Zhivago*

only occasional and rather freakish ornaments. Among these new associates, they learned from the inside how the very, very rich got that way and how they stayed that way. They learned what a bank account in Switzerland or Liechtenstein could mean. As they spent longer and longer periods abroad, their lawyers and tax men acquainted them with some highly agreeable laws which Congress had passed to assuage the feelings of those U.S. citizens who found income tax so onerous that they were willing to go to almost any lengths to void it, including the length of staying out of the country for a year at a time. (Congress can be singularly obliging at times: In 1951 it passed an *ad hoc* law permitting Anna Maria Alberghetti and her family to remain in the United States, although her father was an "involuntary Fascist" under Mussolini). Gene Kelly was the first to discover that if he made pictures abroad for a year, his income would be tax-free up to a limit of $240,000. When word of this got around, the list of those figuratively willing to leave home and mother for the sake of their art all but coincided, by a strange coincidence, with the list of top-bracket stars who were most vulnerable to confiscatory taxation. By the late 1950s not only Culver City and Universal City, but also Beverly Hills and Malibu, began to take on the air of ghost towns.

Unlike Mr. Kelly, who merely spent a year in self-exile, his successors gave every sign of settling in to stay. It must not quite true to say, as someone did, "Knock on any Castle door, there's a star inside," but the star-director John Huston's ducal setup in Ireland gave some substance to the crack. With all Europe, indeed all the world, to choose from, the illustrious fugitives from Internal Revenue chose to huddle together in a few select spots, as if for warmth and moral support. The resulting groupings provided an interesting reflection of the old Hollywood hierarchy of relative star values. Paris, for some reason, attracted those who had specific reasons for absenting themselves from California, but whose reasons had least to do with taxation—Ingrid Bergman, Jean Seberg, Olivia de Havilland. Switzerland was the haven for the top earners and those on a lower salary level with the shrewdest advisers—Charlie Chaplin, Gregory Peck, the Richard Burtons, Gina Lollobrigida, Burt Lancaster, Mel Ferrer and Audrey Hepburn, William Holden, James Mason, George Sanders, Yul Brynner, Peter Ustinov, David Niven; a partial list only. Rome, which had been the original Mecca for errant Hollywoodites because of its well-equipped studios, came to fill a peculiar function, the function once filled by Republic and Monogram. It became the haven for fallen stars, and for stars who never quite made it to the top in the States. Rome, it may have been said, is an old city, and it has been known to sack its sackers. The Romans proved to be expert in exploiting assets created elsewhere. Esther Williams, Fernando Lamas, Guy Madison, John Barrymore, Jr., and Anita Ekberg were names still viable in the European market, and if their Italian films could also get a small release in the United States on the strength of their old reputations, that was velvet. Rome has even become a sort of way station for youngsters on their way up. It has become almost the custom for ambitious beginners, after a few TV and movie roles, to try their luck in Rome, where the appetite for all things American seems to assure a welcome for any young player who even *looks* as if he belongs in Hollywood. Then he can go back and say he has worked for Fellini or Antonioni. This experience, coming at the beginning rather than the middle or the end of a career, provides youthful American thespians with some of the education and some of the pleasures of the grand tour. Said Robert Wagner: "Look, I bought a car, nothing special, just a great car. Well, I love that car. It has taken me all over—France, the Alps, Sicily—and I'd never done any of that before. Now, in Hollywood, someone else would get a new model and maybe I wouldn't—you know. And in the States if you worry about wines, people think you're queer or something."

In 1962 Congress set a limit of $35,000 on the amount of income a citizen could preserve tax-free simply by absenting himself from the country. Possibly the howls of Hollywood unions about "runaway" production had something to do with this *volte-face,* or possibly the mutters of American tourists, spending their heavily taxed incomes on holiday in Europe, where they saw the stars adding astronomical sums to theirs with no taxation at all. It was trumpeted at the time that now the runaways would return, settle down in California where they belong, and listen to the advice of reputable Hollywood tax men instead of those Swiss financiers. A good many did come back, the ones who found themselves ill at ease in cosmopolitan life, who longed for the Hollywood cocoon, where it was a relief *not* to have to worry about wines. But many others had put down roots in Europe, acquired what they considered to be, among their many mansions, their home place, and married or otherwise found their way into the weave of European life. It hardly matters what decision they make. Movie production remains international, nor is it conceivable that it will ever again become as parochial as it once was. Whatever they call home, the stars today are by the nature of the profession long-distance commuters.

THE TELEVISION SYMBIOSIS 5

The pilot fish accompanies the shark with impunity because the shark is not quick enough to get at him. The original relation between television and the movies has already been suggested. Since the movie shark could not devour television, it simply hoped, in the teeth of all probability, that television would go away. Meanwhile it held fast to its own: Any and every movie star in good standing was absolutely prohibited from making any sort of television appearance on pain of professional death. This left television with slim pickings at the start. The original TV actors were drawn from the Broadway stage, but most of them failed to become audience favorites for the same reason that they had never become movie stars—they didn't photograph very well. Television of course had its parent medium to draw on, radio and the vaudeville tradition which radio had conserved and extended, but not all of the great radio personalities were viable on video, not by a long shot. In its effort to get off the ground, TV in its early days gave wholesale employment to ex-movie stars, those who no longer had anything to lose by defying the studios' ban. Even before *Sunset Boulevard* restored her to national attention, Swanson had a brief fling in the new medium, and Wendy Barrie, Betty Furness, Faye Emerson, and other amoebae of the 1930s attained national and even international fame, not as the romantic or dramatic figures they had failed to become on the screen, but as saleswomen. This stalemate did not last very long. As always the young came up, and the young found in television a unique opportunity. The roads to acting success on Broadway or in pictures had long since hardened into a rigid pattern, the principal characteristic of which was the long tedium of waiting for a break. But here was a new medium starved for talent, as susceptible as any of the older ones to youth and freshness, and if the young were inexperienced before the TV cameras, so in a sense was everybody else. By the early fifties, television was fashioning its own stars.

The stars who came out of the TV hopper differed materially from picture stars. Following the pattern established by radio, and essential in a medium which had to entertain all day every day, drama, comedy, and variety emerged in the form of series rather than one-shots. The favorites whom the public sieved out from these categories had the appeal we associate with comic-strip characters rather than that of the more electric stars of Hollywood and of the theater. They embodied the reassuring values of repetition, of everyday familiarity and intimacy. They did not ignite, they endeared. To be sure, some of them flamed into sensations when transferred to the theater screens, but Grace Kelly, James Dean, Joanne Woodward, and Charlton Heston were not television stars but only television apprentices when the movies snapped them up. Their success gave a good many people to think, and as early as 1954 Leonard Goldenson, head of the Paramount theater chain, was suggesting that the movie industry deliberately and consciously regard television as a proving ground for new talent, a substitute for the contract system and a pendant to the new training school provided by internationalized production. Exactly that has happened. Producers no longer need depend on the word of a talent scout that he has spotted an amateur in the Bozeman, Montana, Little Theater who will undoubtedly prove to be star material after a couple of years' training and build-up. They can sit in their living rooms and choose the stars of tomorrow for themselves, and the training and build-up are accomplished at the expense of the networks.

To be sure, in addition to watching their television screens, they must watch even more closely the Trendex ratings. In waiting to see whether a promising newcomer establishes himself in the affections of viewers, it is not wise to wait so long that he actually becomes a big star on the air, an object of bargaining among networks and sponsors. If producers do wait that long before making their overtures, they are going to confront, not a malleable aspirant, but a cold-eyed veteran who considers himself already up there among the bankable names, wants a piece of the action, and in general is quite prepared to teach his grandmother to suck eggs, as happened when James Garner was taken up by Hollywood after the long success of "Maverick." Not that that was any real deterrent in the case of Mr. Garner or anyone else of like standing among television talent. Bankable names are valuable and scarce.

The symbiosis between the two original antagonists has been greatly furthered by the concentration of television production in Hollywood. All the major studios and many independents are deeply involved in making TV programs, and they naturally tend to use the same players in both television and film work when contracts permit. But the permutations and combinations within the symbiosis are many and some of them are mysterious. The living-room audience and the theater audience widely overlap, but they seem to approach the home screen and the downtown screen in quite different moods. Richard Chamberlain was a five-year hit as the television Dr. Kildare, and his popularity seemed steadily to increase in spite of his long exposure. Middle-aged ladies accorded him the same morbid devotion their grandmothers felt toward the matinee idols of old stock company days. But neither his reputation nor his screen performances did much to bolster the box office of the movies he made. As a movie star he decidedly failed to realize the potential everybody felt was in him. In spite of the stratospheric success of "Dragnet," Jack Webb was a downright flop in films. Conversely, Lucille Ball was a secondary attraction in pictures for fifteen years, a valued adjunct to dozens of films rather than their main asset. With lamer lines and coarser material than those of her movies, she achieved the historic success of "I Love Lucy." Perhaps Miss Ball needed stage center to bring out her comic genius, for that is certainly what it proved to be. In the case of Fred MacMurray, it was the theater screen which turned out to be the proving ground for TV. Walt Disney's establishment of MacMurray as a father figure in many films paved the way for his wide popularity in the same role in "My Three Sons." Contemplation of what has happened to Barbara Stanwyck gives the experienced observer of show business the feeling that he is loose from his moorings. Miss Stanwyck was substantially finished as a star by the mid-fifties, a fact underlined by her appearance in support of Elvis Presley. She seemed also to have withdrawn into self-chosen isolation, deliberately cutting the ties of personal friendship which bound her to the studios and to professional life. She had been one of the long-time holdouts against television, and when she finally took the plunge it seemed much too late. But because of the particular character and appeal of her program, "The Big Valley," the white-haired Miss Stanwyck is now a teen-age favorite; her life, loves, and marriages of two generations ago to Robert Taylor and Frank Faye are rehashed in the fan magazines month in and month out. And how pleasant to see the plump still-prettiness of Joan Blondell, as bartender-earth mother in another popular TV series.

Whatever the box score of hits, runs, and errors, the mutual dependency of the movies and television is now complete and permanent, never mind which is the proving ground for which. Mr. Schenck and his fellow magnates of the early days of crisis could not have been wronger. Today, 70 per cent of the polled audience emphatically votes that movies, new and old, are its best TV entertainment.

THE STARS THE SUN SHINES ON 6

Douglas Fairbanks' ebullience spilled itself all over the place, chiefly, toward the end of his career, in the direction of elevating and dignifying what he had come to think of as the art of the motion picture. One of the ideas he tossed off at the rate of a dozen a week was that there ought to be, in Hollywood, some sort of respectable and dignified institution which would signalize by the very fact of its existence that the movies had at last arrived, that they were no longer beyond the civilized pale. If the groves of academe could not then be induced to acknowledge the existence of the film as a force to be seriously reckoned with, then the movies should have their own Academy, yes, goddammit, of Motion Picture Arts and Sciences, and let him snicker who will. The elders of the industry, if such they may be called, Louis B. Mayer, Cecil B. De Mille, Joseph M. Schenck, and Will H. Hays thought well of this idea for strategic reasons of their own, and joined their influence to Fairbanks' enthusiasm: The money was raised, the studios were committed to the project, some of them to their considerable bewilderment. In 1927, with an odd combination of flamboyance and sheepishness, the founding of the Academy of Motion Picture Arts and Sciences was announced to a mildly amused world.

Such few members of the press as responded to this intelligence found their questions answered in the vaguest of terms. It appeared that the announcement of the Academy's existence had preceded any but the most nebulous formulation of its future functions. Whom would the Academy teach? Well, that was hard to say. Presumably, it would instruct future actors, directors, writers, technicians—but the theatrical craft unions, with their strict and nepotistic membership rules, might take a dim view of this sort of training. The new Academy could, of course, devote itself to "technical research and the exchange of artistic and scientific views," as David Selznick put it many years later. But such artistic views as were held by the directors, writers, and actors of the day they were mostly ill equipped to put into words, and as for the producers—! But the exchange of scientific *information,* being much more tangible, was also obviously much more feasible, and the arrival of sound coincidentally with the arrival of the Academy itself meant that such an exchange met a felt want. For several years it appeared that the chief function of the Academy would be to provide a forum for conversations in scientific Choctaw among the wizards who, invisible to the public, made the technical wheels of the movies go round.

Who first thought of the Academy Awards is lost in the mists of the Academy's beginnings, which are misty indeed. This unsung genius forgot one thing, a crucial thing: He omitted to suggest the inclusion of an award for the smartest publicity trick of the year. Perhaps it was just as well; had he done so, this award would inevitably have been won every year by the Awards themselves. But this was not apparent at the outset. In keeping with the idea that the Academy's function was to win respect for the industry, not dollars, major weight was at first given to the scientific and technical awards. But few, even in Hollywood, were capable of appreciating the true inwardness of such awards as that to Burton F. Miller and Warner Brothers for "an equalizer to eliminate relative spectral energy distortion in electronic compressors" or even that to Marty Martin and Hal Adkins of RKO for "equipment providing visual bullet effects." The spotlight soon shifted to where it really belonged in an art of this nature. The press saw to that. From the very first Academy dinner, held on May 16, 1929, it focused relentlessly on the awards for "Best Picture," "Best Actor," and "Best Actress," with "Best Direction" and "Best Screenplay" trailing and the vaunted, prestigious scientific and technical awards hardly rating mention. This redirection of emphasis, while something of a betrayal of Fairbanks' original ideals for the Academy, must have allowed a lot of the movie colony to relax and enjoy themselves. That was inevitable, again to quote Selznick, "in a group whose creative opportunities were then as now dependent upon public applause." From the moment when Janet Gaynor and Emil Jannings won the first awards for *Seventh Heaven* and *The Last Command,* a professional choice which coincided with public opinion, the giving of the Awards became the prime function of the Academy, and as far as the public was concerned the only one. Over the years the Awards have taken their place with the World Series and the presidential elections as feature attractions in the national circus.

The Academy's method of selecting award winners is a peculiar one, arrived at after considerable heartburn and aimed at reconciling a variety of insistently conflicting interests. Five nominees for Best Actor and Best Actress are chosen by all the actors in Hollywood, from bit players on up, presumably on the basis of expert knowledge and out of that sincere admiration which is another name for envy. But the final choice from among these craft-selected nominations is made by the entire membership of the Academy, meaning every kind of worker in film production, including those scientific technicians whose knowledge of wet printing and the multiple-cable remote-controlled winch can hardly be said to equip them to judge the fine points of histrionic achievement.

424

Inevitably the results have reflected a mixture of professional judgement, personal popularity, an eye to the main commercial chance—and pressure. If any one factor in this mélange can be said to be controlling, it has probably over the years been personal popularity. Though her claims to the trophy were small, it is something of a marvel that Marion Davies was never even nominated as Best Actress.

The choices made under these conditions provide a fascinating index to the psychology of Hollywood. Some of them ought rightly to come under the heading of Obligatory Awards, based not on the quality of a particular performance but on the fact that, in the circumstances of a given year, any other choice was simply unthinkable. Stern judges of the art of acting might consider Mary Pickford's work in *Coquette,* though highly creditable, less deserving of the accolade than such other performances of 1929 as Ruth Chatterton's in *Madame X,* Jeanne Eagels' in *The Letter,* or Betty Compson's in *The Barker.* But Miss Pickford had staked her prestige and long supremacy on appearing in a grown-up role in her first talking picture, and the sympathy, respect, and awe which the entire industry felt for her dictated a hands-down victory. Some of the same feelings were responsible for Joan Crawford's Oscar for *Mildred Pierce* in 1945. Again, her performance was excellent, probably her best, but what really won Miss Crawford her award was her courage in defying both Metro-Goldwyn-Mayer and Warner Brothers and staying off the screen for two years at the risk of never coming back to it, in order to secure a story that would extend her life as a box-office star. In rewarding her tough intransigence, the Academy electorate was paying off a lot of old scores. Elizabeth Taylor won the award in 1960 for *Butterfield 8* primarily because she *didn't* win it in 1957 for *Raintree County,* in 1958 for *Cat on a Hot Tin Roof,* or in 1959 for *Suddenly Last Summer,* though she had been nominated in all three years. It was simply high time that this uneven actress but box-office bonanza was given the tribute people thought was due to her position in the stellar pantheon. Similarly, Ronald Colman and Gregory Peck got the nod not because their work in *A Double Life* or *To Kill A Mockingbird* was the best of their respective years, or even the best of their careers, but simply because both had waited so long.

The most notorious of these consolation prizes was Bette Davis's award for *Dangerous* in 1935. *Dangerous* can be seen on television today, and it must mystify film buffs naïve enough to suppose that the Awards always represent the sincere admiration of the Hollywood people for the skill of a fellow craftsman. Through no defect of her own, but entirely because of faulty writing, the drunken actress Miss Davis plays in this weak film is one of her least interesting characterizations, and her admirers could name at least ten Davis performances which better it. She won just the same, despite the competition of Elizabeth Bergner's sensational performance in *Escape Me Never* and Katharine Hepburn's admirable one in *Alice Adams.* The reason was an open secret. The year before, she had lifted herself by her own bootstraps out of a four-year rut of mediocrity with her startlingly conceived and beautifully controlled Mildred in *Of Human Bondage* (*not* to be seen on television, for legal reasons). There was no question of the high caliber or of the importance of Miss Davis's work in this picture; it set a new standard for naturalistic acting in talking pictures. But something happened in 1934 that never had happened before. A "sleeper" of sleepers, an almost-quickie called *It Happened One Night,* starring Clark Gable and Claudette Colbert in what both thought of as a routine assignment (their casting in this secondary attraction was in fact something of a profes-

Oscar's Holy of Holies.

Ingrid Bergman won her Oscar for *Anastasia* by acclamation

Margaret Herrick, long-time secretary of the Academy, says that in a fit of whimsey she named the Award statuette after her Uncle Oscar, after it had gone nameless for too long. Different but similar claims have often been made by Hollywood seekers of columnar space. Much more likely is the legend that some unknown wit dreamed up the name to express his derision for this dubious honorific, and for the look of the thing itself. Its design is indeed symbolic of the ignorant cultural aspirations of Hollywood in the late twenties. The net worth of this chunk of metal is about $60, so few ex-stars are likely to pawn theirs unless they are really desperate. Instead they laughingly disparage them while displaying them as conspicuously as possible. But all jokes aside, and despite their constantly increasing number, the statuettes will undoubtedly end up as collector's items with a going price far above their metallic value. They are already the primitives of Pop art, and they stand for real values in American civilization. To be voted "the best" in the esteem of others is, now more than ever, adequate compensation for a lack of self-esteem.

(Below right) Oscar's primary function. The studio caption says: "Following her annual custom of having the Academy Award winners appear on her ABC show, Louella O. Parsons listens while Olivia de Havilland tells her story. That's Broderick Crawford holding his prize."

(Below) A paradox of the Award system: in 1947, the Award for Best Supporting Actor was won by a non-professional, Harold Russell, for his "work" as the paraplegic veteran in *The Best Years of Our Lives*, but who will say he didn't deserve it?

sional demotion), took the national and world movie public by storm. Its dialogue passed into the language, its favorite scenes were mimicked in daily conversation, and it was booked and rebooked and re-rebooked in virtually every theatrical situation in the land. *It Happened One Night* was more than a box-office gusher; it provided a needed key to the new tastes of Depression-struck audiences, one which the movie men had every intention of using to unlock the gates of fortune for themselves. The picture swept the Academy field as no film had ever done before: Best Production, *It Happened One Night;* Best Direction, Frank Capra; Best Writing, Robert Riskin—and Best Actor and Actress, Clark Gable and Claudette Colbert. Everyone knew that Miss Colbert's work, excellent though it was, was far from equal to Miss Davis's Mildred, but everyone also knew that *Of Human Bondage* was the mildest of mild successes, while *It Happened One Night* was *It Happened One Night.* The voting in this instance brought partially into the open and into the orbit of the press something previously known only in Hollywood itself, what David Selznick later referred to as "the gigantic monetary value of the Awards." By the early thirties the studios had discovered that an award for Best Picture of the Year was a priceless advertising adjunct. Directors became aware that they were accorded much greater respect and freedom of decision and action when one of their films copped the prize. Stars found that if their contracts came up for renewal during the year in which they were honored, they could virtually write their own tickets. As this grew clear, the competition for votes became intense, the pressures blatant. Studios used every threat and promise at their command to sway this volatile and alas, venal electorate in the direction of a picture which, if it didn't actually deserve the award, certainly needed it. As for the players themselves, the late Nick Adams heads the list of actors who would go to any arm-twisting length, including the considerable length of expensive paid trade-paper advertising, to corrupt their colleagues. Voting threatened to become a permanent horse trade, a continuous collusion: Scratch my back this year and I'll scratch yours next. Since the bribery in the nature of things could not be covert, the situation threatened to become an open scandal, and worse, a national joke. The board of governors of the Academy, foreseeing the consequencies of this self-defeating evil, tried to remedy it by tightening the voting rules, but in the last analysis what has saved the voting from becoming a joke and a scandal is what saves your voting and mine. After all the thunderous logrolling, the balloting is secret. Influential individuals, as well as the studios, found frequently that though they paid through the nose for votes, they didn't in the end get them, and that sometimes pressure boomeranged in the form of an adverse verdict. The Academy Awards may not represent the objective judgment of the electors, but they are an accurate seismograph of their real feelings.

Uncomfortably aware of the boners which sometimes occurred in the emotional atmosphere of the voting, the Academy quite early in the game tried to meet the situation by creating a catchall category known as the Special Awards. These were intended not only to honor unclassified achievement but also, tacitly, to rectify past injustices and compensate, or overcompensate, for oversights. Sometimes they only succeed in underscoring the ironies they were intended to erase. In the same year that Bette Davis received her consolation prize for *Dangerous,* David Wark Griffith was given a Special Award for "distinguished creative achievements as a director and producer and his invaluable initiative and lasting contributon to the motion picture arts." At this time Mr. Griffith hadn't made a film for four years, nor in spite of the award was he ever to make one again. It seemed there was no market for the initiative and creativity which had just been retrospectively honored. An equal irony brought to light by the Special Awards is the astonishing fact that neither Charles Chaplin nor Greta Garbo ever received awards as Best Actor or Best Actress. Mr. Chaplin's performance in *City Lights* was thought to be inferior to that of Lionel Barrymore in *A Free Soul,* his Hitler-Tramp in *The Great Dictator* was less meritorious than James Stewart in *The Philadelphia Story,* and his *Monsieur Verdoux* lost out in favor of Ronald Colman's consolation prize for *A Double Life.* Similarly, Garbo's *Anna Christie* could not equal Norma Shearer in *The Divorcee,* her *Camille* was no match for Luise Rainer as Anna Held in *The Great Ziegfeld,* and her *Ninotchka* failed to measure up to Ginger Rogers' *Kitty Foyle.* It is true that, in the very first year of the Awards, Chaplin received the first Special one for "versatility and genius in writing, acting, directing, and producing *The Circus."* But this simple, just recognition of his unique position was never followed up in later years by even a nomination for writing, acting, directing, or anything else. Thirteen years after she made her last picture, Miss Garbo was at last granted recognition in the form of a cryptic Special Award "for unforgettable performances." The voters apparently were able to remember her performances at any time except the year in which they were given.

It would be charitable to speculate that these two great twentieth-century artists were considered by their colleagues to be so completely *sui generis* that to place them in competition with their inferiors would be subtly insulting, not to say ludicrous. It would be charitable, but it would probably be untrue. When the neglect of Garbo first became glaring, about the time of *Conquest* (1938), the author published an article called "No Awards for Garbo," in which he revealed that the Academy membership not only didn't think her the greatest of screen actresses, it was the opinion of many of them that she could not act at all. On which a noted theater critic of the day commented: "It may be that Miss Garbo cannot act, but what she does instead is more interesting than any acting I have ever seen." A fan magazine editor capped this when he said that, in any case, it was impossible to imagine Garbo at the jollification dinner, beaming at the camera as she held her Oscar aloft.

In all likelihood Garbo and Chaplin paid the price for their self-chosen status as outsiders, isolated from the community of Hollywood and aloof from the daily traffic of the studios. Snubbing, they were snubbed when opportunity arose. At that, they ended up exactly where they belonged, in a category apart.

Indeed, the idiosyncratic Special Awards reveal some remarkable opinions, or superstitions, among the folk of Hollywood. It is evidently their belief that not only Garbo cannot act, neither can children, any children. In the year of her first tremendous hit, Shirley Temple was presented with a Special Award "in grateful recognition of her outstanding contribution to screen entertainment during the year 1934." Since the now Mrs. Black was then five years old, this was just enough, but it seems to represent a settled belief that child actors are, whatever else they are, not actors at all. Special rather than best acting Awards were made to Deanna Durbin and Mickey Rooney in 1938, Judy Garland in 1939, Margaret O'Brien in 1944, Peggy Ann Garner in 1945, Claude Jarman, Jr., in 1947, and, as late as 1960, to Hayley Mills. This peculiar custom may represent a defense mechanism. After all, the founder of the Academy, Fairbanks himself, had said many years ago, "The best movie actors are children and animals," and if child actors were let under the wire, the award for best acting might next go to Lassie or Elsa.

It might readily be supposed that those stars who have won the acting award more than once reflect the popularity-contest aspect of the annual choosing-up. But it appears that the case is the oposite. There are certain tacit rules in this matter. No star, however much admiration or affection he may inspire, has ever won an award more than twice; Oscar is too valuable a property to be lavished on the already honored. On the whole, it seems that the twice-chosen star really earns his triumphs in the opinion of the voters. True, Spencer Tracy was the most beloved of Hollywood actors, but his two awards for *Captains Courageous* and *Boys' Town* constituted startled recognition that this hitherto routinist actor was an artist of the highest capabilities. True, Gary Cooper was extremely popular in the film colony—but his first award, for *Sergant York,* was reluctant, almost grudging recognition that a star whom everybody had typecast as a mere personality had developed into a first-class professional. But the ungregarious Fredric March and Ingrid Bergman were never particularly popular in Hollywood; the latter's second award for her competent performance in *Anastasia* was undoubtedly intended as recognition of her courage in defying the studios over Rossellini, and as a tacit welcome back to the fold. As for Olivia de Havilland and Bette Davis, these fractious and sharp-tongued ladies unquestionably rolled up their votes against the grain of a great deal of personal dislike. The strange case of Luise Rainer was strange indeed. It might almost be said that she was in pictures too short a time for the majority to make up their minds whether they were with her or against her as a person. She made her American film debut in 1935, won her first Oscar for *The Great Ziegfeld* in 1936, her second for *The Good Earth* in 1937, and, as a result of this quick double triumph, was in 1938 a very big star indeed, one of the brightest in M-G-M's crown. By 1939 she was out like flout. A more meteoric rise and plunge has never been recorded. Looking back on her acting in the aggregate, in search of a clue to this somersault in public and professional favor, it can be seen that Miss Rainer's work, though skilled, was monotonous. It added up to a sort of cry, a piteous demand for sympathy, which was at first appealing, then uncomfortable, and finally repellent. Her sole attempt at a comeback, in *Refugees* (1943), confirms the impression. She played a battered victim of Nazi horrors, a sympathetic role if ever there was one, and at just the right moment too. But it was evident that Miss Rainer's excessive sympathy for herself made ours superfluous; her self-pity turned the audience's heart to stone.

The Academy Awards, of which the acting awards are the most eagerly awaited, are given at ceremonies consisting of a "dinner" for the entire membership followed by a formal presentation in a local auditorium. Considering the people involved, the arrangements for these affairs were for a long time strangely amateurish. Getting the members to the dinners and then to the distant theater on time and en masse was a problem in generalship seemingly beyond the powers of the staff of the Academy or even those of the big-shot producers on its board of governors. Even after the Awards were put on television, delays, unexpected contretemps, and general awkwardness often characterized the evenings, in full view of the public. The persistently unprofessional aspect of the ceremonies may have represented a clinging to the vestigial belief that the Academy is or ought to be an unworldly body whose deliberations should be conducted like those of scientists or statesmen, and not as if they were part of a song-and-dance act. If such a belief did indeed persist, the networks and the public soon punctured it. Television audiences tuned in the Awards because they wanted to see a show (theater men have long been resigned to empty houses on Award nights), and they insisted that it be a good show. As a result, the award winners now have to give away for nothing the skills and abilities for which they are ordinarily paid astronomical sums. The dialogue lavished on the Academy audiences would earn any writer a year's wages. The gimmicks the stars dream up to dramatize their acceptances, and the performances they deliver, are certainly among their highest histrionic achievements. But nobody can say that the Academy is strictly commercial, that it has no artistic integrity. In nearly forty years before the camera, John Wayne has never won the award for best acting. But then, neither did John Barrymore.

THE 7 CANNIBALS

Pour in sow's blood, hath eaten
Her nine farrow . . .
Macbeth

Primitive peoples eat the bodies of their fathers and grandfathers in order to acquire their virtue. The stars of the new Hollywood seem to adopt the same attitude toward their stellar ancestors. Since the 1940s, a recurrent production motif has been the picture which attempts to resuscitate the legend of a great figure from the period of the heyday of the stars as a vehicle for a promising star of the present. It is very evidently the intent of all concerned to burnish the newcomers with a reflected glory, in the hope that somehow they will acquire a new luminescence they can call their own. The results are usually ironic. Writing about the two Hollywoods as seen in *Sunset Boulevard,* James Agee said: "The lost people are given splendour, recklessness, an aura of awe; the contemporaries, by comparison, are small, smart, safe-playing, incapable of any kind of grandeur, good or bad." Incapable, even, of *acting* grandeur. Even for audiences to whom Valentino, Harlow, and Jeanne Eagels were only names—and legends—it was apparent that Anthony Dexter, Carroll Baker, and Kim Novak were really nothing at all like these personages of the movie and theatrical past; it was apparent also that they would never create any legends on their own. These latecomers had not the stomach to eat their ancestors; like Saturn, like the witches' sow, the ghosts of the illustrious dead devoured their children.

Really to re-create the era of vainglory, it has been necessary to use Gloria Swanson, Bette Davis, Joan Crawford, or Mary Astor in fictional stories which were essentially re-creations of their own past selves. Their magnetism and their intensity, even the ruin of their beauty, draw a sharp line between themselves and their day and the present and upcoming generations of stars. Something has happened. Whether it be a trick of genetics, the diet of the orange juice generation, a prolonged fashion for ordinariness, or a combination of all three, no one who has come up in the past twenty years has been able to achieve that deep-etched, almost three-dimensional individuality of appearance and, as it seemed, of actual being which once was the hallmark of the great star. Agee, again on *Sunset,* speaks of "Miss Swanson watching her young face in an old movie and standing up into the murderous glare of the projector to cry: 'They don't make faces like that any more' (they certainly don't and it is our loss)."

James Cagney as Lon Chaney as Mother O'Grady in *The Man of a Thousand Faces*

Kim Novak as Jeanne Eagels and Jeff Chandler in *The Jeanne Eagels Story*

432

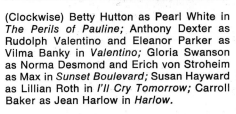
(Clockwise) Betty Hutton as Pearl White in *The Perils of Pauline;* Anthony Dexter as Rudolph Valentino and Eleanor Parker as Vilma Banky in *Valentino;* Gloria Swanson as Norma Desmond and Erich von Stroheim as Max in *Sunset Boulevard;* Susan Hayward as Lillian Roth in *I'll Cry Tomorrow;* Carroll Baker as Jean Harlow in *Harlow.*

8 "MISLIKE ME NOT FOR MY COMPLEXION"

The rash of race-relations films which erupted in the late 1940s seemed at the time just another of Hollywood's recurrent topical cycles, a—largely though not wholly—catchpenny attempt to capitalize on the remnant of wartime egalitarian emotion. The cycle spent itself in the space of three years and that, everybody was pretty much agreed, regretfully or otherwise, was that. Indeed, the final film in the series went almost unnoticed. That was a mistake. *No Way Out* seemed to endorse the idea that the *only* way out of the racial impasse was race-rioting. And it introduced Sidney Poitier to the screen.

At about the same time there emerged a much longer-lived cycle, itself a by-product of World War II, of Korea, and of subsequent world events in which Americans were deeply involved. It consisted of films about the experiences of young American GIs in Europe, the Pacific, Japan, Korea, and eventually southeast Asia. Foremost among these newly dramatized experiences was that of a new sexual relation between white American men and dusky beauties of several racial or national varieties. The dusky beauty of course had long been a screen fixture, but her old role was that of villainess, siren, Lilith; the Dragon Lady well represents the position she used to occupy in popular culture and still does in its substrata. But now, on top of the old sexual mystique, exotic and menacing, she appeared in the role of potential wife, mother, and, most radical, potential citizeness of the U.S.A., to be accepted as an equal and on her own terms. The revolution in human relations which these films implied was validated and solemnized by the marriage of Marlon Brando and Anna Kashfi. Brando's peculiar position as a popular idol, the special characteristics of his avant-garde personality seemed to relegate the idea and the fear of miscegenation to the ranks of the squares and fuddy-duddies (where of course it remains virulent and endemic). In his short-lived, hysterical union with Miss Kashfi, Brando may have struck a more effective blow for his personal ideals than in any of his earnest attempts to do so on the screen.

The screen could only dramatize the revolution in domestic and overseas race relations because the revolution was taking place in actual American life, if on the smallest of scales. Its next movie manifestation was the great increase during the fifties and sixties of roles filled by Negroes and Asiatics—no longer shown as menials or figures of fun or menace, but as casual human components of the familiar everyday scene. This development was in fact less revolutionary than it may seem. Such roles, however much footage they may occupy, are still essentially ghettoized; they are rarely central to the drama of any particular film. And their multiplication on the screen results from pressure rather than demand. Commercial art, art that has to sell tickets, has a way of going to the root of the matter, and the root of the matter here is the question whether a Negro or an Oriental can become a popular favorite—a star—legitimately, by right of request, and not as a result of pressure or bad conscience. And the root of *that* matter is sex. Sidney Poitier's rich talent, Harry Belafonte's more limited one are not crucial to their emergence as popular stars, any more than the particular shades of their skins; what seems to have been controlling in their case is the Caucasian bone structure of their face. Which seems to imply that as far as the mass audience and its instinctive tastes are concerned, some degree of accommodation, via implied past miscegenation, is necessary if colored players are to achieve that identification, that kinship with their audience which has always been necessary to the idea and fact of stardom.

434

Or it may be that the case is rather more the opposite. In their arduous progress toward acceptance as popular favorites, dark-skinned players still remain at something of a distance—from the people in the audience, from the people around them on the screen. However much sympathy and empathy they arouse, they are by definition, visible, evidential, ocular definition, alienated. That may be the source of their primary appeal, in the second half of the twentieth century, to all sorts and conditions of men. And women.

IT SHOULD HAPPEN TO YOU 19

That thirst for applause, if the last infirmity of noble minds, is also the first infirmity of weak ones.   Ruskin

That omnivorous study of popular culture which has proceeded as far as the comic strips, and thrown up pop art as a by-product, has yet to extend to the fan magazines. Even the voracious scholars, famished for new fields, have so far shied away from the pablum offered a readership which, in the words of one fan magazine editor, is still generally supposed to consist of "adolescents whose intelligence has been blighted by seeing their first movie too soon after birth." According to the fan magazines' own studies of their readership, the composite reader is a housewife of twenty-six, married to an industrial worker, who looks back somewhat wistfully upon her own adolescence as a time before the shadows of the prison house had drawn about her. It seems therefore a more refined estimate to say that the fan magazine appeals to the adolescent who, like the baby, is within every adult. We read it or material just like it in our self-betraying moods of self-indulgence. Women acknowledge this; the evidence of the beauty parlor compels them to do so. Lacking such evidence, men are more reticent—and it seems manlier to acknowledge reading *Playboy*. Sooner or later all confess to some degree of interest in this dream stuff, with varying degrees of wry self-disparagement. The graph of the fan magazine's development from its beginnings till now provides a key to the development of the adolescent within under modern conditions. An extended study of the field is overdue, as becomes uncomfortably apparent in an era which acknowledges the lifestyle of adolescence as a sort of ideal, and bends before its new economic power.

The only facts on record so far are those detailed by the aforementioned fan editor, Norbert Lusk, in his aptly titled autobiography, *I Love Actresses!* He begins at the time of the first of several crises which have gradually shaped the magazines to the form we know today.

The upheaval and its consequences which I shall attempt to describe left Will H. Hays editor-in-chief of the magazines, Walter Winchell the unknowing cause of his election to a place more powerful than the nominal editor who only fiddles with material and determines the order in which shall appear. The influences which precipitated the crash gathered slowly. Before the rising tide had reached a climax, the magazines jogged along at a fairly even and generally profitable pace. They informed readers of the beauty, charm, talent, magnetism and wit of stars; their taste in reading, sports, food; their early hardships and crowning success, the stress of present work, the exciting promise of films in the making and reviews of current ones, with a running fire of humorous anecdote.

Mr. Winchell found something else that interested the public. He discovered a new

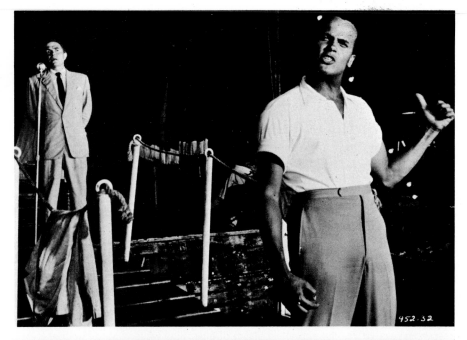

As social analysis, *Island in the Sun,* 1957, was a fruity mish-mosh, but it was a turning point just the same. For in it, Harry Belafonte, a black man, *ridicules* James Mason, a white one.

The rash of "pro-Negro" pictures which broke out in Hollywood in the late forties were considered daring then, but they seem singularly prudent against the backdrop of today. Note the lighting and line-up prominence given Jeanne Crain over Ethel Waters in this scene from *Pinky,* 1949.

(Right) The daughter of Dr. Fu Manchu (usually played by Warner Oland) was portrayed by two different actresses in 1932. The Caucasian Myrna Loy (who made a good thing of Oriental roles for many years before her stardom) is seen here with Charles Starrett as Miss Fu Manchu, in *The Mask of Fu Manchu,* while the same part was played in *Daughter of the Dragon* by a genuine Chinese, Anna May Wong. She is shown here, right, with Sessue Hayakawa, brought back briefly from obscurity for a role in *Daughter of the Dragon.* The studio caption says they are reminiscing over a print of one of Hayakawa's old silent films in which Miss Wong played a bit.

437

Sessue Hayakawa was the only silent player of other than white skin to become a star. The Japanese actor is here seen in *The Beggar Prince*. A great favorite of early audiences, he was virtually forgotten until his brilliant return in *The Bridge on the River Kwai,* 1957, above left. In movie terms the racial revolution is now complete. In the course of this book's preparation, Sidney Poitier became the hottest box office "property" in the world. His progress toward that goal signalizes the evolution of the Negro film stereotype during the past two decades. In *Guess Who's Coming to Dinner,* 1968, right, he is again a doctor but is now a glossy success story, slightly superior to the troubled liberals around him. As for miscegenation, his young fans today would probably have to look it up in the dictionary. He is seen here with his affianced bride, the lovely Katharine Houghton, and her confused father, Spencer Tracy.

(Right) Lloyd Hamilton in *His Darker Self,* with Irma Harrison. While Negroes were cast in bit roles in early films, important Negro roles were always played by white actors in blackface because the Negro was not supposed to have the skill or intelligence to play himself.

(Bottom) King Vidor's *Hallelujah* displeased many Negroes because it portrayed black joy, sorrow, and degradation in isolation from the white environment which conditioned them, but it still lives as a great picture in the memory of many who saw it.

(Below) Stepin Fetchit was vastly popular with white audiences, and ultimately reviled by his fellow blacks, for his perennial portrayal of an apparently brutishly stupid, but actually sly and witty, Negro good-for-nothing. He is seen here in a Charlie Chan movie, with Warner Oland, the most popular of the several Charlie Chans, who generally specialized in Oriental roles. Oland was a Dane.

note in the reporter's scale, a shriller, livelier note. He related items more intimate than had ever been printed: anticipated marriage, birth, divorce; by innuendo boldly touched the untouchable, peeped through the keyhole or over the transom. Sooner or later his column was read by all who knew the alphabet.

This hurt the magazines. Beside Mr. Winchell's fearless audacity, they were timid, tame, their only advantage being space for details and photographs of the undraped female form divine. But legs were only a substitute for Mr. Winchell's specialty. You could only look at pictures; you talked about news.

The magazines felt the velocity of an ill wind. Gradually, without concerted action, they competed by offering confessions, inside stories, secret history, spiteful criticism, wholesale debunking of Hollywood.

Readers did not say "Please disillusion us," did not request revelation of a star's lovelife or the lowdown on any marriage or divorce. But their letters indicated a new sophistication, and their flagging interest in magazines that once had been indispensable sounded the knell of a parting day, the end of the age of innocence. Readers might be young, but they knew a thing or two, including the facts of life, and they wanted to know about the facts of life in Hollywood, which they suspected were more hectic than any-where else.

Stars who found themselves the subject of disturbing stories protested. Something had to be done to curb this evil and make the fan magazine an instrument of good, construc-tive phantasy, perfect escape from reality for stars and public alike. Enter Mr. Hays cloaked as rationalizer, mediator. Exit Mr. Hays a dictator, benevolent but watchful and firm. This lightning change was witnessed by editors and publishers brought together for the first time, except at cocktail parties, and forced to face each other as equals at Mr. Hay's conference table. Not that they privately acknowledged equality. They refused when one of them stated that he never had complaints about anything published in his magazine. All of them knew that recently he had stopped his presses to kill a story which implied that a star and her mother were united in Sapphic devotion. They were sure they could not be equals when another, later under court sentence for falsifying circulation figures, protested that her magazine could not be like the others because it was "different." However, they were united in knowledge that nothing would be the same with the fan magazine any more. The good old days were defunct. That realization was driven in by individual receipt of a document headed with the ominous word "Resolu-tions" and signed by all the studios.

The said resolutions constituted a dictatorship of virtue exactly parallel to that im-posed on films themselves in the form of the Production Code adopted in the same year, 1934. This prepublication censorship spelled itself out in terms of great exactitude:

Whereas the undersigned members of this Committee (the Studio Publicity Executive Committee of the Motion Picture Producers and Distributors of America) seek to curb the inaccuracies, misrepresentations, and exaggeration of facts by certain fan magazine writers, which tend to create false impressions in the mind of the public in regard to motion picture personalities, and which result in much unfavorable public reaction, the Committee herewith adopts the following resolutions, effective immediately:

That, in future, all fan magazine interviews, stories or symposiums which involve studio contract players, whenever or wherever obtained by fan magazine representatives or free-lance writers, shall be submitted to the studio publicity director, or his properly designated representative, for approval before publication;

That each writer shall first obtain approval of the studio publicity director or his representative, of any idea upon which an interview is to be based before such an interview is granted;

That, insofar as practicable, a third party, representing the studio, shall be present during all interviews between players and writers;

That any writer violating these definite rulings of the studios shall be denied admission to the studios thereafter, and all further cooperation.

This highly enforceable censorship, complete with threat of blacklist and loss of livelihood, left the magazines at sea. There was no turning back to the age of innocence—especially since Walter Winchell and his countless emulators were not subject to the dictates of the studios. The company publicity departments, and behind them the stars themselves, found their new absolutism hollow; not even the fan magazines would print the innocuous pap they passed, and certainly no one else would. Inevitably a compromise was arrived at, and as with all censorship, it took the form of a smirking and unpalatable innuendo. "The recapture of lost circulation," says Lusk, "was thought to depend upon romance. Which meant that any two players of the opposite sex seen in public were living together, or planning to. A photograph of a couple at a night club table was implication of an affair. But it must be only a hint in the accompanying caption. The picture would tell the story to the sophisticated." This was, of course, just the sort of thing which the Hays Office had originally intervened to suppress, but in the course of time it was considered not only acceptable but routine, as long as it was managed. Managed, and manufactured. Under this dispensation the corpus of Hollywood press agents formed a sort of unofficial dating service, scrambling and unscrambling their male and female clients as the requirements of publicity dictated, and ever under pressure to supplant an old romance with a new "item." In response, each of the fan magazines now sported "our own photographer," fearless, intrepid in his exploration of the night clubs, but every scoop eyed by stars and studios before release.

The unstately minuet of partner-changing was winked at by the myrmidons of Will Hays and later of Eric Johnston as long as it was expressed in slippery innuendo. But it was not enough to fill the fan magazines to complete reader satisfaction, and the editors hardly knew where to look to find a complement for it. Partly through experience, partly perhaps as a consequence of their own earlier decisions, they had come to the conclusion that fans were only interested in reading about Hollywood personalities as sex symbols, virtually devoid of other human attributes. And the only other available sexual arena, besides the night club table hopping that could be translated into bed hopping, was that of marriage. But marriage in this transitional period still connoted humdrum domesticity and children to excitement-starved moviegoers. It connoted responsibility, the shouldering of the burdens of life, just the sort of thing audiences sought escape from via the screen and through reading about its gods and goddesses. How to equate marriage with glamour? The solution adopted by the magazines was to concentrate exclusively on the honeymoon phase of married life, and to keep all its other aspects firmly in the background. It was all right to publish a funny photograph of a male star the *first* time he put on his wife's apron to help wash the dishes, but after that he had to resume his original personality as a desirable, and by implication an available, sex object, and so did his wife if she was also a star. When children arrived, their births were noted chiefly

The Look of Now: Raquel Welch as Lust in *Bedazzled*

(Clockwise) *I Was a Teen-age Werewolf,* the first film produced specifically for adolescent audiences, was a put-on which took itself seriously; Ronald Reagan as a civic official in *Hell's Kitchen;* Hedda Hopper insisted that mystery was an essential component of star glamour, but she did more to destroy stellar mystery than any individual except Walter Winchell; Claudia Cardinale in *Don't Make Waves.* Water is a good, safe substitute for nudity in conveying libidinous effect via the printed page; Judy Holliday as Gladys Glover in Garson Kanin's *It Should Happen to You;* Jane Fonda in *The Game is Over.* Note to the reader: This is the closest to a nude picture of Miss Fonda which the author or the publishers could secure. Though she competes with her fellow newcomers to see who can go nudest on the screen, neither she nor her competitors will permit any actual nude still photographs of themselves to be circulated for publication.

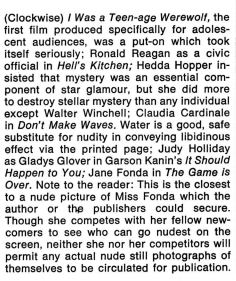

443

as evidence of prior sexual activity; the children themselves were for the most part kept out of sight, on the excuse of their parents' righteous desire to protect them from the glare of the spotlight. Divorce, when it came, could not of course be hidden, not with Mr. Winchell about, but it was played down as an unhappy accident, nobody's fault really, just an evidence of the cruelty of chance and the vanity of human wishes. It was also portrayed as a sort of "King's X," a breathing space for the star before he or she re-entered the lists of love, ready to start not only afresh but right from the beginning, revirginated so to speak, accompanied in the new pursuit of Miss or Mr. Right neither by wounds, regrets, nor the mellow wisdom of experience.

This version of marriage and divorce was the most artificial of the fan magazine conventions, because it contradicted the most universal of common experiences. Hollywood, even the ignorant knew, was not *that* different from everyday life. But the convention remained as long as the studios could enforce their official attitude that the stars who, on the screen, enjoyed such perilous, reckless, exciting, and sometimes immoral adventures were, off the screen, and after they sowed their wild oats, essentially pillars of society. The attitude only changed when the stars no longer had anything much to gain or lose from studio approval or disapproval. The downfall of the old studio system before the onslaught of television gave the stars more than their professional independence. It freed them to behave off-screen in a way which pleased the majority of paying customers without regard to the opinion of the official guardians of a dying morality.

II

Je ne dois qu' à moi seul toute ma renomée.
    Corneille—*L'Excuse à Ariste*
Fame is made by me.
    Aretino

In 1953 Garson Kanin wrote an original screenplay called *It Should Happen to You,* which Columbia produced with Judy Holliday in the starring role of Gladys Glover. This little girl from Gloversville, New York, comes to Manhattan in the time-honored tradition to assault the citadel of fame, Broadway. She has neither the talent nor the training to make it big, but she *has* got sense enough to realize her lack and to make the prudent decision to go home where she belongs. But just before she does so she spends the remnant of her savings to rent a billboard on which she has painted her own name. GLADYS GLOVER. That and nothing more. And, like Byron, she awakes the next morning to find herself famous. There is of course immediate speculation about her throughout New York: Who *is* she, what has she *done,* who does she *know,* thus to acquire such conspicuous display? But, and this is Mr. Kanin's important point, before inquiry can establish that she *is* no one at all, never has *done* anything, and *knows* nobody who is anybody, she has already become famous. The famished presses, and the desperation of those who try to feed them, have seen to that. Her citywide celebrity instantly becomes national celebrity; she is catapulted onto television, where the intimacy and informality of the interview and panel shows put the novice and the amateur on an equal footing with the practiced professional. As an overnight "television personality," she is immediately offered all the perquisites of fame, is invited to the cocktail parties of the movers and shakers, given the place of honor at night clubs, and her paid endorsement is sought for nationally advertised products. She is a success by virtue of being "heard-of," and her fame can in the last analysis only be explained by the method of Gertrude Stein: Gladys Glover is Gladys Glover is Gladys Glover.

Mr. Kanin's Voltairian fable was timely. The early fifties seem in retrospect to be the precise moment when the attention and interest of movie audiences shifted away from what stars did and were on the screen toward what they did and were in their own persons. The potentiality of this shift had always existed, being in the nature of the movies and of stardom itself. John Gilbert or Pola Negri or Clara Bow or Gloria Swanson were in a vague way supposed to be the same *kind* of persons in real life that they portrayed on the screen. Conversely, any radical departure from established type in stellar acting on the screen, while it was given lip service as evidence of versatility, was always considered potentially dangerous to a career. After World War II, after the changes in life-style which came in its wake, the shift away from the image on the screen to the image conjured up by the news media became, first noticeable, then endemic, then decisive. Its first conspicuous example is perhaps that of Errol Flynn. Mr. Flynn's screen self created an ideal ego image of derring-do for small boys with great success for many years. As a screen lover, he was uninspired and even maladroit (he confessed that love scenes embarrassed him). But neither his original screen self of a bold adventurer nor his later one of a worn-out drunk became the final image of Errol Flynn now printed on our memories. That came from his publicized private life. "In like Flynn" has passed into the language. And if only by a coincidence of headline-making, the image of the international playboy-star became involved with politics so early in the game. In 1941 the contemporary troubadour Richard Dyer-Bennet delighted his night club audiences with an up-to-date broadside:

Two Flynns, both recently in the news,
Are on their way to Hades—
The one for laying paving blocks,
The other, minor ladies.

Despite the anguish of his studio and of the Johnston Office, Flynn's constant involvement in sexual lawsuits, his almost exclusive phallic identification, did not damage his career; the contrary in fact. But Ingrid Bergman's cosmic romance with Roberto Rossellini in 1950 seemed not only to spell her own doom, it shook the film firmament to its foundations. That this genuinely illustrious star should throw away her pre-eminent position for a runaway romance involving flagrant adultery and flagrantly illicit motherhood was simply incredible to Hollywood and to the American public—especially when the first issue of her collaboration with Rossellini was a picture so feeble as to rouse further speculation as to how star and director were spending their vital forces while making it. After titillation, incredulity remained the constant of the general reaction to Miss Bergman's folly. It was simply not to be believed that *anyone* should turn her back on all that money, all that fame—and also, somewhat incidentally, on her legal husband and her daughter by him. What no one seems to have taken into account at the time is that Miss Bergman was not your average star. She was a European artist trained in the tradition of the Swedish film and theater world and loyal to its standards. She had for some time been restive with the conventional roles she was playing and at odds with her Hollywood associates. "The trouble with you, Ingrid Bergman," said one of her directors, Sam Wood, "is, you think." Miss Bergman herself was quoted at the same time as saying: "I don't like security. I want to change and meet new people." When Rossellini's

Open City and *Paisan* put him in the avant-garde of film directors, it was she who suggested their collaboration—an amazing (and precedent-setting) act of condescension for a Hollywood diva of those days. And indeed, in spite of the *Sturm und Drang* of their personal life and the furore which surrounded it, their professional collaboration did bear better fruit than *Stromboli,* in the remarkable *Europa '51* and *Un Viaggio in Italia*— which, however, because of the tacit ban on the mass distribution of any Bergman-Rossellini film, were seen in this country only in a few art houses and only in mutilated form. Meanwhile, and in spite of the shrill indignation of the guardians of morality, the American public followed the further adventures of Bergman and Rossellini, their marriage, the successive births of their children, and their eventual sad parting, with what, it became increasingly obvious, was an increasing sympathy. After some years, even conservative, family-minded people began to say that Bergman had been "punished enough." As for the young, pretty much indifferent to the matter because Miss Bergman belonged to the "older" generation of stars, what *they* said indicated that she was chiefly interesting to them on account of, not in spite of, her unconventional behavior.

It was Buddy Adler of 20th Century-Fox who first perceived that nobody could really confuse Ingrid Bergman with the Whore of Babylon, and who invented a method of easing her back into the fold with minimum abrasion. When *Anastasia,* produced in Paris, was received here entirely on its merits, after Miss Bergman's subsequent European-produced pictures had done well in the American market, it was clear that a new day had dawned. Miss Bergman did not venture back to Hollywood itself until recently (possibly because she didn't want to), but she nevertheless in effect resumed her position as a leading star, her luster slightly dimmed, it is true, by the passage of time, but not by the tarnish of immorality. As a result, there was a sense abroad that something had been proved, that a fanatical minority could no longer impose its views on the mass of morally indifferent paying customers (it is from this period also that we date the decline of the Production Code into a dead letter). There were many other straws in the wind. Robert Mitchum's career survived his jail sentence for marijuana use. Walter Wanger, who had shot his wife's agent out of jealousy, returned from prison to the welcoming arms of Joan Bennett and to a Hollywood ready and willing to restore him to the ranks of producers, whatever the reaction of the righteous. The case of Lana Turner was crucial. When her daughter stabbed her lover, Miss Turner was revealed to her public, chiefly composed of women by this time, in a new light. Far from consigning her to oblivion, Miss Turner's notoriety seemed rather to bolster her fading career.

None of these scandals, for so they would have been termed in an earlier day, was hidden from the public; they couldn't be. The press gave them due coverage, but no unfavorable reaction toward motion pictures resulted, except for the customary editorial tut-tutting. No concerted drive to "clean up" motion pictures, such as would certainly have eventuated in the twenties or thirties, materialized. No fans proclaimed their "disillusionment" with their former idols, either in print or at the box office. Instead they watched the Hollywood scene with even more fixed attention, waiting to see what would break next. They were soon rewarded. As if she had been waiting in the wings to cap the climax, Elizabeth Taylor proceeded to provide an international scandal of dimensions sufficient to eclipse all previous sensations throughout the history of show business. Her early marriages and divorces seemed simply a continuation of the grand tradition of multimarriaged stars, and each was dramatized by the fan press. But when, while recovering from her heartbreak over the death of Mike Todd, she deliberately, successfully, and in full view of the public took another star's husband, when the progress and triumph of her campaign were reported day by day in minute segments, even the fan magazines were at a loss to provide rationalized sympathy. There was just no way of softening or playing down Miss Taylor's obvious arrogant defiance of public sensibilities. Even her illnesses, real and dangerous though they clearly were, seemed to symbolize an irresponsible indifference to criticism which, it had always been thought, was simply not available to a popular idol. When, through her liaison with Richard Burton, she took Eddie Fisher's scalp from her belt and flung it in his face, the incredible Liz turned the ultimate screw. There was nowhere left to go, no further way to outrage the old conception of how a movie star, or indeed anyone in public life, should conduct herself.

She thought so herself. She says in her book that after the completion of *Cleopatra,* and even after their marriage, she and Burton were convinced that they had alienated the affections of the entire world, and were perforce resigned to a future existence of all for love and the world well lost. And while the goings-on in Rome were still going on, there was indeed a roar of disapproval. The press feigned shock even while it worked overtime to feed the scandal. The various churches thundered in their various voices. The matriarchy expressed particularly poignant revulsion because Miss Taylor had for so long exemplified girlish and adolescent innocence on the screen. As these feelings got voiced, there was a sense of the impending doom of a career, of a lull before the storm. But the lull proved permanent, the storm never broke. One is tempted at this point to speculate about what went on behind the scenes—in the offices of publishers and of those national organizations like the American Legion and the General Federation of Women's Clubs which had proved so potent when one or another screen personality had roused their antagonism at earlier moments of movie history. The obvious way to damn Miss Taylor was to damn *Cleopatra* at the box office—no loss to art, considering the empty film it inevitably turned out to be. But a lot more was at stake than the burning of a twentieth-century witch. The fate of 20th Century-Fox was at stake. It was well known and widely trumpeted that unless the jinxed *Cleopatra* earned back at least a large part of its incredible cost, the company would go to the wall. And that would never do. In a capitalist society, it was simply immoral to destroy a large corporation for reasons of mere morality. A turning point was reached in the moral history of the country in this year of grace 1963. Economic considerations had not deterred the churches, women's clubs, and patriotic organizations from destroying the careers of Mabel Normand and Roscoe Arbuckle in the twenties or from attempting to destroy that of Chaplin in the forties and fifties through a theater boycott of their pictures, with resulting great financial loss to themselves and their producers. But the fate of *Cleopatra* was left to the operation of the free market. And the free market's verdict was that nowadays, anything goes. The very matriarchs whose triple chins quivered with fury at Miss Taylor's flouting of the sacred home fires could not get to the theaters fast enough to see what she had that they never had had—or, as one of them put it, "What she's got that makes her think she can get away with it."

What Miss Taylor had, after *Cleopatra,* was plenty of cash. Her earnings from *Cleopatra* itself are still in litigation, but her reward for successfully getting away with it was and is fees of two and three million dollars per picture (her husband gets one million), plus, as they say, "perks." *Cleopatra* established two things, of related and equal importance. First, that a star today can indulge with impunity in any form of sexual behavior short of open perversion—and that may be just around the corner. And second, that such behavior, if sufficiently publicized, becomes the principal element in any star's box-office lure. Taylor and Burton, separately and together, earn their millions today almost solely on the basis of a public image established by their offscreen life, a serial story the continuing episodes of which exercise endless fascination. Burton is a very fine actor, but so he was for the ten years of his relative obscurity. His wife is an improving actress —very much improved since the day when, as Hollis Alpert said, "her acting is more convinced than convincing"—but people do not go to her pictures to assess her betterment in her art. They go to see whether she looks as fat on the screen as she does in publicity photographs, and to ask themselves how long she thinks she can hold Burton at that rate.

Such an attitude toward movie stardom did not form overnight. What crystallized around *Cleopatra* and its aftermath was already slowly becoming apparent in the late fifties. It showed up on the fever chart of Hollywood in the phenomena associated with the Clan. The idea of the Clan appears to have been the invention of, of all people, Humphrey Bogart, whose aristocratic individualism might have been expected to turn him against any and all manifestations of the herd instinct. But it was one of his perverse conceits late in life to establish the Holmby Hills Rat Pack, centering around himself as Director of Public Relations. This disorganized organization boasted Lauren Bacall as Den Mother and enunciator of policy. "We had principles," she said of the Rat Pack after Bogart's death. "You *had* to stay up late and get drunk, and all our members were against the PTA." The compulsive social psychologist will find a double whammy in this adolescent defiance. Being against the PTA is defiance of stuffy society, but staying up late and getting drunk is an infraction of the iron movie rule that you must face the morning camera at your physical best. That accorded well with Bogart's anarchic romanticism; he prided himself on his remarkable ability to lead a roistering life yet meet all professional responsibilities without turning a hair. When Frank Sinatra assumed the leadership of the Rat Pack after Bogart's death, and transformed it into the Clan, it took a different turn. In *Hollywood,* Leo Rosten spent many words successfully demonstrating that the parvenus of the movies modeled their social, cultural, and financial lives on the patterns established by Eastern aristocracy and plutocracy at Newport, Bar Harbor, and Tuxedo Park round about 1900. Under Sinatra—and "under" is the right word, for as *Time* said, to the Clan "there is no Frank but Frank"—under Sinatra, the Clan completely reversed this long-time pattern. It set up for emulation by all the world, from jet set to teeny-boppers and possibly even hippies, the goals and life-styles of show business itself. Yesterday's strolling players, a suspect and excluded social group, have become today's most "in" insiders, *arbitri elegantiarum* in clothes, cars, money-making, and speech—especially speech. The Clan was rigidly exclusive, as any elite must be which wishes to arouse envy; those close to it but not really in it were the Mouse Pack, described as non-conformists who could only afford Chevrolets. Non-conformity was indeed the talisman of this exclusive elite, but, continued *Time,* "their non-conformity must be of an especially tailored type. They stand amazed as their own dialogue. They die for publicity but distrust reporters and the press in general. They live for applause but bitterly resent the intrusion of rubes, punks, jerks, and creeps." This paradoxical secretiveness may have something to do with Sinatra's preference for gamblers and gangsters, itself a recognition that the power lines and money lines of this country are no longer the preserve of the Baptist Church. Which, by a not altogether obscure process of association, leads us, through the Clan, to another power cluster, American politics itself.

"They don't want to be counted," lamented J. Robert Rubin of M-G-M when he was appointed head of that division of the Republican National Committee which was charged with fund raising among show-business personalities. Theater people had traditionally stayed aloof from public political commitments for fear of antagonizing one or another section of their audience. In the thirties and forties Melvyn Douglas's marriage to Republican Helen Gahagan Douglas, and his own intense interest in politics, were non-existent facts as far as the fan magazines were concerned, or any other organs that the Hays Office could control. In the fifties, the only actor openly identified with political affairs was George Murphy, and even the general public was pretty much aware how this had come about. Mr. Murphy had made and lost his bid for movie popularity in the early thirties. He survived as an actor in pictures solely because his conservative views exactly coincided with those of Louis B. Mayer and other right-wing industry leaders, and because he was useful to them as an errand boy. His artificial status was an open secret, and something of a joke, in Hollywood. The 1960s *ont changé tout cela*. The change came about at the time of the arrival of the Kennedys on the presidential scene, and the immediate connection was Peter Lawford's double membership in the Kennedy clan and in the Clan clan. The Clansmen plunged into JFK's California campaign against Richard Nixon with a vigor and a personal identification unkown in any previous epoch of movie history. Apparently the only people who were shocked by this were not members of the public but the few hardy pioneers who had preceded the Clan in giving voice to their civic convictions. "I don't know who can stave off this rush of professional showmen into politics," said Dore Schary, "but somebody had better do it right away." In view of Mr. Schary's own long-time political involvement, for which he had in an earlier day been severely criticized within the industry, his attitude may seem both surprising and ungenerous. The minor actress Mercedes McCambridge, who for years had worked hard for the Democrats and harder still for Kennedy, voiced a certain disillusionment: "I'm tired of democracy. We should have a monarchy, with Tuesday Weld as one of the princesses and a nice couple from Armpit, Nevada, to reign. I have a Citizen Kane feeling about Daddy Kennedy sitting out here directing the show from Marion Davies' house."

Miss McCambridge's latent seriousness was out of key with the new era, and especially with the show-business terminology and jargon which now, by a sort of osmosis, began to penetrate the political scene. After the Kennedy victory, narrow though it was, the Clan and its myriad supporters and emulators were jubilant. It was clear that all concerned thought that they, their personal popularity, and their shrill interjection of themselves into a presidential campaign had turned the hesitant tide. *Time,* which avidly followed and reported all these manifestations, said: "Clansman Dean Martin began to put out word that Pres.-Elect Kennedy was going to appoint him Secretary of Liquor. Sammy Davis, Jr., a convert to Judaism, had other ambitions: 'Sinatra will be Ambassador to Italy,' he said. 'I'm hoping for Jerusalem, but I'll be lucky if I get Kenya.' "

Stars became fixtures in the social galaxy surrounding the new President and his family. And if any thought them mere court buffoons, and that their participation in politics was a passing phase, a mere reflection of campaign fever, the subsequent career of Ronald Reagan has surely given them pause. It is as if both national parties, having tried to use the mass media themselves for political effect, with only fair success, now have turned to professionals who have the expertise to use them in a way that is sure to gain popular attention and affection. Whatever the consequences of the campaign of 1960 for the body politic, it established a new fact about contemporary stardom: Fame is not only the spur, it is the self-sufficient goal.

Unlike Gladys Glover all the members of the Clan as it existed, with the possible exception of Lawford, had a claim to fame on the basis of outstanding achievement in their several histrionic, musical, or comic arts. But their professional accomplishments, gained by talent and hard work over a long period, no longer count as much with the public as the selves revealed by their private lives—private lives now lived in public. The mask and the face have changed places. It has become the task of the writers of their roles to provide them with material which projects personalities made familiar to their audience by events outside their official "work." This is particularly true of television, but also of the screen. "The Dean Martin Show" is not "about" the comedian who used to be a skillful, effortless straight man for Jerry Lewis; its "content" is bibulous, amiable, ostentatiously good-for-nothing Dean himself. Similarly, his Matt Helm movie series, nominally centered around a character based on the private eye and James Bond stereotypes, get its laughs and thrills through the incongruity of showing our Dean in situations which in his own life our Dean would avoid. "Screen characters," which from the time of Douglas Fairbanks on were based on a quirk of personality, on some magical affinity between the camera and the human material put before it, have now completed their evolution. A film based on such a screen character today approaches the quality of being a documentary of his own life.

To the degree that this is so, Gladys Glover has triumphed. She was famous only because she was famous, but her fame would shortly have propelled her into a high-pressure world where her amorous adentures, her victories and defeats, blown up to billboard size by the news media, would shortly have provided her with a ready-made identity suitable for dramatization on screens both large and small. And, whatever Kanin's equivocations about the matchless character he created, he leaves little doubt that Gladys was all the more acceptable to her sudden public because she was so much like themselves, and got where she was without any of the qualifications such as talent or training which were once supposed to be the prerequisites of renown. "My consumers, are they not my producers?" asked James Joyce. Miss Glover's lesson has not been lost on the young.

10 FAME IS AN ACCIDENT

Fame, we may understand, is no sure test
of merit but only a probability of such;
it is an accident, not a property of a man.

Carlyle

You will any day now
Have this revelation;
"Why, we're all like people
Acting in a play."

                    Auden

In her column, her books, and on the air, the late Hedda Hopper never tired of preaching to her juniors in the acting profession that mystery, glamour, a psychic distance between performer and public were essential to the fundamental illusion of show business. To the end of her days Miss Hopper was oblivious to the glaring fact that she herself, in concert with Louella Parsons, the fan magazines, and, of course, Mr. Winchell, had made the preservation of any sort of mystery about, or even ignorance of, the private lives of actors an impossibility. Indeed, it was Miss Hopper's adoption on the air of Winchell's machine-gun delivery, plus his lively lubricity and malice, which made her a real threat to Louella and which eventually revolutionized the fan magazines even more thoroughly than he had done. Her ability to live with this paradox is testimony to the power of the human mind to compartmentalize its contents. Pietro Aretino, the fifteenth-century prototype of the publicist who is also a blackmailer, said "Fame is made by me." Hedda, Louella, and their sister scribblers said to the stars, give me news or else. The "else" included not only banishment from their columns; it implied the threat of fabrication of news of a derogatory character, either by innuendo or straight out. So the stars were on notice to manufacture their lives, either as a substitute for the real thing or, increasingly, as a continuous claim on the public attention and interest which they could not survive without. From manufacturing a life for publication to living a manufactured life was only a step. The step has been taken.

We left the fan magazines chafing under the prior censorship established by Will Hays and enforced by the studios and the stars themselves, a censorship which had reduced the contents of the magazines to innocuous pap, spiced by an occasional hint that more went on in Hollywood than putting out the cat and kissing baby goodnight. The dissolution of the studio contract system, and the new "New Freedom" of the 1950s, turned the occasional spicy hint into the staple and exclusive diet of the fan magazine reader. The magazines did not defy Eric Johnston, did not overtly throw off restraint. There was no need. The Magazine Code collapsed at the same time as the Production Code, and under the same barrage of multileveled events. With every publication in existence trumpeting the continuous-performance news of Wanger-Bennett, of Robert Mitchum, of Lana and Stompanato, of Liz and Eddie and Debbie and Burton, it would have been absurd to pretend any longer that the fan mags could remain innocent and keep their circulation. Some feeble protest was indeed made by the faltering guardians of rectitude that since the fan magazines were primarily directed at adolescent girls, and discontented postadolescents, they ought to be tempered to tender ears—or eyes. The adolescents themselves met that one head on, and they used an argument which has never been successfully countered in this country. The manufacturers of popular commodities of all types had discovered that there now existed a teen-age market, with independent purchasing power, and consequently able to dictate its own terms in disregard of parental wishes or any other wishes. Significantly, this discovery showed up early in the movies themselves, and more significantly, it was first recognized at the exhibition level where audience demand takes on an imperative note not always audible

HUNDREDS OF INTIMATE PICTURES!

Modern Screen

AUGUST
10
CENTS

THE LARGEST
CIRCULATION
OF ANY SCREEN
MAGAZINE

BETTE
DAVIS

JACKIE COOGAN'S
OWN STORY
"I WANT MY MONEY!"

movie TV secrets

MARCH 1969 35¢

LAUGH-IN'S WILD, SOCK-IT-TO-ME WORLD

HOROSCOPE BONUS: Turning The Stars on Robert Stack

ABOUT THEIR NEW DADDY

JACKIE TELLS THE CHILDREN

CAROLINE AND JOHN ANSWER

PAUL NEWMAN: THE "ARRANGEMENT" THAT MAKES HIS MARRIAGE WORK

BARBARA PARKINS: You've Come A Long Way, Baby

Screenland

35¢

How Mia Farrow discovered that Ava Gardner still loves Sinatra

How the Beatles got themselves off drugs! We have the story!

PLUS TV-LAND JANUARY

Connie Stevens weeps to Eddie: **"ALL YOU DREAM OF IS LIZ!"**

PHOTO SCREEN

JAN. 35¢

EDDIE'S FRIENDS TURN AGAINST HIM AS CONNIE FIGHTS TO KEEP HER BABY!

Indian priest casts hypnotic spell —
MIA LURED AWAY FROM FRANK!
LIZ' NEW FEARS ABOUT BURTON!
JACKIE FLIES TO ORIENT!

Carol Burnett's heartbreaking life story:
HER RUN-AWAY FATHER, HER ALCOHOLIC MOTHER, AND THE STRANGER WHO SAVED HER FROM HER PAST!

PHOTOPLAY

FEB 50¢

Pix of Jackie & Onassis Necking   IS SHE EXPECTING?

What The Nixon Girls Have That Luci & Lynda Didn't

MIA'S SHOCK AND SHAME OVER LOVE SCENES WITH LIZ!

— PLUS —

Psychiatrist Discusses Pros & Cons Of Sinful Movie

SILVER SCREEN

JANUARY 35¢

How Cary Grant's wife was tempted by Frank Sinatra's offer...

Why the Beatles wouldn't go to Brian Epstein's funeral

Mia Farrow ∗ Patty Duke ∗ Sally Field ∗ Hayley Mills
WHAT OLDER MEN HAVE THAT YOUNG GIRLS CRAVE

Deborah Walley: "I ALMOST GAVE MY SON AWAY!"

Screenland

Why Sidney Poitier switched from black women to white women

Ex-wife's own story: "Ryan O'Neal is trying to destroy me!"

PLUS TV-LAND FEBRUARY

WHY LAWRENCE WELK IS SO DESPERATE TO HAVE A GRANDSON

BURTON TELLS ONASSIS: "Keep your hands off my wife!"

Does Jackie know?

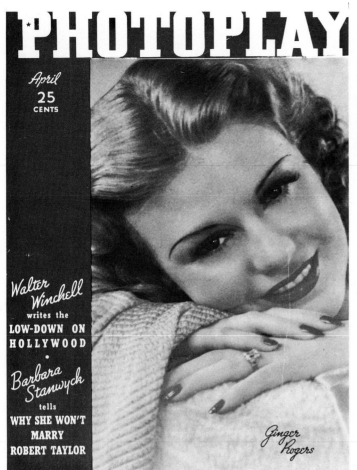

PHOTOPLAY

April
25
CENTS

Walter Winchell writes the **LOW-DOWN ON HOLLYWOOD**

Barbara Stanwyck tells **WHY SHE WON'T MARRY ROBERT TAYLOR**

Ginger Rogers

Burton In Panic! Liz Seeks Help! Sybil Gives It

MOTION PICTURE

APRIL 35

Come With Us To Annette's Wedding

The Day Lady Bird Hurt Jackie

and didn't mean to...

WHEN PRIMA DONNAS MEET! see page 36

ModernScreen

JULY
10
CENTS

THE LARGEST CIRCULATION OF ANY SCREEN MAGAZINE

MADELEINE CARROLL

LUISE RAINER —THE REBEL

SCREENLAND

July

15c

A Real Day with Tyrone Power
Carnival Nights in Hollywood
Greatest Sports Thrills of the Stars

to West Coast ears. In 1958 Elmer Rhoden, Jr., president of the Commonwealth Theater chain in Kansas City, began to finance the production of films, such as *I Was a Teenage Werewolf,* designed exclusively for teen-age tastes. Mr. Rhoden was not particularly ambitious to enter production on his own; he was simply responding to the fact that he could not get enough such films for his theaters to fill the demand, a demand which in his experience was the only one he could steadily rely on. His judgment has been borne out by the development of the teen-age movie into a staple, year-in year-out genre, like the Western or the "woman's picture," and consisting of horror films, motor-cycle gang films, and high school sex films, anything exciting or titillating, with a super-ficial overlay of sophistication and the smallest possible admixture of moral indignation —invariably directed at adults, preferably parents, whose prior sins are always held responsible for anything noxious in the behavior of the teen-agers depicted on the screen.

When outside restraint evaporated, the fan magazines took similar cognizance of the tastes and viewpoint of those whom they knew to be their dominant readers. Adoles-cence is a floating world in which events succeed one another with dizzying rapidity, and with no particular weight or significance except the significance of frenetic change itself. Such values find reflection in the traditional disarray of the emotional lives of famous actors, a disarray now no longer concealed but actually flaunted. The flaunting that goes on in the fan magazines would curl the hair, not only of our ancestors, but of our own selves of a very few years ago—though, to be sure, the editorial pattern the maga-zines now follow is nothing new. Such cover lines as" Julie Andrews: My Own Mother Gave Me Two Men to Love" and "Paul McCartney Boasts About Taking LSD—Risks Brain Damage" have long been familiar in the tabloids and the true confession maga-zines. What is new about "Connie and Eddie's Secret Baby—How Connie Will Tell Her Baby About Its Father" is that it is based on facts known to all, which no one bothers to conceal and which the fan magazines hardly bother to rationalize. What is also new is that these things happen, not to the obscure protagonists of the dramas in *True Story* and the New York *Daily News,* but to the sort of personages whom by long habit we once tended to idolize and deify. In his journalistic ambience, Miss Hopper's treasured mystery and glamour could not possibly survive.

The change in ambience shows up throughout the fan magazines, but most clearly and strikingly on their covers. A single photograph (or painting) was once thought sufficient to motivate the fan to plunk down (in those gone days) his dime, but to part one from his contemporary half dollar the magazines consider it necessary to flood their fronts with eight to ten cover lines and at least three, preferably more, photographs of people-who-are-being-talked-about. The sole exception to this iron rule is the lady who once was known as Mrs. John F. Kennedy but who can now be referred to by anybody anywhere as Jackie with the assurance of instant comprehension. In 1967 she appeared solo on the cover of no less than four issues of *Motion Picture Magazine,* and this is typical. Although she has never appeared in a movie, the widow of the martyred Presi-dent is the greatest of movie stars so far as this branch of movie journalism is concerned. Her potency is so great that she brought Lord Harlech within the orbit of the fan magazines and gave his reputation a currency such as none of his considerable prior achievements commanded. It is obvious that if Bertrand Russell should have had the good luck to spend a week or so in Jackie's company, he too would have become a fan magazine celebrity, with resultant increase in the influence of the world pacifist movement he headed, by the same process through which Mia Farrow made Maharishi Mahesh Yogi the most famous mystic in the world.

Mrs. Kennedy's decision to marry Aristotle Onassis catapulted him into the fan-magazine orbit, and also had the result of transmogrifying him from one kind of world figure into another—a figure named "Ari." It is doubtful if a single one of their readers had ever heard of him before, even in connection with Winston Churchill, still less with the other, less publicized members of his superstratospheric jet set. Like everybody else above, the fans fiercely debated Jackie's "right" to make this marriage without regard to their feelings—and the debate was fiercer in this dreamworld than anywhere else. The magazines had to work hard over this one, and not only because they were starting from scratch. The photographed evidence being ineluctably what it was, there was nothing to do but make Onassis into a sort of father figure, with paradoxical over-tones of Levantine vice. It is an uncertain trumpet that the fan magazines blow here, and the end is not yet; nobody can be sure how many of Jackie's fans have quietly dropped away. But the real example of her puissance was and remains Lord Harlech, and it is an example not lost on young aspirants to movie stardom. If the accident of Lord Harlech's friendship with Jaqueline Kennedy transformed him into a world celebrity, rather against his inclinations, one gathers, that such accidents are obviously the *real* way to fame and its incidental, fortune. New actors have been thoroughly indoctrinated in the belief that they must at the beginning of their careers go through a long and rigorous training to achieve the maximum in physical perfection, as well as the most thorough grounding in the dramatic arts and crafts; even as technical standards and popular requirements of technical standards decline (witness the sales of pop records cut by non-singers) the players themselves do everything in their power to meet such standards to the optimum of their abilities. But once thoroughly groomed and grounded, where do they go from there? There is little any one of them can do on the screen itself to make him stand out from the constant flux of newcomers.

Following in the footsteps of the Carroll Baker of yesteryear (was it only yester-year?), Jane Fonda now heads the list of youngsters and not-so-youngsters engaged in a marathon contest to see who can achieve maximum nudity in how many scenes for how long. But the prevalence of this on-screen gimmick only demonstrates that acting skill, beauty, chic, "glamour," anything and everything that goes to make up the vivid impact of a personality on the camera, are no longer sufficient to lift a mere "star" up onto the Olympian heights of fame inhabited by those whom the fan magazines and their readers now call "superstars." The way up that is both surer and easier is to get yourself talked about through something you do, or something that happens to you, in what you laugh-ingly call your life. All you have to do is shovel yourself into the stream of Hollywood marriage, parenthood, divorce, remarriage, and re-remarriage and wait for the lightning to strike. You too can be Connie Stevens if you can induce Eddie Fisher to get you pregnant. Or, if that seems too drastic, it costs little in time and expense to fly to India for a little instant meditation with the Maharishi. As *Motion Picture* put it, "That seems to be a helpful factor in the Indian mystic's technique. He asserts that your regeneration can happen without interrupting your schedule." (Miss Fonda, fortunately, on the evi-dence and plaudits of *They Shoot Horses, Don't They?* may make it the rest of the way while clothed.)

Twelve years ago the author wrote: "The pitiless glare which had beat on Hollywood so long had revealed every publicity device for what it was. But if people no longer dreamed of movie stars as gods and goddesses of legendary romance, they could still identify with them as successful Americans whose professional secrets they knew and whose private lives were a façade beyond which they did as they pleased, which was pretty well understood to be what you and I would please, if we were they."

"If we were they." The line between "we" and "they" has narrowed to the vanishing point in the ensuing decade. And the façade of private life has become translucent, a light medium, in fact. Any star today who wants, against the grain, to preserve some semblance of privacy must, in order to repel publicity, resort to publicity itself. A favorite device of this nature, which the fan magazines immediately spotted, is the "cover romance." If Barbara Parkins is seen everywhere with Tony Perkins these days, that means that she is really interested in John Phillip Law. This stratagem, borrowed from the James Bond world, is immediately nosed out by the magazines, and discovery is attended by triumphant screech. So Miss Parkins, at whatever emotional cost, reaps a double harvest of publicity. Which one is she *really* in love with, Perkins or Law? Who's covering for whom? We are supposed to hang upon the answer. And well we may, for the answer is about all that matters about Miss Parkins and her numerous sisterhood. They can all learn to act, if they work hard enough; the technical wizards can confer beauty and glamour on them; their directors can give their screen personalities a momentary authority and effectiveness. But all that can make one of them stand out from the ruck of the others is fame, and fame is an accident.

THE COOL 11

He is a hero by the grace of un-reason and un-feelingness, and as such a very modern hero indeed.—Iris Barry on Buster Keaton

The resemblance between the look of the popular screen today and the look of it in the late silent days cannot but strike the battle-scarred diagnostician. The visual equation between wild parties and happenings, between the jazz night club and discotheque, the jump cuts and multiple superimpositions of today and the "double exposures" and "montage effects" of then is at first arousing and at last monotonous. The prevalence of youth, specifically identified as such, in the non-star and all-star no-star films of nowadays is significant. And it is the appearance and behavior of young people on the screen which most impressively recalls the late twenties. Scott Fitzgerald's description of the flapper has already been cited: "Pretty, impudent, superbly assured, as worldly wise, briefly clad and 'hard-berled' as possible." Substitute "cool" for the horribly dated "hard-berled" and the identification is very nearly complete. No doubt a good deal of the overlap is due to latter-day eclecticism; as knowledge of film history spreads, directors dare to revive forgotten or disused cinematic devices in their quest for what seems to be a New Look. But chiefly the cool of the screen today is the reflection of a fashionable state of mind. The one component of the visual equation between past and present which is conspicuously absent is "emoting," that hard-breathing histrionism which made a player's face a map of his interior. Today's young players are apt to express their feelings, if at all, in what they do, or fail to do. There is in this a romantic element, the tradition of the stiff upper lip, of hidden heartbreak, the resolve to approach thirty, the foothills of old age, with flags still defiantly flying. All this is highly acceptable to a minority audience, consisting chiefly of the sophisticated young, who see on the screen a projection of their own life-style, or what they would like their life-style to be.

But in terms of the advancement of the individual career, the new frozen-faced convention is a definite handicap. The cool screen and its cool players play to an audience which is cool in two senses. It doesn't feel much of anything about what it watches—or about whom. The box office reveals that the mass audience, as opposed to the minority audience, has yet to take any of these sensuous automata to its large and still sentimental heart. Emotions not visibly expressed have no effective existence in dramatic terms, and a gap has widened between the people in the seats and the people on the screen. That subtle identification with his audience which Buster Keaton (a revived idol) once achieved is missing now; his successors and imitators lack the art to produce it. They look to us as if seen through the wrong end of the telescope. Indeed, it would appear that that psychic distance which was once supposed to exist between the private life of a star and his public, and which has vanished, has been transferred to the screen itself.

12 HARD-DOLLAR

Every year the industry trade magazine *Motion Picture Herald* asks the nation's exhibitors, who constitute the bulk of its subscribers, to vote for the ten biggest box-office stars of the year. Be it admitted at the outset that this, like all polls, is inaccurate, and that, like others, it reflects whim and prejudice as well as business judgment. But it is probably as accurate a litmus paper as can be devised to test the real popularity of the stars. It is, after all, their own livelihood that the exhibitors are voting on. When these annual polls are reconstituted in terms of decades, as we have done below, the results of the voting take on new pattern and meaning.

The combined winners of the first polls, taken in the 1930s (the polls began in 1932, so the record is for eight years rather than ten), were: 1. Clark Gable 2. Shirley Temple 3. Will Rogers 4. Janet Gaynor 5. Joan Crawford 6. Marie Dressler 7. Wallace Beery 8. Robert Taylor 9. Astaire and Rogers 10. Mickey Rooney. Of these, only three, Janet Gaynor, Joan Crawford, and Wallace Beery, were products of the 1920s. The other seven gained official stardom in their own decade of top popularity; they were with it in the sense that as soon as they were moved into leading roles where the public could see them and express its preference, they became stars.

In the decade 1940-49, the winners were: 1. Bing Crosby 2. Bob Hope 3. Gary Cooper 4. Betty Grable 5. Abbott and Costello 6. Clark Gable 7. Spencer Tracy 8. Humphrey Bogart 9. Mickey Rooney 10. Greer Garson. Here the situation begins to reverse itself. only two, Betty Grable and Greer Garson, were products of the decade. The rest were all thirties stars, with the exception of Gary Cooper, left over from the twenties.

1950-59: 1. John Wayne 2. James Stewart 3. Martin and Lewis 4. Gary Cooper 5. Bing Crosby 6. William Holden 7. Rock Hudson 8. Bob Hope 9. Betty Grable 10. Marilyn Monroe. This set shows a slight gain in contemporaneity, with three products of the decade rather than two: Marilyn Monroe, Rock Hudson, and Martin and Lewis.

Star longevity, however, continues to increase, with two stars who began in the 1940s, William Holden and Betty Grable, four from the thirties, Wayne, Stewart, Hope, and Crosby, and with Gary Cooper, stretching all the way back to the distant silent days.

The 1960s tabulation extends only to the middle of the decade and is consequently subject to upset later on. It shows Doris Day as Number One, followed by 2. Rock Hudson 3. John Wayne 4. Cary Grant 5. Elizabeth Taylor 6. Jack Lemmon 7. Elvis Presley 8. Sandra Dee 9. Sean Connery 10. Jerry Lewis. By now, death and old age have taken their toll; Gable and Bogart and Monroe have gone, and so has Gary Cooper, the last link with the pioneer days. But still only two stars, Sean Connery and Sandra Dee, are actual products of the 1960s. Day, Hudson, Lemmon, Presley, and Lewis come from the fifties and Elizabeth Taylor from the forties, while mighty John Wayne and Cary Grant, both in their sixties and both at the absolute peak of their popularity to date, made their first film appearances in 1931.*

* A composite of the above four polls, though highly artificial because of the long period involved, yields the following not too unlikely tabulation of the all-time champs of the talkie period: 1. John Wayne 2. Bing Crosby 3. Clark Gable 4. Gary Cooper 5. Rock Hudson 6. Bob Hope 7. Doris Day—with Shirley Temple, Betty Grable, James Stewart, and Martin and Lewis in a dead heat for the remaining three places. The reader may draw his own conclusions about the supremacy of the male, and ask himself if the movie audience is really a woman's audience as alleged, but he had better be wary.

These are the hard-dollar stars, the screen personalities whom the largest audience of all have demonstrably taken to their hearts. Aside from the mystique of star quality, which is likely to remain a mystique, are there utilitarian conclusions to be drawn from the votes cast by the theater men in the 1960s so far? There are. Of the top ten, only Elizabeth Taylor can be said to owe her position to her publicized offscreen activities. Miss Taylor today combines notoriety and sex appeal—despite her increasing plumpness, she's still got plenty. But she had even more in the forties and fifties; it was not until she confounded the moral establishment that she finally established her supremacy. She is obviously the model for all the young stars who believe that a manufactured or flaunted private life is the key to making it. They will have to do a lot of flaunting to come to seem anything but pale imitations of the unbelievable Liz. Sean Connery is an actor who was around a long time before the blindest of blind luck made him known throughout the world. It is James Bond, and not Connery himself, who is responsible for the latter's place among the top ten, and it is Connery's absolute rightness for the Bond character which is going to be his chief handicap as a potentially lasting star. The next few years will tell whether Connery can draw out of himself a new personality not only to obliterate, but to replace, the Bond image. Sixth-placer Jack Lemmon is in a class by himself. A relative newcomer to the top ranks, he is the last surviving representative of the old order of stars who owed their place on the screen solely to what they offered on the screen. People go to see him because they think his presence in a picture guarantees them a worthwhile evening's entertainment, which is saying a lot considering what it takes, the devious things it takes, to get an audience into a theater these days. But the most interesting, baffling, and very probably the most significant member of the top ten is Elvis Presley. How he got there and why he stays there tell a lot about the new patterns into which the movies are settling, after the mold was broken nearly twenty years ago.

1930s

Clark Gable

Shirley Temple

Wallace Beery

Joan Crawford

Janet Gaynor

Mickey Rooney

Marie Dressler

Robert Taylor

Will Rogers

Fred Astaire and Ginger Rogers

Bing Crosby and Bob Hope

Gary Cooper

Betty Grable

Abbott and Costello

Clark Gable

Spencer Tracy

Greer Garson

Humphrey Bogart (with Lauren Bacall)

1950s

John Wayne

James Stewart

Martin and Lewis

Gary Cooper

Bing Crosby

Rock Hudson

William Holden

Marilyn Monroe

Betty Grable

Doris Day

Elizabeth Taylor

Jack Lemmon

Jerry Lewis

Sandra Dee

470

Rock Hudson

Elvis Presley

Sean Connery

John Wayne

Cary Grant

13 THE MYSTERY OF ELVIS

If ever there was a born flash in the pan, Elvis Presley is that flash. Everything about his shoot upward signaled to the signal-wise that his descent would be so quick as to be all but invisible. As a singer he had nothing to offer but a shimmy which had caused no great sensation before live audiences in the South, though it did serve to single him out from his literally numberless rivals among country singers. His notoriety arose when he brought his shimmy to television, an event which happened to coincide with the moment in the 1950s when the new, intense teen-age desire to *épater les parents* came out into the open. The parents, suckers as always, duly deplored in editorial and pulpit this intrusion of pelvic sex into the sacred "family medium," and the teen-agers, as duly, went out and bought enough records to make Elvis the top recording star. By all the odds, that ought to have been that. It figured that Presley, having served the turn of one set of rebellious young, would have been cast off in favor of a new idol by the next wave—to retire on his millions or find whatever secondary or tertiary place in show business his extremely modest talents might lead him to. His rise took place at almost the same time as that of Liberace, whose old-biddy audience had slightly more stable tastes and loyalties than the teeny-boppers, and logic and the record seemed to dictate that Elvis should have followed Liberace into, not oblivion exactly, but rather a place in the history of show business, chamber of horrors division.

But Elvis Presley has not joined the ghosts, those ha'nts of the show world whose re-exploitation in one or another of the entertainment forms is usually a signal that somebody has got desperate. He has not developed or improved or learned anything new. He offers today exactly what he offered at the start, and his pictures offer nothing but him, served up in the same old way. But Elvis is that rarest of rare birds of the 1960s, a real star and a *dependable* one. At thirty-four, after thirteen years of fame, his latest films do not make as much money as his early ones. They do not make anything like the unreal-sounding sums earned by *The Sound of Music, Mary Poppins,* or the few other record breakers. But they earn a solid profit which a studio can count on at the end of a year and match against the possible losses of its problematic gambles. And they are "vehicles," just like in the dear dead days that we thought beyond recall. The ads say simply "It's ELVIS," and the people come.

All this is strictly against the current rules. The success of the Elvis pictures owes nothing whatever to the "chemistry" of star combinations. Elvis himself is decidedly not a teen-age idol any more; at best, he remains in their minds as a sort of elder statesman of the revolt industry. The kind of publicity he gets, which nowadays is a mild kind, owes nothing whatever to the international jet set scene, to involvement with politics, or even to the Hollywood dating and temporary marriage whirl. During the six months he spends working in Hollywood, he rarely goes night-clubbing and still more rarely to parties. "He wouldn't know how to act," says an old friend. His films are given the same kind of backhanded press treatment accorded the Gene Autry singing Westerns of the thirties; critics hardly bother to review them. And neither the author nor you, dear reader, has any friends who have ever seen an Elvis picture—not if you can afford the price of this book.

The people who arise and go at the signal "It's ELVIS" are people who so deeply and desperately want to believe that life is simpler than can be that they will suspend disbelief in the teeth of the evidence. The late Siegfried Kracauer pointed out in his

The original Elvis Presley when he was an obscure singer of "country music"

(Left) *Jailhouse Rock.* The denatured screen version of Elvis the Pelvis.

(Above) *Blue Hawaii.* Spanking would be a mild diversion in the Sade-inspired films of the sophisticated young, but it's still titillating enough for some audiences.

Blue Hawaii. Stirring it up for the home folks.

Girls, Girls, Girls. The primeval brute.

474

Theory of Film that systems of taste and preference, as well as systems of ideas, have a long life after death. They are like novas which, even after they have blown up and collapsed into themselves, continue to give out heat and light for millions of years. The Presley films are as simple-minded in structure and values as the melodramas of the Stone Age of the silent era. The Presley hero's character consists entirely of the fact that he looks and acts vaguely like a hood, but turns out to be a right guy in the clinches. Only that and nothing more. He is what would be called in the world of painting a false primitive. The members of his audience are also false primitives. They are by no means as isolated from modern life as their preferences would indicate. Scratch an Ozark hillbilly and you find a television owner. The important thing is they *wish* they were isolated. What most of them would like best is to find a way of stopping the film from running through the projector at about the year—by current readings—1934. They trust Elvis and feel at home with him because he too is at exactly the same point. Having made his zillions, he has had the absolute entree into the megalopolitan world of success. He has chosen instead, and it is obviously a spontaneous choice, to return to the world whence he came. His mansion near Memphis, where he spends half the year, has the pillared portico of the old plantation owners, evidence that making it up there with these lost figures is still, for him and his followers, making it big. But the roses in vases scattered through this antebellum dreamhouse are artificial. He could afford the biggest greenhouse in the world, or have all the flowers of Mentone flown to him every day. But to the marginal folk from whom he sprung, artificial flowers were a symbol of both gentility and permance. Ma Joad would agree.

It might be deduced from the above that the author believes that a star of today who wants to be a star in the old sense would do well to set his sights on the primitive-minded. There is something to be said for this. The illusions about stars which once made stardom a fact rather than a formality cannot survive in the swinging world, but a case can be made out for the contention that the majority of contemporary moviegoers still want to do their swinging in the old way rather than the new. No doubt the basic audience for the Presley pictures is identical with the audience for country music—a large one nowadays—but his fan clubs, and he still has them, are to be found as far away as New Zealand—evidence, perhaps, of a worldwide cult of the defective. But the important fact about this audience, wherever it is found, is that it maintains tastes and values and viewpoints in common, and still intensely felt. A personality which *genuinely* expresses that viewpoint can still inspire adoration and loyalty of a degree which has thought to be lost. That is the solution to the mystery of Elvis. What his example means for other stars is that they must match their own self-image with the self-image of at least a large minority group of pronounced outlook and feeling. Short of that, an oncoming player may achieve much in the way of fame and success, but classical stardom will not be among his achievements.

SELECTED SHORT
SUBJECTS VII

Marilyn Monroe

Zasu Pitts

Brigitte Bardot

Rita Hayworth

Jean Shrimpton and Paul Jones

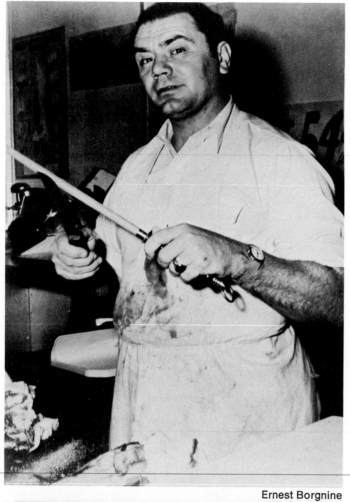

Ernest Borgnine

Jean-Paul Belmondo

Lee Marvin

Melina Mercouri and James Garner

Orson Welles

Marlene Dietrich

Angela Lansbury

Monica Vitti

Katharine Hepburn and Katharine Houghton

Zsa Zsa Gabor

Julie Christie

Gina Lollobrigida

Anthony Quinn

482

The Beatles

Montgomery Clift and David McCallum

Charlie Chaplin

Orson Welles, Margaret Rutherford and Jeanne Moreau

Rock Hudson

Ann-Margaret and John Forsythe

Mia Farrow and Elizabeth Taylor

Julie Andrews

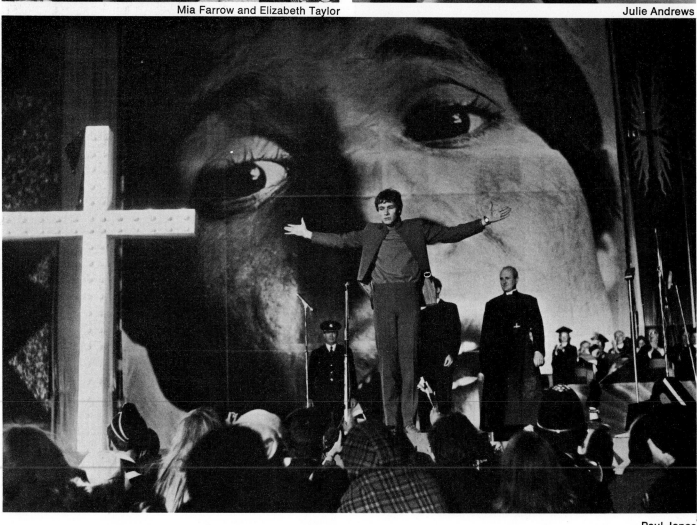

Paul Jones

George Raft

MAE WEST

"IT AIN'T NO SIN"

with ROGER PRYOR, John Mack Brown, Duke Ellington & Band • Directed by Leo McCarey

Ad for *It Ain't No Sin*, 1934

Frank Sinatra and Bing Crosby

Mario Lanza

Sean Connery

CONCLUSION

In the summer of 1969 occurred a series of events almost without precedent in American screen history. It consisted of the successive premieres, within a few weeks or months of each other, of *Easy Rider, Midnight Cowboy, Putney Swope, Medium Cool, Last Summer,* and *Alice's Restaurant.* None of these films is, taken by itself, sufficient to revolutionize the world of film, or the world outside film. In the aggregate, they seem to represent an event of enormous portent. Just what that portent may be, it is—writing in the midst of the events themselves—extremely foolhardy to guess. But the *impact* of these films, coming at us so fast, one after another, is so great that the temptation to guess is irresistible—even though guessing is a desperate attempt to choose between bales of hay: a summing up? a coming of age? or a new birth of freedom?

Parturition or maturation, there is no doubt about the summing up. Very like the New Wave films from France which broke over us a decade earlier, these fresh American films derive from a whole spectrum of disparate sources, purposes, inspirations. The impulses they represent have been gathering force for years, and disparate though they are, they share a common factor to which our moviegoing has been gradually accustoming us. That factor is a starkly critical attitude toward this our life in these United States and in the Western world—"the way we live now."

Perhaps some of it began with Tennessee Williams. True, Williams only projected to a larger audience what readers of Faulkner already knew, but his steady, persistent debunking of moonlight and magnolias effectively ensured the demise of that part of our national romance; the legend of the Old South is, now and forever, gone with Margaret Mitchell. But Williams was only a prologue. The curtain really rose on the revelation in *Dr. Strangelove* and *Seven Days in May,* that our betrayers could be, not Communist or other alien agents from within or without, as we were told to think in the fifties, but our own anointed leaders; that is, from among ourselves. The portrayal of the President of the United States as an ineffectual handwringer would have been literally unthinkable in any previous period of movie making—it is slightly unthinkable even in retrospect—yet it occasioned no great outcry, even from superpatriots. The films swept on from that point. *The Ugly American* represented our foreign policy as a perennial bungle. *To Sir with Love* and other films depicted elementary and high school education as a struggle with juvenile delinquency and authority. Then, just before campus unrest became a full scale national issue, Mike Nichols' *Who's Afraid of Virginia Woolf?* portrayed the higher reaches of the academic and married life as a sort of hell of jealous self-seeking and drunken self-anesthesia. And the same Nichols presented *The Graduate,* in which a young man rejected the adult world for which the university was meant to painstakingly prepare him in all its aspects—economic, familial, and the not-so-lightsome realms of love.

The success of *The Graduate* paved the way for the 1969 wave of critical films and made their production possible even as *The Sound of Music* was demonstrating that the largest movie audience of all still prefers cotton candy. *The Graduate*'s amazing box office record was proving equally conclusively that there was a second-largest audience not only prepared but actually eager to have served up to them as "entertainment" the abrasive subject of the generation gap—or chasm, as it has now become. For indeed it is the gaps—chasms—fissures—in American life which are the real subject of these new young films. The gap between the American dream and any decent realization of it is the overt theme of *Midnight Cowboy.* Totally conditioned by advertising and the media, its young Buck can see no way of achieving upward mobility except by selling his sex. As sex is his sole asset in a covetous world, who shall call him unrealistic? Lacking even that asset, his pathetic companion, Ratso, has no hope at all except the hope of helping him sell it. In its powerful rendering of the milieu through which they move, *Midnight Cowboy* seems to say that main goals of the denizens of the lower depths are no longer wealth and power, nor even an autonomous life, but simply a kind of mindless excitement, paid for by somebody else—or gratuitously provided by the System. Something of the same theme infects *Putney Swope,* a notorious fantasy of black power with a surprising admittance of self-doubt. At its end, money, the Almighty Dollar, is immolated in a rite of desperation; the angry idealists who made this film seem to signal that they are afraid of what will happen to their ideals if they ever get their hands on the long green in sufficient quantity. Doubt, self-doubt, enters into the closed world of seemingly self-sufficient youth as we see it in *Last Summer* and *Alice's Restaurant.* The "free" teen-agers of *Last Summer,* liberated by their parents' indifference to them, discover that their freedom is only a freedom to get lost in the maze of their conflicting urges. The older youth of *Alice's Restaurant,* who stand together so proudly and successfully against the hostile adult world, also learn, after their victory, that they have no place to go. This joyful elegy to the "aging children" seems, in its penultimate scene, to indicate a preference for death to the compromises of growing up. So does *Easy Rider,* by all odds the most popular of these films with the new audiences . . .

Editor's Note

Here the author's writing broke off.

The man who so movingly and amusingly and shrewdly characterized the characters we call the movie stars, and who regretted the passing of the old stars and perhaps even the gorgeous nonsense of the old star system, passed from our eyes himself. But Dick Griffith had written his book. It was about—as his original outline said—such matters as "the haughty stars of the theater who first condescended to 'pose' for the movie camera"; how the "new movie public chose its own stars on its own terms"; the sources of stars, from worldwide searches to stage mothers, from beauty to It, through the machinery of the star-making mechanism itself. He had identified and organized his stars by type and by box office, in commonly understood categories and in surprising ones.

He was interested, as we have seen, in the stars as they grow old, in the dead stars who continue to fascinate the living, in "the cannibals" who play in reflected glory parts which are "biographies" of stars long gone. He had noted his growing conviction that notoriety and scandal, far from being fatal to a stellar career as they have been in instances in the past, seem today to be indispensable to it; and such phenomena as "the cool young stars," with their "deliberate emotional inexpressiveness, the reflection, among other things, of a fashionable state of mind, involuntarily reminiscent of the jazz age" (and reminiscent, of course, of such frozen faces as Bogart).

It is a safe prediction, Griffith wrote in one draft, that the "stormy future will produce occasional brilliant meteors (blockbusters and quickies don't need stars) and that hero and heroine worship will go on, in some fashion, and that the future will have its own Valentinos, Swansons, Garbos." He had gone over in his mind performers such as Rock Hudson, Audrey Hepburn, Paul Newman, Tony Curtis, Joanne Woodward, Pat Neal, Eva Marie Saint, and all the Fondas, etc., but it was clear that he had come to no real conclusion about which he thought would meet the test.

Which test? At various times, when I would challenge him in conversation or correspondence about the new stars, pointing out that many of us still go to see people on screen in whom we are interested, his response was: The director, the story or vehicle, even the producer or writer has a bigger effect than ever before. The "stars" have less. Yes, you will still go to see an interesting male actor or a striking actress. But you won't go to see them in just anything. Almost none of today's movie actors can do what the old stars did—that is, pull you into a darkened room to see *them,* in pictures good, bad, or, frequently, middling.

When I accused him, by way of devil's advocating, that he was really writing about the rise and fall of the movie star, he wrote back that he was not. He was trying to show life, death, and transfiguration. Griffith added:

"The difficulty is what you describe as 'a matter of tense.' Am I dealing with something that is over and done with? Or something that is about to be over, or nearly done with? . . . The star system is not finished; it has altered, in kind as well as degree. Gilbert Seldes said that the seven lively arts *transformed* themselves into the mass media. Some such metamorphosis has overtaken the making and selling and being of stars. What has happened to the stars is fundamentally a projection of what has happened to ourselves. The psychic distance between the audience and the people on the screen has changed. We still identify with the stars but our identification now takes new forms and has new motives behind it."

And then he turned for the moment from such troublesome matters as what has happened to our stars to consider, for a moment, the pure joy of the photographs herein—which, he always said in self-mockery, were the real reason people would buy the book:

"There arrived today some choice stills from Mrs. Goldwyn, which cheers me . . ."

S.S.V.

498